Problem Solving Courts

Richard L. Wiener • Eve M. Brank
Editors

Problem Solving Courts

Social Science and Legal Perspectives

Springer

Editors
Richard L. Wiener
Department of Psychology
University of Nebraska-Lincoln
Lincoln, Nebraska
USA

Eve M. Brank
Department of Psychology
University of Nebraska-Lincoln
Lincoln, Nebraska
USA

ISBN 978-1-4614-7402-9 ISBN 978-1-4614-7403-6 (eBook)
DOI 10.1007/978-1-4614-7403-6
Springer New York Heidelberg Dordrecht London

Library of Congress Control Number: 2013941655

Printed on acid-free paper

Springer is part of Springer Science+Business Media (www.springer.com)

This book is dedicated to the memory of Professor Bruce Winick whose pioneering work in Therapeutic Jurisprudence made this work possible.

Problem-Solving Courts, Therapeutic Jurisprudence, and Mainstreaming

This is a most important and timely—book. The University of Nebraska's vibrant interdisciplinary program in law and psychology has, in this volume, taken a careful look at "problem-solving courts" and at how their functioning can be facilitated by the application of principles of therapeutic jurisprudence (TJ). The book grows out of a live conference where legal, social science, and philosophical dimensions of problem-solving courts—and of the 'new judging'—were grappled with by an impressive and accomplished group of scholars.

The volume opens with an excellent overview of the area. It then shifts to specific discussions of dependency courts, domestic violence courts, and mental health courts. And, apart from an epilogue, the volume closes with a chapter by my close friend and collaborator, the late Bruce Winick, who wrote on the relationship between problem-solving courts and therapeutic jurisprudence. In his chapter, Winick teases out many of the TJ techniques that courts can use to motivate offenders, to increase compliance with court orders and program requirements, and to foster self-efficacy of participants.

Fittingly, the book is dedicated to Bruce Winick, who worked passionately in TJ—and on his chapter—virtually until his last breath. The conference itself was of great interest to Bruce, and he was in constant contact with Rich Wiener regarding its organization and content. When the conference was finally held, Bruce was too weak to attend physically, but, remarkably, he contributed nonetheless through videoconferencing. Bruce passed away when his manuscript for the conference proceedings was nearly complete; fortunately, Rich Wiener put the final touches on the paper so that it could appear here—playing an exceptionally important part of rounding out the discussion and placing it within a TJ framework.

The volume is exceptionally timely. As I write these words, in late September 2012, the University of Miami's TJ Center, which Bruce founded and directed, is about to sponsor the "Bruce Winick Conference on Problem-Solving Courts" where, in October 2012, an interdisciplinary and international group will continue the important discussion of issues raised here. And only last month, in August, 2012, I had the pleasure of presenting a paper at an Oxford University International Conference on Therapeutic Jurisprudence and Problem-Solving Courts.

The overall topic, then, is of great current interest. However, the global economic crisis is of course playing out in this realm as well. Just last week, for example, the TJ listserv was abuzz with word that, in Queensland, Australia, budgets for problem-solving courts had been slashed, and list members were engaged in intense dialogue as to how to proceed, how to pick up the pieces, where to go from here. Much of the discussion revolved around how the benefits of problem-solving courts and the practices of TJ might be "mainstreamed" in the general judicial system. There is nothing to applaud in the precipitous way in which this issue has been raised, but the "mainstreaming" of problem-solving court knowledge and of TJ techniques is indeed something Bruce would have taken a great interest in. In our coedited book written a decade ago,[1] we wrote:

> Indeed, the proliferation of different problem solving courts, and the development of various "hybrid" models, suggests to us that the problem solving court movement may actually be a transitional stage in the creation of a judicial system attuned to problem solving, to therapeutic jurisprudence, and to judging with an ethic of care.

Either way, the material in this volume should be immensely helpful: in creating and fine-tuning problem—solving courts themselves, the material would obviously be directly applicable. And in the emerging area of "mainstreaming", the knowledge will be equally important: to grapple with the issue of treatments and services in various judicial settings, and with how principles of TJ judging—such as those laid out in Bruce's final chapter—can apply more generally.[2]

David B. Wexler
Professor of Law and Director, International Network on Therapeutic Jurisprudence, University of Puerto Rico, and Distinguished Research Professor of Law Emeritus, University of Arizona.
e-mail: davidBwexler@yahoo.com

September 21, 2012 San Juan, Puerto Rico

---

[1] Winick, B. J., & Wexler, D. B. (Eds.). (2003). Judging in a therapeutic key: Therapeutic jurisprudence and the courts (p. 87). Durham, NC: Carolina Academic Press.

[2] The TJ listserv discussion noted that a "Mainstreaming TJ Project" is already underway—a project that was actually inspired more by a desire to expand on the success of problem-solving courts than to pick up the pieces in the event of their demise. In fact, my own talk at the Oxford Conference in August, was entitled "New Wine in New Bottles: The Need to Sketch a Therapeutic Jurisprudence "Code" of Proposed Criminal Processes and Practices," available at http://ssrn.com/abstract=2065454. I am serving on an informal "mainstreaming" committee with Australian magistrates Pauline Spencer, Michael King, and Jelena Popovic, and with retired Arizona judge Michael Jones, now a full-time faculty member at the Phoenix School of Law. SSRN (The Social Science Research Network) carries recent papers directly on point by Spencer (abstract = 2083370), King (abstract = 1349412; and abstract = 2100632), and Jones (abstract = 2102375).

Contents

Contributors

Richard L. Wiener Department of Psychology, University of Nebraska-Lincoln, Lincoln, USA
e-mail: rwiener2@unl.edu

Leah Georges Department of Psychology, University of Nebraska-Lincoln, Lincoln, USA

Cindy S. Lederman Miami, FL, USA
e-mail: clederman@jud11.flcourts.org

Sophia I. Gatowski Systems Change Solutions, Inc.: Research, Evaluation and Training Consultants, Vancouver, BC, Canada
e-mail: sgatowski@ymail.com

Shirley A. Dobbin Systems Change Solutions, Inc.: Research, Evaluation and Training Consultants, Vancouver, BC, Canada

Alicia Summers Permanency Planning for Children Department, National Council of Juvenile and Family Court Judges, Reno, NV, USA

Victoria Weisz University of Nebraska-Lincoln, Lincoln, USA
e-mail: vweisz1@unl.edu

Barbara A. Babb Center for Families, Children and the Courts, University of Baltimore School of Law, 1420 N. Charles St., Baltimore, MD 21201, USA
e-mail: bbabb@ubalt.edu

Nancy Wolff Center for Behavioral Health Services & Criminal Justice Research, Rutgers University, 176 Ryders Lane, New Brunswick, NJ 08901, USA
e-mail: nwolff@cbhs.rutgers.edu

Anna Williams Shavers University of Nebraska–Lincoln College of Law, Lincoln, NE, USA
e-mail: ashavers@unl.edu

John Petrila College of Public Health, Department of Health Policy & Management, CPH 2139 13201 Bruce Downs Blvd University of South Florida Tampa, FL 33612 USA
e-mail: jpetril1@health.usf.edu

Allison D. Redlich State University of NewYork at Albany, Albany, USA
e-mail: aredlich@albany.edu

Robert F. Schopp College of Law, University of Nebraska, Lincoln, Nebraska, USA
e-mail: rschopp1@unl.edu

Elizabeth Richardson Australian Centre for Justice Innovation, Faculty of Law, Monash University, Monash University Law Chambers, Level 1/555 Lonsdale Street, Melbourne 3000, Australia
e-mail: liz.richardson@monash.edu

Katey Thom Centre for Mental Health Research, University of Auckland, Auckland, New Zealand

Brian McKenna Australian Catholic University and North Western Mental Health, Melbourne, Australia

Bruce J. Winick University of Miami, Coral Gables, FL, USA

Eve M. Brank University of Nebraska-Lincoln, Lincoln, NE, USA
e-mail: ebrank2@unl.edu

Joshua A. Haby University of Nebraska-Lincoln, Lincoln, NE, USA

Chapter 1
Social Psychology and Problem-Solving Courts: Judicial Roles and Decision Making

Richard L. Wiener and Leah Georges

Observations from a Mental Health Drug Court

On a mid-October morning, multiple defendants, their families, observers, social workers, treatment providers, attorneys, the judge, and all the other members of the judge's treatment team packed the mental health drug courtroom. There was a steady stream of offenders entering the courtroom and then leaving after appearing before the judge and the treatment team. During each hearing, an offender made an individual appearance before the judge, often without counsel. The offenders answered any questions that the judge asked and sometimes took the opportunity to directly address the court with his or her own questions, comments, or problems that resulted from participating in the treatment program. Some of the offenders, the ones with new cases or the ones that were not adhering satisfactorily to their treatment plans, arrived at court early (e.g., 8:30 a.m.) and had to stay until their hearings as late as 1:00 or 2:00 in the afternoon. Others arrived shortly before their hearings, answered a few questions, and then were dismissed with a new hearing date, which could have been as soon as the very next week or as late as 3 months down the road. All that depended upon how well the problem-solving court client was doing in treatment and whether the offender was in compliance with the conditions of the agreement between the client and the judge.

Consider Mr. Jones, an offender whom the state had charged with breaking and entering after the police found him in a local drug store at 3:00 in the morning, attempting to steal two boxes of cookies and several candy bars. Jones was not working, he was hungry, and he was wandering the streets of the city depressed and confused about where he was and where he was going. At the time of his apprehension, Jones was high on crystal methamphetamine (meth). The police found him wandering in the drug store mumbling to himself, crying, and trying to open one of the packages of cookies as he tried to exit the store. Prior to his arrest, Jones

R. L. Wiener (✉) · L. Georges
Department of Psychology, University of Nebraska-Lincoln, Lincoln, USA
e-mail: rwiener2@unl.edu

R. L. Wiener, E. M. Brank (eds.), *Problem Solving Courts*,
DOI 10.1007/978-1-4614-7403-6_1,

had been in and out of psychiatric treatment for episodes of clinical depression. When offered the choice between facing charges in the traditional criminal justice system or participating in the mental health drug court, Jones decided to take part in the problem-solving court program and accepted the stated goals of stopping his illegal use of meth and seeking treatment for his mental health problems. He agreed to regularly attend meetings of a 12-step program near his home (Jones lived with his older brother), provide urine samples upon the Court's request to prove that he had not used illegal substances, participate in rehabilitative therapy, and take his prescribed depression medication. In exchange, the court offered to drop the charges against Jones when he graduated from mental health court and established that he was capable (with supervision) of engaging in a substance-free and crime-free lifestyle.

Jones arrived at court at 11:30 for his 12:00 p.m. hearing. Sitting at the state's bench were several attorneys along with representatives from the treatment center he attended, his 12-step program, and the court laboratory responsible for testing his urine drops. One of the assistant state attorneys selected Mr. Jones' file and called out his name. The attorney pulled out several manila folders bound together with rubber bands and paper clips and began to rifle through the materials in preparation to ask questions of the offender and to answer any questions that the judge or other members of the judicial team might ask. At the same time, a case manager standing across the other side of the bench, opened her box of files and pulled out a smaller set of folders summarizing the offender's behavior in his treatment program. As the judge called Mr. Jones' name, the offender walked slowly and deliberately to a podium in the middle of the courtroom, which stood between the state and defense's tables facing the bench. Jones appeared somewhat nervous despite the fact that he had appeared many times before in the preceding 9 months of his participation in the problem-solving court. The judge greeted Mr. Jones and asked how things were going for him. Jones said that he was feeling much better and that he was looking forward to starting a program to complete his GED. Answering additional questions from the judge, he said that he had been clean now for the last 6 months and that he had not missed any of his treatment sessions or 12-step program meetings since his last appearance. The judge asked if Jones was taking his medication and he answered that he was, but the medicines made him dizzy sometimes and took away his appetite. After conferring with the case manager, the judge directed the social worker to make an appointment for Mr. Jones with the psychiatrist to see if there was something that could be done to offset the side effects of the medication. The state's attorney commented that Jones needed to stay on the medication because he had made an agreement to do so with the Court.

Next, the judge turned to the case manager to check on the accuracy of Mr. Jones' statements. The case manager confirmed that Jones was indeed drug free for more than 6 months with a long series of negative urine drops. Furthermore, the laboratory reported that he was taking his medications regularly. Jones had attended enough of the 12-step meetings to be in compliance with his treatment program, but he had missed a few meetings in the last several weeks. Still, Jones' therapist had submitted positive reports stating that the offender was making a solid effort to adhere to this treatment plan and that he was cooperative in therapy and working consistently on the ongoing issues that seemed to trigger his depression episodes. The judge listened intently, but was very aware of the state's attorney signaling that he should start preparing for the next hearing. The judge's caseload was large and required that the hearings keep moving on so that the next defendant would also have his time in front of the judge. The judge looked up at the defendant speaking at the podium and congratulated him for doing so well and making good progress. He warned him not to miss his 12-step program because that was partly why he was able to stay sober and able to stay with his treatment program. The judge told Jones because he was doing so well he would not have to report back to court for an additional 6 weeks. The bailiff looked to the calendar, announced the next hearing for Jones, and handed him a slip of paper with the court date and time. The judge smiled at the offender and asked the rest of the people in the courtroom to join him in applauding Jones for his success. As Jones left the podium, he received loud applause and congratulations for his success.

The first author of this chapter has spent many hours observing problem-solving courts in multiple jurisdictions. The observations that I made of Mr. Jones in mental health drug court are not unique, but instead summarize the typical court hearing appearance when an offender complies with the court treatment plan. The positive reception that Jones received in court is contingent upon successful adherence to the treatment plan and the offender returning negative urine drops. For those defendants who slip back into their sanctioned conduct, those who test positive for substances, those who fail to come to treatment, and those who engage in further nuisance and/or illegal behavior the experience may not be as positive. It is likely to include further sanctioning such as closer monitoring (i.e., shorter times between hearings), harsh lectures during the hearings, additional urine drops, and even being detained in jail for short periods of time. In fact, for defendants who continually fail to comply with their treatment agreements the judge may decide to return their cases back to the regular docket of the criminal court. However, for those who are in compliance the problem-solving court, the experience can be pleasant, motivating, encouraging, and even something to which they look forward. In 2012, problem-solving courts include drug courts, domestic violence courts, unified family courts, mental health courts, veterans courts, and even youth courts. Problem-solving courts exist throughout the United States and some have grown up in other common law countries including Canada, England, Australia, and New Zealand. The purpose of this book is to examine the phenomenon of problem-solving courts through the lenses of law, philosophy, social science, and clinical treatment. We focus on the questions: "What is a problem solving court and how is it different from a traditional criminal court?"

The Revolving Door Problem

For many who suffer from mental illness or substance abuse, and even for some who are perpetrators of family violence, the criminal justice system has become a dumping ground. This extends to veterans who find themselves to function in a stateside culture after having spent months and even years at war in the Middle East theatre. After the courts adjudicate these offenders and they serve their punishments they frequently recidivate and return to the criminal courts with new charges (King 2009). Many offenders display difficulty to treat psychological problems that cause them to act out in disruptive ways, which the criminal justice system cannot effectively address with its punishment-oriented interventions. Indeed, the traditional tools of the criminal justice system are limited to efforts at deterrence, incapacitation, and to a lesser extent punitive rehabilitation, and such techniques do not treat the underlying psychological and social problems that are at the root of many types of maladaptive behavior (Winick and Stefan 2005). Deterrence and incapacitation techniques are ill suited to address the personal and psychological failings of lawbreakers who suffer from underlying social and psychological dysfunction (King 2009). As a result, traditional courts have become revolving doors for people whose criminal behavior arises from psychological and social impairments (King 2009). Problem-solving courts are one response to the revolving door problem.

Problem-solving court judges require offenders to complete services that force the offenders to confront their underlying psychological and social problems (Berman and Feinblatt 2005; Winick and Wexler 2003). Acting with the authority of the state, judges in problem-solving courts have the ability to hold offenders accountable for their actions and make them responsible for their own rehabilitation in a way that other community agents lack the influence to do (Berman and Feinblatt 2005; King 2009; Winick and Stefan 2005). Judges in problem-solving courts go well beyond the metaphor of umpires calling balls and strikes in favor of a team model in which the judge acts similar to the captain of the team.

Judges act as team leaders and form partnerships with community welfare agencies and service providers to address the wider issues that offenders face. In fact, problem-solving judges act as much like case managers as they do as judicial officers. The key component that differentiates them from traditional criminal court judges is that they try to motivate participants to take advantage of the services available for remediation. The process in problem-solving courts is collaborative instead of adversarial, in that attorneys, service providers, and judges work as an interdisciplinary team to develop a treatment plan to serve the interests of the participants and their families. The offenders take active roles in their own rehabilitations (Berman and Feinblatt 2005; King 2009). While the philosophy of problem-solving courts is well-articulated, specific models of how the courts influence offenders remain poorly specified. The current book includes a series of papers that examine the role of court processes in a model of participant rehabilitation that attempts to enable offenders to take control of their own rehabilitation in accordance with the tenets of therapeutic jurisprudence (Winick and Wexler 2003). First, we discuss the traditional rational actor approach to adjudication and then describe a decision-making model more consistent with the philosophies of therapeutic jurisprudence.

Rational Actor Model

Traditional criminal law adopts a rational actor model to explain the conduct of offenders (Korobkin and Ulen 1998, 2000). It assumes that people weigh the costs and benefits of following, or not following the law and based upon the outcome of that calculus deliberately choose a course of action. Therefore, judges in traditional criminal courts rely on punishment to discourage undesirable behavior because they adhere to the rational choice model in which all people assess their material, social, and psychological assets at the time of their choice and act to increase or at least maintain those assets (Hastie and Dawes 2001). Under the rational choice model, the driving force is adaptation so that actors select behaviors with the highest expected utility (Korobkin and Ulen 2000), those that maximize the likelihood of a positive change in one's life assets. Rational actors avoid behaviors that lead to a decrease in their assets and therefore will not engage in behaviors that lead to jail time or fines. Furthermore, by a process of general deterrence others who become aware of the law will avoid those same undesirable behaviors because they too wish to avoid the loss of their own life assets. We argue that the rational utility maximizer model is incomplete for understanding the choice behavior of offenders and potential offenders because it leaves no room for offenders' perceptions of fairness, motivational styles, or emotional reactions to courtroom process or hearing outcomes (Wiener et al. 2006).

To be sure, judges in problem-solving courts do adopt some of the elements of a deterrence-based theory, when they function as compliance monitors ordering offenders to participate in services and then evaluating their progress during review hearings in order to foster public safety and offender obedience. Judges acting in this capacity adopt many of the same techniques, as do their brethren in traditional criminal courts. However, those in traditional courts act only to rule on the attorney motions and in doing so assure that the trial process is consistent with that the rules of procedure and rules of evidence that are controlling within the jurisdiction within which they serve. As an example of how problem-solving court judges use deterrence-based techniques to promote rehabilitation, Rempel et al. (2008) reported on a Brooklyn Domestic Violence Court in which magistrates primarily held review hearings to determine whether offenders were in compliance and therefore could continue to the next hearing without a change in protocol. In that court, judges added additional sanctions when offenders engaged in undesirable and illegal conduct. However, even in the domestic violence and drug courts where judges hold clients to unbending standards of conduct, they still leave room for program participants to "fall off the wagon" and even expect them to deviate from purely rational choice patterns. That is, they expect setbacks, plan for them, and try to shape the behavior of offenders very much similar to behavior management health care providers would do, albeit often without the training of such health care providers.

Nowhere is the inadequacy of the rational actor model as clear as in the policies that traditional courts apply to mentally ill defendants, trying to deter offenders from carrying out additional crimes, and trying to deter others through example from engaging in similar crimes. Typically, these efforts fall short because defendants with mental health issues are often not rational utility maximizers, in part, because they do not recognize the same life assets as do people without mental illnesses, and partly because they do not weigh costs and benefits in the same way as others do. As a result, court-enforced punishment is unlikely to rehabilitate or even deter people with mental illnesses. Instead, those with debilitating mental illnesses frequently recidivate, return to court and overcrowd local jails and regional prisons. Furthermore, mentally ill inmates face jails and prisons which lack treatment resources and are intensely stressful, resulting in further decompensation and increased suffering.

One remedy to the problem of "revolving door" inmates has been to divert individuals from jail into treatment through problem-solving courts (Winick 2003), which are criminal or family courts with separate dockets for those with psychological or social problems. These courts divert offenders from the criminal justice system into treatment (Goldkamp and Irons-Guynn 2000; King 2009; Redlich 2005; Redlich et al. 2006; Steadman et al. 2001). Participants undergo court-ordered treatment, take medication, and participate in community-based services. The court praises success in treatment and sanctions lack of compliance. Participation in mental health courts and other problem-solving courts is voluntary so that offenders can choose to defend themselves in regular criminal court or agree to participate in the drug, mental health, or other treatment regimen (Redlich et al. 2006).

Inasmuch as judges in problem-solving courts facilitate the rehabilitation and psychological well-being of the offenders, this is an application of therapeutic jurisprudence, the basic insight of which is that legal rules, legal practices, and the way legal actors (such as judges and lawyers) play their roles impose inevitable consequences on the psychological well-being of those affected (Winick 2006). Therapeutic jurisprudence is less a theory of human behavior and more a philosophy of nonretributive justice in which the goal is to empower offenders, offer them a way to take control of their own treatment, and help them to make judgments that are rational in the way that the criminal law defines rational choice.

King (2009) argues that principles of motivation are founded in self-determination, the promotion of procedural justice, and offender compliance. Therapeutic jurisprudence-based problem-solving courts inspire motivation and assure treatment compliance by viewing defendants as active processors who adjust their responses to the courtroom according to their perceptions of the fairness of their treatment at the hands of the court, their motivation states induced during hearings, and their anticipated emotions about future hearings (Wiener et al. 2010). Court officers try to create an environment through law and legal process that motivates and encourages offenders to participate in services and to seek positive outcomes, and reinforces offenders for doing so (Winick 2006).

The Psychological Model of Legal Decision Making

Problem-Solving Court Offenders

Wiener et al. (2010) posited a social cognitive model that helps explain how offenders' judgment and decision-making processes deviate from those of a purely rational decision maker. Our model endorses a therapeutic jurisprudence philosophy to understand how problem-solving courts empower clients to take responsibility for their own rehabilitation. We have reproduced the model in Fig. 1.1. It shows how

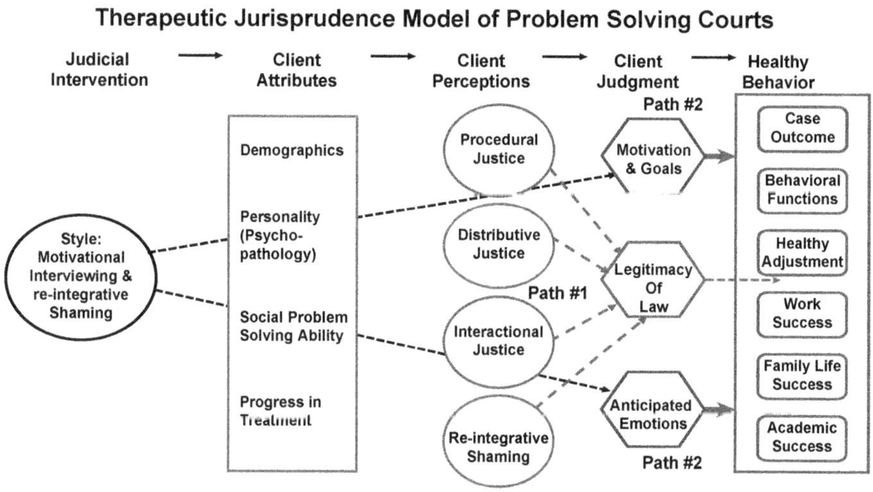

Fig. 1.1 Therapeutic jurisprudence model of problem-solving courts

judicial intervention may or may not produce healthy choices and positive outcomes for problem-solving court offenders.

Figure 1.1 depicts two paths that describe the judgment process of offenders as they choose either to follow the courts orders or to disregard the judge (Wiener et al. 2010). The first path relies heavily on the offenders' sense of justice, fair play, and ultimately the legitimacy of the law. Based upon Tyler and Blader's (2003) group value theory, we hypothesize that when defendants believe that the punishments (or rewards) that they receive are commensurate with their conduct, they conclude that the adjudication outcome was just and therefore the law is legitimate. In other words, if hearing outcomes are consistent with norms of fairness (equality and equity), offenders experience distributive justice and are more likely to follow the court's orders because they perceive the decision outcome to be fair and balanced relative to their own misconduct.

Along the same path (#1)(Wiener et al. 2010) refer to multiple determinants of procedural justice, which rise from offender evaluations of the formal decision-making procedure and whether the process was unbiased. To the extent to which defendants believe that the process was unbiased and the court encouraged them to voice their views in order to influence decision outcomes, the existing research suggests that the offenders will have found the process to be procedurally just or fair (Wiener et al. 2010). Prior research shows that when people experience procedural justice and to a lesser extent, distributive justice, they are more likely to engage in a positive way with the larger defining group (in this case, law-abiding society), adhere to its norms, and respect the society's constraints on their conduct (e.g., Amiot et al. 2007; Blader 2007a, b; Fuller et al. 2006; Gleibs et al. 2008; Hakonen and Lipponen 2008; Mayer et al. 2009).

Monahan et al. (2005) have shown that perceptions of procedural justice lead to perceptions of voluntary choice to participate in programs rather than coercion and thereby help offenders to gain a sense of intrinsic motivation and avoid the negative effects of coercion. Furthermore, Tyler's (2006) work established a link between procedural justice and perceived legitimacy of authority and respect for the law. Thus, problem-solving court participants who find court procedures fair are more likely to engage with authority in a healthy way and voluntarily accept the demands of the court. Following recent work in organizational psychology (e.g., Bernerth et al. 2007; De Cremer et al. 2007; Flaherty and Moss 2007; Forret and Love 2008; Klendauer and Deller 2009), our model further divides procedural justice into a procedural factor (i.e., perceptions of the impartiality the decision process itself) and an interactional factor (i.e., perceptions of respect that the decision maker shows for the recipient of the decision). The literature supports strongly this delineation of the different components of justice (Bies and Moag 1986; Colquitt 2001; Leventhal 1980; Shapiro et al. 1994; Thibaut and Walker 1975; Tyler 1988, 2000, 2003).

Poythress et al. (2002) showed that problem-solving court participants report experiencing high levels of procedural fairness. They administered a measure of procedural justice to defendants in the Broward County Mental Health Court and to a sample of defendants in a criminal court in another Florida jurisdiction and found that participants in the mental health court were more satisfied with the proceedings. The authors explained their findings with the observation that the participants in the problem-solving court thought that they had a greater opportunity to explain their own personal situations. They felt that the judge was more interested in them, treated them with greater respect, and more fairly. Wales et al. (2010) found similar procedural justice results in their study of participants in the District of Columbia's Mental Health Diversion Court.

Finally, research has shown that perceptions of procedural justice helped drunk driver offenders to see the law as legitimate. In a study of alternative dispute resolution procedures (i.e., the Canberra Reintegrative Shaming Experiment), Tyler et al. (2007) demonstrated that increases in procedural justice predicted offenders' belief in the legitimacy of the law. In addition, when friends and relatives in the offenders' lives respected them as individuals and were ready to reintegrate the offenders back into the significant others' own lives, the offenders came to believe in the legitimacy of the law, especially when their friends and family were ashamed of the offenders' conduct. Furthermore, those offenders who regarded the law as legitimate were less likely to drive under the influence as shown in follow-up data. In summary, we expect that if offenders perceive that a problem-solving court is procedurally fair, it produced a balanced outcome, resulted in respect for the offenders, and reconnected them to the positive aspects of their lives, they will view the law as legitimate and comply with judicial orders. That is they do not comply with the law out of a fear of certain and swift punishment, but rather out of a respect for the legitimacy of the law.

The second path in Fig. 1.1 is more direct than the first in that it bypasses a consideration of the legitimacy of the law, operating directly out of the characteristics of offenders' motivational and emotional states (Wiener et al. 2010). Accordingly, offenders who show motivational strategies to increase healthy behavior or who, in a closely linked manner, anticipate positive emotions for succeeding at their rehabilitative work and negative emotions for failing, are more likely to adhere to the judges' orders. More specifically, Wiener et al. (2010) argued that problem-solving court participants can commit two types of decision errors: errors of omission (i.e., failure to participate in ordered therapeutic services such as individual and/or group therapy) or errors of commission (i.e., engaging in antisocial behaviors such as acting out aggressively, substance abuse, or engaging in nuisance behaviors). The research literature in social psychology shows that these two that different types of motivation strategies minimize these errors.

According to Higgins and colleagues' regulatory focus theory research (Higgins 1997, 1998, 2000, 2001, 2002; Camacho et al. 2003; Crowe and Higgins 1997; Higgins et al. 1997), people in a promotion motivational state seek accomplishment and advancement by obtaining matches to desired end states. At the same time, those in a prevention motivational state seek safety and security by avoiding mismatches to the desired end state. High promotion motivation results in people working diligently to accomplish their goals and avoid errors of omission, while prevention motivation increases vigilant action and avoidance of errors of commission (Higgins 1997, 1998, 2000, 2002). Recently, Cesario et al. (2008) showed that promotion and prevention motivation arise from both situational inducements and activation of individual difference traits (see also, Higgins 1997, 1998, 2001, 2005, 2006; Higgins et al. 1994; Lee and Aaker 2004). Arguably, the most serious decision errors that offenders in problem-solving courts can make are errors of commission leading to more illegal conduct and a cycle of recidivism and rearrest. It follows that clients with heightened prevention motivation are most likely to be successful because they will avoid future antisocial acts. However, errors of omission (failing to participate in ordered therapeutic intervention) are also detrimental so that the most successful offenders will also be high in promotion focus, and so as a result are more likely to diligently engage in appropriate goal behavior and follow the courts rehabilitation plan.

Recent work in social psychology suggests that anticipated emotion acts similarly to motivation and may offer a separate route that could explain offender decision making. According to Baumeister et al. (2007), experienced emotion acts as feedback serving to continually update our records of past successes and failures. The proposition that the future anticipation of positive and negative emotion can gain the power to regulate subsequent behavior enjoys empirical support in the literature tested in a variety of situations (Loewenstein et al. 2001). Perhaps most importantly for the distinction we make between the rational actor model and our view, Mellers and colleagues (Mellers 2000; Mellers et al. 1997, 1999) demonstrated that anticipated pleasure explained choices beyond the expected utility inherent in the rational actor model. They showed this in a series of studies that examined decision making in both real world and laboratory contexts (e.g., financial gambles, test scores, and pregnancy tests).

The jump from the Baumeister et al. (2007) feedback model and the accompanying research literature in anticipated emotion to our prediction that offenders who experience positive or negative emotions after court hearings may anticipate the same for future encounters is a short and logical one. However, we go one step further and predict that offenders who anticipate positive (or negative) emotions following their own successes (or failures) in achieving the problem-solving court requirements are most likely to comply with future judicial orders. Thus, the challenge for the problem-solving court judges is to instill the appropriate type of anticipated affect in the clients who come before them.

However, these findings are more complicated because people are inaccurate in forecasting their emotions. This is especially true for problem-solving court participants whose emotional instability likely contributed to the legal violation that triggered court intervention in the first place. The affective forecasting literature suggests that people are generally impulsive (Hsee and Hastie 2006; Slovic 2001) paying more attention to immediate payoffs than to distant outcomes. This is true even when the costs of distant outcomes are greater than the benefits in the immediate payoffs, even when the cost of those outcomes far exceeds the immediate payoffs. As a result, people are inaccurate in predicting the actual emotions that they will eventually experience after both successful and unsuccessful outcomes (Gilbert et al. 1998; Gilbert and Wilson 2000; Wilson and Gilbert 2003, 2005). For example, in Gilbert and colleagues' work, people overestimated the emotional consequences of outcomes of a variety of appetitive choices producing, among other effects, a durability bias, an overestimation of the length of time that one would experience affect after an outcome. Yet, despite the fact that participants in problem-solving courts may anticipate wrongly the feelings that they will experience when they obtain either positive or negative outcomes following hearings, it may be the anticipation of positive or negative emotion and not the actual experienced motivation that determines their likelihood of compliance decisions.

Problem-solving clients likely demonstrate what Wilson et al. (2000) called "focalism" referring to the situation in which people focus too much attention on a future outcome and ignore the other events that occur in their lives simultaneously. In Wilson et al.'s (2000) research, college students overanticipated long periods of happiness or unhappiness when their school football team won or lost a weekend game. Similarly, offenders in problem-solving courts might overestimate the positive (negative) feelings that will follow successful (unsuccessful) experiences in court hearings. Our model suggests that regardless of their actual emotions, offenders will be more likely to comply with court orders and program requirements to the extent that they forecast positive affect (or negative affect) in subsequent court hearings if they follow (or failed to follow) these requirements.

Of course, client demographic, personality, problem-solving ability, psychopathology, and devotion to treatment efforts may moderate and mediate judicial interventions and the influences of procedural, distributive, and interactional justice, re-integrative shaming, offender motivation, and anticipated emotion. Figure 1.1 represents these client attributes as potential moderators and possibly as mediators. In its totality, Fig. 1.1 represents a decision-making process that includes some aspects of the rational actor approach, but goes beyond that to consider a fuller psychological model of judgment and decision making that is more consistent with the therapeutic jurisprudence approach.

Judicial Officers

Under a therapeutic jurisprudence model, problem-solving court judges acknowledge that decision-making processes may not always be purely rational. They endorse a psychological rather than an economic model of human decision making and indeed such a model applies not only to the judgments and decisions of offenders, but also to the judgments and decisions of the judicial officers themselves. That is, the judges' views of offenders as "quasi-" rational and even irrational decision makers demands that they behave differently toward offenders than does a purely rational model of decision making. The quasirational or irrational model requires judges to act to empower clients to make the best choices for themselves, their families, and their communities. For this reason, problem-solving court judges take advantage of the authority that the state imbues them with, even when not acting in the traditional role of judicial officers. Traditional social workers and case managers act with the authority of an agency, which connects only indirectly to the state through a Department of Health and Human Services. For case managers to act with the authority of law, they must work through the courts to obtain the state power that judges bring automatically. Because they wield the authority of the state, judges have the potential to be more effective than are traditional case managers in holding offenders accountable for their own rehabilitation. Equally important, judges have the power to order the services that will assist offenders to address the wider issues that they must confront in order to move forward in resolving the underlying problems that they face (Berman and Feinblatt 2005; King 2009; Winick and Stefan 2005). In assisting offenders to overcome the barriers to a healthy lifestyle, these judges seek out the cooperation of community service providers. They act as team leaders collaborating with community welfare agencies and service providers to address offenders' problems and as such take on some of the traditional roles of case managers. As a result, the process becomes more cooperative than adversarial so that the various actors (attorneys, service providers, and judges) work as a team to meet the best interests of the participants and their families (Berman and Feinblatt 2005; King 2009).

Michael King in his recently published bench book (2009) rejects the term problem-solving courts in favor of "solution focused judging." According to King, rehabilitation is not simply the absence of a negative event—offending—rather it focuses on bringing about a positive outcome, "the ability to lead a happy, constructive and law abiding life in the community" (King 2009, p. 5). King argues that to be successful problem-focused judges must use court process to help bring about a solution to the participants' problems. The goal of the judge ought to be to use court process to empower program participants to determine the essential requirements that they need to lead a happy, constructive, and law-abiding life. To do so the judge should assist the offenders to identify the problems which affect their ability to lead such a life and to facilitate them in developing and implementing solutions to their problems. Respecting the autonomy of the clients, in effect, seeing them as quasirational actors who deviate from simple utility maximization, the judges consider the program participants' needs and wishes, ultimately leading them to provide ongoing support for the clients when at all possible.

Taxonomy of Problem-Solving Courts: Judicial Role and Decision-Making Models

Agency of the Judicial Role

Next we return to the question that began our discussion, "What is a problem solving court and how is it different from a traditional criminal court?" The discussion in the previous sections describes two fundamental dimensions of problem-solving courts, which differentiate them from traditional criminal and civil courtrooms. The first dimension is one of agency and refers specifically to the role of trial court judges. We can think of the trial court judge's role on a continuum with opposite poles labeled as arbitrator and facilitator. The arbitrator judge acts similar to an umpire in a baseball game, objectively calling balls and strikes serving as the final arbitrator of the rules of evidence, trial process, and choice of law. The judge communicates primarily with the attorneys acting as does a referee in a boxing match, making sure that the adversarial opponents follow the accepted rules of procedure. The judge speaks sparingly to the defendants and when speaking the judge represents the authority of the state indifferent to the interests of either the side of the dispute. The judge's decisions pertain only to issues of law and administration of a "fair" trial. If the trier of fact finds the defendant guilty in a criminal trial, only then does the trial judge abandon the arbitrator role during a sentencing hearing to apply the law and sentencing guidelines to assign a punishment. However, even here, the trial judge will apply the law within tight constraints as the legislature intended.

The facilitator judge serves as a case manager or team leader forming partnerships with service providers, the state's attorney, the defense attorney and other court staff in order to understand and find solutions for the underlying social and psychological problems that contributed to the offender's conflict with the law. The goal of the judicial team is to assign the offenders to services that will effectively ameliorate their personal problems, motivate them to engage fully in the services, and to monitor the clients making sure that they do not backslide and once again violate the law. To accomplish this task, judges create therapeutic environments in their courtrooms that relax rules of procedure and evidence, enabling the judicial team to consider the perspective of the offenders as troubled clients. These judges reject many of the elements of the adversarial approach in favor of one in which all parties work toward a common goal—solving the psychosocial problems of the defendants.

Decision-Making Model

The second dimension concerns the model of decision making that the court adopts for understanding the way offenders decide whether to obey or disobey the law. Once again, we can think of the judge's role on a continuum with opposite poles, this time labeled as "economic or rational actor model" and "psychological model". The economic model views people as cost minimizers and benefit maximizers; therefore, trial judges rely heavily on punishment to deter illegal behavior both from the current offender and from others who come to expect swift and certain punishment for their misdeeds. The courts assume that offenders adapt to their circumstances and select behaviors with the greatest benefits and fewest costs. Punishment tips the balance against illegal conduct by increasing the costs relative to the benefits. Furthermore, by a process of general deterrence other potential defendants will avoid illegal behaviors because they wish to avoid the punishments that the courts can and do hand down.

The psychological decision-making model acknowledges that the rational actor model is incomplete because it leaves no room for offenders' perceptions of fairness, motivational styles, or emotional reactions to hearing processes or outcomes (Wiener et al. 2006). The psychological model sees offenders as more complex than simple utility maximizers. It considers the offenders' views of the legitimacy of law, their motivations for following the law, personal dispositions that arise from the offenders' social circumstances, psychological characteristics of the offenders, and the offenders' emotional reactions to the events that occurred before, during, and after their arrests. The psychological model assumes that offenders who take responsibility for their own treatment will be more likely to comply with the judge's orders and will be successful in their rehabilitation process. Wiener et al. (2010) describe one social cognitive model that suggests two paths: a procedural justice to legitimacy path and an emotion and motivational path that can moderate rational choice to predict healthy choice outcomes for clients in problem-solving courts. Other models that endorse a therapeutic jurisprudence philosophy are certainly possible.

A qualifying note about these two dimensions, decision-making model and judicial agency, is in order. The descriptions that we offer represent the endpoints for these two dimensions so that judges in all courtrooms likely fall somewhere between the two endpoints on each dimension endorsing some but perhaps not all the properties of one endpoint of the other. For example, in drug courts, domestic violence problem-solving courts, and in some mental health courts, the judges do take on a more adversarial role approach. They carefully monitor offender conduct throughout the problem-solving court program, admonish clients who backslide, and even sanction some with jail time if they violate the law (e.g., continuing to use illegal drugs, fail to adhere to court orders in domestic violence cases, or refuse to attend treatment activities). Similarly, in dependency courts, domestic violence courts, and unified family courts, the judge may serve some of the arbitrator and the facilitator functions to both help treat offenders and their families while, at the same time, adjudicating the legal issues in the case.

Figure 1.2 displays the two dimensions and shows seven examples of problem-solving courts which vary according to judge's agency role and decision-making Model. The bottom right quadrant, where the judge acts as an arbitrator and the court assumes an economic (rational model) include as the defining exemplary, traditional criminal courts. Falling closer the center of both dimensions are domestic violence courts that have jurisdiction over civil and criminal matters in domestic violence cases where the goal is to hold the offender accountable for his or her actions, treat the violent offender, and offer services to the victims of the violence. Moving up the vertical access (i.e., judge as facilitator with an economic decision-making model) locates drug courts in which the judge acts more in a facilitator role, but still relies heavily on drug use testing, punishment, and deterrence to prevent offenders from engaging in further substance abuse. The lower left quadrant (i.e., judge as arbitrator with a psychological decision-making model) lists dependency court or sometimes family court, which serve to adjudicate abuse and neglect cases. Here the judge assumes some of the traditional role as an arbitrator, ruling on motions, hearing motions, and deciding on issues of law, but does so with an eye toward treatment of the family to promote the best interests of the child. Judges in dependency courts typically give the family the benefit of the doubt and assume that with the correct services, the family will work to change problem behaviors to either retain or regain custody of their child or children. Not everyone considers dependency courts to be problem-solving courts because they, unlike integrated service courts, still operate primarily on an adversarial model, but with relaxed rules of evidence and procedure. However, dependency courts were the starting point for modifications that led to the true problem-solving court structure. Finally, in the upper left hand quadrant (i.e., judge as facilitator assuming a psychological decision-making model) are mental health courts, veterans' courts, and integrated service courts (i.e., courts that combine services offered in dependency courts, mental health courts, and drug courts). In our model, these courts represents the purest of the problem-solving courts because the judge acts as a case manager who uses the power of the state to empower clients to solve their psychosocial problems by making use of a partnership between the court treatment team and service providers in the community. The judge leads the problem-solving team, which works to motivate the clients to participate in services and work toward rehabilitation. The courts rely less on punishment and deterrence and more on fostering procedural and distributive justice, client motivation, and client emotional reactions. The judge uses a more complex model of offender decision making, one similar to our social cognitive model (Wiener et al. 2010).

The chapters in this book generally assume that problem-solving courts are ones in which judges act primarily as facilitators and team leaders, assume clients make complex decisions that go well beyond simple utility maximization, and therefore they consider client perceptions of fairness, client motivations, and client emotions in dealing with offenders' psychosocial problems. The first part of this book that follows this introductory discussion includes three chapters that focus on the lower right hand corner of Fig. 1.2 treating dependency courts as the jumping-off point for problem-solving courts. Chapter 2, "The Marriage of Science and Law in Child Welfare Cases" authored by Judge Cindy S. Lederman sets the stage with the observation that in child welfare cases, dependency court judges make decisions that include clinical components, but always within a developmental context. Lederman argues that to make those decisions, judges must have access to the most accurate and up-to-date findings in the science of child development. In Chap. 3, "Exploring the Value-Added of Specialized Problem Solving Courts for Dependency Cases" Sophie Gawtowski, Shirley Dobbin, and Alicia Summers show how dependency courts are the foundational model for problem-solving courts and highlight the importance of practice guidelines for judges in these courts. They demonstrate this with data that

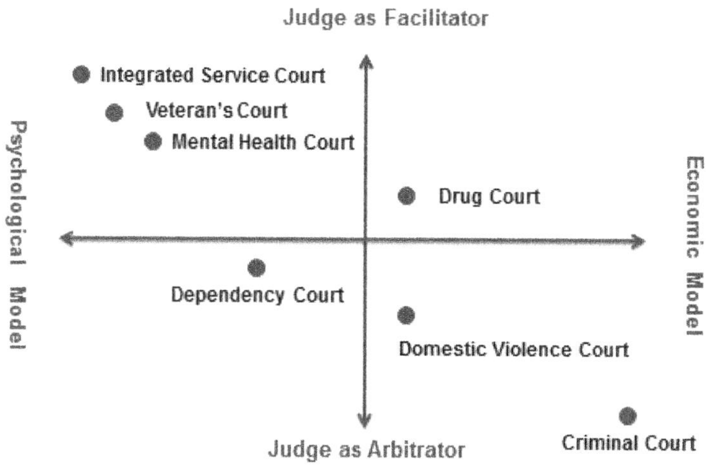

Fig. 1.2 Seven examples of problem-solving courts that vary according to Judge's Agency Role and Decision Making Model

compare the functioning of three different dependency courts in Utah, each using a different type of problem-solving court model. To round out this part, Victoria Weisz (Chap. 4) more critically examines the roles of methodology, data interpretation, and dependency courts' need for timely and accurate research data in a chapter entitled, "Dependency Courts and Science."

The second part focuses on the lower left hand corner of Fig. 1.2 with an in-depth analysis of domestic violence courts. In Chap. 5, "Unified Family Courts: An Interdisciplinary Framework and A Problem solving Approach" Barbara Babb discusses the need for problem-solving courts to help perpetrators and victims cope with the complicated issues of modern families including incidents of domestic violence that too frequently result in conflict with the law. Professor Babb shows how therapeutic jurisprudence is a blueprint for unified family courts and how that model helps judges in those courts respond effectively to problems related to domestic violence. Chapter 6, "Domestic Violence Courts: The Case of Lady Justice Meets the Serpents of the Caduccus" authored by Nancy Wolff first describes the need for domestic violence courts and then goes on to discuss the functions that they serve. She summarizes the courts' attempt to integrate the prosecution, punishment, and deterrence of batterers; rehabilitation of batterers; and protection of victims through the use of protective orders. She explains that part of the value of domestic violence courts is the efficiency of being able to expedite, simplify, and unify the way in which the court responds to domestic violence by addressing both the criminal and civil issues that courts must consider to prosecute the batterer and protect the victim. Rounding out Part II, is a chapter entitled "Gender Issues in Problem-Solving Courts" in which Anna Shavers examines the role of therapeutic jurisprudence as an approach to address the problems of domestic violence in the problem-solving court milieu, especially, as it affects both men and women in a chapter entitled, "Gender Issues in Problem-Solving Courts."

The third part in this book focuses on the upper left hand corner of Fig. 1.2 with three chapters that examine in detail the need for mental health courts, the way that they function, their effectiveness, and the special concerns that they generate. In Chap. 8, "Mental Health Courts May Work, But Does It Matter If They Do?" John Petrila describes mental health courts as nonadversarial forums that work toward meeting the social and treatment needs of mentally ill clients who get into trouble with the law. He goes on to argue that emerging data suggest that mental health courts are effective at improving public safety and better access to treatment, but that finding does not silence other substantive and procedural issues that we need to consider before concluding that these problem-solving courts are worth retaining in the justice system. The rest of the chapter takes on some of these substantive and procedural issues and makes recommendations on how to make the best use of mental health courts. In Chap. 9, "The Past, Present, and Future of Mental Health Courts" Alison Redlich summarizes ten essential elements of mental health courts organized into three global areas: planning and sustainability, precourt enrollment considerations, and in-court considerations. She evaluates the existing research in each of these areas highlighting what we know and what we still need to find out and the uses that analysis to begin to plot the future of mental health courts in the justice system. Rounding out this part is a chapter by Robert Schopp entitled, "Mental Health Courts: Competence, Responsibility, and Proportionality," in which he argues that to be successful mental health courts must reduce recidivism while not undermining any of the important values in the relevant criminal law. He goes on to catalogue the relevant values in the criminal law that might be incompatible with mental health courts and suggests that certain types of psychological impairments might be amenable to treatment in mental health courts without violating the values embodied in the criminal law. He concludes his analysis by showing when these courts might be consistent with legal values and when they might not be.

The fourth part in this book includes two chapters that examine problem solving in a broader perspective. Chapter 11, "The Evolution of Problem-Solving Courts in Australia and New Zealand: A Trans-Tasman Comparative Perspective" coauthored by Elizabeth Richardson, Katey Thom, and Brian McKenna compares existing problem-solving courts in Australia and developing ones in New Zealand with those in the United States. They describe the cultural and structural differences among these countries that contribute to the differences in how these courts function in each jurisdiction. First, the authors argue that the courts in Australia and those developing in New Zealand look more circumspect on the innovative judicial practices that have grown up in problem-solving courts in the United States. The authors discuss the difference between what King (2009) and King (2010) call "solution focused" courts and the function of problem-solving courts in the United States suggesting that these courts should not solve problems for people, but instead they should create opportunities for people to undergo treatment or therapy to address their own problems. This chapter presents an overview of the problem-solving courts currently operating in Australia and New Zealand and it then concentrates on the critical role of collaboration between the legal, health, and welfare sectors in these courts. Chapter 12 is a posthumous work that the late Bruce Winick mostly completed before his premature death. Professors Winick with David Wexler are the founders of the therapeutic jurisprudence school of thought. In his chapter, Professor Winick describes therapeutic jurisprudence as the underlying philosophical foundation for problem-solving courts. He shows how this plays out in drug courts, mental health courts, and domestic violence courts. This chapter includes some additional comments applying Professor Winick's comments to newly emerging veterans' courts. We are honored to have Bruce's final work in our book.

Finally, this book finishes with Eve Brank's discussion of the contribution of the chapters in this book to the state of the field for problem-solving courts. She examines the intended and unintended consequences of problem-solving courts with a particular focus on the unintended consequences because of the current disconnect between legal training and the needs of problem-solving courts. Brank outlines possible solutions to prepare the legal academy for courts that have a therapeutic jurisprudence foundation. In summary, this collection of chapters takes a different look at problem-solving courts, integrating legal and social scientific analysis with focal point of a philosophic lens. Problem-solving courts emerged out of the tenets of therapeutic jurisprudence as the late Bruce Winick wrote so eloquently in his contribution to this book. We hope that this book takes the next step and sharpens some of the important insights of therapeutic jurisprudence in the context of this new innovative merging of social science and law.

References

Amiot, C. E., Terry, D. J., & Callan, V. J. (2007). Status, equity and social identification during an intergroup merger: A longitudinal study. *British Journal of Social Psychology, 46,* 557–577. doi:10.1348/014466606X146015.

Baumeister, R. F., Vohs, K. D., DeWall, C. N., & Zhang, L. (2007). How emotion shapes behavior: Feedback, anticipation, and reflection, rather than direct causation. *Personality and Social Psychology Review, 11,* 167–203. doi:10.1177/1088868307301033.

Berman, G., & Feinblatt, J. (2005). *Good courts: The case for problem-solving justice.* New York: New Press.

Bernerth, J. B., Armenakis, A. A., Field, H. S., & Walker, H. J. (2007). Justice, cynicism, and commitment: A study of important organizational change variables. *Journal of Applied Behavioral Science, 43,* 303–326. doi:10.1177/0021886306296602.

Bies, R. J., & Moag, J. F. (1986).Interactional justice: Communication criteria of fairness. In R. J. Lewicki, B. H. Sheppard, & M. H. Bazerman (Eds.), *Research on negotiations in organizations: A biannual research series* (Vol. 1, pp. 43–55). Greenwich: JAI Press.

Blader, S. L. (2007a). What determines people's fairness judgments? Identification and outcomes influence procedural justice evaluations under uncertainty. *Journal of Experimental Social Psychology, 43,* 986–994. doi:10.1016/j.jesp.2006.10.022.

Blader, S. L. (2007b). What leads organizational members to collectivize? Injustice and identification as precursors of union certification. *Organization Science, 18,* 108–126. doi:10.1287/orsc.1060.0217.

Camacho, C. J., Higgins, E. T., & Luger, L. (2003). Moral value transfer from regulatory fit: "What feels right is right" and "what feels wrong is wrong." *Journal of Personality and Social Psychology, 84,* 498–510. doi:10.1037/0022-3514.84.3.49.

Cesario, J., Higgins, E. T., & Scholer, A. A. (2008). Regulatory fit and persuasion: Basic principles and remaining questions. *Social and Personality Psychology Compass, 2,* 444–463. doi:10.1111/j.1751-9004.2007.00055.x.

Colquitt, J. A. (2001). On the dimensionality of organizational justice: A construct validation of a measure. *Journal of Applied Psychology, 56,* 386–400. doi:10.1037/0021-9010.86.3.386.

Crowe, E., & Higgins, E. T. (1997). Regulatory focus and strategic inclinations: Promotion and prevention in decision making. *Organizational Behavior and Human Decision Processes, 69,* 117–132. doi:10.1006/obhd.1996.2675.

De Cremer, D. M., van Dijke, M., & Bos, A. E. R. (2007). When leaders are seen as transformational: The effects of organizational justice. *Journal of Applied Social Psychology, 37,* 1797–1816. doi:10.1111/j.1559-1816.2007.00238.x.

Flaherty, S., & Moss, S. A. (2007). The impact of personality and team context on the relationships between workplace injustice and counterproductive work behavior. *Journal of Applied Social Psychology, 37,* 2549–2575. doi:10.1111/j.1559-1816.2007.00270.x.

Forret, M., & Love, M. S. (2008). Employee justice perceptions and coworker relationships. *Leadership & Organization Development Journal, 29,* 248–260. doi:10.1108/01437730810861308.

Fuller, J. B., Hester, K., Barnett, T., Frey, L., Relyea, C., & Beu, D. (2006). Perceived external prestige and internal respect: New insights into the organizational identification process. *Human Relations, 59,* 815–846. doi:10.1177/0018726706067148.

Gilbert, D. T., & Wilson, T. D. (2000).Some problems in the forecasting of future affective states. In J. P. Forgas (Ed.), *Feeling and thinking: The role of affect in social cognition* (pp. 178–197). New York: Cambridge University Press.

Gilbert, D. T., Pinel, E. C., Wilson, T. D., Blumberg, S. J., & Wheatley, T. P. (1998). Immune neglect: A source of durability bias in affective forecasting. *Journal of Personality and Social Psychology, 75,* 617–638. doi:10.1037/0022-3514.75.3.617.

Gleibs, I. H., Mummendey, A., & Noack, P. (2008). Predictors of change in postmerger identification during a merger process: A longitudinal study. *Journal of Personality and Social Psychology, 95,* 1095–1112. doi:10.1037/0022-3514.95.5.1095.

Goldkamp, J. S., & Irons-Guynn, C. (2000). *Emerging judicial strategies for the mentally ill in the criminal caseload: Mental health courts in Ft. Lauderdale, Seattle, Bernadino, and Anchorage.* Philadelphia: Crime and Justice Research Institute.

Hakonen, M., & Lipponen, J. (2008). Procedural justice and identification with virtual teams: The moderating role of face-to-face meetings and geographical dispersion. *Social Justice Research, 21,* 164–178. doi:10.1007/s11211-008-0070-3.

Hastie, R., & Dawes, R. M. (2001). *Rational choice in an uncertain world: The psychology of judgment and decision making.* Thousand Oaks: Sage Publications, Inc.

Higgins, E. T. (1997). Beyond pleasure and pain. *American Psychologist, 52,* 1280–1300. doi:10.1037/0003-066X.52.12.1280.

Higgins, E. T. (1998).Promotion and prevention: Regulatory focus as a motivational principle. In M. P. Zanna (Ed.), *Advances in experimental social psychology* (Vol. 30, pp. 1–46). New York: Academic Press.

Higgins, E. T. (2000). Making a good decision: Value from fit. *American Psychologist, 55,* 1217–1230. doi:10.1037/0003-066X.55.11.1217.

Higgins, E. T. (2001).Promotion and prevention experiences: Relating emotions to non-emotional motivational states. In J. P. Forgas (Ed.), *Handbook of emotions* (pp. 186–211). London: Blackwell.

Higgins, E. T. (2002). How self-regulation creates distinct values: The case of promotion and prevention decision making. *Journal of Consumer Psychology, 12,* 177–191. doi:10.1207/S15327663JCP1203_01.

Higgins, E. T. (2005). Value from regulatory fit. *Current Directions in Psychological Science, 14,* 209–213. doi:10.1111/j.0963-7214.2005.00366.x.

Higgins, E. T. (2006). Value from hedonic experience and engagement. *Psychological Review, 113,* 439–460. doi:10.1037/0033-295X.113.3.439.

Higgins, E. T., Roney, C. J., Crowe, E., & Hymes, C. (1994). Ideal versus ought predilections for approach and avoidance distinct self-regulatory systems. *Journal of Personality and Social Psychology, 66,* 276–286.

Higgins, E. T., Shah, J., & Friedman, R. (1997). Emotional responses to goal attainment: Strength of regulatory focus as moderator. *Journal of Personality and Social Psychology, 72,* 515–525. doi:10.1037/0022-3514.72.3.515.

Hsee, C. K., & Hastie, R. (2006). Decision and experience: Why don't we choose what makes us happy? *Trends in Cognitive Sciences, 10,* 31–37. doi:10.1016/j.tics.2005.11.007.

King, M. S. (2009). *Solution-focused judging bench book.* Melbourne: Australasian Institute of Judicial Administration and the Legal Services Board of Victoria.

King, M. S. (2010). Should problem-solving courts be solution-focused courts? Revista Juridica Universidad de Puerto Rico, Forthcoming; Monash University Faculty of Law Legal Studies Research Paper No. 2010/03. Available at SSRN: http://ssrn.com/abstract=1725022. Accessed 20 Sep. 2012.

Klendauer, R., & Deller, J. (2009). Organizational justice and managerial commitment in corporate mergers. *Journal of Managerial Psychology, 24,* 29–45. doi:10.1108/02683940910922528.

Korobkin, R. B., & Ulen, T. S. (1998). Efficiency and equity: What can be gained by combining Coase and Rawls? *Washington Law Review, 73,* 329–348.

Korobkin, R. B., & Ulen, T. S. (2000). Law and behavioral science: Removing the rationality assumption from law and economics. *California Law Review, 88,* 1051–1144.

Lee, A. Y., & Aaker, J. L. (2004). Bringing the frame into focus: The influence of regulatory fit on processing fluency and persuasion. *Journal of Personality and Social Psychology, 86,* 205–218. doi:10.1037/0022-3514.86.2.205.

Leventhal, G. S. (1980). What should be done with equity theory? New approaches to the study of fairness in social relationships. In K. Gergen, M. Greenberg, & R. Willis (Eds.), *Social exchange: Advances in theory and research* (pp. 27–55). New York: Plenum.

Loewenstein, G., Weber, E. U., Hsee, C. K., & Welch, N. (2001). Risk as feelings. *Psychological Bulletin, 127,* 267–286. doi:10.1037//0033-2909.127.2.267.

Mayer, D. M., Greenbaum, R. L., Kuenzi, M., & Shteynberg, G. (2009). When do fair procedures not matter? A test of the identity violation effect. *Journal of Applied Psychology, 94,* 142–161. doi:10.1037/a0013108.

Mellers, B. A. (2000). Choice and the relative pleasure of consequences. *Psychological Bulletin, 126,* 910–924. doi:10.1037/0033-2909.126.6.910.

Mellers, B. A., Schwartz, A., Ho, K., & Ritov, I. (1997). Decision affect theory: Emotional reactions to the outcomes of risky options. *Psychological Science, 8,* 423–429. doi:10.1111/j.1467-9280.1997.tb00455.x.

Mellers, B., Schwartz, A., & Ritov, I. (1999). Emotion-based choice. *Journal of Experimental Psychology, 128,* 332–345. doi:10.1037/0096-3445.128.3.332.

Monahan, J., Redlich, A. D., Swanson, J., Clark Robbins, P., Appelbaum, P. S., Appelbaum, M. D., Petrila, J. D., et al. (2005). Use of leverage to improve adherence to psychiatric treatment in the community. *Psychiatric Services, 56,* 37–44. doi:10.1176/appi.ps.56.1.37.

Poythress, N.G., Petrila, J., McGaha, A., & Boothroyd, R. (2002). Perceived coercion and procedural justice in the Broward County Mental Health Court. *International Journal of Law and Psychiatry, 25,* 517–533. doi:10.1016/S0160-2527(01)00110-8.

Redlich, A. D. (2005). Voluntary, but knowing and intelligent: Comprehension in mental health courts. *Psychology, Public Policy, and Law, 11,* 605–619. doi:10.1037/1076-8971.11.4.605.

Redlich, A. D., Steadman, H. J., Monahan, J., Robbins, P. C., & Petrila, J. (2006). Patterns of practice in mental health courts: A national survey. *Law and Human Behavior, 30,* 347–362. doi:10.1007/s10979-006-9036-x.

Rempel, M., Labriola, M., & Davis, R. C. (2008). Does judicial monitoring deter domestic violence recidivism? Results of a quasi-experimental comparison in the Bronx. *Violence Against Women, 14,* 185–207. doi:10.1177/1077801207312535.

Shapiro, D., Buttner, E. H., & Barry, B. (1994). Explanations: What factors enhance their perceived adequacy? *Organizational Behavior and Human Decision Processes, 58,* 346–368. doi:10.1006/obhd.1994.1041.

Slovic, P. (2001). Psychological study of human judgment: Implications for investment decision making. *Journal of Behavioral Finance, 2,* 160–172. doi:10.1207/S15327760JPFM0203_6.
Steadman, H. J., Davidson, S., & Brown, C. (2001). Law and psychiatry: Mental health courts: Their promise and unanswered questions. *Psychiatric Services, 52,* 457–458. doi:10.1176/appi.ps.52.4.457.
Thibaut, J., & Walker, L. (1975). *Procedural justice.* Hillsdale: Lawrence Erlbaum.
Tyler, T. R. (1988). What is procedural justice? Criteria used by citizens to assess the fairness of legal procedures. *Law & Society Review, 22,* 103–135.
Tyler, T. R. (2000). Social justice: Outcome and procedure. *International Journal of Psychology, 35,* 117–125. doi:10.1080/002075900399411.
Tyler, T. R. (2003). Procedural justice, legitimacy, and the effective rule of law. *Crime and Justice: A Review of Research, 30,* 283–358. doi:0192-3234/2003/0030.
Tyler, T. R. (2006). *Why people obey the law.* New Haven: Yale University Press.
Tyler, T. R., & Blader, S. L. (2003). The group engagement model: Procedural justice, social identity, and cooperative behavior. *Personality and Social Psychology Review, 7,* 349–361. doi:10.1207/S15327957PSPR0704_07.
Tyler, T. R., Sherman, L., Strang, H., Barnes, G. C., & Woods, D. (2007). Reintegrative shaming, procedural justice, and recidivism: The engagement of offenders' psychological mechanisms in the Canberra RISE drinking-and-driving experiment. *Law & Society Review, 41,* 553–586. doi:10.1111/j.1540-5893.2007.00314.x.
Wales, H. W., Hiday, V. A., & Ray, B. (2010). Procedural justice and the mental health court's role in reducing recidivism. *International Journal of Law and Psychiatry, 33,* 265–271. doi:10.1016/j.ijlp.2010.06.009.
Wiener, R., Bornstein, B., & Voss, A. (2006). Emotion and the law: A framework for inquiry. *Law and Human Behavior, 30,* 231–248. doi:10.1007/s10979-006-9025-0.
Wiener, R. L., Winick, B. J., Georges, L. S., & Castro, A. (2010). A testable theory of problem solving courts: Avoiding past empirical and legal failures. *International Journal of Law and Psychiatry, 33,* 417–427. doi:10.1016/j.ijlp.2010.09.012.
Wilson, T. D., & Gilbert, D. T. (2003).Affective forecasting. In M. P. Zanna (Ed.), *Advances in experimental social psychology* (Vol. 35, pp. 345–407). San Diego: Academic Press.
Wilson, T. D., & Gilbert, D. T. (2005). Affective forecasting: Knowing what to want. *Current Directions in Psychological Science, 14,* 131–134. doi:10.1111/j.0963-7214.2005.00355.x.
Wilson, T. D., Wheatley, T., Meyers, J., Gilbert, D. T., & Axsom, D. (2000). Focalism: A source of durability bias in affective forecasting. *Journal of Personality and Social Psychology, 78,* 821–836. doi:10.1037/0022-3514.78.5.821.
Winick, B. J. (2003). Therapeutic jurisprudence and problem solving courts. *Fordham Urban Law Journal, 30,* 1055–1090.
Winick, B. J. (2006). Therapeutic jurisprudence: Enhancing the relationship between law and psychology. *Law and Psychology: Current Legal Issues, 9,* 30–48.
Winick, B. J., & Stefan, S. (2005). Forward: A dialogue on mental health courts. *Psychology, Public Policy and Law, 11,* 507–526. doi:10.1037/1076-8971.11.507.507.
Winick, B., & Wexler, D. (2003). *Judging in a therapeutic key: Therapeutic jurisprudence and the courts.* Durham: Carolina Academic Press.

Part I
Dependency Specialty Courts

Chapter 2
The Marriage of Science and the Law in Child Welfare Cases

Cindy S. Lederman

At this time in our history, courts have become the last resort for families who have been failed by every other institution. These troubled families are pouring in the courthouse doors, many involuntarily, seeking the support they have been unable or unwilling to negotiate in their own communities. Communities have been unable to offer the kinds of social services that families need to preserve and enhance their abilities to function in the open community. The public seems to expect the courts to have answers for problems that our society has been unable to solve: substance abuse, violence, poverty, and crime. A legal institution is hardly the appropriate forum to ameliorate these societal ills, regardless of the demands of the public. Nevertheless, the issues surface daily in our courtrooms and yet court devoid of science and research, is even more poorly equipped to meet the needs of the impoverished. To meet the burdens that society now demands of the courts, judges must learn to critically analyze the most recent literature in the social sciences.

Judges have become experts in human suffering and cumulative disadvantage but that experiential expertise is not enough. It is never enough to deal effectively with the quotidian problems in our dependency courts. The challenges amount to a Sisyphean task. Jurists work with young mothers who have to be taught to smile at their babies.

Jurists learn that the first words of the babies in dependency court are often "stop" and "no". Jurists experience the pain of telling the 7-year-old who was repeatedly severely beaten by her mother why she cannot go home to the mother she misses and loves. Jurists attempt to craft a safe solution so that a mentally retarded mother who loves her baby and has never intentionally hurt her can be reunified with enough safeguards in the home that the child can grow and prosper by living with a parent

---

Fill the seats of justice with men who are good, but not so absolute in goodness as to forget what human frailty is. Thomas Noon Talfourd

---

C. S. Lederman (✉)
Miami, FL, USA
e-mail: clederman@jud11.flcourts.org

R. L. Wiener, E. M. Brank (eds.), *Problem Solving Courts*,
DOI 10.1007/978-1-4614-7403-6_2, © Springer Science+Business Media, LLC 2013

with an intelligence quotient (IQ) of 65. Jurists take children away from their parents every day and put them in placements they hope and pray will be better than the ones from which they have been removed.

Judges in dependency court literally make hundreds of decisions every week, in a matter of moments, with limited information. The typical court has only the information on the record that attorneys and witnesses bring to the judges and few judges have scientific experts to offer to theme the work of the social sciences. Judges, decision makers in family law and mental health fields, remain largely ignorant about several decades of research on child development. Child development researchers and child custody decision makers rarely cross paths, and most of the relevant publications intended for academic audiences are inaccessible to readers (Lamb and Kelly 2000). Yet, decisions are made that often have a long-term effect on the life of a child without being informed by research and science in a forum that seems like an emergency room.[1] The judges must make immediate decisions based only upon the information that that the parties make available to them and they must make those decisions within the time constraints of the typically short hearing.

In juvenile court, success is achieved in fulfilling our legal mandate to reunify and rehabilitate only if the court partners, working together as team can facilitate the modification of human behavior. Keeping children safe, healing children, and reunifying families with *good enough* parents are not traditional legal functions; in fact, these functions are much more difficult to achieve. It is much easier to adjudicate a case than to teach a young mother from chronic, intergenerational impoverishment and deprivation how to be a good enough parent.

There is an additional component to judging in child welfare cases. There is a clinical aspect to most of the decisions made in dependency court where child well-being must be paramount. Decisions have to be made in a developmental context based on the child's age, level of developmental functioning, and emotional health. A case-by-case determination must be made; there is no suitable one size fits all approach. The legal decisions must be informed by the science of child development to avoid harm to the child. Combining science with the law, the concept of Therapeutic Jurisprudence comes to life and the focus is on the law's effect on emotional life and psychological well-being (Wexler 2000, p. 125).

The concepts of problem-solving courts and solution-focused judging, both semantic progeny of the term Therapeutic Jurisprudence, are now commonly used terms in our court system. Therapeutic Jurisprudence is defined as the study of the role of the law as a therapeutic agent (Wexler 1995, p. 220). Can the court, an intervention itself, facilitate healing, protection, and rehabilitation? Can the court stop the intergenerational transmission of child maltreatment? Each day in dependency court and in the child welfare system is an experiment. The courts require valid and reliable information to conduct these experiments in ways that will benefit the families that suffer from the various social and psychological maladies that land them in court in the first place. We need to collect information on the types of clients that come to the

[1] Comment by Judge Valerie Manno-Schurr, R.N., J.D. on her first day presiding in dependency court.

court, the types of services provided, and most importantly, on the outcomes of the services that are provided. In this manner, judges in problem-solving courts might take on some of the paradigmatic approaches that psychologists and sociologists bring to the area of Therapeutic Jurisprudence.

Those of us who work in a juvenile court setting work in the oldest example of problem-solving courts in the USA. The Illinois Juvenile Court Act of 1899[2] authorized the creation of the first juvenile court in Chicago. The juvenile court focused on social welfare and was explicitly charged with the duty of protecting and rehabilitating children. The child's best interest was the prevailing standard of a court system that focused on the child, not the offense. Unfortunately, the juvenile court of the last century has shifted to an institution focused on children's due process rights and on accountability and punishment (Dodge et al. 2006, p. 330). There remains little distinction between a criminal court and the increasingly adversarial juvenile court except that the defendants are younger and smaller and there is no constitutional right to a jury trial. With the advent of the translation of the science that explains adolescent brain development, it is clear that juvenile courts in America must respect the hegemony of science in determining policy and practice. Juveniles are not short adults and cannot be treated as such if the mandate of rehabilitation is to be fulfilled. But judges and lawyers are trained in the law, not science, which is not enough. Judges need to be students of research. When making a decision based on the legal standard of "best interest of the child", there needs to be an element of critical thinking based on the individual characteristics of the child and family, the age and experience of the child, risk factors, protective factors, resilience, level of functioning, and developmental status. Visitation for a baby must not be the same as visitation for a teenager. Shared parental responsibility, shared custody, parenting plans, and placement changes each have developmental implications that must be understood and included in the judge's deliberation to avoid unnecessary iatrogenic effects on the child. These considerations form the basis of Therapeutic Jurisprudence.

One of the simplest yet descriptive definitions of Therapeutic Jurisprudence was written by Professor Christopher Slobogin who defined it as "the use of social science to study the extent to which a legal rule or practice promotes the psychological and physical well-being of the people it affects" (Hora et al. 1999, p. 443). In an adversarial, rights-based system that some characterize as *rights myopic* (Huntington 2006, p. 637), the rush to adjudicate and only adjudicate trumps well-being at almost every turn, in almost every forum. Juvenile court is the welcome exception, at least since 1997 when President Clinton signed the Adoption and Safe Families Act. In 1997, finally, the child, and not the parents, became the center of the child welfare system in America.

The dilemma with problem-solving courts is the failure to incorporate science and evaluation as an integral component. The understanding and use of research and evaluation in a problem-solving court is as important as the understanding and application of the law (See Brank, this book). A problem-solving court devoid of

---

[2] Illinois Juvenile Court Act, 1899 Illinois Laws, 132 et seq. (1899).

science can be dangerous. Centuries ago, Leonardo da Vinci recognized the power of science when he wrote:

> Those who are enamored of practice without science are like a pilot who goes into a ship without rudder or compass and never has any certainty where he is going.

Being without a rudder or compass, guided only by the law, a jurist has both the legal and moral responsibility to ensure the safety, well-being, and permanency of the child. Former Chief Judge Judith Kaye (New York Court of Appeals), a champion of problem-solving courts believes that jurists can and must do much more than process cases. Adjudicating the case is not the same as resolving it (Kaye 2004, p. 126). A case represents a unique human being with unique problems who we know from experience will often be back before the court again and again. Unfortunately, in the American justice system, the quality of the work product of a judge is evaluated based on the outcome measure of how many cases the jurist can close and how quickly. That is the sole, empty, outcome measurement. However, to be effective decision makers, family court judges need feedback in the form of outcome measures, which indicate whether the family has successfully reunited, how well the children are doing at school, how well the children and parents are adjusting to the rigors of everyday social life, and whether or not the family has an adequate economic base from which it may function.

There are many examples of the absence of science and research in the court that have resulted in iatrogenic public policies, examples include direct filing delinquent youth into the adult system, sentencing delinquent youth to boot camps, and universal use of family preservation programs (Chalk and King 1998, p. 8). The failure or refusal to consider decades of research in policymaking has resulted in harm to children and families. In many instances, the consequences the policy was designed to prevent were only exacerbated by enacting public policy based on political considerations not supported by scientific research. In short, some of the interventions that problem-solving court judges have ordered for clients have not proved to be effective and therefore, reflect a waste of time and resources.

One striking example of the absence of science in policy and practice in our court and child welfare systems involves the failure to recognize the importance of a focus on the first few years of life and the needs of maltreated infants and toddlers. Maltreated infants and toddlers were invisible and absent from child welfare policies and practice because of policy makers' ignorance of the science of early child development. Furthermore, young children are not in school, so that they easily drop through the cracks in the social service system. As a result, the opportunity to intervene when it is most efficacious and to change the tragedy of child maltreatment into an opportunity to heal and grow was lost forever. It is now recognized that the science of early brain development established over decades of neuroscience and behavioral research illustrates why child development, especially from birth to age five is the foundation for a prosperous and sustainable society.[3] Yet, our courts

---

[3] *In brief: The science of early child development*, Center on the Developing Child, Harvard University.

virtually ignored these very young children, even though promoting the well-being of every child in the child welfare system was a legal responsibility of the dependency court.

We now know that babies can be depressed, have a long-term memory of trauma and are significantly affected by the mood and affect of their caregiver.[4] The young children who come into our courts have already suffered. Psychoanalytic theory was the first to suggest that early trauma involves the shattering of the young child's protective shield represented by the parent's care and nurturance. When that protective shield is violated by the experience of trauma, there are possible long-term ramifications for the future capacity to place trust in intimate relationships (Lieberman and Van Horn 2009, p. 711). The words "the baby is too young to. . . ." should never be heard in our dependency courts. The culture of absence should be completely reversed with the young child, as an imperative, at the very center of each case. Very young children need active attention and stimulation to grow into healthy school-aged children. Enriching the environments of young children transform them in ways that we now are beginning to understand. They can learn that the world can be a safe place, and that they can trust others and the court can facilitate that healing.

Dr. Jack Shonkoff, Director of the Center on the Developing Child at Harvard University, explains the power of the court this way: the judge actually holds the integrity of the child's developing brain in his or her hands (comment in Shonkoff 2007). The law changes slowly. Problem-solving courts have resulted not from a change in the law, but from a change in jurisprudential practice. Problem-solving courts extend the role of the legal system beyond fact finding and the imposition of sanctions. They attempt to use the authority of the court to maintain the social health of the community (Butts 2001, p. 121). This is a significant change in the jurist's role. As others explain in this book (See Wiener and Georges), judges in problem-solving courts can motivate clients to engage in services and empower them to use those services to modify their troubling behavior.

Judicial leadership inspired by the desire to make meaningful, positive, and permanent changes in the lives of the people who appear in court has created changes in practice. These are the judges who do not want to be measured by how many cases they close how quickly, but by the influence they have in changing the developmental pathway of a life. Justice Benjamin Cardozo believed that the work of a judge is in one sense enduring and in another sense ephemeral. What is good in it endures (Kaye 2004, p. 126). This necessitates a reevaluation of established legal practice and beliefs. The definitions and limitations of neutrality and impartiality and activism and fairness were therefore revised, by practice, not the law. Judges faced with clients that keep returning to court because of their psychological, social, and economic problems require more than the objective judge who acts only to make sure the rules of the game in the courtroom are fair and just. To assist clients to rehabilitate their lives, judges took many of the roles of case managers (See Wiener and Georges, this book). The hope was to facilitate a change in the social health of the court community. Perhaps, the change in the law and then policy will follow.

---

[4] Zero to Three, *What grown-ups understand about child development* (2000).

Perhaps, the good that is done by moving beyond the mere adjudication of a case will endure, as well. The outcomes by which we measure a court as an intervention must be significantly modified to reflect the complexity of the problems and the promise of changing human behavior.

One of the starting points for a more productive legal course would begin with an inquiry about the quality of the services and programs our families are ordered to complete as part of their case plan. Every day, judges order children and families to participate in therapeutic services, substance abuse programs, and programs designed to prevent repeated domestic violence. Judges and child welfare professionals are irresponsible and naive because they believe that each program and service is a quality service and that the service is helping our families. They act as if all services work and that whatever action the court takes in assigning these services is correct. This uncritical belief system can only change when the courts demand valid and reliable measures that the judges can use as feedback to determine when, why, and how services actually benefit (or do not benefit) the consumers of these services.

Every researcher knows that some interventions work, some have no effect whatsoever (known as the null hypothesis), and some services actually harm the people while the services should be helping. In fact, the vast majority of prevention programs, more than 90 %, have no evidentiary support to confirm or deny their effectiveness (Greenwood 2006).

No one asks the simple question: how do we know if this service is effective? The legal requirement of reasonable efforts is not being met in our courts. A service that has no empirical basis, no empirical design, and delivered by poorly trained professionals is not going to help our families stay out of the child welfare system or get their children back. There are good interventions and bad interventions so that the simple act of offering a community service and requiring a family to participate in that service is no guarantee that the family will move toward a successful resolution of the problems that landed them in family court the first place.

Another disturbing example of the failure of the child welfare system to provide the most basic service in a responsible way to families of cumulative advantage with very limited skills is a study of parent-focused interventions or what is commonly called parenting skills. The parents who come into the child welfare system have learned parenting by assimilating the beliefs and experiences of their own families, and, for many of them parenting is far from difficult because it only involves feeding and clothing a child. Almost every parent in our country's child welfare system has a case plan that contains the task of parenting skills. Although there are numerous efficacious parent-focused interventions that change the family environment and improve the lives of children, research has documented that most of the parent-focused interventions currently delivered to families in the child welfare system and most foster parent training do not use treatment strategies with solid empirical support (Horvitz et al. 2010, p. 28).

What do child welfare professionals know about evidence-based practice? Curious about the existence and awareness of evidence-based practices and programs in the child welfare system in Miami-Dade County, members of a Florida nonprofit corporation, Research and Reform for Children in Court, Inc., sought answers by asking questions to over 300 child welfare professionals at an annual child welfare conference in Miami.

Do practitioners understand what evidence-based practice means?

What is the level of awareness by child welfare system professionals regarding how evidence-based practices effect positive change in families?

How can evidence-based practices be best disseminated by professionals and judges making referrals for services in the child welfare system?

Although the answers to these questions are difficult to determine, they are important to the implementation of effective interventions, service delivery, and quality. To assess the perceptions, attitudes, and knowledge of evidence-based practices among those working in the child welfare system, a short survey instrument was developed. The goal of the survey was to identify child welfare professionals' level of understanding of evidence-based practice; their attitudes about the use of evidence-based practice; and to target potential training and educational gaps in the community in order to improve existing systems and encourage the implementation of more evidence-based programs and policies.[5]

In all, 209 members of the child welfare community (i.e., service providers, social workers, attorneys, and judges) in Miami responded to the survey. The responses to the survey pointed to the need for further training in this area as well as a need to revise the criteria by which services for families involved in the child welfare system are selected. A total of 87 % of the respondents who identified themselves as either frontline child welfare professionals or service providers—those who deliver direct services to families or engage in case management and investigative decisions—were unable to define evidence-based practice using the criteria outlined above. Among child welfare workers, 92 % of Case Managers, 90 % of Case Manager Supervisors, and 80 % of Child Protective Investigators were unable to define evidence-based practice. In addition, 97 % of the middle management or program specialists, 60 % of the funders, 50 % of the judges,and all of those in the advocates group were unable to provide acceptable definitions of evidence-based practice (Lederman et al. 2009, p. 24).

Although 88 % of the 209 survey respondents were unable to define evidence-based practice with 87 % believing that evidence-based practice was any approach that resulted in "better outcomes." Of the respondents, 60 % believed that evidence-based practices "improved collaborative decision-making" and 52 % agreed that "the Court thinks these are better programs." Also, 35 % of the 209 respondents recognized that evidence-based practices are "cost-effective" (Lederman et al. 2009, p. 25).

Even if a child or parent is in an evidence-based service, how is successful compliance measured? Judges make reunification decisions based on service completion of case plan tasks. How is successful completion of a service measured? Too often

[5] The survey was administered at the *2008 Miami-Dade Community Based Care Alliance Annual Regional Child Welfare Conference*, held in November of 2008 in Miami, Florida. This conference drew more than 300 professionals who serve families in the child welfare system for training and discussion on current topics and practices in the field.

in our child welfare system, it is measured by attending and attending alone (for an empirical demonstration of this issue see Brank et al. 2002). Every parent who attends all the classes successfully completes the program and is fit to parent. No one fails. Has the parent learned, can she use what she learned to enhance the relationship with her child, is she able outside of the classroom environment to consistently and effectively use the strategies she was taught? What exactly did the parent do to obtain that "certificate of completion" judges see the parents displaying in court? It seems all that is required is that a parent show up and stay awake to meet the completion requirements. Every day, judges jeopardize the safety of children by reunifying parents with their children because a parent has obtained her certificate. It is not possible for a teen mother who has never felt nurtured or safe as a child, who thinks she is spoiling her baby if she picks him up when he cries, to learn how to nurture and understand her baby's needs in a didactic class with no parent–child interaction that is devoid of an empirical basis.

Judges must begin to ask questions and demand a system of care improvement. Judges must ask for proof of learning and the ability to integrate that learning in a natural environment with the child.

There are parenting programs that have been determined to be efficacious. Programs such as multidimensional treatment foster care (MTFC) is an intervention designed for youth and foster parents in foster care settings; the Positive Parenting Program known as Triple P has been shown to decrease behavior problems and dysfunctional parenting styles; and the Incredible Years (IY) parenting curricula has resulted in increases in positive parenting affect, replacement of harsh discipline with nonviolent discipline techniques, and reduced child conduct problems (Horvitz et al. 2010, p. 30).

Child–Parent Psychotherapy (CPP) has been an invaluable tool in the Miami Juvenile Court for a decade. A relationship-based intervention for parents and young children developed by Dr. Alicia Lieberman, and adapted for the Miami Juvenile Court by Dr. Joy Osofsky, has resulted in successes that some might describe as miracles. Parents have been reunified who would never have been able to learn to be a good enough parent before the advent of CPP (Winnicott 1960, p. 585). Despite the intensive, lengthy, and onerous nature of the intervention, lawyers who represent parents in dependency court ask for CPP for their clients. Parents who are defensive and defiant at the removal hearing where their children are taken from them and assure the court that they are good parents find CPP to be life changing. A young mother who needed to be taught to smile at her baby, feel enjoyment being with her baby and praise her baby characterized what she had learned at a court hearing by observing that "my baby loves me now".

CPP is based on the beliefs as stated by Dr. Joy Osofsky that the infant was harmed in the relationship and must be healed in the relationship. The therapeutic work in CPP, which appears to a lay person to involve modeling appropriate parenting behavior, incorporates a broad range of techniques to enhance the mother's awareness and responsiveness to her child's needs because emotional and behavioral problems in infancy and early childhood need to be addressed in the context of primary attachment relationships.

The results are striking. There has been no further reported abuse or neglect in the original 57 dyads. Overall, important improvements in both parental sensitivity to the children and in the children's emotional responsiveness and behaviors were observed (Osofsky et al. 2007, p. 259). This intervention may be one of the most effective tools in our dependency courts to stop the intergenerational transmission of child maltreatment.

The incentive to spur innovation in human services is a chronic problem in the child welfare system where there is no profit motivation and where there has not been a strong focus on knowledge development (Horvitz et al. 2010, p. 32). Evidence is the apple pie of decision-making, who could be against it (Peterson 2001, p. 191)? Well, in the crisis nature of child welfare work, the low social status attributed to those whose career involves helping these families, the high caseloads and frequent turnover, and knowledge development, is regarded as a luxury. The research is not accessible, available, or translated in a way that child welfare workers or most officers of the court find helpful.

Dr. Katherine Dill, the creator of PART-Ontario, an organization that promotes knowledge translation and evidence-informed practice in child welfare in Canada believes that there is hope. The shift towards the use of research evidence in practice has marked an important turning point in a field like child welfare where practitioners have been traditionally separated from academic research and have implemented interventions based on customary practices as opposed to what has been demonstrated to be effective (Dill and Shera 2010). Dr. Dill has developed a network of almost 30 Children's Aid Societies in Canada that contract with PART to receive assistance in informing their work with research. She provides multiple types of educational opportunities including webinars, periodic 3-page translations of relevant research articles called PARTICLES, online access to highly respected academic journals and even the services of a "researcher on call". After 3 years, 76 % of her PART partners believe that research is informing practice in their individual agencies.[6]

The challenges to healing families in the child welfare system seem overwhelming. Without science and meaningful evaluation in our problem-solving courts the challenges will never be overcome. Judges want to make better decisions, being informed not only by what they feel or think, but more importantly by what they know. However, the quality of the judges' decisions requires that that the choice calculous be based upon valid and reliable information. Judges and social scientists must work together to make this type of information available and accessible to the child welfare system.

References

Brank, E. M., Williams, A. L., Ray, R. E., & Weisz, V. (2002). Parental compliance: Its role in termination of parental rights cases. *Nebraska Law Review, 80,* 335–353.

Butts, J. A. (2001). Problem-solving courts. *Law & Policy, 23,* 121–124.

[6] PART evaluation results 2010.

Chalk, R., & King, P. (1998). *Violence in families: Assessing prevention and treatment programs*. Washington, DC: National Academy Press.

Dill, K., & Shera, W. (2010). *Pushing the envelope: Future directions for evidence-informed practice*. Toronto: PART & University of Toronto.

Dodge, K., Dishion, T., & Lansford, J. (2006). *Deviant peer influences in programs for youth*. New York: Guilford Press.

Greenwood, P. (2006). *Changing lives: Delinquency prevention as crime control policy*. Chicago: The University of Chicago Press.

Hora, P., Schma, W., & Rosenthal, J. (1999). Therapeutic jurisprudence and the drug treatment movement: Revolutionizing the criminal justice system's response to drug abuse and crime in America. *Notre Dame Law Review, 74*(2), 439–527.

Horvitz, S., Chamberlain, P., Landsverk, J., & Mullican, C. (2010). Improving the mental health of children in child welfare through the implementation of evidence based parenting interventions. *Administration and Policy in Mental Health, 37*(1–2), 27–39.

Huntington, C. (2006). Rights myopia in child welfare. *UCLA Law Review, 53,* 637–699.

Kaye, J. (2004). Delivering justice today: A problem-solving approach. *Yale Law and Policy Review, 22,* 125–151.

Lamb, M., & Kelly, J. (2000). Using child development research to make appropriate custody and access decisions for young children. *Family and Conciliation Courts Review, 38*(3), 297–311.

Lederman, C., Gomez-Kaifer, M., Katz, L., Thomlison, B., & Maze, C. (2009). An imperative: Evidence based practice within the child welfare system of care. *Juvenile and Family Justice Today, Fall,* 22–25.

Lieberman, A., & Van Horn, P. (2009) Giving voice to the unsayable: Repairing the effects of trauma in infancy and early childhood. *Child and Adolescent Psychiatric Clinics of North America, 18,* 707–720.

Osofsky, J., Kronenberg, M., Hammer, J., Lederman, C., Katz, L., Adams, S., Graham, M., & Hogan, A. (2007). The development and the evaluation of the intervention model for the Florida Infant Mental Health Program. *Infant Mental Health Journal, 28,* 259–280.

Peterson, M. A. (2001). Evidence: Its meaning in health care and law. *Journal of Health Politics, Policy and Law, 26*(2), 191–193.

Shonkoff, J. (2007). *Helping babies from the bench: Using the science of early childhood development in court*. Washington, DC: Zero to Three.

Wexler, D. (1995). Reflections on the scope of therapeutic jurisprudence. *Psychology, Public Policy and the Law, 1*(1), 220–236.

Wexler, D. (2000). Therapeutic jurisprudence: An overview. *Thomas. M. Cooley Law Review, 17,* 125–134.

Winnicott, D. W. (1960). The theory of the parent–infant relationship. *International Journal of Psychoanalysis, 41,* 585–595.

Chapter 3
Exploring the Value-Added of Specialized Problem-Solving Courts for Dependency Cases

Sophia I. Gatowski, Shirley A. Dobbin and Alicia Summers

Examining the Value-Added of Specialized Problem-Solving Courts for Dependency Cases

When people think of problem-solving courts within the dependency or child abuse and neglect case context, the "specialized" problem-solving courts that divert a sub-population of their cases to receive special handling come most readily to mind (e.g., dependency drug courts or family treatment courts). Although dependency courts are themselves specialized in the sense that they focus on child abuse and neglect cases, they are nonspecialized problem-solving courts in the sense that they apply an individualized, problem-solving approach to *all* cases that come before them. Dependency courts that follow "best practice" problem-solving guidelines (i.e., nationally recognized recommendations for handling child abuse and neglect hearings developed by experts such as those promulgated by the National Council of Juvenile and Family Court Judges 1995 and 2000) have considerable promise for improving the judicial branch's ability to respond positively to the needs of its constituents—that by treating all children and families that come under the court's jurisdiction with a therapeutic, multidisciplinary, collaborative approach, improved child safety, timely permanency, and positive well-being outcomes will result (see Lederman, this book). However, this promise cannot be fully realized until we know more about the functioning and effect of problem-solving court features or standards for case processing in the dependency court context. While there are numerous studies of specific dependency court programs and interventions (e.g., Burford and Hudson 2009; Gatowski et al. 2005; Litchfield et al. 2003; Summers et al. 2008; Thoennes 1997, 2008 to cite just a few), there are far fewer evaluations of "best practice" case processing elements

S. I. Gatowski (✉) · S. A. Dobbin
Systems Change Solutions, Inc.: Research, Evaluation and Training Consultants, Vancouver, BC, Canada
e-mail: sgatowski@ymail.com

A. Summers
Permanency Planning for Children Department,
National Council of Juvenile and Family Court Judges, Reno, NV, USA

R. L. Wiener, E. M. Brank (eds.), *Problem Solving Courts*,
DOI 10.1007/978-1-4614-7403-6_3, © Springer Science+Business Media, LLC 2013

(Dobbin et al. 2003; Gatowski et al. 2002a, b). More comprehensive research needs to be undertaken on foundational or ostensibly "best practice" problem-solving features of dependency court processing with findings from that research feedback into reforms and the training of judicial and dependency court stakeholders (Summers et al. 2008). Considerably more research is needed, for example, on the operation of foundational problem-solving court practices that can tie those practices to specific outcomes. As Judge Lederman notes in her chapter in this book, the gap that exists between research and practice in the dependency court arena needs to be bridged.

In this chapter, we provide an orientation to the widely recognized theory of "best practice" framework for dependency case processing as it requires a collaborative problem-solving approach to the resolution of child abuse and neglect cases. We compare and contrast this foundational "best practice" dependency court model with family drug courts (FDCs), which are the most prevalent specialized problem-solving courts in the child abuse and neglect case context. We also present research exploring the different procedures and outcomes associated with the implementation of three problem-solving court models in one state (foundational best practice, FDC, and a therapeutic justice court, TJC). This research provides insight into the operation of problem-solving court features in the dependency court context and sheds light on how best to coordinate between cases handled by a traditional dependency court process and those assigned to specialized models such as FDCs in order to maximize the use of specialized models for those individuals who need them most. The research also suggests ways to enhance the "best practice" model by adapting elements of the drug court model to apply to all dependency cases (rather than growing more and more specialized courts) and suggests areas in need of further research.

The Evolution of the Dependency Court

The first juvenile court was established in 1899 in Chicago, Illinois with the "intention of creating a statewide *special* court with unique jurisdiction over predelinquent and delinquent youth . . . the court was created to extend protection to troubled children in general, including those who are abused, neglected, dependent or in need of supervision" (Roush 1996). Today, "dependency court" refers to a special branch of juvenile or family court dealing with civil child abuse and neglect. Dependency courts grew out of the recognition that courts had failed to respond to the needs of abused and neglected children in a way that ameliorated the underlying problems that brought the family before the court—resulting in reemergence of the problem and repeated court intervention. Instead, a special branch of court was needed that would not just litigate a wrong-doing, but resolve the underlying family problems, ending the "revolving door" that keeps bringing the family back to court. Dependency courts adjudicate whether child abuse or neglect has occurred, and when it has, orders services to prevent its reoccurrence. When services fail, the court will work toward termination of parental rights and a permanent, safe placement alternative for the child. Dependency courts make important decisions regarding the child's placement (in the home or out of the home), the necessary services and resources to assist the child(ren) and family, when it is safe enough for the child to return home, and the termination of parental rights and final permanency outcome (Lecklitner et al. 1999).

Efforts to improve dependency courts have been steadily underway since the Adoption Assistance and Child Welfare Act of 1980 (PL 96-272), one of the first major steps in formalizing the juvenile dependency court process. This was followed by a number of key events in the 1990s, which sought to further enhance the system (such as the Omnibus Budget Reconciliation Act of 1993, for example, which included the federal State Court Improvement Program (CIP), and was enacted to systematically reform the juvenile dependency court). In 1995, the National Council of Juvenile and Family Court Judges (hereinafter the National Council), the nation's oldest judicial membership organization,[1] published the *Resource Guidelines: Improving Court Practice in Child Abuse and Neglect Cases* (hereinafter the Guidelines). The Guidelines document provided the foundation for dependency court improvements not only by establishing court hearing "best practices," but also by making recommendations for enhancement of the juvenile dependency system as a whole. The critical leadership role of the judge (both on- and off-the-bench) is stressed in this "best practice" orientation, as is the role of the court more broadly, and the need for systems-wide collaboration to improve outcomes for abused and neglected children (Portune et al. 2009). "Best practice" in this context refers to an approach to handling child abuse and neglect cases that requires, among other activities, active judicial inquiry and oversight, frequent and direct engagement of parties by the judge, early appointment of counsel, the conduct of substantive hearings, and collaboration by the judge with system partners for court improvement. The Guidelines were developed by an expert committee of judges, child welfare administrators, and attorneys, and drew heavily from the experiences of juvenile courts that had undergone considerable reform. The final Guidelines publication and the recommendations for dependency practices contained therein were subsequently endorsed by the Conference of Chief Judges, the American Bar Association, and the Board of Trustees of the National Council.[2] The "best practices" referred to in the Guidelines should not be confused with "evidence-based" practices. Evidence-based practices are based on a foundation of empirical research, whereas "best practices" referred to in the Guidelines are recommendations derived from the consensus of experts in the handling of child abuse and neglect cases.

The publication of the Guidelines was quickly followed by the Adoption and Safe Families Act passed by the U.S. Congress in 1997 (ASFA, Public Law 105-89), which codified most of the recommendations of the Guidelines document and established permanency, safety, and well-being of children as the primary outcomes

---

[1] The national council of juvenile and family court judges was founded in the United States in 1937 (www.ncjfcj.org).

[2] The original Guidelines document was supplemented by the *Adoption and Permanency Guidelines: Improving Court Practice in Child Abuse and Neglect Cases*, which was published by the National Council in 2000 to more fully cover best practices as they relate to the latter stages of the dependency case process (i.e., termination of parental rights and adoption).

to achieve in child welfare cases (NCJFCJ 2009). The intent in passing ASFA was to prevent children from languishing in foster care and to prevent foster care drift by moving children out of foster care and into safe and permanent placements as quickly as possible. ASFA shortened the timeframes for case processing and called upon the nation's courts and social service agencies to make the health and safety of children the paramount concern in placement and permanency decisions. ASFA placed stringent requirements on the courts and child welfare systems, holding them accountable for both the protection and permanent placement of children and for assistance with families. ASFA placed further pressure on courts to find innovative ways to resolve cases and promote timely permanency. The Guidelines and federal legislation such as ASFA increased the responsibility and accountability of judicial officers, requiring them to ensure both the safety and the best interest of the child and procedural fairness for parents, all the while moving the case along in a timely fashion.

Since its publication in 1995 and dissemination till date, the Guidelines have grown in their power of influence through the widespread acceptance of what have become foundational judicial "best practices" in child abuse and neglect cases that reinforce the appropriateness of the problem-solving approach for this case type. Two significant ways the Guidelines have been implemented and served to influence dependency court practice is through the national Model Courts project and through the federal State CIP. With the development of the Guidelines, the National Council received funding from the U.S. Department of Justice, Office of Juvenile Justice and Delinquency Prevention to support implementation of the best practices in specific project sites, through its national Model Courts project. The "Child Victims Act Model Courts Project" began with a small number of courts and a very specific focus on supporting the development of judicial leadership, implementing court-based best practices from the Guidelines, and building collaborative relationships between the court and the child welfare agency (Portune et al. 2009). Today, there are 36 participating Model Courts representing the largest dependency court jurisdictions in the country (i.e., New York City, Los Angeles, and Chicago) as well as suburban, rural, and tribal jurisdictions. Although these courts continue to focus on the best practices of the Guidelines as the foundational component of their reform efforts, the range of system partners involved in collaborative efforts in each site has grown and increasingly complex issues are being addressed. The Guidelines have also informed judicial and system stakeholder trainings conducted in every state through their federal State CIP. The CIP was created as part of the Omnibus Budget Reconciliation Act of 1993 (Public Law 103-66), which designated a portion of state funds to child welfare agencies and tribes for grants to state court systems to examine their foster care and adoption laws and judicial processes, and to develop and implement plans for system improvement. A common feature of state court improvement plans has been multidisciplinary stakeholder training on the Guidelines' best practices, evaluation of current practice against those recommended in the Guidelines (e.g., National Council of Juvenile and Family Court Judges 2005), and the implementation of "best practice/model" courts that use the Guidelines' recommendations to design reforms.

The Dependency Court as a Problem-Solving Court

In a study of judges who were asked to consider the transferability of specialized problem-solving court principles to conventional courts, juvenile delinquency and dependency courts were widely cited as perhaps the most appropriate venues for problem solving, particularly for practices such as addressing the problems that contribute to recidivism, using a team-based approach, and interacting directly with all parties (Farole et al. 2005). In their study, Farole et al. (2005) convened focus groups with judges in California and New York with extensive experience presiding over problem-solving courts. The judges were to consider which problem-solving court practices are most easily applied in conventional courts and which type of courts are most amenable to those problem-solving practices. All of the 29 judges in the study agreed that juvenile delinquency and dependency courts held the most potential for problem solving to be practiced (Farole et al. 2005).

In fact, the juvenile court is arguably the original problem-solving court as juvenile court judges have always been tasked with attempting to identify services and strategies to rehabilitate children, youth, and family members (Edwards 1992; Berman and Feinblatt 2005). The strong judicial oversight and substantive review of services' associated with problem-solving court models is consistent with dependency court federal (e.g., ASFA) and state law (e.g., California's Standard of Judicial Administration 2005) that require the same of dependency court judges. Although problem-solving courts such as drug courts, mental health courts, and veterans courts require judicial leadership to bring the court system and service providers together and to create a collaborative environment to produce timely resolution of cases, this has long been the traditional role of dependency court judges who are conveners of court systems and communities on behalf of children and families (Edwards 1992; Berman 2000). Dependency court reform efforts (the ASFA, Resource Guidelines, Model Courts, and the federal CIP) further reinforced the need for problem-solving approaches in dependency case processing—engaging parents early on in the case, for example, to encourage timely compliance and responsibility; ensuring the educational and medical needs of the child are met to promote well-being during a difficult time for children and families; and taking an active role in ensuring that family relationships and attachments are not severed by addressing visitation with parents and siblings.

A closer look at the best practice framework for dependency cases articulated in the Guidelines reveals how similar they are to the guiding principles of problem-solving court models (i.e., the guiding principles of both drug courts and other specialized models as well as the principles of therapeutic jurisprudence more generally). The dependency court "best practices" set a framework that supports information sharing and timely decision making, parent involvement in case planning, and an overall problem-solving approach to the handling of child abuse and neglect cases:

- *Judicial leadership*: Judicial leadership is the cornerstone of the Resource Guidelines' principles—both on-the-bench in individual cases and off-the-bench in the broader community. Judges in both dependency best practice courts and problem-solving court models assume a leadership role in specific cases when requiring timely and comprehensive access to appropriate services. They also assume a leadership role off-the-bench when engaged in the collaboration with system partners and the larger community. In fact, the driving Guidelines' principle, on which all other principles are based, is the need for judicial leadership to provide comprehensive and timely judicial action in child abuse and neglect cases. Without this vitally important cornerstone, best practice principles cannot be fully implemented and achieved. Committed, knowledgeable judicial leaders are crucial to the success of best practice and reform efforts in both dependency courts and in the problem-solving court model.

- *Problem-solving judicial orientation*: Dependency court requires active, judicial involvement in cases—explicit use of judicial authority to motivate, monitor progress, and compliance. The proactive role of the judge in problem-solving courts is also consistent with the best practice recommendations of the Guidelines. Judges are encouraged, in both the best practice framework and in the problem-solving court models, to ask more questions, seek more information about each case, explore a greater range of possible solutions, and motivate parents to engage in services.
- *Therapeutic jurisprudence approach to processing cases*: Problem-solving courts and the Guidelines approach to handling dependency cases use the principles of therapeutic jurisprudence to enhance their response to cases and the individuals involved in those cases. Problem-solving and Guidelines-based dependency courts, for instance, employ key principles of therapeutic jurisprudence such as ongoing judicial intervention, close monitoring, and immediate response (e.g., through frequent and proactive judicial review of cases), multidisciplinary involvement, and collaboration with community-based and government agency organizations (Winnick and Wexler 2003) to enhance the functioning of the court.
- *Early and active engagement of parties*: Early engagement of parents in the dependency court process is stressed in the best practice approach as critically important to handling these cases. Engagement in this "best practice" context is not just something that happens at a single point in time—engagement is not just involving the family—in this context, engagement is also the process of developing and maintaining an interest in a relationship, often initiated through the identification of a common goal or mutual interest. Engagement is facilitated through mutual respect, clear and consistent communication, and information sharing. Ideally, multiple levels of engagement are involved that include individual, social, and system processes. Direct interaction with respondent parents in court hearings is stressed in a "best practices" framework, as it is in problem-solving court models, as a way to encourage compliance with court orders and case plans, enabling judges to motivate individuals to make progress, and to bring to light the needs of the parties.
- *Early, active, and collaborative approach to court intervention*: A collaborative problem-solving approach to resolve child abuse and neglect cases is emphasized in the "best practice" orientation in response to concerns that overly adversarial proceedings can result in delays in case processing which ultimately delays permanency for children. Adapting to the nonadversarial role in best practice dependency

courts and problem-solving courts can be difficult for attorneys and is often cited as a stumbling block implementing a problem-solving court model (e.g., Casey 2004; Ogletree 1993; Quinn 2001; Simon 2003). A central component of the collaborative model in dependency cases is the concept of "front-loading" which sets in place procedures to ensure that all parties to the court proceeding begin actively participating at the *earliest* point possible and are doing all they can to minimize the length of time for which children remain in temporary placement and their families remain court involved. Front-loading is designed to address these concerns by establishing a process that encourages early problem solving and cooperation at the onset of court proceedings. Examples of front-loading of dependency cases include the use of expanded, substantive preliminary protective hearings; early appointment of counsel for parents and children; prehearing or pretrial settlement conferencing; early alternative dispute resolution such as mediation or family group conferencing; and early identification of services to children and families.

- *Judicial continuity (one family/one judge)*: Best practice Guidelines recommend that dependency courts function under a one family/one judge case assignment system in which one judicial officer presides over all of the court hearings in a dependency case. The aim is that when a single judicial officer hears all matters related to a single family, (he or she) will gain knowledge of the family's circumstances and their past response to court orders, will be able to identify behavior patterns, and can help to ensure there is consistency and continuity in court orders and case plans. A one family/one judge case assignment system also helps to minimize the number of times a person is required to appear in court because it allows for multiple cases for one individual or family to be heard together. In the dependency context, for example, a one family/one judge case assignment system would allow the judge to address matters related to the dependency matter as well as the child's delinquency and any parental orders of protection in one hearing. Although the dependency best practices approach and the problem-solving court model may require more hearings because frequent review of case progress is considered important, the need to add further hearings for other matters is reduced under a one judge/one family case assignment system.
- *Outcome focus*: In a dependency court best practice framework, judges and system stakeholders are just as concerned with improving outcomes for the children and families that come under the jurisdiction of the court as they are with case processing. Although timeliness of case processing is certainly an important court performance goal, dependency courts should be equally concerned with the safety, permanency, and well-being outcomes associated with the cases under their jurisdiction.
- *Not limited to a narrow dispute*: Traditional courts limit their attention to the narrow dispute in controversy, whereas dependency courts attempt to understand and address the underlying problem that is responsible for the immediate dispute. The goal is to help the individuals before the court to effectively deal with the problem in ways that will prevent recurring court involvement.
- *Creates the need for information*: The nature of the decision-making process in dependency cases creates a demand for more and varied information about family

problems, what is in the best interests of the child(ren), and what resources, interventions, or services are best to resolve those problems. Although this demand has significantly improved the quality and quantity of information brought before the court, as Judge Lederman notes in her chapter, bridges still need to be built between research and the practice needs of dependency courts.

The most prevalent *specialized* problem-solving court model in the dependency context is the family drug or family treatment court (U.S. Bureau of Justice Assistance 2005)—"specialized" because those dependency courts focus on a specific issue or presenting problem, in this case—substance abuse. While most of the parents' substance abuse is typically reviewed by the FDC team (e.g., domestic violence, parenting skills, mental and physical health, pending criminal charges, housing, child care, and employment or education), FDCs "specialize" by focusing and concentrating their efforts on determining the individual treatment needs of substance-abusing parents whose children are under the jurisdiction of the dependency court. Although a significant percentage of families that come under the jurisdiction of dependency courts are drug or alcohol involved (U.S. Department of Health and Human Services 2005; Young and Otero 2005), FDCs typically only serve a small portion of that population because of capacity and resource limitations. The professional stakeholders in the FDC work with these parents in an effort to rehabilitate them, so that they can become competent caretakers and have their children safely returned to their care (U.S. Bureau of Justice Assistance 2004; U.S. Department of Justice 1998). As in other problem-solving courts (including the traditional dependency court), judicial leadership is key and case reviews are frequent.

Although traditional dependency courts and specialized dependency problem-solving courts such as FDCs share a number of features, they also differ in some significant ways. As previously mentioned, traditional dependency courts were not established to deal with a specific problem such as substance abuse or domestic violence, but with *all* presenting problems of the children and families that come under the court's jurisdiction. Judges in traditional dependency courts may also not see (or define) themselves as therapeutic agents to the extent that judges in specialized problem-solving courts view themselves. Unlike traditional judges functioning in traditional dependency courts, judges in specialized problem-solving court models consciously view themselves as therapeutic agents (Young et al. 2003). In fact, because the role is unique, judges should participate in additional training before assuming their role on the bench of a specialized problem-solving court—training which includes a focus on the judge's therapeutic role and specific strategies for enacting that role (Young et al. 2003). As a result, the therapeutic jurisprudence function of specialized dependency court judges is much more visible.

Outstanding Questions About Problem-Solving Dependency Courts

Our experience observing and facilitating the development of dependency courts as problem-solving courts over more than 15 years has left us with some outstanding questions. For instance, are the widely adopted and recognized best practices truly "best"? What outcomes can be associated with these best practices to move beyond theory to evidence-based practice? What is the value-added of "specialized" problem-solving courts such as FDC when dependency court best practice is followed or is the norm? What do specialized problem-solving courts do to enhance the experience and outcomes for individuals involved with the court that cannot be achieved in a dependency court following a best practice framework? If dependency court incorporates critical elements of "specialized" problem-solving court models into daily practice with *all* cases, can positive outcomes associated with drug court models diffuse to more cases and more families? FDCs serve a relatively small proportion of the overall population of parents that come before the juvenile court with substance abuse problems—Are there FDC strategies that can be adapted, within overall caseload and resource constraints, to the broader population of parents involved in the dependency court system? How do we take what is being learned in courts serving subpopulations of cases and use that information to bolster or improve practice and outcomes in the dependency court as a whole?

An Evaluation of Utah Juvenile Court Problem-Solving Models

The Utah Juvenile Court provided us with a unique context within which to empirically study problem-solving models in dependency courts and their influence on case outcomes. At the time of the study in 2006, three distinct models of problem-solving courts were operating in Utah, each using somewhat different strategies—court reviews of varying frequencies, differing screening procedures and areas of focus for service, different engagement strategies to involve parents in case planning, and different collaborative arrangements with the Division of Child and Family Services and treatment providers (Dobbin et al. 2006).

The Three Problem-Solving Models

The Traditional Utah Juvenile Court Process The traditional dependency court process in the Utah Juvenile Court—from the initial shelter hearing held within 72 h of removal, through the achievement of permanency and case closure—is built on the best practice recommendations of the Resource Guidelines. Past performance measurement data and evaluation findings show that hearings in the traditional juvenile courts are substantially compliant with statutory and federally required timeframes for case processing (Dobbin et al. 2003). These Guidelines-based courts reflect the key principles and processes of the problem-solving model approach, including a focus on judicial leadership, collaboration with system partners to improve outcomes, and frequent case review. Study sites representing the traditional court model in Utah were the Second Judicial District (urban) and Eighth Judicial District (rural) dependency courts.

Family Drug Courts FDCs in Utah were first implemented in 2000 with the goal of creating a problem-solving process to support parental sobriety and timely permanency for children. The Utah FDCs use a combination of frequent court oversight, frequent drug-testing, multidisciplinary treatment team meetings, priority placement for substance abuse treatment services and clinical and judicial rewards and sanctions (including jail time for noncompliance in some instances). The drug court review hearings were attended by all FDC clients so that each parent could observe and learn from the interactions taking place, with the aim of shaping their own behavior and building group support for sobriety. Judges presiding over the FDC also preside over the dependency hearings for the drug court clients (i.e., the same judge hears both the drug court reviews and the underlying dependency matter). Study sites representing the FDC model in Utah were the Fourth Judicial District (urban) and Seventh Judicial District (rural) dependency courts.

Therapeutic Justice Court The TJC was first implemented in Salt Lake City, Utah (an urban and suburban court jurisdiction) in 2002. The aim of the TJC is to apply a therapeutic justice model to all of the child protection cases assigned to one courtroom (i.e., assigned to one judge), irrespective of the family's presenting problem. The primary goal is the achievement of family reunification or other permanency for children in less than the maximum allowed time of 12 months from removal, while maintaining safety. Achievement of this goal is facilitated through early screening and assessments, early linkages to services, early engagement of parents in case plan development and the permanency planning process, the creation of a problem-solving atmosphere in court hearings, and a cohesive legal model that supports and is supported by a cohesive clinical and service model. The TJC aimed to adopt the case coordination strategy from the FDC model, the frequent predisposition court reviews from the FDC model, and the FDC's cohesive clinical and service model, and to apply those strategies in an individualized approach to each family as needed.

All of the problem-solving courts in Utah were implemented within a strong framework of court and agency "best practice." Within the Utah Juvenile Court, Guidelines' best practices have been implemented throughout the state, with extensive judicial and multidisciplinary training. Furthermore, the Rules of the Juvenile Court have incorporated the Guidelines' recommendations for case processing (Utah Rules of Juvenile Procedure 1995). Since the FDC and TJC were built on a traditional court model that had at its core the Guidelines' best practices, and previous research we had conducted in each of the three jurisdictions of interest had indicated that their case processing timeframes were highly compliant with statutory and federal timelines (Dobbin et al. 2003), the baseline timeliness performance against which the FDCs and the TJC were measured could already be considered high. In addition, the research we had previously conducted (Dobbin et al. 2003) included extensive court observation in which hearings were compared with the standards recommended by the Resource Guidelines for the conduct of high quality hearings. All three of the jurisdictions in the problem-solving court study were found, in the earlier study, to be strongly compliant with the recommendations of the Guidelines for best hearing practice (Dobbin et al. 2003). As a result, any gains found in a study of the new problem-solving courts would be compared against strong foundational practice, rather than against practice that could be considered inferior or not in compliance with mandated practices let alone "best practices." What also made this research opportunity particularly intriguing was that one of the models (the TJC) was established because the judge wanted to tweak or enhance some features of her traditional or Guidelines-based court process to see if the same positive outcomes attributed to FDC models could be obtained.

For the purposes of this Chapter, the methods employed by this research are only briefly summarized below—the reader is referred to the final study report by Dobbin et al. 2006, available online at www.ncjfcj.org for more detail with respect to method and analyses.

Research Goals

In evaluating the different problem-solving models operating in the Utah Juvenile Court, we hoped to determine the impact of these various models on the timeliness of case outcomes, permanency, and the overall quality of the process. The specific research goals were to:

- Clearly describe the defining characteristics of the general problem-solving models operating in Utah, identifying the specific policies and procedures in each model designed to facilitate safe, timely permanency for children (e.g., to what extent, if any did procedures and policies differ across project sites and to what extent, if any did these models change the role of the judges and other professionals (attorneys, case workers) in the dependency process.

Investigate the extent to which these various problem-solving models influence case-processing timeliness, permanency outcomes, and the quality of hearings. Quality of the process was operationalized as hearing practice that adhered to the best practice recommendations of the Resource Guidelines such as active judicial oversight of case planning, frequent court reviews that substantively address case progress and work to ameliorate barriers to that progress, and active parental engagement in the case process.

Methods

A number of qualitative and quantitative methods were used in an assessment of each of the problem-solving court models of interest to this study, including:

- *Interviews with professional stakeholders*. In order to fully describe the problem-solving model, judges, court coordinators, social work case managers, and attorneys were interviewed in each problem-solving court (focus was on role; nature of interaction with other professionals, children and parents; challenges and opportunities presented by the model; and extent to which role has changed or is different from traditional view). Interview respondents were also asked to comment on the quality of the case process under each model.

- *Interview with parents*. In order to assess the level of parental engagement under each model, parents with open or recently closed cases were interviewed. The interviews covered their experience in the specific model (including their level of input into the development of service plans, whether they felt they were treated with respect and had an opportunity for voice (Lind and Tyler 1988), the perceived appropriateness of services, and agency compliance with the delivery of services).
- *Focus group with adolescents*. As an additional measure of process quality and parental engagement, focus groups were conducted with youth whose parents had been involved in each of the three problem-solving court models. Youth were asked for their perception of their parents' involvement with the court, parental engagement of services, and their parents' overall success.
- *Observation of hearing and nonhearing events*. As a measure of quality of the case process and to provide a rich description of the practices and stakeholder roles operating in each model, hearing and nonhearing events were observed in each project site using a structured observation instrument. In each project site, the number and type of hearings to observe was determined in collaboration with court administrators, but were selected to be the representative of the dependency case process generally and the specific problem-solving court model specifically. Among the items coded during the hearing observations was the presence of parties, role of the parties, role of the judge, level of engagement of parties, specific issues discussed, and formality of procedures. In addition, a number of nonhearing processes (e.g., case staffings) were observed in each site, where the breadth of issues and services discussed, and interactional dynamics were assessed. Observations were conducted with teams of observers, and coding was checked for interrater reliability. Using Holsti's coefficient, a commonly accepted measure of interrater reliability, the average interrater reliability was 0.87. All variables ranged from 0.8 to 1, demonstrating good interrater reliability across items.
- *Case file review*. Court records in each site were examined using a structured coding instrument for case process (specific petition allegations, the substance of hearings, parties present, issues discussed, quality and scope of orders, etc.) and outcome variables (final disposition of the case, safety and permanency outcomes, compliance with case plans, and timeliness of case processing). Case files were coded by a team of coders, with coding checked for interrater reliability (using Holsti's coefficient, the average interrater reliability was 0.84
- *Court and Department of Children and Family Services database analysis*. For each project site, data were collected from both the court and agency databases regarding case processing outcomes (e.g., final disposition of the case, safety and permanency outcomes, compliance with case plans, timeliness of case processing, and reentry into the dependency court system after case closure).

Every attempt was made to ensure that cases were comparable across sites. This was relatively straightforward as the majority of each court's caseload involved substance abuse with primarily methamphetamine (crystal-meth) involved families. In addition, the state of Utah is fairly homogenous with most racial and ethnic diversity in Salt Lake City (the location of the TJC). Although random assignment of cases to a specific problem-solving court model or control group would have been ideal for our research purposes, this was not possible because of the specific intake or case assignment processes already in place in each site. These intake practices may have created some differences, albeit small, in the population of cases addressed by the different problem-solving court models. In drug court model, for example, all parents were assessed at intake or petition filing by the drug court coordinator for inclusion in the drug court program. Criteria for selection into the drug court were "significant" substance abuse issues and a willingness to participate. In this way, the drug court program excluded those parents whose substance abuse was not considered to be a significant concern and/or who refused to participate. In contrast, all cases that were assigned to the judge overseeing the TJC model, regardless of degree of substance abuse or willingness to participate in a specific program, were subjected to the TJC procedures.

Summary of Process Findings: Three Problem-Solving Court Models

1. *The traditional dependency court model*

   While the following problem-solving features and processes were present in the traditional dependency court they were also *common* to all three models:

   (a) Early and active judicial oversight of cases as exhibited by frequent court review—every three months after disposition (although less frequent court reviews were implemented predisposition in the traditional model).

   (b) One family/one judge case assignment (including in the FDC where the drug court judge also heard the underlying dependency matter and presided over drug court review hearings and regular dependency proceedings).

   (c) Early appointment of counsel at the initial hearing (i.e., the shelter hearing which took place within 72 h of removal of the child) to ensure that all parties to initial proceedings have appropriate legal representation at the outset (e.g., each of the models used dedicated attorney teams, with counsel assigned to specific courtrooms, facilitating continuity of counsel in cases).

   (d) Dedication of sufficient court time for initial proceedings to allow for substantive discussion on matters related to reasonable efforts, the continued need for out-of-home placement, alternative placement options, service needs, visitation, the need for protective orders, child support, identification of putative fathers, establishment of paternity and other matters. Shelter hearings (the initial hearing in a case) lasted an average of 40 min across all sites with a range from 30 to 55 min.

   (e) Judges who required timely and comprehensive reports to the court and who did not accept requests to continue or delay proceedings because reports were not available. This served to clearly place expectations on all parties to ensure that parents are ready from the onset of the court process to engage in detailed discussions of case specifics and that all parties provided the court with sufficient information to make rulings on these matters. Prior to the shelter hearing (the initial or first hearing in a dependency case), a multidisciplinary team conference was held to review the investigative finding and basis of the petition, the status of the case, permanency placement and visitation options, and service needs.

2. Features of the *family drug court (FDC)*
   In addition to the traditional dependency court features noted above, the FDC model included the following features (for more detail, please see Dobbin et al. 2006):
   (a) Emphasis on early screening of parents for services—the FDC emphasized early screening of parents through additional multidisciplinary case staffings (this is in addition to the multidisciplinary team conferences, which were common to all three models). During the screening process, the client's potential motivation to succeed in drug court and commitment to the recovery process is assessed. Once clients are selected for drug court, staffing meetings are used for discussions between the FDC team and the judge about the status of each case, the progress of the client in treatment, results of drug tests, overall client progress, compliance with FDC process and requirements, possible service needs, and possible rewards and sanctions.
   (b) Parent involvement in case planning—parent involvement in case planning was demonstrated through clear and consistent communication of expectations and requirements, and the use of an FDC agreement or behavioral contract. A judge–parent therapeutic relationship was also fostered through frequent appearances (ranging from once every week in early phases of the program to once per month in latter phases), direct inquiry and discussion with the parents about their progress, and displaying empathy and support.
   (c) Priority access to substance abuse treatment services—parents involved in the FDC were given priority access to substance abuse treatment services, as well as other services such as mental health assessments and treatment, housing, and employment resources.
   (d) Expanded role for the judge—the judge in the FDC model had more input into the overall progress of the case (not only in the legal decisions, but in discussions about the provision of treatment, the use of sanctions and rewards, and in direct and frequent interactions with the parents). The FDC judges participated in staffing meetings, discussing necessary services, level of parental compliances and all decisions made. Judges directly questioned and supported the drug court parents—judges reflected their thoughts, as well as the FDC team's thoughts on client progress back to the parent and the larger group of FDC clients who attended the hearing. Judges demonstrated pleasure when clients demonstrated success, expressed empathy over client struggles and concerns for clients' children, and effectively admonished clients' for lack of progress or compliance as needed. Judges were "team-oriented"—although they maintained authority for final decision making, decisions in the FDC reviews were consensus based.

(e) Frequent court review—the number of court appearances in the FDC were greater than the number of court appearances in the traditional model. Formal court reviews of the underlying dependency matter are the same in the traditional and FDC models, but "appearances" before the judge are increased (via additional hearings to discuss parents' recovery and progress through the drug court program). The frequency and time of those appearances are increased or decreased based on compliance with treatment protocols and client progress. Similar to most drug courts, drug court hearing or appearance frequency is organized around program phases. In the Utah model, court appearances happened every 2 weeks for the first 2–4 months and once a month during later stages of treatment. Compare this to the traditional model where hearings occurred at 72 h post removal, at 60 and 90 days, and then every 3 months postdisposition.

3. *Therapeutic justice court (TJC)*
   In addition to the features of the traditional dependency court model, the TJC model had the following features (for more details, please see Dobbin et al. 2006):

(a) Application of procedures to all cases—unlike the FDC model, in which potential clients are screened for eligibility and acceptance into the program, all cases appearing before the TJC judge during "intake" or shelter week (when cases first come into the court system with a removal of a child) are processed using the TJC model—all families assigned to the judge, whether new families or families that are returning to the system, are part of the TJC model (there are no prescreening and eligibility criteria).
(b) Early assessment of respondent parents is conducted for all individuals (regardless of presenting problem) by a TJC Coordinator at the initial shelter hearing (the first hearing in a case). This initial contact leads to several meetings in which the Coordinator builds a supportive relationship with the parents through early discussion of their service needs. This discussion was broad in focus and while substance abuse treatment needs may be addressed, they were not the primary reason for the early screening and assessment discussion. Parents' attorneys must consent to this early screening (this was by far the norm due to the collaborative nature of the model, which was already built on a collaborative "traditional" best practice model).
(c) The TJC judge has a critical leadership role but does not participate in multidisciplinary staffing. Unlike the FDC model, the TJC judge does not participate in any form of treatment and service-oriented discussion with parties outside of the formal court hearing itself. However, substantive discussion is had in the hearing with all parties present about treatment, service needs, client progress and overall compliance with case planning. The judge also interacts directly with parents in hearings, addressing questions directly to them.
(d) Frequent court review—in practice, all three models reviewed the underlying dependency case with the appropriate level of frequency, often 3–4 months postdisposition (as per Guidelines' best practice recommendations). In the

TJC model, the overall number of reviews of the underlying dependency is increased over the traditional model, especially at the early stages of the case. And, in both the FDC and TJC models, the increased court review begins much earlier in the case compared with the traditional model. In the TJC model, these reviews afforded the judge an opportunity for ongoing judicial supervision, with the judge using this opportunity to encourage appropriate behavior and to discourage inappropriate behavior. During observations, the research team observed the TJC judge praising parents for doing well and effectively admonishing parents for failure to engage their case plans and make progress (a finding that was corroborated by other interviews with court stakeholders about the judge's behavior and with interviews of the parents themselves). During the first 8 weeks of the case, the court holds a review at least once a month, sometimes more frequently. Beyond the first 8 weeks, reviews are held every 90 days or as otherwise needed to meet the needs of the family. In contrast to the FDC model, the review hearings were more reflective of formal review hearings (although they occured predisposition). In the early reviews conducted as part of the TJC model, only the parent(s) whose case is being discussed was present (i.e., there is no gallery of peers to observe the process as in the FDC model). Thus, the group dynamic effect of the FDC is missing in the TJC model. However, the impact of an authority figure in rewarding progress and admonishing noncompliance was very much present in the TJC model. Although parents did not benefit from seeing the response of the court to other clients, the TJC review hearings provided an opportunity for more in-depth discussion of the specific case, and more specific feedback on parents' overall progress from the judge and from attorneys and caseworkers. There was also more time spent tying the consequences of the parents' compliance or noncompliance to their parenting role and the long-term permanency and safety of their children than was evident in the FDC reviews.

(e) Parental engagement—although at a different level of intensity, the initial contact between the TJC Coordinator and the parent, serves somewhat of the same engagement function as the initial outreach to a potential FDC client. The judge begins the engagement process at the initial shelter hearing (although the judge is not formally screening parents for possible participation in a specialized program, the judge does clearly explain the overall dependency process, ASFA timeframes and consequences for noncompliance, and expectations for conduct directly to the parent(s)). In subsequent hearings, the TJC judge also discusses progress, empathizes with struggles, expresses concerns for client's children, and demonstrates pleasure over successes. The judge does address parents directly and engages in dialogue with the parent (attorneys will interject or prevent the parent from responding if necessary to protect their client's rights). Although formal rewards and sanctions were not used, the judge used verbal praise and admonishments to help motivate parents and modify their behavior. Considerable focus was given to tying the consequences of the parents' compliance or noncompliance to their parenting role and the long-term permanency and safety of their children.

Summary of Outcome Findings: Three Problem-Solving Court Models

When compared with the traditional "best practice courts," both the FDC and the TJC had more effectively engaged parents early-on, involved more parties in case planning, had more positive ratings of overall quality from stakeholders and consumers (i.e., professionals, parents and youth), and had more enhanced system integration (this was especially true for the FDC model). When compared with the traditional and TJC model, the FDC had earlier access to substance abuse services and more involvement of service providers in case planning (see Dobbin et al. 2006).

Little effect for the models on case processing timeframes was found, with no significant difference among the models. For all cases studied, regardless of project site, case processing timeframes were well within state and federal timeframes. This finding was not surprising since all of the models were built on a foundational best practice framework that emphasizes the efficient and timely processing of cases. However, there was a significant increase ($p < 0.05$) in the number of reunifications in both the FDC (78 %) and TJC (82 %) as compared with the traditional court (61 %) suggesting that those problem-solving models (that enhanced foundational best practice) may have had an impact on increasing the number of reunifications in those jurisdictions. There was no significant difference found between the FDC and the TJC with respect to reunification rates. We were also interested in safety outcomes associated with each of the models. In the dependency court context, maintaining safety can be operationalized as closing a case and having no further substantiated allegations of abuse or neglect which cause the case to "re-enter" the court system. We found a significant difference in reentry rates between traditional, TJC and FDC models, with the TJC and FDC models having significantly fewer reentries into the dependency court system after case closure due to a reunification outcome than the traditional model (measured at 6 and 12 months after case closure; $p < 0.01$). This suggests that the TJC and FDC problem-solving models were more successful at helping families maintain safety after case closure (at least in the short term). No significant difference was found between the FDC and TJC with respect to reentry rates.

Lessons Learned About the Value-Added of Specialized Problem-Solving Court Models

The results of this study of three problem-solving court models provides insight into the feasibility of applying critical elements of the specialized problem-solving court models, such as drug courts, to all dependency cases. The most striking resource difference among the three models was the early access to and provision of intensive substance abuse services allocated to the FDC model. These were resources prioritized for FDC clients and not as readily available for parents in either of the other models. In order to "go to scale," dependency courts would need to work collaboratively with their community treatment providers to develop resources and funding to widen the availability and access of drug and alcohol services to parents whose substance abuse is a primary reason for their court involvement, but who are not in a drug court program. Findings from the study also reinforce the need for key "front-loading" strategies implemented in both the TJC and FDC models to be adopted for all dependency cases, such as strategies that would facilitate earlier screening, assessments of parents, and provision of services. Short of implementing a time and resource intensive multidisciplinary case staffing process, such as that used in the FDC, this can be accomplished by assigning a resource person to attend all shelter hearings and to hold more frequent predisposition court reviews on dependency matters (as implemented in the TJC model). The engagement of parties was also a critically important element of both the TJC and FDC models and opportunities to engage parties should be developed and capitalized upon in all dependency cases. This can be achieved, for example, by encouraging direct interaction between judges and parents in hearings (including providing immediate feedback to parents on their progress) and to ensure parents are meaningfully involved in case planning and have a voice in decisions made about their families. In addition, ways to create the "group effect" that is so effective in drug court models should be explored—perhaps through a noncourt setting such as through a "peer–parent mentoring program" which teams successful dependency system "graduates" with respondent parents for support. In order to go to scale with features of specialized problem-solving courts, ways to support the caseworker–parent relationship should also be considered. When asked to identify the most critical element of the FDCs, by far the feature identified as most helpful by parents and youth we interviewed was the parent's relationship with their caseworker.

Bridging the Gap: Ongoing Research to Practice Challenges

Unlike the child welfare system, which has long benefitted from and been informed by research and program evaluations designed to determine effective interventions and preventions, research used to inform the juvenile dependency court system is still emerging. A substantive review of the nature and scope of dependency court-related research we conducted in 2007 (reviewing both quantitative and qualitative studies published in peer-reviewed academic journals, nonpeer-reviewed technical assistance publications, and government reports) found much work of value to our understanding of effective dependency court functioning but also some serious areas of deficiency (Summers et al. 2008). The majority of studies we reviewed were descriptive, with few employing experimental designs and most lacking in statistical rigor. We found a clear lack of studies related to the core work of dependency courts—foundational hearing processes, one family/one judge concept (the role of judicial continuity on case processing and outcomes), representation practice (especially studies of effective parent and children's representation), and studies evaluating the operation of best practice elements and their impact on case outcomes. There was also a lack of research on judges and judging, such as the nature and complexity of judicial best-interest decision making, the judicial workload required for best practice in dependency cases, and the impact the dependency court judge has on parental engagement. The interaction between the problem-solving court judge and the individual seems to be an important ingredient in program success, and more empirical work should probe how this occurs.

More theory-driven and outcome-oriented (meaningful outcomes) research is needed to examine the effectiveness of the "best practice" Resource Guidelines model we have described in this chapter. An understanding of therapeutic jurisprudence's approach, procedural justice variables, and psychological principles at work can provide considerable help in structuring dependency courts, further defining and reinforcing the role played by judges functioning within them, and identifying the specific judicial training needed to improve outcomes for children and families under the court's jurisdiction.

In this chapter, we presented one example of an examination of dependency courts' problem-solving processes and outcomes, but more research is clearly needed—not only with respect to the impact of "best practice" features on case process and outcomes, but also on how to diffuse critical elements of problem-solving models to all dependency cases. In order to help bridge the gap between research and practice, more collaboration between academic researchers (with expertise in theory and statistical rigor) and applied researchers (with expertise in systems' knowledge and applied methods) is needed. Research funding for dependency courts needs to become a priority so that methodologically sound and practically useful research for juvenile dependency courts can be implemented. All research in this context should be disseminated in a manner that allows for the broadest possible audience to benefit. There is a lack of opportunity to learn from research that has already been done and apply the findings in a meaningful way. Because the majority of the research in this field is conducted by applied researchers who produce reports directly for the court or other funders, many of the research reports are not widely disseminated and accessible. Ultimately, for research to assist in moving our understanding of dependency problem-solving courts forward, it must be tied to theory, be systematically tested so that the underlying mechanisms of change can be identified, and widely disseminated so that it contributes to a growing knowledge base and is applied in practice.

In this chapter, we presented research exploring the different procedures and outcomes associated with the implementation of three problem-solving court models in dependency cases in one state (foundational best practice, FDC and a TJC). There are many challenges to operating problem-solving courts, from staffing, space, and budgets to the interdisciplinary challenge of coordinating the efforts of diverse agencies to try to tackle complex issues. Because specialized problem-solving courts such as drug courts are heavily staff and resource intensive, they are not able to serve all of the families that could benefit from them. The research we present offers insight into how *all* dependency cases can be handled with elements of specialized problem-solving court models in such a way as to capitalize on their benefits—specifically by adopting and enhancing features of the best practice dependency court approach, which is its own type of problem-solving court model.

References

Berman, G. (2000). What is a traditional judge, anyways? *Judicature, 84*(2), 78–85.

Berman, G., & Feinblatt, J. (2005). *Good courts*. New York: The New Press.

Burford, G., & Hudson, J. (Eds.). (2009). *Family group conferencing: New directions in community-centered child and family practice*. New Brunswick: Transaction Publications.

California Judicial Council. (2005). *Standard of judicial administration 24*. Washington: West Publishing.

Casey, T. (2004). When good intentions are not enough: Problem-solving courts and the impending crisis of legitimacy. *SMU Law Review, 57,* 1459–1483.

Dobbin, S., Gatowski, S., Litchfield, M., Maxwell, D., & Oetjen, J. (2003). An evaluation of Utah court improvement project reforms and best practices: Results and recommendations. *Technical Assistance Bulletin, VII*(1). U.S. Department Of Justice, Office of Juvenile Justice and Delinquency Prevention and the National Council of Juvenile and Family Court Judges. www.ncjfcj.org.

Dobbin, S., Gatowski, S., Litchfield, M., & Padilla, J. (2006). *Evaluating front-loading strategies in child abuse and neglect cases: Are we improving outcomes for children and families*. Reno: National Council of Juvenile and Family Court Judges. www.ncjfcj.org.

Edwards, L. (1992). The juvenile court and the role of the juvenile court judge. *Juvenile and Family Court Journal, 43*(2), 25–32.

Farole, D. J., Puffet, N. K., Rempel, M., & Byrne, F. (2005). Applying problem-solving court principles in mainstream courts: Lessons for state courts. *Justice System Journal, 26*(1), 57–75.

Gatowski, S., Dobbin, S., & Litchfield, M. (2002a). The Portland model court expanded second shelter hearing process: evaluating best practice components of front-loading. *Technical Assistance Bulletin, VI*(3), U.S. Department of Justice, Office of Juvenile Justice and Delinquency Prevention and the National Council of Juvenile and Family Court Judges. www.ncjfcj.org.

Gatowski, S., Dobbin, S., Litchfield, M., Halemba, G., Siegel, G., & Gunn, R. (2002b). The El Paso, Texas 65th Judicial district children's court: Evaluation of model court activities (1999–2001). *Technical Assistance Bulletin, VI*(4), U.S. Department of Justice, Office of Juvenile Justice and Delinquency Prevention and the National Council of Juvenile and Family Court Judges. www.ncjfcj.org.

Gatowski, S., Dobbin, S., Litchfield, M., & Oetjen, J. (2005). *Mediation in child protection cases: An evaluation of the Washington, D.C. family court child protection mediation program*. U.S. Department of Justice, Office of Juvenile Justice and Delinquency Prevention and the National Council of Juvenile and Family Court Judges. www.ncjfcj.org.

Lecklitner, G. L., Malik, N. M, Aaron, S. M., & Lederman, C. S. (1999). Promoting safety for abused children and battered mothers: Miami-Dade County's model dependency court intervention program. *Child Maltreatment, 4,* 175–182.

Lind, E. A., & Tyler, T. R. (1988). *The social psychology of procedural justice: Critical issues in social justice*. New York: Plenum.

Litchfield, M., Gatowski, S., & Dobbin, S. (2003). Improving outcomes for families: Results from an evaluation of Miami's family decision-making program. *Protecting Children, 19*(1–2), 48–52.

National Council of Juvenile and Family Court Judges (NCJFCJ). (1995). *Resource guidelines: Improving court practice in child abuse and neglect cases*. Reno: National Council of Juvenile and Family Court Judges.

National Council of Juvenile and Family Court Judges (NCJFCJ). (2000). *Adoption and permanency guidelines: Improving Court practice in child abuse and neglect cases*. Reno: National Council of Juvenile and Family Court Judges.

National Council of Juvenile and Family Court Judges (NCJFCJ). (2005). *Washington State CIP re-assessment final report*. Reno: National Council of Juvenile and Family Court Judges.

National Council of Juvenile and Family Court Judges (NCJFCJ). (2009). *The resource guidelines: Supporting best practices and building foundations for innovation in child abuse and neglect cases*. Reno: National Council of Juvenile and Family Court Judges.

Ogletree, C. (1993). Beyond justifications: Seeking motivations to sustain public defenders. *Harvard Law Review, 106,* 1239.

Portune, L., Gatowski, S., & Dobbin, S. (2009). *The resource guidelines: Supporting best practices and building foundations for innovation in child abuse and neglect cases.* Reno: National Council of Juvenile and Family Court Judges.

Quinn, M. C. (2001). Whose team am I on anyway? Musings of a public defender about drug treatment court practice. *N Y U Journal of Law and Social Change, 26,* 37–56.

Roush, D. W. (1996). Part I: Historical perspective—Advent of the juvenile justice system. In D. W. Roush (Ed.), *Desktop guide to good juvenile detention practice—Research report.* Washington: U.S. Department of Justice, Office of Juvenile Justice and Delinquency Prevention.

Simon, W. H. (2003). Criminal defenders and community justice: The drug court example. *American Criminal Law Review, 40,* 1595–1599.

Summers, A., Dobbin, S., & Gatowski, S. (2008). *The state of juvenile dependency court research: Implications for practice and policy.* Administrative Office of the California Courts and the National Council of Juvenile and Family Court Judges. www.ncjfcj.org.

Thoennes, N. (1997). An evaluation of child protection mediation in five California counties. *Family and Conciliation Courts Review, 35*(2), 184–195.

Thoennes, N. (2008). What we know now: Findings from dependency mediation research. *Family Court Review, 47*(1), 21.

U.S. Bureau of Justice Assistance. (2004). *Family dependency treatment courts: Addressing child abuse and neglect cases using the drug court model.* U.S. Bureau of Justice Assistance, December.

U.S. Bureau of Justice Assistance. (2005). *Drug court activity.* U.S. Bureau of Justice Assistance, BJA Drug Court Clearinghouse and American University, January.

U.S. Department of Health and Human Services. (2005).*Child maltreatment 2003.* Washington: DHHS.

U.S. Department of Justice. (1998). *Juvenile and family drug courts: An overview.* Office of justice programs drug court clearinghouse and technical assistance project.

Winnick, B. J., & Wexler, D. B. (2003). *Judging in a therapeutic key: Therapeutic jurisprudence and the courts.* Durham: Carolina Academic Press.

Young, N. K., & Otero, C. (2005). *Current substance abuse issues impacting child abuse and neglect.* Fifteenth National Conference on Child Abuse and Neglect, Washington, D.C. (April).

Young, N. K., Wong, M., Adkins, T., & Simpson, S. (2003). *Family drug treatment courts: Process documentation and retrospective outcome evaluation.* Irvine: Children and Family Futures.

Chapter 4
Dependency Courts and Science

Victoria Weisz

The stakes in dependency courts are extremely high, both for the welfare of involved children and for the fundamental rights of both children and families. These cases involve the state reaching into a family and, at the minimum, forcing parents and children to engage in activities and services not of their voluntary choosing. Further, state action often includes removing children from their parents' care and placing them in the foster care system. Although, in the past, dependency court stakeholders may have viewed foster care as a benign alternative that held few risks when compared to a potentially unsafe family situation, recent research has illustrated the harms inherent in growing up in foster care (Fowler et al. 2009; Lawrence et al. 2006). Finally, in a small but significant percent of cases, the state moves on to terminate the parent's rights to his or her children, and subsequently the children's ability to have a relationship with his or her parent.

Given the high stakes, and the large number of involved citizens,[1] the dearth of social and behavioral science research that is relevant to dependency court (not surprisingly related to limited federal funding for this area of research) is notable. The previous chapters (Lederman and Gatowski in this volume) illustrate two significant, but different, ways that dependency courts might utilize social/behavioral science to improve their work. Gatowski et al. in this volume (Chap. 9) describe evaluation research that tests the effectiveness of dependency court accepted "best practices." They wisely suggest that just because there is a consensus from professionals on a best practice that empirical validation of the effectiveness of the practice is needed before courts should be confident that the practice will likely result in desired outcomes. These researchers focus on court processes themselves, including, for example, timing of hearings, frequency of hearings, judicial involvement, and parent engagement

[1] 400,540 children were in foster care on Sept. 30, 2011 (Casanueva et al. 2012).

V. Weisz (✉)
University of Nebraska-Lincoln, Lincoln, USA
e-mail: vweisz1@unl.edu

R. L. Wiener, E. M. Brank (eds.), *Problem Solving Courts*,

DOI 10.1007/978-1-4614-7403-6_4,

in three court models: a traditional dependency court model, a family drug court model, and a therapeutic justice court model.

Judge Lederman, also in this volume (Chap. 9), does not focus on the court process itself, but instead makes an argument for judges to be mindful of the scientific basis for the evidence they consider (e.g., assessments, recommendations for interventions). She expresses legitimate concerns for the lack of scientific foundational support for most court-ordered services for parents and children. She describes evidence-based psychological assessments and interventions (Lederman and Osofsky 2008) that she is able to rely on in her court and how those interventions contribute to desired outcomes for children and parents. Judge Lederman calls upon judges to require scientific underpinnings for the services they require for parents and children.

As noted by Gatowski (Chap. 9), since 1980 dependency courts have had oversight responsibility over the state agency that is charged with caring for the children, providing rehabilitative services to the parents, and working to keep children in their homes, return them to their parents, or find another permanent family. Courts depend on others to bring them information, in particular caseworkers, attorneys, and treatment providers. In most states, the rules of evidence are relaxed for disposition and review hearings, so that information that comes in can be quite informal, hearsay ridden, and subjective. In some states, the courts have a fair amount of authority over the state agency. In many states, the courts have quite limited authority.

These two papers make strong arguments for the need for more research regarding court processes as well as research regarding the validity of assessments and the effectiveness of services that courts utilize in making far reaching decisions in the lives of parents and children. This chapter will briefly discuss some challenges that might be considered as courts and social–behavioral scientists work together to build a dependency court system that meets its expectations for a fair and efficient court process. Additionally, the chapter will address potential challenges and recommendations for judges who expect that court referred services have a sound scientific basis.

Challenges in Isolating Dependency Court Process Features

Gatowski et al. describe a wide range of broad features of best practice dependency courts that include judicial leadership, a problem-solving judicial orientation, a therapeutic jurisprudence approach, early and active engagement of parties, a collaborative approach, etc. They compared a general best practice dependency court with two specific problem-solving courts (family drug court and therapeutic jurisprudence court) and found the two specialized courts to have significantly better outcomes with higher reunification rates and lower re-entry (into the child welfare system) rates. There were no differences in case processing timeframes, which were all well within federal and state timeframes. This comparison of types of best practices is a good first step in assessing the effectiveness of various court procedures and Gatowski et al. do an admirable job in describing the aspirational features of these best practice courts. It is difficult, however, to tease out which factors may be contributing to the outcomes. Is the higher reunification rate and lower re-entry rate for family drug courts related to features of the court process or simply to the fact of prioritization for drug treatment? The relative similarity of outcomes for the drug court and therapeutic jurisprudence cases suggest that perhaps the group participation aspects of the drug courts are not critical. Then again, it may be that the group dynamic is critical for substance abusing parents but not for the general child welfare population that includes but is not limited to substance abuse problems. It is also not clear whether some of the effects are individual judge variables rather than court process variables (difficult to untangle in the best practices model emphasis on the significance of judicial leadership).

One approach that might help move the field along would be to reduce the number of features that are being tested. Gatowski et al. describe nine broad principles. Perhaps, the field leaders who have promulgated these best practice principles could identify a handful of important features that could be validly and reliably operationalized. Gatowski et al. have already made progress in this area. For example, a problem-solving orientation is described as asking questions, seeking more information, etc. Early and active engagement is described as including direct interaction with respondent parents in court hearings. A therapeutic jurisprudence approach includes frequent and proactive judicial review (frequent hearings, individualized court orders—not rubber stamping the agency's recommendations). More foundational work seems needed to identify, operationalize, and validate measures of important best practice features that may (or may not) contribute to desired judicial practice outcomes. Further, researchers would need to then systematically study these factors either one or two at a time, with more sophisticated statistical models that can handle multiple variables, or in some combination of both approaches.

Court cases are complex. A multitude of factors can potentially affect outcomes for children and families, including features of the court process, activities of the child welfare system, and behaviors of the parents or children. A systematic study of the court variables is needed to identify which of them are the ones that contribute to the desired outcomes.

Challenges in Selecting and Measuring Outcomes for Dependency Court Process Reform

Gatowski et al. (Chap. 9) report on three sets of outcomes: case processing timeframes, percentage of reunifications, and re-entries into the system. Reducing case processing timeframes is an important management outcome for courts, many of those over the past decade have had to manage increasing caseloads with decreasing resources [US Department of Justice (DOJ) 2008]. Further, if one assumes that mandatory court involvement is an intrusion into family life, then limiting the length of that intrusion seems to be desirable (Sankaran 2010; Guggenheim 2005). More efficient resolution of child welfare cases so that they do not linger in the court system appears to be a reasonable outcome [National Council of Juvenile and Family

Court Judges (NCJFCJ) 1995] and its measurement seems relatively straightforward (DOJ 2008). Similarly, the percentage of reunifications is relatively straightforward to measure and it also reflects the legal framework that reunification should be the goal in most cases (DOJ 2008; Sankaran 2010). Re-entry into the system, considered a proxy for child safety is, on the one hand, perhaps the most critical outcome and also the one that contains the most measurement challenges that will be discussed below.

The outcomes in the reported study are included in the broader array of court performance measures that are included in the *Toolkit for Court Performance Measures in Child Abuse and Neglect Cases* (DOJ 2008). The development of the *Toolkit* reflects an interest in a variety of national groups to develop uniform measures for court performance measures, many of which could be considered outcomes. The *Toolkit* identifies 30 measures of child safety, child permanency, due process, and judicial timeliness that are considered representative of desired outcomes.

The safety measures include (a) the percentage of children who are abused or neglected while under court jurisdiction and (b) the percentage of children who are abused or neglected within 12 months after the case is closed following a permanent placement. Unlike some of the other outcomes (e.g., there are differences of opinion as to whether it is better for children to take longer for permanency if they can eventually be reunified with their parents as compared to more speedy permanency that involves termination of their parent's right and adoption; Guggenheim 2005), the goal of child safety is uncontroversial. Gatowski et al. measure of re-entry is an example of this safety outcome measure.

Although re-entry is one measurement that can be used to assess child safety, the *Toolkit* also suggests emergency removal orders, custody transfer orders, and written agency reports for children still under court jurisdiction. For children who have been released from court jurisdiction, the *Toolkit* recommends child welfare "hot line" reports on children, new petitions alleging maltreatment, and/or judicial findings of abuse or neglect. While broadening the official information sources makes it more likely to detect further maltreatment of children, these sources all require that the maltreatment has come to some public attention. Further, facts about the family situation must support shifting community perspectives, policies, and politics regarding thresholds for state identification and involvement (Institute of Medicine and National Research Council 2012). Researchers that study child maltreatment have noted that gathering information directly from children and parents, in addition to the public sources, strengthens the accuracy of maltreatment measurement (Everson et al. 2008; McGee et al. 1995; Stockhammer et al. 2001). Further maltreatment to children could more accurately be measured if court researchers used methods and instruments developed in the social science arena. For example, the National Survey on Child and Adolescent Well-being (Casanueva et al. 2012) has three measures that address child maltreatment: Violence Exposure Scale, injury questions from the Child Health and Illness Profile, and an adapted Parent–Child Conflicts Scale that gathers specific maltreatment information. This information is gathered directly from children and families through phone interviews. Direct reports from children and parents would strengthen the measurement of child safety, even though the accuracy of those self-reports may also be limited—by the children and parent's willingness to tell the truth. Because of the importance of the safety outcome in determining the effectiveness of various court processes and procedures, the use of reliable and valid multimodal (official records and child/parent instruments) measurement methods would considerably advance our understanding of the impact of various court processes and innovations. A first important step in developing a multimodal approach might focus on a single court and set of children. Various approaches of measuring safety could be undertaken and the extent to which the different measures of safety agree could be assessed. If there is not an agreement among different approaches that measure the same phenomenon (e.g., child safety), then more work would be needed to refine the approach. Without this foundational work, we risk misplaced confidence that certain court processes make children safer, when in fact they may not be doing so.

Challenges in Raising the Bar for Science in Dependency Court

Lederman (Chap. 9) discusses scientific knowledge that should inform dependency courts; in particular that infants and toddlers can be psychologically harmed by maltreatment; that relationship focused interventions for them can successfully address the harm; and that many types of parenting training are ineffective although effective models do exist. She could have also noted that substance abuse treatment programs vary in their adherence to evidence-based practice and in their effectiveness (Miller 2007; Garner 2009). Lederman also describes a recent survey that suggests the vast majority of social workers and other stakeholders in the child welfare field do not understand what evidence-based practice means and would presumably not be able to critically evaluate the potential effectiveness of typical child welfare services (Lederman et al. 2009).

The effectiveness of court-ordered child welfare services is critically important. When children are maltreated and the state intervenes, the role of the court and the agency is a rehabilitative one. The agency, with the court's approval, must determine what changes a particular parent needs to make to be able to nurture her child and keep him safe. Next, the agency needs to determine what services could help the parent to make these changes. Choosing the appropriate services should include a determination of the relevance of the service to the change the parent needs to make, and the effectiveness of the service in helping parents make that change. As Lederman argues, required judicial findings that the agency has made reasonable efforts to reunify a child, must include an assessment that the offered services are effective and relevant and will reasonably assist the parent in ameliorating the problems that resulted in the state's intervention. If offered services are not evidence based—if they have not been shown to effectively address the type of problem the parent needs help with—then the court may, and should, exercise its authority and make no reasonable efforts findings.

How are judges to know whether particular services are evidence based or whether particular children and parents need the services? Monahan and Walker (2011) have, over the past several decades, developed a scheme for judicial uses of social science. Although the rules of evidence are typically relaxed in the dispositional phases of dependency cases, looking to Monahan and Walker's (2007) discussion of how social science research can be used as social framework may be instructive. For social framework information, social science provides a context for a particular situation. In dependency court, for example, general research about the vulnerabilities of maltreated infants and toddlers, or the features associated with evidence-based interventions could provide the court the context to make judgments in the individual case before him or her. Monahan and Walker (2007) outline steps that judges can take in using social science that includes:

> If the parties or amici do not submit social science studies, request such studies from the parties or amici, or obtain them from the court's own sua sponte investigation of published sources. (p. 162)

Thus, they would suggest that judges may routinely ask for information about the evidence basis for any service that he or she is asked to order,[2] about demonstrations that the local intervention has fidelity to the evidence-based model, and about the success rates of programs.

If a judge knows that the majority of services in his or her jurisdiction are not evidence based, what can he or she do? Judge Lederman presides in a relatively service-rich urban area with excellent universities, a medical school, and many well-trained professionals. Most dependency courts do not have access to as wide a range and as high a quality of services as that. Courts cannot build services. However, the judges can provide community leadership to encourage growth of such services. Judges can routinely question whether a proposed service is evidence based. Judges can also make "no reasonable efforts"[3] findings to accurately communicate that parents have not been provided services that would help them rehabilitate as well as put pressure on the agency to develop appropriate services.

Conclusion

The two previous chapters develop a nice frame for using science to address some of the challenges faced by dependency courts. Gatowski et al. explore research methods that can provide important empirical tests for the consensus best practice

[2] The California Evidence-Based Clearinghouse for Child Welfare (http://www.cebc4cw.org/) and SAMHSA's National Registry of Evidence-based Services and Practices (http://www.nrepp.samhsa.gov/) are two resources that readily provide information about the empirical foundation of a broad range of services.

[3] 42 U.S.C. Section 671(a)(15)(B) The Child Welfare Agency has a duty to provide timely and appropriate services to the family to make it possible for the child to safely return home. The court is required to make findings as to whether the state's provision of services meets the reasonable efforts standard.

recommendations that are currently driving dependency court reforms. This line of research is aimed toward determining scientifically supported effective court processes and practices, that is, clearly defined court practices that are linked to clearly defined desired court outcomes. In contrast, Lederman looks to research to improve the quality of judicial decisions and orders. She challenges courts to ensure that they order effective interventions that have a reasonable chance to ameliorate the problems that brought the family into the system. Both approaches face challenges, as this discussion has detailed. Still, it is laudable and hopeful that dependency courts are looking at science to assist them in improving processes as well as judicial decisions. One hopes for a growth in relevant social and behavioral scientific research to assist the courts in this endeavor.

References

Casanueva, C., Smith, K., Dolan, M., Tueller, S., & Lloyd, S. (2012). NSCAW II Wave 2 Report: Safety. OPRE Report #2013-07. Washington, DC: Office of Planning, Research and Evaluation, Administration for Children and Families, U.S. Department of Health and Human Services. http.://www.acfhhs.gov!sites/defauJt/files/opre/nscaw_child_sa.fety.pdf. Retrieved from 24 April 2013.

Everson, M. D., Smith, J. B., Hussey, J. M., English, D., Litrownik, A. J., Dibpwotz, H., et al. (2008). Concordance between adolescent reports of childhood abuse and child protective service determinations in an at-risk sample of young adolescents. *Child Maltreatment, 13*(1), 14–26.

Fowler, P. J., Toro, P. A., & Miles, B. W. (2009). Pathways to and from homelessness and associated psychosocial outcomes among adolescents leaving the foster care system. *American Journal of Public Health, 99*(8), 1453–1458. doi:10.2105/AJPH.2008.142547.

Garner, B. R. (2009). Research on the diffusion of evidence-based treatments within substance abuse treatment: A systematic review. *Journal of Substance Abuse Treatment, 36*(4), 376–399. doi:10.1016/j.jsat.2008.08.004.

Guggenheim, M. (2005). *What's wrong with children's rights*. Cambridge: Harvard University Press.

IOM (Institute of Medicine) and NRC (National Research Council). (2012). *Child maltreatment research, policy, and practice for the next decade: Workshop summary*. Washington, DC: The National Academies Press.

Lawrence, C. R., Carlson, E. A., & Egeland, B. (2006). The impact of foster care on development. *Development and Psychopathology, 18*(1), 57–76. doi:10.1017/S0954579406060044.

Lederman, C., Gomez-Kaifer, M., Katz, L., Thomlison, B., & Maze, C. (2009). An imperative: Evidence based practice within the child welfare system of care. *Juvenile and Family Justice Today, 18*(4), 22–25.

Lederman, C., & Osofsky, J. D. (2008). A judicial-mental health partnership to heal young children in juvenile court. *Infant Mental Health Journal, 29*(1), 36–47. doi:10.1002/imhj.20164.

McGee, R. A., Wolfe, D. A., Yuen, S. A., & Wilson, S. K. (1995). The measurement of maltreatment: A comparison of approaches. *Child Abuse & Neglect, 19*(2), 233–249. doi:10.1016/0145-134(94)00119-F.

Miller, J. C. (2007). 12-Step treatment for alcohol and substance abuse revisited: Best available evidence suggests lack of effectiveness or harm. *International Journal of mental Health and Addiction, 6*, 568–576. doi:10.1007/s11469-008-9146-4.

Monahan, J., & Walker, L. (2007). A judges' guide to using social science. *Court Review,* (43) 156–163.

Monahan, J., & Walker, L. (2011). Twenty-five years of Social Science in Law. *Law and Human Behavior, 35*(1), 72–82. doi:10.1007s10979-009-9214-8.

National Council of Juvenile and Family Court Judges (1995). *Resource guidelines: Improving court practice in child abuse & neglect cases.*

Sankaran, V. S. (2010). Representing parents in child welfare cases. In D. N. Duquette & A. M. Haralambie (Eds.), *Child welfare law and practice: representing children, parents, and state agencies in abuse, neglect, and dependency cases* (2nd ed.) Denver: Bradford.

Stockhammer, T. F., Salzinger, S., Feldman, R. S., Mojica, E., & Primavera, L. H. (2001). Assessment of the effect of physical child abuse within an ecological framework: Measurement issues. *Journal of Community Psychology, 29*(3), 319–344.

U.S. Department of Health & Human Services, Administration for Children and Families. (2012). https://www.acf.hhs.gov/sites/default/files/cb/afcarsreport19.pdf. Retrieved from 24 April 2013.

U.S. Department of Justice, Office of Justice Programs, Office of Juvenile Justice and Delinquency Prevention (2008). Court performance measures in child abuse and neglect cases. from https://www.ncjrs.gov/pdffiles1/ojjdp/223567.pdf. Retrieved from 24 April 2013.

Part II
Domestic Violence Specialty Courts

Chapter 5
Unified Family Courts: An Interdisciplinary Framework and a Problem-Solving Approach

Barbara A. Babb

> [W]hile the challenges of a contemporary . . . family court docket may be fierce, we can unquestionably find ways to meet them and do better. I am simply unwilling to adopt a despairing and defeatist attitude that 'nothing works' or—put another way—'everything stinks, but don't change a thing.'[1]

Introduction

State court caseload statistics reveal that people increasingly are using the courts to resolve their family legal disputes.[2] For example, in Maryland, nearly 45 % of the total trial court filings involve family and juvenile cases, exceeding the portion devoted to either criminal or tort cases.[3] Further, the majority of family law litigants are not represented by attorneys, a recent phenomenon that presents special challenges for courts.[4]

---

[1] Judith S. Kaye, *Delivering Justice Today: A Problem-Solving Approach*, 22 Yale L. & Pol'y Rev. 125, 147 (2004).

[2] Family law matters are defined to include divorce, annulment, and property distribution; child custody and visitation; alimony and child support; paternity, adoption, and termination of parental rights; juvenile cases (juvenile delinquency, child abuse, and child neglect); domestic violence; criminal nonsupport; name change; guardianship of minors and disabled persons; and withholding or withdrawal of life-sustaining medical procedures, involuntary admissions, and emergency evaluations. *See, e.g.*, Del. Code Ann. tit. 10, §§ 921–925, 927–928 (West 2010).

[3] *2008–2009 Statistical Digest*, MD Courts.Gov, http://mdcourts.gov/publications/annualreport/reports/20082009/statisticaldigest.pdf (last visited August 18, 2010); *see also Annual Statistical Report 2009*, Courts.Alaska.Gov, http://www.courts.alaska.gov/reports/annualrep-fy08.pdf (last visited August 18, 2010) (51 %); *2009 New Case Filings and Reopened Cases*, Courts.MT.Gov, http://courts.mt.gov/content/dcourt/stats/2009/case_filings.pdfwebsite (last visited September 2, 2010) (49 %).

[4] Barbara A. Babb, *Fashioning an Interdisciplinary Framework for Court Reform in Family Law: A Blueprint to Construct a Unified Family Court,* 71 S. Cal. L. Rev. 469, 472–473 (1998) [hereinafter Babb, *Fashioning an Interdisciplinary Framework for Court Reform in Family Law*].

B. A. Babb (✉)
Center for Families, Children and the Courts, University of Baltimore School of Law,
1420 N. Charles St., Baltimore, MD 21201, USA
e-mail: bbabb@ubalt.edu

R. L. Wiener, E. M. Brank (eds.), *Problem Solving Courts,*
DOI 10.1007/978-1-4614-7403-6_5, © Springer Science+Business Media, LLC 2013

In addition to the increasing number of family law cases, the problems associated with family legal issues are complex. Many families now regularly face challenges related to unemployment, poverty, homelessness, substance abuse, mental illness, and domestic violence, to name a few.[5] Dramatic changes in the structure and function of the family, including new reproductive technologies and increased life expectancy,[6] also complicate the resolution of family law matters. Adjudication of these matters challenges the court process, which often is ill equipped to handle the volume and scope of family law cases in contemporary American society.

> [T]he judicial system present in most states ... contributes to the demise of the family unit. Under the current system, it is not uncommon to have a family involved with one judge because of an adult abuse proceeding, a second judge because of the ensuing divorce, with still another judge because of child abuse and neglect allegations, and a fourth judge if the abuse allegations led to criminal charges. The fragmented judicial system is costly to litigants, inefficient in the use of judicial resources, and can result in the issuance of diverse or even conflicting orders affecting the family. Also, "too often courthouse resolutions resolve only the legal conflicts, leaving unaddressed the underlying personal relationship and psychological disputes."[7]

One court reform that attempts to address these issues is a concept receiving increasing consideration and about which I have written extensively is the unified family court.[8]

---

[5] Barbara A. Babb, *An Interdisciplinary Approach to Family Law Jurisprudence: Application of an Ecological and Therapeutic Perspective,* 72 Ind. L.J. 775, 777–780 (1997) [hereinafter Babb, *An Interdisciplinary Approach to Family Law Jurisprudence*].

[6] *Id.* at 777.

[7] Paul A. Williams, *A Unified Family Court for Missouri*, 63 UMKC L. Rev. 383, 383–384 (1994) (citation omitted) (quoting Ann L. Milne, *Family Law From a Family System Perspective—The Binary Equation*, 21 Pac. L.J. 933, 934 (1990) (detailing Missouri's legislative efforts to create a unified family court).

[8] *See* Babb, *Fashioning an Interdisciplinary Framework for Court Reform in Family Law*, *supra* note 4, at 477 (proposing a model structure to create a unified family court based on an ecological and therapeutic approach to family law adjudication); Barbara A. Babb, *Reevaluating Where We Stand: A Comprehensive Survey of America's Family Justice Systems*, 46 Fam. Ct. Rev. 230 (2008) [hereinafter Babb, *Reevaluating Where We Stand*] (updating the surveys conducted in Barbara A. Babb, *Where We Stand: An Analysis of America's Family Law Adjudicatory Systems and the Mandate to Establish Unified Family Courts*, 32 Fam. L.Q. 31, 34 (1998) [hereinafter Babb, *Where We Stand*] (presenting a comprehensive overview of a nationwide survey determining how each state's courts handle family law matters, illustrating the inconsistency in how America's courts process family law cases, and suggesting that states consider implementing unified family courts); *see generally* Babb, *An Interdisciplinary Approach to Family Law Jurisprudence*, *supra* note 5 (detailing changes in the structure and function of the American family in the past few decades and proposing a paradigm for family law jurisprudence that utilizes an ecological and therapeutic perspective to family law decision making). For further literature, see Developments in the Law—The Law of Family and Marriage, 116 Harv. L. Rev. 2099, 2099–2122 (2003); Richard Bolt & Jana Singer, Juristocracy in the Trenches: Problem-Solving Judges and Therapeutic Jurisprudence in Drug Treatment Courts and Unified Family Courts, 65 Md. L. Rev. 82 (2006) (examining the developments in the unified family court and drug treatment court systems); James W. Bozzomo & Andrew Schepard, Efficiency, Therapeutic Justice, Mediation and Evaluation: Reflections on a

[A unified family court is] a single court system with comprehensive jurisdiction over all cases involving children and relating to the family. One specially trained and interested judge addresses the legal and accompanying emotional and social issues challenging each family. Then under the auspices of the family court judicial action, informal court processes and social service agencies and resources are coordinated to produce a comprehensive resolution tailored to the individual family's legal, personal, emotional, and social needs. The result is a one family–one judge system that is more efficient and more compassionate for families in crisis.[9]

Although the American Bar Association, the Association of Family and Conciliation Courts, and the National Council of Juvenile and Family Court Judges all advocate for the creation of unified family courts,[10] my own research over time has revealed many states have not adopted this model, nor do they have any specialized system to handle family law matters.[11]

Reacting to similar challenges, criminal justice systems in many states have addressed issues like those facing family justice systems—burgeoning numbers compounded by complex social problems—by creating specialized problem-solving courts. As discussed by the other authors in this volume, "[p]roblem-solving courts are part of the formal criminal justice system. They seek not to divert cases out of the system but rather to reengineer the system itself."[12] Beginning with the first drug treatment court established in Miami, Florida, in 1989, "[t]here are now more than 2,000 problem-solving courts."[13] While the most well-developed problem-solving courts are community courts, domestic-violence courts, and drug courts, "there are no fewer than eleven different kinds of problem-solving courts."[14] These include, for example, "mental-health courts, reentry courts, juvenile drug courts, DWI courts,

Survey of Unified Family Courts, 37 Fam. L.Q. 333 (2003) (detailing the progression of unified family courts in the 21st century); Deborah J. Chase, Pro Se Justice and Unified Family Courts, 37 Fam. L.Q. 403 (2003) (discussing how the complexity of domestic issues and the increase in pro se litigants has pushed courts toward a unified family system); Jane C. Murphy, Revitalizing the Adversary System in Family Law, 78 U. Cin. L. Rev. 891 (2010) (discussing unified family courts' ability to resolve family conflicts through therapeutic and adversarial approaches); Jane M. Spinak, Adding Value to Families: The Potential of Model Family Courts, 2002 Wis. L. Rev. 331 (2002) (reviewing New York and other states' family court systems through different perspectives).

[9] Williams, *supra* note 7, at 384.

[10] Symposium, *American Bar Association Policy on Unified Family Courts*, 32 Fam. L.Q. 1 (1998); *Resolution Regarding the Unified Model Court Concept Paper of the NCJFCJ Cross-Over Committee*, NCJFCJ.org, http://www.ncjfcj.org/images/stories/dept/resolutions/cross-over.comm.resolution.pdf (last visited August 18, 2010).

[11] Babb, *Reevaluating Where We Stand, supra* note 8, at 231; Barbara A. Babb, *Where We Stand Redux: Another Look at America's Family Law Adjudicatory Systems*, 35 Fam. L.Q. 627 (2002) [hereinafter Babb, *Where Stand Redux*]; Babb, *Where We Stand, supra* note 8, at 39–40; Babb, *Fashioning an Interdisciplinary Framework for Court Reform in Family Law, supra* note 4, at 483–485.

[12] Greg Berman & John Feinblatt, Good Courts: The Case for Problem Solving Justice 42 (2005).

[13] *Id.* at 9.

[14] *Id.* at 7.

family-treatment courts, homeless courts, and youth courts."[15] The common element to all of these specialized courts is "working to ensure not just that the punishment fits the crime . . . but that the process fits the problem. These innovative courts encourage judges and attorneys to think of themselves as problem solvers rather than as simply case processors."[16]

This chapter advocates that family law cases also deserve and require this type of problem-solving justice. *Introduction* of the chapter summarizes my interdisciplinary approach to family law decision-making and to court reform in family law through the application of a therapeutic jurisprudence. In *Therapeutic Jurisprudence and Family Law Court Reform,* I continue in a similar vein by focusing on the developmental psychology research on the ecology of human development. *The Ecology of Human Development and Family Court Reform* reviews my blueprint for the creation of a model unified family court that incorporates the interdisciplinary perspective. *Blueprint for an Interdisciplinary Unified Family Court* provides brief concluding remarks about the importance of applying the general problem-solving court philosophy to my blueprint for unified family courts.

Therapeutic Jurisprudence and Family Law Court Reform

"Family law cases focus on some of the most intimate, emotional, and all-encompassing aspects of parties' personal lives."[17] The law is intervening explicitly by determining how families and children live. Because of this unique and powerful aspect of these cases, the legal process should seek a way to address effectively the legal and nonlegal issues, as well as a method to account for all the competing influences on the parties' lives. Therapeutic jurisprudence, a concept from mental health law that now is applied internationally and to broad areas of the law,[18] suggests how courts should proceed if they intervene in people's lives. The ecology of

---

[15] *Id.* at 8.

[16] *Id.* at 5.

[17] Babb, *Fashioning an Interdisciplinary Framework for Court Reform in Family Law, supra* note 4, at 471; *see also* Steven H. Hobbs, *In Search of Family Value: Constructing a Framework for Jurisprudence Discourse*, 75 Marq. L. Rev. 529, 530 (1992). Hobbs describes the character of family law jurisprudence:

> Each case is the real-life drama of a family working out what is valuable and important to it, while at the same time remaining within the bounds of the law. When our lives interact with the law, a discourse arises about who we are, what our hopes and dreams are for our family, how we form companionate relationships, and how we view raising children.

Id.

[18] *See generally* Bruce J. Winick et al., Judging in a Therapeutic Key: Therapeutic Jurisprudence and the Courts (2003); Dennis P. Stolle et al., Practicing Therapeutic Jurisprudence: Law as a Helping Profession (2000); Law in a Therapeutic Key: Developments in Therapeutic Jurisprudence (David B. Wexler & Bruce J. Winick eds., 1997); Bruce J. Winick, *The Jurisprudence of Therapeutic Jurisprudence, in* Law in a Therapeutic Key: Developments in Therapeutic Jurisprudence 645 (David B. Wexler & Bruce J. Winick eds., 1997) [hereinafter Winick, *The Jurisprudence of Therapeutic Jurisprudence*]; David B. Wexler et al., Essays in Therapeutic Jurisprudence (1991); David B.

human development,[19] a research paradigm from the social sciences, offers to family law attorneys and decision-makers, as well as to court reformers, an analytical tool to account for the many factors affecting parties' lives. When these constructs are applied together, they empower the justice system to provide more effective solutions to contemporary family legal issues. I address therapeutic jurisprudence in this section and address ecology of human development in the next.

Professor David Wexler, one of the co-founders with Professor Bruce Winick of the concept of therapeutic jurisprudence, defines it as follows:

> Therapeutic jurisprudence is the study of the role of law as a therapeutic agent. It looks at the law as a social force that, like it or not, may produce therapeutic or anti-therapeutic consequences. Such consequences may flow from substantive rules, legal procedures, or from the behavior of legal actors (lawyers or judges).
> The task of therapeutic jurisprudence is to identify—and ultimately to examine empirically—relationships between legal arrangements and therapeutic outcomes. The research task is a cooperative and thoroughly interdisciplinary one.[20]

Therapeutic jurisprudence applied in the family law context requires that the court focus on achieving outcomes that help the individuals and families involved in family law cases.[21] The individual's own viewpoint is important in determining what constitutes a therapeutic outcome, something attorneys and decision-makers must attempt to honor.[22] Nonetheless, "what is ultimately regarded as 'therapeutic'—and the law's role in promoting therapeutic aims is a socio-political decision, decided by legal-political decision-makers, with... important input given to consumers or recipients of the law's therapeutic aims."[23] Therapeutic jurisprudence calls for an understanding of "the extent to which a legal rule or practice promotes the psychological and physical well-being of the people it affects."[24]

A therapeutic jurisprudential approach to family law practice and decision-making and to court reform in family law aims to improve the lives of families and children

---

Wexler et al., Therapeutic Jurisprudence: the law as a Therapeutic Agent (1990); International Network on Therapeutic Jurisprudence, http://www.law.arizona.edu/depts/upr-intj/ (last visited August 19, 2010).

[19] *See generally* Urie Bronfenbrenner, The Ecology of Human Development (1979).

[20] David B. Wexler, *Putting Mental Health Into Mental Health Law: Therapeutic Jurisprudence, in* Essays in Therapeutic Jurisprudence 3, 8 (David B. Wexler & Bruce J. Winick eds., 1991) (citation omitted).

[21] Babb, *Fashioning an Interdisciplinary Framework for Court Reform in Family Law, supra* note 4; Babb, *An Interdisciplinary Approach to Family Law Jurisprudence, supra* note 5.

[22] *See* Winick, *The Jurisprudence of Therapeutic Jurisprudence, supra* note 18, at 653.

[23] David B. Wexler, *Reflections on the Scope of Therapeutic Jurisprudence, in* Law in a Therapeutic Key: Developments in Therapeutic Jurisprudence 811–12 (David B. Wexler & Bruce J. Winick eds., 1997) [hereinafter Wexler, *Reflections on the Scope of Therapeutic Jurisprudence*] (citations omitted).

[24] Christopher Slobogin, *Therapeutic Jurisprudence Five Dilemmas to Ponder*, 1 Psychol. Pub. Pol'y & L. 193, 196 (1995). But see Wexler, Reflections on the *Scope of Therapeutic Jurisprudence, supra* note 23, at 827 ("[R]esearch into the therapeutic or antitherapeutic consequences of various arrangements applying or administering existing law has not received very much attention. This is... a most promising avenue of microanalytic therapeutic jurisprudence.").

as a result of their involvement with the family justice system.[25] To accomplish this, attorneys and decision-makers must contemplate legal outcomes intended to produce more effective functioning on the part of families and children.[26] As I have written, "[i]n the field of family law, therapeutic jurisprudence should strive to protect families and children from present and future harms, to reduce emotional turmoil, to promote family harmony or preservation, and to provide individualized and efficient, effective justice."[27] As Professors Wexler and Winick caution, however, "[t]herapeutic jurisprudence in no way suggests that therapeutic considerations should trump other considerations. Therapeutic considerations are but one category of important considerations, as are autonomy, integrity of the fact-finding process, community safety, and more."[28]

Accepting therapeutic jurisprudence as a goal of family law practice and decision-making requires insisting upon this therapeutic orientation for all professionals involved in the process, including attorneys, judges, mental health professionals, special masters, and mediators, among others.[29] This orientation "has the potential to facilitate problem-solving and to positively enhance the quality of the parties' daily lives, thereby rendering a more effective outcome for individuals and families."[30] In addition, "[s]ociety as a whole must begin to acknowledge that this type of intervention and support is therapeutic for families, rather than viewing the intervention as an indication that families have failed."[31]

For example, Randall Kessler describes a few experiences he has had in a Georgia Unified Family Court in which the judges and attorneys have approached cases holistically and with the goal of closure.[32] Kessler described cases where the judges and attorneys worked together to avoid long appeals process and embarrassment for the parties.[33] The "one-stop judicial shopping" provided by a unified family court results in a more efficient system where families only appear before one judge even if there are a variety of ongoing and current legal issues (e.g., domestic violence protection petition, child support proceedings, divorce,

---

[25] Babb, *Fashioning an Interdisciplinary Framework for Court Reform in Family Law*, *supra* note 4, at 509–514; Babb, *An Interdisciplinary Approach to Family Law Jurisprudence*, *supra* note 5, at 798–801.

[26] *See* Winick, *The Jurisprudence of Therapeutic Jurisprudence*, *supra* note 18, at 655.

[27] Babb, *An Interdisciplinary Approach to Family Law Jurisprudence*, *supra* note 5, at 800.

[28] Winick, *The Jurisprudence of Therapeutic Jurisprudence, supra* note 18, at 714; David B. Wexler & Bruce J. Winick, *Patients, Professionals, and the Path of Therapeutic Jurisprudence: A Response to Petrila*, in Law in a Therapeutic Key: Developments in Therapeutic Jurisprudence 707, 708 (David B. Wexler & Bruce J. Winick eds., 1997) (citation omitted).

[29] *See* Lynne M. Kenney & Diane Vigil, *A Lawyer's Guide to Therapeutic Interventions in Domestic Relations Court*, 28 Ariz. St. L.J. 629, 635–38 (1996).

[30] Babb, *An Interdisciplinary Approach to Family Law Jurisprudence*, *supra* note 5, at 802.

[31] *Id.* at 805 & n.187.

[32] Randall M. Kessler, *Unified Family Court: A Practitioner's Perspective on Unified Family Courts: Case Studies,* 46 Fam. Ct. Rev. 279–281 (2008).

[33] *Id.* at 281.

etc.).[34] The rationale behind the "one-stop" approach rests on the idea that the myriad of legal issues a family can experience are very often interrelated and interdependent[35] and coordination of efforts should result in a system that has less duplication and is more effective.[36]

The Ecology of Human Development and Family Court Reform

To be most effective and helpful to family law litigants, the family law process must allow for a comprehensive understanding of all the legal and nonlegal issues the parties face. I have proposed the application of a theoretical research paradigm from the social sciences, "the ecology of human development,"[37] as a valuable framework to structure this holistic approach to both the family legal process and court structure. This section outlines the relevant underpinnings of this Professor Urie Bronfenbrenner's model, which promotes consideration of the interaction among individuals, institutions, and the social environment; assists with the identification of problems; and contributes to the development of solutions.[38] The ultimate aim of the ecological approach is to strengthen the connections among these interactions, institutions, and influences to improve families' and children's functioning.[39] Bronfenbrenner "sees the social environment as a grand human experiment, and thus invites our efforts to improve it, to make it better."[40]

---

[34] Andrew Schepard, *Editorial Note: Special Issues on Unified Family Courts: "The White Flame of Progress,"* 46 Fam. Ct. Rev. 217–222 (2008).

[35] *Id.* at 218.

[36] Claudia Wright, *Representation of Children in a Unified Family Court System in Florida,* 14 U. Fla. J.L. & Pub. Pol'y 179–192 (2003).

[37] *See generally* Bronfenbrenner, *supra* note 19.

[38] Gary B. Melton, Child Advocacy: Psychological Issues and Interventions 64 (1983); *see also* Gary B. Melton et al., Community Mental Health Centers and the Courts: An Evaluation of Community-Based Forensic Services (1985). This book offers a comprehensive examination of the relationship between the mental health professions and the legal system, with suggestions for strengthening that relationship.

[39] James Garbarino & Robert H. Abramowitz, *Sociocultural Risk and Opportunity, in* Children and Families in the Social Environment 35 (James Garbarino et al. eds., 2d ed. 1992). Application of an ecological perspective may present challenges:

> It would be easy to cast aside the many interconnections and pretend that there is *just* the developing child, or *just* the family as a social unit, or *just* the community power structure, or *just* the professional delivering human services. It would be easy, but we believe it would not be enough. Rather, we seek to capture the whole tangled mass of relationships connecting child, family, and social environment.

James Garbarino & Mario T. Gaboury, *An Introduction, in* Children and Families in the Social Environment 1 (James Garbarino et al. eds., 2d ed. 1992) [hereinafter Garbarino, *An Introduction*] (emphasis in original).

[40] Garbarino, *An Introduction*, *supra* note 34, at 3.

Bronfenbrenner accounts for the competing influences on people's lives by arranging the settings within which individuals live from smallest to largest[41]—"as a set of nested structures, each inside the next, like a set of Russian dolls."[42] The most immediate context within which people live is the "microsystem,"[43] such as the husband–wife relationship, the parent–child relationship, and sibling relationships. The next level or setting is the "mesosystem,"[44] or the relationships between microsystems, such as the interconnections between a child's school and his home setting or between a child's school and the neighborhood setting. The "exosystem"[45] is the next largest setting and encompasses those setting that have power over one's life but in which one does not participate, such as the influence of a parent's workplace on a child's life. Finally, the overarching ideological patterns of a culture or subculture, or shared assumptions and social policy, are known as the "macrosystem."[46] Bronfenbrenner believes that increasing the number and extent of individuals' and families' connections among these various systems can function as positive influences on family life.[47] He also imposes a life-course perspective with regard to the lives of families and children, recognizing that situations and their effects on individuals and families may change over time.[48]

---

[41] Bronfenbrenner, *supra* note 19, at 7, 22.

[42] *Id.* at 3.

[43] *Id.* at 7, 22.

[44] *Id.* at 7–8, 25.

[45] *Id.*

[46] James Garbarino & Robert H. Abramowitz, *The Ecology of Human Development*, *in* Children and Families in the Social Environment 11, 27 (James Garbarino ed., 2d ed. 1992) [hereinafter Garbarino, *The Ecology of Human Development*].

[47] *American Families: Trends and Pressures, 1973: Hearings on Examination of the Influence that Governmental Policies Have on American Families Before the Subcomm. on Children and Youth of the Senate Comm. on Labor and Public Welfare*, 93rd Cong. 31962, 31964–65 (1973) [hereinafter *Hearings*] (statement of Urie Bronfenbrenner, Professor of Human Development and Family Studies and Psychology, College of Human Ecology, Cornell University).

[48] Garbarino, *An Introduction*, *supra* note 34, at 9–10; Garbarino, *The Ecology of Human Development*, *supra* note 41, at 29–30. The following illustrates the need for a life-course perspective:

> Since most data are a cross-sectional snapshot of families, families are assumed to be static. A more realistic (though much more difficult) approach is to recognize and analyze the fluidity, change, and transitions as individuals live in a variety of family patterns. There are periods in the life cycle when an individual family may be one in which the father works and the mother stays home with the children. This stage is relatively short-lived when the total family life course is analyzed. There are periods, also, when women (and men) find themselves raising a family without a spouse present, but again, for many this is a transition period. None of these types or stages, however, should be viewed as the dominant or "ideal" family type. No one family type is superior to another or to be favored over others. Effective policies and services should be sensitive to the needs and stresses of certain types of families and recognize that some families are at greater risk (statistically) than others.

Applied to family law decision-making, the value of this ecological approach is "that it reveals connections that might otherwise go unnoticed and helps us look beyond the immediate and the obvious to see where the most significant influences lie."[49] Further, "the ecological perspective on human development offers a kind of map for steering a course of study and intervention."[50] Bronfenbrenner suggests that each level of the ecology can produce benefits or risks, and he urges strengthening these natural interactions or interconnections to enhance individual and family functioning.[51] Applying the ecology of human development paradigm to families' legal problems can assist lawyers, judges, and other professionals involved with the family justice system to identify the breadth and scope of factors affecting people's lives and allow them to have a holistic view of families' functioning. Court professionals can "look beyond the individual litigants . . . to holistically examine the larger social environments in which participants live, and to fashion legal remedies that strengthen a family's supportive relationships."[52] This expanded knowledge permits all family justice system professionals to intervene more effectively, thereby promoting more therapeutic outcomes for families and children.

In practice, this holistic approach encourages court personnel to consider the variety of influences on the family in order to provide more effective solutions.[53] For example, the courts would consider the organizations and relationships the family members have with their neighborhoods, religious organizations, and schools.[54] Although the courts may not be able to change the family's mesosystem, it would be able to consider it in deciding how to apply the law in a way that is best for the family. That means the entire court process would do a better job of accommodating the complex factors that contributed to the family being within the court system.[55] One way that unified family courts do just this is through the "one-stop" approach. Many families who are in need of court interventions are also dealing with employment and financial strains. By considering these strains and making the process more efficient, the families will have a better chance at success.

Likewise, the court structure itself must assist decision-makers to consider the various systems affecting the family. Courts must be guided to view schools, neighborhoods, places of employment, religious organizations, and other institutions within which family members participate as potential influences upon a family's

---

Robert M. Maroney, Families, Social Services, and Social Policy: The Issue of Shared Responsibility 50 (1980).

[49] Garbarino, *The Ecology of Human Development*, *supra* note 41, at 19.

[50] *Id.* at 28.

[51] Bronfenbrenner, *supra* note 19, at 214; *Hearings*, *supra* note 41, at 157 (statement of Urie Bronfenbrenner).

[52] Babb, *An Interdisciplinary Approach to Family Law Jurisprudence*, *supra* note 5, at 803.

[53] Barbara A. Babb & Judith D. Moran, Substance Abuse, Families, and Unified Family Courts: The Creation of a Caring Justice System, 3 J. Health Pol'y & L. 1, 25–33 (1999) [hereinafter Babb & Moran, Substance Abuse, Families, and Unified Family Courts].

[54] *Id.*

[55] *See* Babb, *Fashioning an Interdisciplinary Framework for Court Reform in Family Law*, *supra* note 4.

legal matters. I have created a blueprint for a particular court structure, the unified family court, with the theoretical underpinnings of therapeutic jurisprudence and the ecology of human development set within the general problem-solving template, as the mechanism to achieve this structured consideration of families' and children's lives, thereby assisting in the fashioning of more effective resolutions to families' legal problems.[56]

Blueprint for an Interdisciplinary Unified Family Court

A unified family court is one that coordinates the work of independent forums and agencies, each of which has some limited role to resolve family legal matters.[57] This section describes the blueprint for a model unified family court framed by the ecology of human development and driven by therapeutic jurisprudence. This interdisciplinary framework empowers the family justice system to fashion the most appropriate outcomes for families and children. The section also describes certain aspects of the current design of America's family justice systems based upon the results of a national survey, which I have conducted in 1998,[58] 2002,[59] and most recently in 2008.[60]

Separate Court Structure

It is imperative to consider family law issues within a specialized court due to the diversity of and relationships among the legal problems, as well as the intimacy of the participants and the effect of these problems on the stability of people's lives.[61] As one scholar has noted, "a single court could examine the entire relationship between parent and parent, parent and child, child and child, family and in-laws, and family and the public. And, having explored the whole complex of relationships, a single court could provide consistent and continuing consideration of each aspect of the problem."[62]

---

[56] *Id.*

[57] *See* Roscoe Pound, *The Place of the Family Court in the Judicial System*, 5 Nat'l Probation & Parole Ass'n J. 161 (1959).

[58] *See* Babb, *Fashioning an Interdisciplinary Framework for Court Reform in Family Law*, *supra* note 4; Babb, *Where We Stand*, *supra* note 8.

[59] *See* Babb, *Where Stand Redux*, *supra* note 11.

[60] *See* Babb, *Reevaluating Where We Stand*, *supra* note 8. These surveys involved a written survey, telephone interviews, and e-mail exchanges with court personnel in all the states including D.C. The goal was to develop an understanding of each state's system and the way each state defined family law matters and understanding the way the cases are assigned and handled in each state.

[61] Babb, *Fashioning an Interdisciplinary Framework for Court Reform in Family Law*, *supra* note 4, at 514.

[62] Lindsay G. Arthur, *A Family Court–Why Not?* 51 Minn. L. Rev. 226 (1966) (citation omitted) (advocating, in an early article, consolidation of family law litigation and court treatment of the entire family problem).

Courts within the last decade have begun to restructure their processing of family law cases by creating separate specialized courts or by creating divisions or departments of existing courts, known, for example, as family divisions or family departments.[63] In fact, only 13 states currently operate without some form of family court in existence somewhere within the state, although the rest do not necessarily have a unified family court system.[64] Given the numbers of family law cases our nation's justice systems are handling, along with the importance of family legal matters in people's lives and their effects on society, it is imperative that any family court, regardless of its structure, be established at the same level and receive the same resources and support as a trial court of general jurisdiction.[65]

> Another issue related to court structure is that of judicial specialization. As I have written, ... judges assigned to specialized family courts must themselves be specialized family court jurists. The types of choices required by decision-makers to resolve family legal matters compel the need for judicial specialization. Not only must these judges fully understand the intricacies of the entire body of family law, but they also must possess an appreciation for and understanding of the social settings within which family members function, including any problems attendant to each of these settings, such as substance abuse and domestic violence.[66]

Because of the complex nature of the cases, family court judges equipped to fashion the most effective or therapeutic outcomes for families and children are those educated about relevant social science literature, including child development, family dynamics, domestic violence, mental illness, substance abuse, and other issues related to family law cases.

Length of judicial assignment is another issue critical to court structure. "In order to fully comprehend the breadth of family law proceedings, as well as to understand from an ecological focus the various settings within which family law litigants live their lives, family law judges must remain within the family court system for significant periods of time."[67] In my most recent survey of America's family justice systems, I have found that in those states with some form of family court, the length of a judge's term ranges from 1 year to a life-term assignment.[68] In the majority of jurisdictions, family court judges generally serve for a term ranging between 2 and 10 years.[69] Some scholars estimate the minimum length of judicial assignment to a

---

[63] Babb, *Reevaluating Where We Stand*, *supra* note 8, at 232 (nearly 75 % of states have some form of family court).

[64] *Id.* The thirteen state include: Alabama, Arkansas, Idaho, Iowa, Mississippi, Montana, Nebraska, Oklahoma, South Dakota, Tennessee, Utah, Virginia, and Wyoming are without a family court. *Id.* at 240 app. a.

[65] *Id.* at 231; Babb, *Fashioning an Interdisciplinary Framework for Court Reform in Family Law*, *supra* note 4, at 516.

[66] Babb, *Fashioning an Interdisciplinary Framework for Court Reform in Family Law*, *supra* note 4, at 514–15.

[67] *Id.* at 515 (footnote omitted).

[68] Babb, *Reevaluating Where We Stand*, *supra* note 8, at 234, 249 app. c.

[69] *Id.*

family court at 4 years,[70] but we do not yet have any empirical evidence that provides guidance on what would be the ideal term or even the ideal way to train these judges.

Comprehensive Subject Matter Jurisdiction

To enable a unified family court to address a family's legal and related nonlegal problems holistically, rather than in a fragmented and unrelated manner, the court should have comprehensive subject matter jurisdiction over the full range of family law issues.[71]

A court without this power will struggle to fully strengthen the family's interactions among the various systems within which it functions. Similarly, the court would not be at liberty to resolve related family problems, which severely interferes with the effectiveness of the court's intervention.

Unified family courts must be equipped to respond as comprehensively as possible to these related legal matters. Subject matter jurisdiction should include dissolution and related matters, such as distribution of marital property, separation, and annulment; child custody, visitation, modification, and interstate custody cases; child support establishment, modification, enforcement, and uniform interstate family support cases; determination of paternity; child abuse and neglect; termination of parental rights; domestic violence proceedings; adoption; juvenile delinquency proceedings; adult and juvenile guardianship and conservatorship; mental health matters, including civil commitment and confinement; legal-medical issues, including right to die, abortion, and living wills; emancipation; and name change.[72]

Although experts differ about whether to include the criminal jurisdiction over intrafamilial issues as unified family court subject matter jurisdiction, such as child abuse and domestic violence,[73] some states are experimenting with integrated

---

[70] Sanford N. Katz & Jeffrey A. Kuhn, Recommendations for a Model Family Court 4–5 (1991). *But see H.* Ted Rubin & Victor Eugene Flango, Court Coordination of Family Cases 77 (1992) (estimating the minimum length of judicial assignment to a family court should be 12 months).

[71] *See supra* note 2 (defining comprehensive family law subject matter jurisdiction).

[72] Babb, *Fashioning an Interdisciplinary Framework for Court Reform in Family Law*, *supra* note 4, at 518 (footnote omitted); *see, e.g.*, Md. Code Ann., Md. Rule § 16–204 (West 2010).

[73] *See* Katz & Kuhn, *supra* note 60. The authors discuss the arguments for and against including criminal jurisdiction over intrafamilial matters as part of the family court:

> [w]hile proponents for inclusion of this jurisdiction in family court argued that such a system promotes coordinated delivery of services to the family and discourages multiple interviewing of victims, as well as fragmented delivery, those arguing against such jurisdiction cited possible due process violations and community pressure for a more punitive stance toward offenders as rendering such jurisdiction inappropriate for the family court.

Id. at 8–9. *See also* Linda Szymanski, Theresa Homisak & E. Hunter Hurst, III, Policy Alternatives and Current Court Practice in the Special Problem Areas of Jurisdiction Over the Family 8–9 (1993). The authors suggest additional arguments against including criminal jurisdiction in the family court:

domestic violence courts.[74] Integrated Domestic Violence courts hear all civil and criminal cases involving a family with domestic violence concerns.[75] The aim of these courts is to protect and assist victims and to promote defendant accountability,[76] but there are possible due process issues that the courts must address.

According to my most recent survey of America's family justice systems, of the 38 states (including District of Columbia) that have some form of family court, 24 states and the District of Columbia assign their family courts comprehensive subject matter jurisdiction.[77] Empowering unified family courts with the most inclusive subject matter jurisdiction feasible allows courts to respond as comprehensively as possible to all of a family's related legal and nonlegal matters. This promotes a more holistic assessment of a family's problems and facilitates the fashioning of more effective outcomes for the family.

Specialized Case Management and Case Processing System

In order to prevent family legal problems from remaining unresolved and escalating, it is important for these cases to receive prompt attention from the justice system. Case management and case processing, or the method by which cases proceed from initial filing through resolution, should proceed without undue delay and with active, hands-on participation from court personnel as early as possible.[78]

> A judge, a professional court administrator, a trained intake worker, or a team of these personnel can evaluate each case filing or intake and can determine whether the parties require immediate attention. The initial evaluation process also can result in referral of the parties to appropriate [social] services, as well as scheduling an early status conference. At

---

> [i]nclusion of criminal jurisdiction within the family court can present a host of problems . . . First, there is a philosophical divergence between juvenile court and criminal court. Juvenile court's intervention is justified on the basis of protecting the child and is not intended as punishment but as remediation. Criminal proceedings seek to punish offenders without regard to family interests. Adult criminal proceedings require the availability of jury trial with the increased administrative burden on the restructured court system, unless the criminal jurisdiction is limited to misdemeanors.

Id. (citation omitted).

[74] Kaye, *supra* note 1, 143.

[75] *Id.*

[76] *Id.*

[77] Babb, *Reevaluating Where We Stand, supra* note 8, at 233, 245 app. b. (Arizona, Delaware, District of Columbia, Florida, Georgia, Hawaii, Kansas, Kentucky, Maine, Maryland, Massachusetts, Michigan, Minnesota, Nevada, New Hampshire, New Jersey, North Carolina, North Dakota, Oregon, Pennsylvania, Rhode Island, South Carolina, Vermont, Washington, Wisconsin all assign their family courts comprehensive subject-matter jurisdiction).

[78] Babb,*Fashioning an Interdisciplinary Framework for Court Reform in Family Law, supra* note 4, at 519–520.

> this conference, the parties, their attorneys, and the judge can frame the issues in the case, discuss settlement possibilities, and consider alternatives to an adversarial trial or hearing.[79]

The active case management process is ongoing throughout the life of the case and requires constant monitoring.[80] For example, in New York, the judge has an active role in leadership and the team approach with the case conferences. These case conferences allow for a more efficient approach that can better accommodate timely and appropriate interventions.[81]

A related aspect of case management and case processing necessitates considering who should become familiar with the history of each case, as well as how this historical and holistic knowledge can be acquired. The one judge–one case method, or the individual assignment system, of case management means that the same judge oversees a case from start to finish.[82] This method facilitates more therapeutic and ecological decision-making because a judge develops a more comprehensive awareness of the family's problems, allowing for the fashioning of more effective outcomes. For example, if a judge knows that a particular intervention was not helpful or effective in the past, she will have a better idea of the types of interventions that may be better suited for the family. Another type of case management is the one judge–one family approach, where the family appears before the same judge every time the parties come to court and on any number of cases.[83] While this approach offers the same benefits as the one judge–one case method, there is concern that the judges' impartiality will be compromised due to "judicial overfamiliarity" with the parties.[84] In other words, the characteristics that make the one judge–one case method appealing can also be a source of criticism if the judges do not guard against becoming so familiar that they are no longer unbiased. A third method of case management, the one family–one team approach, ensures consistency in processing a family law case due to the same team of court administrators' involvement in a family's case every time the family utilizes the court system.[85] The advantages of this method are the same as the other two case assignment methods.

My 2008 family justice system survey reveals that of the 38 jurisdictions that have some form of family court, 12 jurisdictions apply the one judge–one family case assignment method.[86] Five states currently use the one judge–one case assignment

[79] *Id.* at 520 (footnotes omitted).

[80] *Id.* at 520–21 (footnote omitted).

[81] **Spinak at 359 (see footnote 8?)

[82] Robert F. Peckham, *A Judicial Response to the Cost of Litigation: Case Management, Two-Stage Discovery Planning and Alternative Dispute Resolution*, 37 Rutgers L. Rev. 253, 257 (1985); Babb, *Reevaluating Where We Stand, supra* note 8, at 253 app. d.

[83] Babb, *Reevaluating Where We Stand, supra* note 8, at 253 app. d n.3.

[84] Ann H. Geraghty & Wallace J. Mllyniec, *Tempering Enthusiasm with Caution*, 40 Fam. Ct. Rev. 435, 439 (2002).

[85] Babb, *Reevaluating Where We Stand, supra* note 8, at 231.

[86] Babb, *Reevaluating Where We Stand, supra* note 8, at 234, 253 app. d. *See supra* note 56 for the list of jurisdictions that do not have a family court. The 12 jurisdictions that apply the one judge–one family case assignment method include: District of Columbia, Arizona, Delaware, Georgia,

method.[87] Four states[88] assign cases through the traditional calendar method.[89] The remaining 16 states employ a variety of case assignment methods.[90]

Operating a unified family court with a therapeutic and ecological approach requires a high level of administrative coordination, including providing a family court administrator and an administrative or presiding family court judge.[91] "The court management system, including nonjudicial personnel, must aim to resolve disputes in a timely manner, to supply and to coordinate efficiently the necessary resources or services, and to network appropriately with other courts in the system to share information about families that allows for consistent judicial decision-making."[92] This type of court administration, coupled with the specialized case management and case processing systems detailed above, promotes more effective resolutions for family legal proceedings.

An Array of Services

It is essential for a unified family court to have available an array of services it can offer families in order to fashion the most helpful outcomes. These services can assist judges in the family law case management process and can aid their understanding of the entire context of a family's legal problems, including any underlying social and psychological issues related to the family's functioning.[93] "This informed decision-making enables a judge to fashion a creative resolution to the family problem . . ."[94] In addition, "[t]he accelerated and coordinated provision of social services is . . . unified under the authority of the family court, as is coordination of collateral and ancillary matters . . . for family members not directly before the court."[95]

Hawaii, Kentucky, New Hampshire, New Jersey, North Carolina, North Dakota, Ohio, Oregon, and Wisconsin. *Id.*

[87] *Id.* The jurisdictions that use the one judge–one case assignment method include: Alabama, Massachusetts, New Mexico, Rhode Island, and West Virginia. *Id.*

[88] *Id.* These jurisdictions include: California, Connecticut, South Carolina, and Vermont. *Id.*

[89] The traditional calendar method is defined as the standard procedure utilized by the clerk of court to assign all civil matters to the respective judges on a daily, weekly, monthly, or other regularly scheduled basis. *Id.* at 253 app. d n. 1.

[90] *Id.* at 234. These jurisdictions include: Colorado, Florida, Illinois, Indiana, Kansas, Louisiana, Maine, Maryland, Michigan, Minnesota, Missouri, Nevada, New York, Pennsylvania, Texas, and Washington. *Id.*

[91] Babb, *Fashioning an Interdisciplinary Framework for Court Reform in Family Law*, *supra* note 4, at 521–22.

[92] *Id.* at 521.

[93] *Id.* at 522.

[94] *Id.* at 523 (footnote omitted).

[95] Stephen Cribari, *Therapeutic Power and Judicial Authority*, Unified Fam. Chron., Spring 1999, at 1.

Alternative dispute resolution procedures, such as negotiation, mediation, neutral case evaluation, and other informal processes, should be part of any family court's functioning because they all work together to distance the case from the traditional adversarial system.

> The earlier the court incorporates these alternatives into family law proceedings, the more successful the court becomes at circumventing the adversary process and locating services to assist families. In contrast to . . . programs existing independent of the court system, court-connected programs are likely to gain greater acceptance by the parties; they tend to view procedures in this setting as unbiased . . . ."[96]

The nature of the services can vary, depending upon the needs of the court clientele and community.[97] Services can be court-supplied or court-connected, where the court links the parties to existing services within the community, a more fiscally prudent process.[98] Examples of services, in addition to alternative dispute resolution efforts, include assessment and evaluation, counseling, parent education, children's programs, supervised visitation, neutral drop-off centers, substance abuse services, domestic violence victim advocacy and representation, and assistance for self-represented litigants.[99] But the number of services is not the ultimate answer; courts should be seeking empirical evidence on what types of services are most effective for particular situations and family's needs. Unified family court judges are likely to be better equipped to consider the empirical evidence because of their specialized knowledge and commitment to social science research.

The provision of appropriate services requires the unified family court to work closely with the community, creating a court–community connection. Whatever services are deemed appropriate for a given family within a particular court setting, the earlier the family members receive the services, the more likely they are to

---

[96] Babb, *Fashioning an Interdisciplinary Framework for Court Reform in Family Law, supra* note 4, at 522 (footnotes omitted).

[97] Under Md. Code Ann., Md. Rule § 16–204(a)(3) (West 2010), the following services must be available through the family division: "mediation in custody and visitation matters, custody investigations, trained personnel to respond to emergencies, mental health evaluations and evaluations for alcohol and drug abuse, information services, including procedural assistance to *pro se* litigants, information regarding lawyer referral services, parenting seminars, and any additional family support services for which funding is provided." *Id.* The Family Division of the Circuit Court of Baltimore City offers the following programs: substance abuse services, supervised visitation program, medical services office, neutral drop-off, family mediation service, Domestic Violence Ex Parte Project, Protective Order Advocacy and Representation Project, Assisted Pro Se Litigation Project, parenting seminars, Children's Group, and the Volunteer Attorney Settlement Panel. Babb & Moran, *Substance Abuse, Families, and Unified Family Courts, supra* note 53.

[98] Md. Code Ann., Md. Rule § 16–204(a)(3)(C) (West 2010) (every jurisdiction must possess a Family Services Coordinator and follow specific designated tasks); A.B.A. Presidential Working Group on the Unmet Legal Needs of Children and Their Families, America's Children at Risk: A National Agenda for Legal Action 54 (1993).

[99] Babb & Moran, *Substance Abuse, Families, and Unified Family Courts, supra* note 53, at 25–32; *see also* Babb, *Fashioning an Interdisciplinary Framework for Court Reform in Family Law, supra* 4, at 523 n. 293.

benefit from them and thus to reap the therapeutic outcomes these courts should provide.[100]

A User-Friendly Court

Given the enormous volume of family law cases,[101] it is essential for the unified family court to remain accessible to users and be user-friendly. The unified family court also must account for the tremendous numbers of self-represented litigants.[102] A unified family court should be centrally located,[103] and it should be child- and family-oriented, including maintaining appropriate waiting rooms for children and witnesses, separate interview rooms for privacy, and adequate courthouse security.[104] Creating a user-friendly court also means that courts are designed for the convenience of the clientele and that all court personnel are trained to treat the clientele courteously.[105] One relatively recent improvement involves new technologies that permit courts to install computerized kiosks that disseminate prepared legal forms[106] and to make form pleadings available via the internet and in courthouse centers for family law matters.[107]

Although no one court design is adaptable to every jurisdiction, this blueprint for a unified family court, grounded in a therapeutic and an ecological perspective, most closely approaches the model court defined by the Standard Family Court Act in 1959 but never established in the necessary comprehensive sense.

> To protect and safeguard family life, in general, and family units, in particular, by affording to family members all possible help in resolving their justiciable problems and conflicts

---

[100] Rubin & Flango, *supra* note 60, at 9.

[101] Berman & Feinblatt, *supra* note 12, at 24 (The National Center for State Courts reported that the largest increases in case filing from 1984–1998 were in areas of domestic relations, which grew by 75 %, and juvenile cases, which grew by 73 %).

[102] *See* Murphy, *supra* note 8.

[103] *Letters: Family Court must be in a Center City location*, The Philadelphia Inquirer, http://www.philly.com/inquirer/opinion/99215824.html (last visited August 21, 2010).

[104] *See* Katz & Kuhn, *supra* note 60; *see also* Laura Duncan, *Courthouse Day Care Programs Increasing*, A.B.A. J., Oct. 1995, at 22–23 (describing some features of the more than 30 child care centers within American courthouses and noting that California, Massachusetts, and New York have legislatively appropriated funding to construct these centers).

[105] *See* Stephen P. Johnson, Just Solutions: Seeking Innovation and Change in the American Justice System 234 (1994).

[106] *Id.* at 29. *See also* Office of the Clerk of the Circuit Court of Cook County, The 21st Century Clerk's Office: A Blueprint for Change 5 (2001), http://www.cookcountyclerkofcourt.org/gifs/transitionreportfinal.pdf; Task Force on Pro Se & Indigent Litigants, Reports and Recommendations of the Supreme Court of Ohio 18 (2006), http://www.supremecourt.ohio.gov/Publications/prose/report_april06.pdf.

[107] Department of Family Administration, 2006 Annual Report 31 (2006), http://mdcourts.gov/family/pdfs/annualreports/annualreport06.pdf.

> arising from their interpersonal relationships, in a single court, with one specially qualified staff under one leadership, with a common philosophy and purpose working as a unit, with one set of family records, all in one place, under the direction of one or more specially qualified judges.[108]

Because more effective resolution of family legal matters can benefit the entire society by strengthening individuals' and families' functioning, it is imperative that all lessons learned are applied to family justice system reform. The interdisciplinary unified family court model proposed in this chapter is enhanced by applying principles from the recently established problem-solving courts.

Conclusion

Why is it vitally important to consider unified family courts within the problem-solving or specialty court context? I believe the unified family court idea is the best way to address the myriad of issues that families bring to the legal system. Family law matters touch on every aspect of a person's life; having a court system that can more holistically address those matters is vitally important. By using the problem-solving court template and my blueprint for the unified family court we can better approach the whole of the family rather than piecemeal tactics that will continue to fall short. A unified family court that comprehensively approaches the needs of families from an interdisciplinary perspective and is able to do so in a user-friendly way will meet the current challenges of overburdened courts and families that desperately need their help.

---

[108] Committee on the Standard Family Court Act of the National Probation and Parole Association, *Standard Family Court Act—Text and Commentary*, 5 Nat'l Probation & Parole Ass'n J. 99, 106 (1959).

Chapter 6
Domestic Violence Courts: The Case of Lady Justice Meets the Serpents of the Caduceus

Nancy Wolff

> I am a victim of domestic violence. I suffered many years at the wrong side of my husband's fist and vicious tongue. I wasn't only battered physically but also abused mentally, emotionally, and verbally by the man who I thought loved me and who I loved more than myself.
> ~ M.H. (serving 30 years for killing her abusive husband)

Domestic violence is prevalent across the United States. Each year in the United States approximately 1.5 million women experience 4.8 million physical or sexual assaults committed against them by their intimate partners (Tjaden and Thoennes 2000) and an estimated 3.3 million children witness these episodes of domestic violence (American Psychological Association 1996). Over a lifetime, one in four American women experience at least one incident of domestic violence (Tjaden and Thoennes 2000). Intimate partner abuse most often occurs in the privacy of the home, goes unreported, is repeated, and often escalates, resulting in the loss of self-esteem, loss of health and well-being, and, for some, the loss of life (Fritzler and Simon 2000; Healey and Smith 1998).

The human and social consequences of domestic violence, defined as a "constellation of physical, sexual, and psychological abuses" between intimates (Healey et al. 1998, p. 3) is unbounded. It has primary and immediate effects on the female victim[1] measured in terms of her loss in emotional, mental, and physical health, as well as ability to perform normal functions in the home and on the job. Secondary effects include the harm to the children in the household who witness and may also be direct victims of the batterer's wrath and cruelty (Simon 1995). These children may experience proximal losses to their health and emotional well-being, as well as more distal effects as future victims or perpetrators of domestic violence (American

[1] Women are most often the victims of domestic violence, although men also report being battered by their female partners. In 2001, 15 % of domestic victimizations reported were against men (Rennison 2003).

N. Wolff (✉)
Center for Behavioral Health Services & Criminal Justice Research,
Rutgers University, 176 Ryders Lane, New Brunswick, NJ 08901, USA
e-mail: nwolff@cbhs.rutgers.edu

R. L. Wiener, E. M. Brank (eds.), *Problem Solving Courts*,
DOI 10.1007/978-1-4614-7403-6_6, © Springer Science+Business Media, LLC 2013

Psychological Association 1996; Cappell and Heiner 1990; Ehrensaft et al. 2003; Magdol et al. 1998; Rosenbaum and O'Leary 1981; Widom 1989a).

The social costs of domestic violence include the medical costs associated with treating the victim's broken limbs, internal bleeding, head trauma, and damaged kidneys; mental health costs of treatment for the victim's posttraumatic stress disorder (PTSD), anxiety, depression, and general sense of worthlessness; productivity losses due to her lost work days and cut-down days because of physical or emotional injuries and employment termination; the criminal justice costs associated with police responding to repeated 911 calls, court costs for processing restraining orders and criminal charges, prosecution costs for charges of assault, destruction of property, stalking, harassment, and murder; and the intangible costs resulting from living in fear and the human loss of life. The annual direct cost of domestic violence in the United States is estimated at US$ 5.8 billion, with more than 70 % of these costs (US$ 4.1 billion) associated with medical and mental health care services (National Center for Injury Prevention and Control 2003).

It is because of the pervasiveness of domestic violence and its combined social unacceptability *and* imposing, recurring social and human consequences that domestic violence legislation and eventually courts emerged. The rationale for domestic violence legislation and courts grew out of the feminist movement in the 1960s that focused national attention on women as victims of partner-related violence (Epstein 1999; Moore 2009). Activist feminists from grass-roots organizations succeeded in redefining domestic violence as a crime, not a private matter and characterized it as an issue of control and dominance, where male partners used their power to dominate and control "their" women (Healey et al. 1998; Turgeon 2008). Through the lens of sexism, domestic violence was recast in the 1970s and 1980s as a social problem requiring a social policy remedy, and created the impetus for incremental legislative changes that eventually culminated in 1994 with the passage of the Violence Against Women Act,[2] which earmarked federal funding for specialized interventions (e.g., domestic violence courts) to protect women from violence.

Yet long before federal legislation, states and localities responded to the issue of domestic violence through policy and legal changes affecting policing and prosecution practices. At the state and local level, the criminal justice response to domestic violence began in the 1970s and included specialized police training, mandatory arrest laws, and special prosecution units (Buzawa and Buzawa 1996; Zorza 1992). These interventions trained police to deescalate and contain violence between intimates that had resulted in emergency calls, while the law required police to arrest batterers. In turn, prosecutors were expected and did prosecute batterers on criminal charges ranging from harassment to assault. According to Fagan (1996, p. 9), "by 1980, 47 States had passed domestic violence legislation mandating changes in protection orders, enabling warrantless arrest for misdemeanor assaults, and recognizing a history of abuse and threat as part of a legal defense for battered women who killed their abusive husbands." Those convicted of domestic violence often received

[2] Violence Women Act of 1994. Pub. L. No. 103-322,108 Stat. 1902.

sentences with special conditions requiring participation in batterer programs, creating a new intervention modality that was intended to enhance batterer accountability, and prevent future acts of violence against intimates (Healey et al. 1998).

The impact of these interventions on the court system was nontrivial; arrests related to domestic violence and their prosecution, along with the applications for restraining orders grew significantly in the 1970s and 1980s (Hirschel et al. 2008; Moore 2009), inundating the courts with domestic violence cases (Buzawa and Buzawa 1996; Epstein 1999). In response, the judiciary introduced analogous domestic violence specialization. The first domestic violence court was implemented in Dade County, Florida in 1992, with New York State, under Chief Justice Judith Kaye, introducing the most comprehensive state-wide judicial response in 1994 (Casey and Rottman 2003; Mazur and Aldrick 2003). Today there are more than 200 specialized courts in the United States that focus on issues related to domestic violence (Labriola et al. 2009). These courts are geographically concentrated in four states: New York ($n = 66$), California ($n = 34$), Washington ($n = 24$), and Florida ($n = 24$) (Labriola et al. 2009).

Broadly speaking, domestic violence courts attempt to integrate three parallel tracks associated with the 30-year social trend of criminalizing domestic violence: prosecution, punishment, and deterrence of batterers; rehabilitation of batterers; and protection of victims through the use of protective orders (Fagan 1996). They also attempt to expedite, simplify, and unify the processing and monitoring of domestic violence cases that frequently involve both criminal and civil issues associated, respectively, with prosecuting the batterer and protecting the victim (Keilitz 2004). The overarching goal of these courts is not to eschew punishment, but rather to ensure that punishment is efficiently and fully exacted on batterers in ways that hold them accountable for their crimes against intimates and to deter future acts of domestic violence in part through prosecution and in part through rehabilitation, while, at the same time, protecting the victim of domestic violence.

According to a national survey of domestic violence courts in the United States, the primary goals of these courts are victim safety and offender accountability, followed by "other" goals that include deterrence, rehabilitation, and administration of justice (Labriola et al. 2009). Of the 13 goals identified by participating courts, victim safety and offender accountability were the most strongly endorsed goals by court respondents and prosecutors. By contrast, endorsement was the weakest for the goal of offender rehabilitation, with prosecutors being less likely than court respondents to view this goal as extremely important (27 vs. 37 %). More than one-third (35 %) of court respondents identified rehabilitating offenders as "not a goal" (19 %) or "somewhat important (15 %)." There was, however, geographical variation among courts regarding the importance of offender rehabilitation. Court respondents in New York were significantly less likely to report that offender rehabilitation was extremely important, compared with California (19 vs. 57 %) and other states (19 vs. 49 %). Offender rehabilitation was the least selected of the 13 goals by New York courts, whereas it was ranked as fourth among California's respondents and fifth by courts in other states.

Although rehabilitation is not a high-priority goal of domestic violence courts, they are nonetheless categorized as a "problem solving" court, most commonly exemplified by drug or mental health courts (Mazur and Aldrich 2003; Shelton 2007). Problem-solving courts rest on the legal foundation of therapeutic jurisprudence (Wexler and Winick 1991, 1996) that "looks at the law as a social force that, like it or not, may produce therapeutic or antitherapeutic consequences" (Wexler 1991, p. 8). Because of the antitherapeutic consequences of incarceration for defendants that commit crimes *because of* or *as a consequence of* a treatable behavioral health problem, problem-solving courts order therapeutic treatment instead of incarceration. Their goal is to stop the criminalization of treatable behavioral health problems, particularly drug addiction or mental illness (Berman and Feinblatt 2001; Casey and Rottman 2003). Indeed, first-generation problem-solving courts such as drug and mental health courts systematically diverted defendants with behavioral health problems to supervised treatment in the community in lieu of incarceration (Goldkamp and Irons-Guynn 2000; Nolan 2001). In sharp contrast, domestic violence courts seek to "increase the certainty and severity of legal responses" (Fagan 1996, p. 3) (enforcing offender accountability) against batterers while protecting the victim from their harm.

In theory and practice, domestic violence courts primarily focus on victim safety and, as such, appeal to principles of restorative justice, the need to repair or heal the victim (Braithwaite 2002; Dignan 2005) rather than principles of therapeutic jurisprudence, the need to rehabilitate the offender through behavioral health intervention. Goals of offender rehabilitation and recovery have been downplayed by domestic violence courts in part because there is a lack of consensus regarding whether batterer behavior is remediable through behavioral health intervention, reflecting how little is known about its etiology, and in part because historically the focus has been on helping the victim, not the batterer (Turgeon 2008). While attending a batterer program is typically required as a special condition of sentencing by domestic violence courts, the evidence on the effectiveness of batterer programs in terms of changing offender behavior is weak (Gondolf 2011; Saunders 2008; Stover et al. 2009), which draws into question the extent to which these programs seek to rehabilitate behavior (Turgeon 2008). It is for this reason that batterers programs are more often considered a systems intervention, not behavioral health treatment (Gondolf 2011).

Even though there are more than 200 domestic violence courts operating in the United States, there is no consistency among these courts in terms of structure and process (Labriola et al. 2009; Weber 2000), and their effectiveness on relevant outcomes such as recidivism and victim safety remains uncertain (Casey and Rottman 2003; Moore 2009; Shelton 2007; Turgeon 2008). The evidence on the performance of domestic violence courts is clearest on outcomes measuring case processing. Significant reductions in days lapsed between case filing and disposition were found for misdemeanor domestic violence courts compared with nonspecialized misdemeanor courts in Milwaukee, Manhattan, and San Diego (Angene 2000; Davis et al. 2001; Eckberg and Podkpacz 2002; Peterson 2004). The opposite was found in the single evaluation of a felony domestic violence court; case processing increased, it was argued, because the issues within the indictment were more severe (Newmark et al. 2001).

The research evidence becomes more ambiguous for performance outcomes measuring offender accountability, recidivism, and victim safety. Although holding perpetrators responsible for their conduct is a priority of domestic violence courts, the evidence here is mixed. Of the six evaluations of domestic violence courts, three studies found conviction rates increased (Goldkamp et al. 1996; Davis et al. 2001; Eckberg and Podkopacz 2002) and three found no significant change in conviction rates (Angene 2000; Newmark et al. 2001; Peterson 2004). The effect of domestic violence courts on sentencing is equally ambiguous, but less reliable because there is considerable variation both in sentencing laws among states where the studies were conducted and in the research designs across the studies (Moore 2009). Compared with nonspecialized courts, however, domestic violence courts have been found to more consistently order special conditions such as batterer programs, substance abuse treatment, drug testing, and intensive probation supervision as part of sentencing (Angene 2000; Harrell et al. 2007a; Newmark et al. 2001).

Although safety of victims is the primary goal of domestic violence courts, their ability to significantly reduce recidivism has not been consistently documented in studies using either quasi-experimental or experimental designs. Of the ten evaluations using quasiexperimental designs, three studies found small to significant reductions in rearrests, five found no reductions or increases, and two, focusing on a single court site, found no significant reductions in one study and a significant reduction in the other, a result attributed to the incapacitation of offenders who, as a consequence, had less time "at risk" in the community (for a review, see Moore 2009). Four randomized trials of domestic violence courts explored the effects of sentencing offenders to batterer programs on recidivism. Consistently, these studies found batterer programs performed no better than community service or probation alternatives on rates of reoffending (Davis et al. 2000; Dunford 2000; Feder and Dugan 2002; Labriola et al. 2005). This finding is not too surprising in light of the weak empirical support for batterer programs (Gondolf 2011; Saunders 2008; Stover et al. 2009).

The effects of domestic violence courts on victims are mixed as well. Compared with nonspecialized courts, domestic violence courts are more likely to connect victims with local victim services such as advocacy groups (Harrell et al. 2007a; Henning and Klesges 1999; Newmark et al. 2001) and to be favorably perceived in terms of case processing and procedural fairness (Eckberg and Podkopacz 2002; Harrell et al. 2007a; Henning and Klesges 1999). In terms of victim safety, victims affiliated with domestic violence courts in Massachusetts, Michigan, and Wisconsin did not report higher levels of perceived safety compared with women who were not receiving advocacy services (Visher et al. 2008). Given the weak effect of domestic violence courts on recidivism, this finding should be viewed as an appropriate response on behalf of victims.

Overall, the research jury is still out regarding the outcome effectiveness of domestic violence courts (Casey and Rottman 2003; Moore 2009; Turgeon 2008). Deliberations are currently impeded partially by the lack of evidence (there have been relatively few studies of domestic violence courts) and partially by the methodological limitations associated with the studies thus far completed. Methodological problems often limit the generalizability and validity of evaluation research. In the case of domestic violence courts, these problems include the natural variation in the (a) design and structure of the court intervention itself (i.e., lack of intervention integrity); (b) sentencing laws across states influencing the flexibility of domestic violence courts; (c) culture of the local legal system that influences judicial, prosecutorial, and policing practices toward offenders and victims; and (d) depth and breadth of the service system that courts draw upon when mandating special conditions to the offender and to assist and advocate for the victim. Natural variation such as this creates uniqueness within the intervention being evaluated limiting generalizability and noise within the experimental design drawing into question the validity and reliability of findings. Other more traditional methodological problems also plague this literature including short follow-up periods; sample selection bias; lack of control for other confounding components; incomplete or unreliable sources of outcome data (e.g., reliance on official reports or self-report for reoffending outcomes); variation in study designs; and inconsistent measurement of outcomes. For these reasons, although there is some encouraging news regarding the potential effectiveness of domestic violence courts, there is good reason to expect that there will be reasonable doubt about their outcome effectiveness for the foreseeable future.

While diversity among and within these courts contributes to their ambiguous performance, it will be argued herein that domestic violence courts will likely remain a weak harm reduction/prevention intervention for several reasons. First, at the foundation of any effective intervention is a well-articulated and empirically supported theory of the behavior to be changed (Andrews and Bonta 2006). Theories of offending behavior are often explained in terms of individual pathology, social learning, structural conditions, and rational choice, among others (McGuire 2002). Indeed it is the absence of an empirically supported theory of domestic violence that predicts the unlikely effectiveness of domestic violence courts (methodological problems notwithstanding). Domestic violence courts similar to batterers programs were developed as a reaction to a social problem and without benefit of a research base regarding the underlying causes of domestic violence as a process within a relationship or as behavior of individuals who are party to the relationship. For this reason alone, if domestic violence courts are to have a reasonable chance for crime reduction and safety effectiveness, they must rest on an empirically informed understanding of the etiology of domestic violence (a dyadic dynamic), batterer behavior, and victim behavior. Second, most efforts to stop domestic violence have focused on a single intervention such as a domestic violence court or batterer program. This notion of a "magic bullet" reflects both an unnuanced understanding of domestic violence as a phenomenon and a behavior and the historical practice of "one dose will do" and "one size fits all." In recent years, the practice of a single, uniform dosing of a domestic violence intervention has been challenged, with a growing call to tailor responses to the needs and risks of the offender *and* victim (Stuart et al. 2007b) and to coordinate a multilayered and sequenced response that addresses the acute and chronic needs and risks of the family unit (Coulter and VandeWeerd 2009).

At a minimum, more research is needed to support the foundation and intervention strategies of domestic violence courts. To the extent that the phenomenon of domestic violence is anchored in individual pathology such as past trauma, substance abuse, and mental illness, Lady Justice may need to reach with greater commitment to embrace the therapeutic potential of the Caduceus of the Serpents on behalf of the victim *and* the batterer.

To explore these issues, I begin in "Characteristics of Domestic Violence Courts Shaping Performance," by defining domestic courts in terms of their characteristics that may enhance and hinder performance. In "Principles of Therapeutic Jurisprudence Applied to Domestic Violence," domestic violence courts are assessed through the lens of therapeutic jurisprudence. Here I address the "schisms of extremes" underpinning these courts and how they forestall Lady Justice's reach toward and embrace of the Caduceus' therapeutic potential. "A Holistic, Therapeutic–Restorative Approach to Domestic Violence Courts" develops an alternative strategy for judicial intervention for domestic violence; a strategy that employs a more holistic and balanced approach and addresses the needs of both the batterer and the victim, while holding the batterer accountable for his behavior. Finally, "Promise, Limitations, and Future Research" makes recommendations for improving the potential of domestic violence courts and for future empirical experimentation.

Characteristics of Domestic Violence Courts Shaping Performance

Defining a domestic violence court is challenging because there is no standard domestic violence court model or set of developmental guidelines (Weber 2000).[3] In general, a domestic violence court has a specialized docket that adjudicates criminal offenses involving intimate partners and components that include a dedicated judge and specially trained court personnel that advocates and coordinates resources for victims. They differ in terms of whether the court is located in the civil or criminal division of the judiciary; has one or multiple judges with a special or mixed docket; integrates civil and criminal proceedings; monitors offenders through judicial review or probation supervision; and coordinates with other divisions of the judiciary, units of the criminal justice system, and community-based services.[4] In practice, the efficiency, deterrence, and protection performance of these courts is determined by their characteristics of mission, process, orientation, and structure. In this section, characteristics that are likely to enhance and hinder the performance (i.e., goals of

[3] For example, variability within drug court model is somewhat controlled by the availability of drug court-specific developmental guidelines. The National Association of Drug Court Professionals developed a manual identifying ten components of successful drug programs, which was then published and distributed by the Office of Justice Programs (Office of Justice Programs 1997).

[4] For more details on the structure and operations of domestic violence courts, see Labriola et al. (2009), Casey and Rottman (2003), Karan et al. (1999), and Karan et al. (2000).

offender accountability, victim safety, and recidivism) of domestic violence courts are explored and related to principles of restorative and therapeutic justice.

Characteristics Enhancing the Performance of Domestic Violence Courts

Three characteristics of domestic violence courts can be expected to enhance their performance: court mission, operational efficiency, and specialized training. The characteristics of mission and operational efficiency motivate the implementation of a domestic violence court and draw primarily on principles of restorative justice—restoring the victim (Fritzler and Simon 2000), whereas specialized training enhances the mission and operational efficiency performance of the court (Moore 2009). Each of the characteristics of domestic violence courts are described in turn below.

Court Mission The mission of a domestic violence court is to hold batterers accountable for their crimes against their intimate partners and to protect the victim from the batterer (Labriola et al. 2009; Weber 2000). These courts use target-specific criminal processing to prosecute batterers and civil orders to protect victims, although not necessarily in an integrated fashion. Criminal and civil remedies are used to stop current and deter future criminal activities by the batterer against the victim (applying principles of deterrence theory), while providing relief to the victim through the provision of protective orders and coordination of victim-related resources (applying principles of restorative justice). The goals of the court are consistent with the interests of the public (and victim) insofar as batterers stop their criminal behavior against the victim. In theory, targeting domestic violence through a purposeful mission that increases the likelihood of detecting and prosecuting a batterer, everything else equal, is expected to enhance the capacity of the court to deter current and future acts of domestic violence. Likewise, providing the victim with injunctive relief, victim advocacy, and instrumental resources is expected to enhance the protective capability of the court (Karan et al. 1999; Weber 2000).

Operational Efficiency It is not uncommon for domestic violence cases to "fall through the cracks" because they seek remedy in both criminal and civil courts, which are typically processed by different judges and involve different court procedures and remedies (Karan et al. 1999; Weber 2000). The fragmented court system itself is a liability for the victim and an asset for the batterer. For this reason, specialized domestic violence courts were designed to improve the (a) identification of domestic violence cases (i.e., target specificity) and (b) efficiency of related court procedures to ensure that victims are not lost in the shuffle within and between different divisions of the court (Berman and Feinblatt 2001; Kaye 2002). The goal here is to make court procedures more victim-friendly and responsive (Keilitz 2004). Identifying a relevant case is critical, as is its timing. As a matter of practice, domestic violence courts work with court clerks to identify cases of domestic violence. Court clerks often screen for domestic violence cases and refer them immediately to intake units that become the first point of contact for victims. These units help victims apply for protective and child custody orders, arrange for a victim advocate, and connect victims with safe housing, child support, and other family-related resources as needed. By identifying a domestic violence case earlier and assigning victim advocates at point of intake, the court process used by domestic violence courts is expected to be made easier, faster, less overwhelming, and more comprehensible for victims of domestic violence (Mazur and Aldrich 2003; Moore 2009; Weber 2000). Operational efficiency, as practiced by domestic violence courts, is fully consistent with the court's overarching mission of protecting the victim.

Specialized Training in Domestic Violence Domestic violence cases are challenging because of their social and emotional complexity (Fritzler and Simon 2000). These cases often involve intimates with strong emotional and financial interdependencies, dependent children, broader family dynamics and interests, and heated emotions. Batterers, in addition to being violent, often have thinking styles that are manipulative and deceptive (Fritzler and Simon 2000; Jasinski and Williams 1998; Moore 2009). Some batterers attempt to use court proceeding to further harass their inmate partners or avoid responsibility for their behavior (Mazur and Aldrich 2003; Simon 1995). For example, batterers may fail to appear in court or engage in behaviors that require more court appearances in an effort to inconvenience or intimidate the victim. To protect victims from further manipulation by their batterers, domestic violence court personnel, including judges, court clerks, case coordinators, and prosecutors, receive specialized training on topics related to the nature and dynamics of domestic violence, the criminal justice response to domestic violence, the profile of batterers and victims and their respective behavioral tendencies, and the risks that victims face when they confront their batterer through legal means (Cissner 2007; Keilitz 2004).[5] Court personnel also receive information on resources and services available to victims in the community and the importance of victim advocacy. Having more informed court personnel works to more effectively hold the batterer responsible for his criminal behavior and to protect the victim from the batterer, while expanding her financial and emotional resources so that she can break her dependence on the batterer.

Not surprisingly, domestic violence courts perform best on outcomes measuring operational efficiency and procedural justice. In general, domestic violence courts have been found to improve outcomes related to victim satisfaction with procedural processes and the availability of services; access to information; and decision making by judges (Casey and Rottman 2003; Eckberg and Podkopacz 2002; Harrell et al. 2007a; Henning and Klesges 1999; Moore 2009; Newmark et al. 2001; Turgeon 2008). More specifically, evaluations of domestic violence courts have shown consistent reductions in the rate of case dismissals and increases in the rates of guilty pleas, batterer compliance with judicial orders, and victim access to services and information (Moore 2009).

[5] For example, the Judicial Institute in White Plains, New York provides a 2-day training for court personnel with additional training on special topics.

By contrast, these evaluations have shown weak improvements in outcomes related to recidivism. In terms of reoffending, three studies found significant, albeit small, reductions in reoffending associated with domestic violence courts (Angene 2000; Gover et al. 2003; Harrell et al. 2007a), with another study reporting a drop in the rearrest rate from 8 to 4.2 %, which was attributed to a lack of opportunity among the study participants who, during the observation period, spent more time in jail (Harrell et al. 2006). Other studies have found no reductions or increases in rearrests over the study period (Henning and Klesges 1999; Newmark et al. 2001; Peterson 2004; Harrell et al. 2007b; Quann 2007). Victims participating in domestic violence courts have not reported a greater sense of safety, nor has batterer behavior or their recidivism been found to change in consistently positive ways (Moore 2009). The lackluster performance of domestic violence courts on safety and recidivism outcomes can be understood best in the context of court characteristics that hinder the application of therapeutic intervention.

Characteristics Hindering the Performance of Domestic Violence Courts

There has been only a desultory application of therapeutic jurisprudence principles in the development, design, and implementation of domestic violence courts. Therapeutic intervention as practiced in domestic violence courts is framed as rehabilitation and focuses exclusively on the batterer, and is often used by judges as a compliance tool, not for behavioral change (Labriola et al. 2009; Turgeon 2008). The justification for this profoundly circumscribed application of therapeutic intervention rests on the following assumptions underpinning domestic violence courts: (1) batterer behavior is caused by sociocultural factors that condition men to use their power against and over women; (2) batterers bear the full responsibility for domestic violence; (3) any remedial or rehabilitative intervention should focus on the batterer; (4) all batterers are equal in motivation, pathology, and behavior; and (5) batterers are rational decision makers and will stop behaviors in which their costs exceed their benefits. Characteristics of the court that reflect these assumptions include: problem definition and intervention orientation.

Problem Definition Domestic violence is a phenomenon that involves two people–the batterer and the victim. Because the batterer (man) harms the victim (woman), the incident, through the application of the law, is narrowly and cleanly dichotomized into sides of blame and innocence, which serves to polarize the court's intervention and remedy. This practice of dichotomization is further justified by appealing to a gender power interpretation of domestic violence: Patriarchal values within the prevailing social structure condition men to use power and control tactics in an effort to dominate over women by whatever means necessary. However, while patriarchal values may be a necessary condition for domestic violence, they are certainly not sufficient given that most men in society do not engage in domestic violence and some women perpetrate violence against their male and female partners (Dutton 1995; Healey et al. 1998; O'Leary 1993).

Although power asymmetries within gendered roles have been used to define and conceptualize domestic violence, it has not been validated as a causal model of batterer behavior (Day et al. 2009). For a domestic violence court to reduce recidivism, it must have an active ingredient that, at least in theory, is expected to change offender behavior. However, assuming a causal model of batterer behavior without empirical validation introduces an internal bias into the court; a bias whereby effectiveness is based on luck (guessing right), not science (proving right). For this reason, Day et al. (2009) advocate for the development of domestic violence interventions that are informed by a "greater sophistication in how domestic violence is understood" and that are sensitive to "identifying the needs of treatment participants, and delivering programs in ways that are engaging and motivating for men to change" (p. 211).

Therapeutic Orientation Batterers are the primary focus of rehabilitative intervention within domestic violence courts. These courts typically require that batterers complete a batterer program, known as the "sanction of choice" (Turgeon 2008). Groups, comprised of 8–15 members, meet for usually 40 h over a time period ranging from 8 to 36 weeks (Stover et al. 2009). Batter programs attempt either to resocialize the batterers thinking about sex roles, power dominance, and control or teach them new cognitive skills for managing tensions that may trigger violence (Healey et al. 1998). Batterer programs using the resocializing approach, most frequently associated with the Duluth Curriculum, seek to raise the gender consciousness of batterers usually through tactics that are confrontation; they aggressively challenge participants on issues of power and control, while building new skills for interacting with women on egalitarian terms. Alternatively, the cognitive-behavioral therapy (CBT) approach to batterer treatment is focused on the individual and interprets his violence as a way for the batterer to release tension, avoid internal discomfort, or manage stress. This form of batter treatment stresses skill building in areas of relaxation techniques for stress and tension management; identifying and neutralizing anger-provoking thinking for anger management; and managing other triggers that lower impulse control for violence prevention (Babcock 2004). Some courts also mandate additional special treatment conditions including substance abuse treatment, mental health counseling, parenting classes, and anger management (Cissner 2007; Labriola et al. 2009; Moore 2009).

The research on the effectiveness of batterer programs is mixed and largely inconclusive (Jackson et al. 2003). There have been more than 40 evaluations of batterer programs (mostly those following the Duluth curriculum or the CBT approach). In general, these programs have been found to have no effect or extremely modest effects on recidivism (i.e., an average 5 % reduction in reassault for those who complete the program relative to those who do not), while no differences have been detected in recidivism outcomes between the Duluth and CBT approaches (Babcock et al. 2004; Day et al. 2009; Gondolf 2011; Levesque et al. 2012; Saunders 2008; Stover et al. 2009; Turgeon 2008).[6]

---

[6] For a review of the literature on the effectiveness of batterer programs and their design, see Babcock et al. (2004); Day et al. (2009); Gondolf (2011); and Stover et al. (2009).

The weak effectiveness evidence for these batterer programs can be partially explained by study design limitations including small sample sizes, lack of control groups, attrition, underreported or uneven monitoring of recidivism, and other anomalistic attributes associated with socially complex interventions (Babcock et al. 2004; Day et al. 2009; Wolff 2000, 2001), and by the absence of an empirically validated theoretical model of battering behavior supporting these programs. While these limitations may partially explain the inconclusive findings, an outcome of "no effect" is to be expected when treatment effects require motivation toward outcomes by the person being treated. Similar to alcohol and substance abuse treatment, for batterer interventions to work, the batterer must be motivated toward the outcomes of the intervention, that is, to change his cognitions and behavior in ways that stop his battering behavior (DiClemente 1999; DiClemente et al. 1999). When outcomes are averaged across batterers with opposing motivations toward treatment and who are compelled by court mandate, outcomes will likely net out, yielding no detectable effect. Domestic violence courts can mandate batterers to treatment, but that alone does not motivate batterers to the outcomes of these programs. More specifically, courts can compel batterers to comply with the special conditions of treatment, but cannot mandate batterer's receptivity to the goals of treatment.

Undaunted by the weak effectiveness of batterer programs, domestic violence courts continue to order batterer programming as the sanction of choice. The rationale for their use, however, has been reframed as a monitoring strategy (Labriola et al. 2009; Turgeon 2008); batterer programs simply provide a mechanism by which the court can supervise the batterer and monitor his compliance with the sanction, not as a therapeutic intervention to change his behavior.

Principles of Therapeutic Jurisprudence Applied to Domestic Violence

Because of their atheoretical design, the potential of domestic violence courts to rehabilitate batterers and protect victims is constrained. Their lack of potential is further constrained by an imbalance within these courts between principles of therapeutic jurisprudence and restorative justice; an imbalance that stems from their bias toward punishment combined with their narrow application of therapeutic intervention. In this section, I address the "schisms of extremes" underpinning domestic courts and argue for a broader application of therapeutic intervention that is more in keeping with the tradition of problem-solving courts.

Divisive polemics are endemic within domestic violence courts. In reviewing the literature, one is struck by the extreme values and opinions underpinning their development and implementation. Indeed much of the theory and practical orientations of domestic violence courts rest on "either/or" scenarios: abuser or victim; punishment or rehabilitation; judgment or understanding; sociocultural conditioning or individual pathology; and individual or couple. These extremes are reinforced by equally uncompromising rhetoric that eschews "blaming the victim" and espouses "punishing the abuser." Similarly, theories and evidence related to violence and victimology are classified as either domestic violence or general violence and victimization, bifurcating the relevant overlapping literatures and arbitrarily limiting the reach of the extant knowledge base to inform the design and potential of domestic violence courts (Fagan 1996). For example, it has been argued that general theories of criminal behavior, particularly theories of violence, may be useful in designing interventions for batterers (Howells and Day 2002) to the extent that batterers engage more broadly in antisociality, that is, their battering behavior is part of a broader pattern of violence exhibited in the community at large. A batterer who falls into a generalist offender category would likely have criminogenic risks and needs that parallel those of violent offenders and, as such, might benefit more from interventions that more generally address violent behavior, not just violence exhibited within a domestic setting (Day et al. 2009).

Extreme, and often normative, positions, such as the schisms of extremes, sharply limit the court's ability to intervene in ways that recognize the complexity and heterogeneity of violence between intimates. Rarely if ever are social phenomena, such as domestic violence, caused by a single independent factor or remedied by a single-focused intervention (Coulter and VandeWeerd 2009; Walker 2001). Changing a social interactional phenomenon most often requires a holistic understanding of its multidimensionality and dynamic qualities, and how static and dynamic factors contribute to its manifestation and prevention (Stover et al. 2009). Under identification, as well as the over simplification, of the factors characterizing and contributing to violence between intimates constrains the ability of the court to prevent domestic violence. If the goal, therefore, is to strengthen the potential of domestic violence courts, it is critical to step back from these normative positions and reexamine domestic violence through a therapeutic lens.

Domestic Violence Through a Therapeutic Lens "It takes two to tango" and it takes two to create the conditions that culminate in an incident of domestic violence. While one principal may strike, the other principal is present when the strike occurs. Many principals of abusive relationships are not unfamiliar with violent intimate relationships. They witnessed violence in their families or were the victims of child abuse themselves (Gortner et al. 1997). Abuse in childhood is strongly correlated with adult victimization and criminality (Browne et al. 1999; Chesney-Lind 1997; Dutton and Hart 1992; Ehrensaft et al. 2003; Goodman et al. 2001; Ireland and Widom 1994; Magdol et al. 1998; McClellan et al. 1997; Rosenbaum and O'Leary 1981; Siegel and Williams 2003; Smith and Thornberry 1995; Widom 1989a,b). For example, in exploring the question of whether childhood abuse leads to adult criminal behavior, Widom and Maxfield (2001) find that childhood abuse increased the odds of delinquency and adult criminality. Leading these authors to conclude that "today's [child] victims of neglect may well be tomorrow's violent offenders" (p. 7). The interpersonal trauma literature also shows that men and women have different patterns in their experiences of and reactions to interpersonal violence over the life cycle (Cutler and Nolen-Hoeksema 1991; McClellan et al. 1997; Widom and Maxfield 2001; Widom and White 1997). More generally, childhood physical and sexual abuses have been linked to emotional problems and substance abuse in adulthood (Kendall-Tackett et al. 1993; Malinosky-Rummell and Hansen 1993; Messman-Moore and Long 2000).

Interpersonal trauma contributes to the development of mental disorders (Ballanger et al. 2004; Hegarty et al. 2004; Kramer et al. 2004; Widom et al. 2007). Overall, roughly 15–24 % of individuals who experience a potentially traumatic event will develop posttraumatic stress disorder (PTSD; Breslau et al. 1998). The vast majority of men (88 %) and women (79 %) with lifetime PTSD have a history of at least one additional mental disorder (Kessler et al. 1995). Other psychiatric disorders associated with PTSD include affective disorders, other anxiety disorders, phobias, conduct disorders, somatization, and substance use disorders (Kessler et al. 1995; Kendall-Tackett et al. 1993). PTSD and substance abuse also commonly cooccur (Jacobsen et al. 2001) and recent evidence suggests a causal connection (Chilcoat and Breslau 1998).

A strong research base links substance abuse and interpersonal violence. Among perpetrators of interpersonal violence, rates of co-occurring substance abuse range from 40 to 92 % (Brookoff et al. 1997; Easton et al. 2000; Wilt and Olson 1996). In a study of men enrolled in batterers programs, Stuart et al. (2007a) found that 68 % of those men engaged in hazardous drinking and more than half reported use of an illegal substance in the past year. Use of alcohol or drugs often occurs prior to a violent episode. Fal-Stewart (2003) found that men enrolled in batterer programs were 20 times more likely to abuse their partners on days they were drinking heavily compared with nondrinking days.

Combined together, this literature suggests that principals of domestic violence may have learned their roles in intimate relationships through childhood abuse (i.e., they were once victims of trauma or neglect or witnessed familial violence) and manifest adult-coping strategies that predispose them to behaviors that harm themselves (e.g., substance abuse, abusive relationships) or others (e.g., violence). This literature also suggests that the principals of domestic violence may be similar in their etiologies, but different in how these similarities are manifested in adult behavior.

While there is compelling evidence to suggest there may be causal and treatable behavioral health factors underlying the dynamic of domestic abuse, there are other characteristics of the principals that also may be relevant to their treatability, including criminal or victim thinking styles; power orientation; personality disorders (e.g., narcissism, borderline, and antisocial personality); treatment motivation and tolerance; and violence history (Healey et al. 1998; Mauricio et al. 2007; Simon 1997). Because of the likely nonequivalence among batterers, "profiling" batterers, although not victims, has been recommended as a method for improving the target efficiency of batterer intervention programming (Walker 2001).

The notion that "all batterers are equal" has long been criticized by violence experts (Cardin 1994; Healey and Smith 1998; Holtzworth-Munroe et al. 2000; Tolman and Bennett 1990). Also, in recent years, in an effort to improve treatment effectiveness, typologies of batterers have been developed and empirically tested (Eckhardt et al. 2008; Hamberger and Hastings 1986, 1991; Heckert and Gondolf

2000, 2005; Holtzworth-Munroe and Meehan 2004; Holtzworth-Munroe et al. 2000; Saunders 2008; Waltz et al. 2000). Batterer typologies attempt to group batterers into more homogenous subgroups that better predict treatment completion and reduced recidivism. Such typologies often include data on demographics; psychopathology and psychopathy; criminal and violence history; prior abuse (direct or witnessed); family of origin dynamics; and methods for resolving conflict in relationships.[7] Although several batterer typologies have been developed, they have not been found to substantially and consistently predict outcomes (Gondolf 2011).

Other researchers suggest classifying batterers by their criminogenic risks, not batterer typologies, in an effort to more generally identify the static and dynamic risk factors that more reliably predict violent behavior (Day et al. 2009). This argues for classifying batterers as a general class of violent offender and drawing on the stronger theoretical and empirical base underpinning the classification of offenders by level of risk (Andrews and Bonta 2006). The advantage of this method of classification is that criminogenic risks translate into criminogenic needs (identified as risks that are amenable to change or dynamic), and these needs, when targeted for intervention, have been found to reduce risk (Andrews and Bonta 2006). Among the areas of criminogenic needs relevant to offenders of (domestic) violence are psychopathic personality, trauma history, presence of PTSD and other mental disorders, substance/alcohol abuse, criminal thinking style, and treatment motivation. Focusing on criminogenic needs expands the scope of intervention, particularly therapeutic intervention, and, in so doing, rebalances the blend of deterrence and therapeutic jurisprudence underpinning the mission of domestic violence courts.

Profiling victims has not received equal attention, even though they are principals to the incident of domestic violence. While victims may not be criminally responsible for the incident, they may have behaviors that contribute to its dynamic elements, and their ability to free themselves from the abusive relationship is often weakened by the effects of abuse on their self-esteem, self-worth, and self-efficacy (Little and Kaufman Kantor 2002; Messman-Moore and Long 2000). By the time some women seek help from the courts, they have experienced severe and repeated abuse, which leaves them weakened in spirit and terrified. They are so accustomed to being told what to do by their partners that their sense of self has retreated and, in the extreme, been erased. If they seek injunctive relief, it is often to stop the violence, not end the relationship. One woman (M.H.) serving a 30-year sentence for killing her abuser recounts that:

> by the time I was arrested I could no longer think or do anything for myself. I needed his permission and/or authorization to do anything; so much so that after I was arrested and at the Prosecutor's Office, I refused to sign my Miranda card because I needed his permission. I would get in trouble for doing anything without his knowledge and permission.

---

[7] Measures often used in the development of batterer typologies include but are not limited to the Millon Clinical Multiaxial Inventory-III (Millon 1997); Conflict Tactic Scale (Straus 1979); Family Adaptability Cohesion Evaluation Scale (FACES III) (Olson et al. 1985); and the Adult Attachment Scale (Collins and Read 1990).

Further, she acknowledges her dependency on her abuser:

> I loved him so much that even after a few years of incarceration and counseling I still would have gone home with him knowing that after we had got home I would be beat for not being at home and having his food prepared and waiting for him. He controlled every aspect of me and my life for 17 years. Without him there was no me. I was his wife and he was my love, my life, my world... I couldn't think for myself and I no longer had my husband telling me what to do, I was lost.

Many theories are offered for why victims of abuse stay with their batterers (Cunningham et al. 1998). Some reasons include learned helplessness, traumatic bonding, fear of retaliation, practical barriers, and emotional shock (Dutton and Painter 1981; Fagan and Browne 1993; Finkelhor and Browne 1985). Victims' decisions to stay and leave are complex and influenced by a multitude of factors. For this reason, it is unrealistic to think that a short-term intervention by the court and a victim advocate with or without instrumental resources will change the behavior of the principal receiving the abuse. Given her likely history of childhood abuse and perhaps substance abuse problems combined with years of cultivated dependence on the principal who abuses her, she may lack the ability to act in an empowered fashion to protect herself from him. It may also be unrealistic to think that she has the emotional resiliency to walk away from the man she loves and wants to please. She, too, may need insight and skills to help her get and keep herself safe. Her ability to stay safe requires building her sense of self-determination and allied skills. Depending on the court (or an advocate) for her safety is as misguided as depending on her partner to stop abusing her. Healing and skill building are also part of the recovery process for the principals of abuse. They, too, must look within themselves to heal. According to M.H.:

> Shortly after coming to prison I started one-on-one counseling for domestic violence so that I could become a stronger woman and learn how and possibly why I had to suffer through all I did. It was a long and hard process... Through my years of counseling I was able to look inside of myself to find that one little spark of me that had survived all the years with my controlling husband who abused me. It wasn't easy. There were a lot of ups and downs along with a lot of pain. During those years I truly cried an ocean full of tears... Little by little as the days have turned into years my spark has turned into a flame that grows brighter and stronger with each passing day. I have learned not only to like myself but love myself and I will never allow anyone including myself to abuse me in anyway.

Creating scientifically rigorous "victimogenic" risks and needs, analogous to those for offenders, are vitally important. Principals of abuse may each have behaviors that would benefit from treatment. Likewise, they each may benefit from building cognitions and coping skills that could empower their independence and keep them safe and away from relationships that are harmful. Identifying the risks and needs of the principals of domestic violence is central to developing interventions that reliably reduce violence.

Another common characteristic between principals of domestic violence is their readiness for change. Victims will often return to their abusive partners and abusive partners often resume their abusive behaviors once reunited; this recycling of behaviors is referred to as the "cycle of violence." Responsivity to change is considered key to any behavioral change according to the transtheoretical model of behavior change (Prochaska et al. 1992), which models change as a process that moves through five stages: precontemplation, contemplation, preparation, action, and maintenance (Prochaska and DiClemente 1983). According to this model, people are more likely to change their behaviors when interventions are tailored to their stage of readiness. Thirty years of research has identified processes that facilitate change in the different stages and show that tailoring interventions to these stages enhances effectiveness (Noar et al. 2007). Research on domestic violence has focused on the readiness of batterers to change in an effort to address poorer outcomes for "resistant" batterers, particularly those who drop out of batterer programs. From the few studies conducted thus far, there is little support for using the Stages of Change model to predict program completion (Gondolf 2011); however, there is a growing literature showing that stage of change is associated with behavioral indicators of change such as weighting of pros and cons of ending violence, accepting responsibility, and establishing of positive working alliance in groups (Babcock et al. 2005; Eckhardt et al. 2008; Murphy and Ting 2010).

Motivating change, however, is different from identifying the stage of change. Two research literatures are relevant here. The first focuses on client engagement, often framed in terms of therapeutic alliance, which is defined as concurrence between the client and therapist on treatment goals and tasks and a positive affective connection between them (Bordin 1979). Across a variety of intervention types, therapeutic alliance has been found to successfully predict treatment success in two extensive meta-analyses (Horvath and Symonds 1991; Martin et al. 2000). Consistent with this finding, several studies of batterers have found measures of therapeutic alliance to predict treatment completion, controlling for other personal characteristics of batterers (Cadsky et al. 1996; Rondeau et al. 2001). The second relevant literature is motivational interviewing (Miller 1983). Motivational interviewing is a process of engaging people in change and it uses a variety of communication techniques to evoke change through the development of a respectful, person-centered partnership. Techniques used include expressing empathy, rolling with resistance, supporting the person's capacity to change, and developing discrepancies between the client's behavior and goals. Individual change is internally motivated through respectful engagement that explores and resolves ambivalence, not externally driven by coercion or confrontation. Motivational interviewing, while intended as a style of interaction that encourages change, has been developed into a type of intervention, called motivational enhancing treatment (MET). Across a variety of addictive behaviors (alcohol and drug, cigarette smoking, and pathological gambling), MET has been found to improve treatment outcomes (Davis et al. 2003; Colby et al. 1998; Wulfert et al. 2006). In a study of highly resistant batterers, Scott et al. (2011) found that clients receiving a 6-week MET program followed by 10 weeks of a standard batterer program had significantly higher rates of completion compared with resistant and nonresistant clients in the standard intervention program, although there was no significant differences found in counselor reports of clients' group participation across the groups. It appears that MET may improve completion rates, but not change offending behavior.

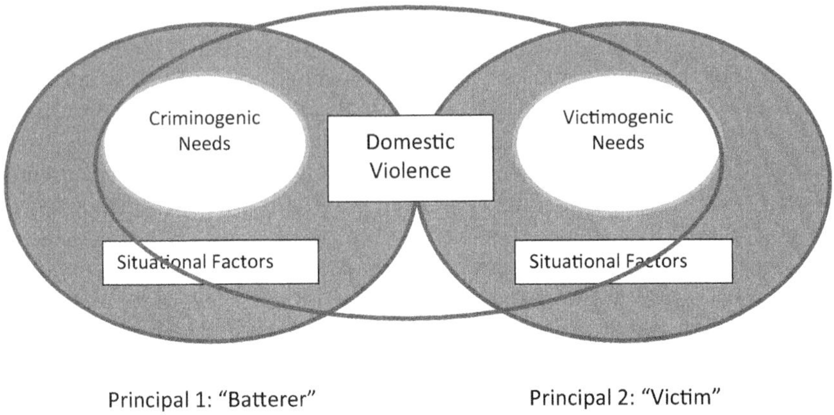

Fig. 6.1 Model of the conjoint dynamic of domestic violence

Efforts to motivate batterers to change their behavior have experimented with techniques designed to internally motivate change, although to a lesser extent than the efforts to externally drive change through treatment mandates or punishment. Similar experimentation is absent in terms of changing the behavior of victims. This omission reflects an attempt to avoid any appearance of blaming the victim for the abuse. Judge Timothy Lawliss, in a Roundtable discussion on court responses to domestic violence, ventured to say "at least one politically incorrect thing," which was:

> For violence to occur both people have to be in the same place at the same time. Some instances of violence are caused by one person making a decision to track down the other person wherever they are, but other times people voluntarily get together and then the act of violence occurs .... Couldn't we develop a program that would help educate the victim to see the negative consequences of her decision? (Turgeon 2008, pp. 364–365).

Political correctness may perpetuate violence if, indeed, the victim's behavior contributes to either the opportunity for an abusive event or its onset. Perhaps by stepping outside the political correctness box and objectively exploring if and how episodes of domestic violence arise and, in so doing, independent contributions of each principal are identified, we might find a more sensible balance in the development of interventions for each of the principals that, together, yield greater overall success in preventing subsequent events of domestic violence (Kaufman Kantor and Jasinski 1998). If, for example, domestic violence were modeled as a conjoint dynamic, as shown in Fig. 6.1, driven by the criminogenic and victimogenic needs and situations unique to each principal, we might develop more successful interventions.

A Holistic, Therapeutic–Restorative Approach to Domestic Violence Courts

Domestic violence courts as they are currently designed and implemented are weak interventions in terms of recidivism and safety (Moore 2009). Yet that does not mean that they cannot be made more effective. If their goal is to stop domestic abuse, rethinking these interventions, starting with their foundational principles, is unavoidable. Toward this goal, as researchers, we need to step outside our normative straightjackets and experiment with alternative interventions within the court. This does not mean that the principles of deterrence and/or restorative justice should be discarded. Nor does it mean that battering should be condoned or trivialized, or that batterers should not be held accountable. It is more about how this conjoint dynamic is best understood, treated, and prevented, not whether it is to be punished.

The core challenge in strengthening the performance of domestic violence courts is balance; finding the "right" blend of punishment, restoration, and therapeutic intervention to stop and prevent the escalation toward harm between intimates. Incorporating principles of therapeutic jurisprudence into domestic violence courts provides an opportunity to enhance the court's use of evidence-based treatments for trauma, psychopathology, and addiction, while also empirically testing whether such integrated interventions improve the outcome performance of these courts. The application of trauma-informed therapeutic intervention does not in any way condone or trivialize battering; rather, it suggests that to stop the dynamic process underlying the violence both principals must be viewed as part of the problem and the solution. In this way, principals of domestic violence are assumed to (a) each play a role in the dynamic leading up to the battering incident and (b) each would benefit from behavioral health treatment that could help them to better understand their roles and the etiology underpinning these roles, and to build coping skills to avoid and protect themselves against future harm. Having a role does not confer or imply blame; it simply says that each has a responsibility to understand why they were at the scene of a crime and what can be done to prevent being there in the future. Therapeutic jurisprudence does not negate the assignment of blame or punishment; it only allows the court to mandate effective behavioral treatment in an effort to stop future harm as part of sentencing and its efforts to practice restorative justice.

In this section, I proffer an outline for an alternative strategy for judicial intervention for domestic violence; a strategy employing a more holistic and balanced approach that addresses the needs of both principals of domestic violence, while holding the batterer accountable for his behavior. This alternative version of domestic violence courts embraces the complexity and dynamism of domestic violence by assuming the following: (1) principals of domestic violence, individually and collectively, made choices that contributed to a dynamic that culminated in violence between them; (2) personal accountability is expected of the principals; (3) principals of domestic violence are trapped emotionally and cognitively by behaviors that they do not understand or have control over; (4) principals of domestic violence differ in their motivation, pathology, trauma histories, and behavior, requiring the identification of crimogenic and victimogenic needs of the principals and targeted interventions that blend punishment, restoration, and recovery; (5) recovery is the goal for the principals of domestic violence; and (6) there are stages of change associated with any changed behavior and recovery process, which can be enhanced through client engagement approaches such as therapeutic alliance or motivational interviewing.

Holistic Therapeutic Orientation Domestic violence is a dynamic phenomenon that affects the principals, as well as their children. Indeed, their children may model their behavior in future intimate relationships, creating an intergenerational contagion of domestic violence. For this reason, the principals and their children are the focus of therapeutic intervention. Therapeutic intervention may include **individual psychotherapy**, focusing on the individual's current and past experiences, problems, thoughts, feelings, or relationships; **psycho-educational and cognitive-behavioral group therapy**, identifying problems, behaviors, and cognitions and building new skills for coping and staying safe; **couple therapy**, focusing on the couple and their problems, while building their communication and problem-solving skills; and **family therapy**, focusing on the family unit with the goal of helping the children understand what they experienced, express their feelings toward their parents, and learn that abuse is wrong, while healing the relationships between child and parent by reestablishing bonds of trust, respect, and safety. The combination and order of therapeutic intervention will depend in part on the couple (i.e., whether they have children, want to stay together as a couple) and in part on the needs and risk assessments of the principals.

Screening Assessment and Need Identification Assessment focuses on the family unit, inclusive of the adult principals and their dependent children. The purpose of assessment is to determine the health, emotional, psychological, instrumental, and safety needs of the principals[8] and their children, as well as to identify the criminogenic and victimogenic risk and protective factors that are likely to predict future harm and the success of therapeutic intervention. Needs assessment typically collect information on (a) the health and behavioral health of the principals, inclusive of measures of self-efficacy, self-esteem, resiliency, and self-control and impulsivity, as well as substance and alcohol use history and history of the other types of addictive behaviors; (b) the availability of instrument resources, inclusive of safe housing, transportation, financial support, social networks, and so forth; (c) problem areas requiring legal remedy such as legal assistance for restraining orders, child custody, or separation or divorce proceedings; and (d) safety concerns for self or others. By assessing needs holistically, steps can be taken immediately to prioritize and address the needs of each principal and the affected children, while also laying the foundation for subsequent tailoring of interventions to needs. Methods used by family court to assess the wellness of the family may be instrumental in this process. Prioritizing needs would focus on identifying areas remedial by therapeutic intervention as well as treatment readiness. Areas relevant to treatment-related targeting include psychopathology, psychopathy, addictive behaviors, trauma and violence history, coping and functioning skills, resiliency, motivation to change, and criminogenic

[8] Coulter and VandeWeerd (2009) describe a comprehensive screening procedure for batterers that includes questions regarding the batterer's demographics, family history of violence, childhood history, employment history drug and alcohol history, violence history, prior treatment history, as well as their perception of the domestic violence incident. Standard tools such as the Psychopathy Checklist-Revised and the LSI-R are commonly used instruments for the identification of criminogenic risks and needs.

factors such as criminal thinking styles, and prior arrest, delinquency, and violence. Identifying criminogenic and victimogenic needs based on this information would be used to tailor treatments to subgroups of principals, enhancing target efficiency, and perhaps overall outcome performance.

Targeted Therapeutic Interventions Matching the needs of principals to interventions presumes that an array of interventions, varying in intensity and focus, is available. Models of early intervention for first-time batterers might focus first on education. In cases involving minimal violence, domestic violence courts could mandate that both principals attend a day-long domestic violence course (at locations that differ depending on the participant's role in the domestic violence).[9] Expanded awareness, through education, may yield better decision making on behalf of the principals, especially with respect to the need for therapeutic help. For those principals ready to address the underlying causes of domestic violence and their role in it, the first line of *therapeutic* intervention might include building safe coping skills that also address addictive behaviors such as substance abuse, self-abuse, or risky behaviors. Here the therapeutic intervention might focus on understanding domestic abuse, the cycle of violence, and its underlying causes and triggers, while building skills to identify triggers and prevent future situations of harm. Experimenting with therapies that (a) are gender-specific and compassionate to the person (not the behavior), (b) group principals by their roles in the domestic violence, and (c) use psycho-educational and CBT approaches to build skills might follow. This type of first stage therapeutic intervention would not be predicated on confrontation nor would it invoke a harsh-style of interpersonal interaction. In the spirit of practicing civility and developing person-centered partnerships with clients, the therapeutic environment would attempt to engender feelings of safety and respect among clients, while addressing behaviors that are deemed unacceptable. From here, principals may be encouraged to participate in individual therapy to understand core problems or experiences that put them at risk; couple therapy to understand problems within the relationship and to build better problem-solving skills (if the couple decided to stay together); and family therapy to help the children heal from the trauma they experienced and to repair their relationships with the principals. For those principals who are not ready to address their roles in domestic violence, more punitive approaches may be required including loss of liberty and loss of child custody in an effort to protect those harmed by domestic violence from future harm and to motivate those who are complicit in its manifestation to engage in therapeutic remedy. Making the therapeutic intervention within domestic violence courts more recovery and healing oriented may invite greater participation and yield better performance outcomes, requiring less social control.

Coordinated and Continuous Intervention One-dose interventions are rarely enough to solve complex, dynamic problems such as domestic violence. Nested

[9] This recommendation is modeled on the requirement that people convicted of driving under the influence (DUI) attend DUI School and those who want to lower their insurance premiums can attend a defensive driving course.

within domestic violence are co-occurring individual pathologies including PTSD, depression, narcissism, antisocial personality disorder, substance and alcohol abuse, along with housing, employment, and financial insecurity, criminal histories, and social vulnerabilities. It is naive to think that single doses of incarceration, therapy, or their combination can intercede in ways that will eradicate it. Recovery is the only real solution, and recovery requires education, skills, practice, mentoring, and the tried-and-true philosophy of one-day-at-a-time. It requires building the capacity of the principals to understand their problems, experiences, feelings, and thoughts; to identify and manage their triggers, and to form and maintain healthy relationships. It requires a holistic view of the problem and coordinated set of treatment solutions that address the problems in ways that build the capacity of the principals to manage life in healthy and safe ways. However, similar to the problems themselves, the services addressing them must be coordinated and balanced to be effective. If any part of the therapeutic service complex is missing or inadequate (e.g., trauma treatment, substance abuse treatment), the overall effectiveness of available treatments will likely suffer. Court-based interventions will likely rise or fall on their ability to identify, access, coordinate, and sustain the "right" balance of treatment services and, as appropriate, punitive sanctions for the batterer.

Promise, Limitations, and Future Research

The reliance of domestic violence courts on punishment, ineffective treatment programming for batterers, and short-term restoration of victims is just not enough to achieve the mission of the courts. This is confirmed by the fact that recidivism is unabated and harm continues with or without the court's intervention (Moore 2009).

Does this mean that domestic violence courts should be eliminated on grounds of ineffectiveness on outcomes relevant to the court's mission? The answer: it depends. If domestic courts continue as usual, their performance statistics simply do not support their replication or maintenance, especially in light of their higher staffing and processing costs. If, however, their design, problem orientation, and therapeutic intervention are open to modification in ways that bridge the schisms of extremes that currently limit the court's reach into the therapeutic realms, then the jury remains out until further experimentation. Indeed the potential of domestic violence courts has not been fairly assessed because the design of these courts have not (a) been informed by the relevant literatures on violence, victimization, and trauma; (b) incorporated therapeutic interventions for both principals of domestic violence that rely on evidence-based needs and risk assessment instruments and interventions; or (c) used assignment strategies based on empirically validated risk and needs for batterers or victims that may make treatment assignments more target specific and efficient.

The *intervention* of domestic violence courts would benefit from more science and less opinion. In summarizing the literature regarding "what works" among correctional programs, Levesque et al. (2012), reflecting earlier work by Andrews and Dowden (2007), provide a roadmap for scientific inquiry:

> Two decades of research have found correctional program outcomes are moderated by whether programs address offender *risk* (did the program provide the most intensive services to the highest risk offenders?), *needs* (did the program target needs, such as alcohol, abuse, associated with increased likelihood of reoffending?) and *responsivity* (did the program adapt the intervention to individual characteristics, such as strengths, motivations, preferences, personality, age, gender, and culture?) (p. 2).

Applying their roadmap to domestic violence courts would begin the process of improving their effectiveness. From a research perspective, we are at the beginning of a long journey as much remains unknown about the potential of domestic violence courts. Whether they can be effective remains an empirical question; one that merits scientific investigation that tests general and specific theories of violence and victimization and a more holistic approach that includes both principals and the extant research evidence on causes and etiologies of violence and victimization and their treatment alternatives. What these courts are currently doing is clearly not enough. However, before they are labeled as ineffective, more experimentation is warranted. This can best be achieved by broadly reviewing the extant literature, generating hypotheses, and testing them through intervention research.

The more holistic model of intervention for domestic violence courts offered in the previous sections provides a template for future research and innovation. At the outset, some may reflexively argue that this model is infeasible because it will likely cost too much. Inarguably, adding more direct costs for assessment and tailored and multistaged and multiprincipal programming will add to costs. However, justifying the status quo by focusing only on direct costs is shortsighted for two reasons. First, these additional direct costs must be considered against the social costs, which are staggering, associated with continuing the current response to domestic violence. Although the direct costs of the current response, borne by localities, may appear affordable, they do very little to offset the larger social cost, as they yield little in the way of remedy. Second, developing more effective interventions and targeting their use more efficiently may not only decrease per person cost in the long run, it may also increase the benefit side of the cost effectiveness equation by significantly decreasing recidivism. To efficiently allocate scarce resources toward the prevention of domestic violence, emphasis is placed on cost-effectiveness from a societal perspective, not cost minimization from a locality perspective.

As researchers, our task is not to focus on the cost of change, but to develop interventions that are based on a coherent and empirically supported theory of behavior and to test their cost-effectiveness. The holistic response to domestic violence offers a wealth of researchable questions including (1) what factors contribute to a domestic violence event; (2) are there unique criminogenic and victimogenic risks and needs that predict domestic violence events; (3) what factors motivate principals of domestic violence to change their behavior; (4) what are the marginal and relative impacts of program content and client engagement approaches on intervention effectiveness; (5) what combination of interventions and in what sequence performs best in terms of the cessation of domestic violence; and (6) what is the strongest, most engaging stage-matched intervention for principals with particular criminogenic and victimogenic needs.

The human and social consequences that domestic violence exacts on the principals, their children, and society are far too great, as is the court's potential effect on reducing these consequences, to allow the schism of extremes to yield acceptable ineffectiveness. Lady Justice needs to reach with greater commitment to embrace the Caduceus of the Serpents if we are ever to know the potential of domestic violence courts.

Acknowledgments This study was supported by a grant from the National Institute of Mental Health (Grant #5P30MH079920).

References

American Psychological Association, Presidential Task Force on Violence and Family. (1996). *Report of the APA presidential task force on violence and the family*. Washington: American Psychological Association.

Andrews, D. A., & Bonta, J. (2006). *The psychology of criminal conduct* (4th ed.). Newark: LexisNexis.

Andrews, D. A., & Dowden, C. (2007). The risk-need-responsivity model of assessment and human service in prevention and corrections: Crime-prevention jurisprudence. *Canadian Journal of Criminology and Criminal Justice, 49,* 439–464.

Angene, L. (2000). *Evaluation report for the San Diego County domestic violence courts*. San Diego: San Diego Superior Court.

Babcock, J. C., Green, C. E., & Robie, C. (2004). Does batterers' treatment work? A meta-analytic review of domestic violence treatment. *Clinical Psychology Review, 23*(8), 1023–1053.

Babcock, J. C., Canady, B., Senior, A., & Eckhardt, C. I. (2005). Applying the transtheoretical model to female and male perpetrators of intimate partner violence: Gender differences in stages and processes of change. *Violence and Victims, 20,* 235–251.

Ballanger, J. C., Davidson, J. R., Lecrubier, Y., Nutt, D. J., Marshall, R. D., Nemeroff, C. B., Yehuda, R. (2004). Consensus statement update on posttraumatic stress disorder from the international consensus group on depression and anxiety. *Journal of Clinical Psychology, 65,* 55–62.

Berman, G., & Feinblatt, J. (2001). Problem-solving courts: A brief primer. *Law & Policy, 23,* 125–140.

Bordin, E. S. (1979). The generalizability of the psychoanalytic concept of the working alliance. *Psychotherapy: Theory, Research & Practice, 16*(3), 252–260.

Braithwaite, J. (2002). *Restorative justice and responsive regulation*. Oxford: Oxford University Press.

Breslau, N., Kessler, R. C., Chilcoat, H. D., Schultz, L. R., Davis, G. C., & Andreski, P. (1998). Trauma and posttraumatic stress disorder in the community: The 1996 Detroit area survey of trauma. *Archives General Psychiatry, 55,* 626–632.

Brookoff, D., O'Brien, K. K., Cook, C. S., Thompson, T. D., & Williams, C. A. (1997). Characteristics of participants in domestic violence. Assessment at the scene of domestic assault. *The Journal of the American Medical Association, 277*(17), 1369–1373.

Browne, A., Miller, A., & Maguin, E. (1999). Prevalence and severity of lifetime physical and sexual victimization among incarcerated women. *International Journal of Law and Psychiatry, 22,* 301–322.

Buzawa, E., & Buzawa, C. (1996). *Domestic violence: The criminal justice response* (2nd ed.). Thousand Oaks: Sage.

Cadsky, O., Hanson, R. K., Crawford, M., & LaLonde, C. (1996). Attrition from a male batterer treatment program: Client-treatment congruence and lifestyle instability. *Violence and Victims, 11,* 51–64.

Cappell, C., & Heiner, R. B. (1990). The intergenerational transmission of family aggression. *Journal of Family Violence, 5,* 135–152.

Cardin, A. D. (1994). Wife abuse and the wife abuser: Review and recommendations. *Counseling Psychologist, 22,* 539–582.

Casey, P. M., & Rottman, D. B. (2003). *Problem-solving courts: Models and trends*. Williamsburg: National Center for State Courts. Retrieved from http://community-corrections-fall09.wiki.uml.edu/file/view/Problem+Solving+Justice+Overview.pdf. Accessed 1 May 2013.

Chesney-Lind, M. (1997). *The female offender: Girls, women, and crime*. Thousand Oaks: Sage.

Chilcoat, M. D., & Breslau, N. (1998). Posttraumatic stress disorder and drug disorders: Testing causal pathways. *Archives of General Psychiatry, 55*(10), 913–917.

Cissner, A. B. (2007). *Bringing domestic violence best practices to New York's town and village courts*. New York: Center for Court Innovation. Retrieved from http://www.courtinnovation.org/_uploads/documents/T_V_Court_report.pdf. Accessed 1 May 2013.

Colby, S. M., Monti, P. M., Barnett, N. P., Rohsenow, D. J., Weissman, K., Spirito, A., Lewander, W. J. (1998). Brief motivational interviewing in a hospital setting for adolescent smoking: A preliminary study. *Journal of Consulting and Clinical Psychology, 66*(3), 574–578.

Collins, N. L., & Read, S. J. (1990). Adult attachment, working models and relationship quality in dating couples. *Journal of Personality and Social Psychology, 58,* 644–663.

Coulter, M., & VandeWeerd, C. (2009). Reducing domestic violence and other criminal recidivism: Effectiveness of a multilevel batterers intervention program. *Violence and Victims, 24*(2), 139–152.

Cunningham, A., Jaffe, P., Baker, L., Dick, T., Malla, S., Mazaheri, N., & Poisson, S. (1998). *Theory derived explanations for male violence against female partners: Literature review and related implications for treatment and evaluation*. London: London Family Court Clinic.

Cutler, N. J., & Nolen-Hoeksema, S. (1991). Accounting for sex differences in depression through female victimization: Childhood sexual abuse. *Sex Roles, 24,* 425–438.

Davis, R. C., Taylor, B. C., & Maxwell, C. D. (2000). *Does batterer treatment reduce violence: A randomized experiment in Brooklyn*. Washington: National Institute of Justice.

Davis, R. C., Smith, B. E., & Rabbitt, C. R. (2001). Research notes, increasing convictions in domestic violence cases: A field test in Milwauke. *The Justice System Journal, 22*(1), 61.

Davis, T. M., Baer, J. S., Saxon, A. J., & Kivlahan, D. R. (2003). Brief motivational feedback improves post-incarceration treatment contact among veterans with substance use disorders. *Drug and Alcohol Dependence, 69*(2), 197–203.

Day, A., Chung, D., O'Leary, P., & Carson, E. (2009). Programs for men who perpetrate domestic violence: An examination of the issues underlying the effectiveness of intervention programs. *Journal of Family Violence, 24,* 203–212.

DiClemente, C. C. (1999). Motivation for change: Implications for substance abuse. *Psychological Science, 10,* 209–213.

DiClemente, C. C., Bellino, L. E., & Neavins, T. M. (1999). Motivation for change and alcoholism treatment. *Alcohol Research & Health, 23*(2), 86–92. Retrieved from http://pubs.niaaa.nih.gov/publications/arh23-2/086-92.pdf. Accessed 1 May 2013.

Dignan, J. (2005). *Evaluating restorative justice from a victim perspective: Empirical evidence. Understanding Victims and Restorative Justice* (pp. 132–161). Maidenhead: Open University Press.

Dunford, F. W. (2000). The San Diego Navy experiment: An assessment of interventions for men who assault their wives. *Journal of Consulting and Clinical Psychology, 68,* 486–476.

Dutton, D. G. (1995). *The domestic assault of women* (2nd ed.). Vancouver: University of British Columbia Press.

Dutton, D. G., & Hart, S. D. (1992). Risk marker for family violence in a federally incarcerated population. *International Journal of Law and Psychiatry, 15,* 101–112.

Dutton, D. G., & Painter, S. L. (1981). Traumatic bonding: The development of emotional attachments in battered women and other relationships of intermittent abuse. *Victimology: An International Journal, 6,* 139–155.

Easton, C., Swan, S., & Sinha, R. (2000). Motivation to change substance use among offenders of domestic violence. *Journal of Substance Abuse Treatment, 19*(1), 1–5.

Eckberg, D., & Podkpacz, M. (2002, November). Domestic violence court in Minneapolis: Three levels of analysis. Presentation. American Society of Criminology Annual Conference, Chicago, IL.

Eckhardt, C., Holtzworth-Munroe, A., Norlander, B., Sibley, A., & Cahill, M. (2008). Readiness to change, partner violence subtypes, and treatment outcomes among men in treatment for partner assault. *Violence and Victims, 23,* 446–475.

Ehrensaft, M. K., Cohen, P., Brown, J., Smailes, E., Henian, C., & Johnson, J. G. (2003). Intergenerational transmission of partner violence: A 20-year prospective study. *Journal of Consulting & Clinical Psychology, 7*(4), 741–753.

Epstein, D. (1999). Effective intervention in domestic violence cases: Rethinking the roles of prosecutors, judges and the court system. *Yale Journal of Law and Feminism, 11,* 3–50.

Fagan, J. (1996). *The criminalization of domestic violence: Promises and limits* (National Institute of Justice Research Report). Retrieved from http://www.ncjrs.gov/pdffiles/crimdom.pdf. Accessed 1 May 2013.

Fagan, J., & Browne, A. (1993). Violence between spouses and intimates: Physical aggression between women and men in intimate relationships. In A. Reiss Jr. & J. Roth (Eds.). *Understanding and preventing violence: Vol. 3. Social and psychological perspectives of violence.* Washington: National Academy Press.

Fal-Stewart, W. (2003). The occurrence of partner physical aggression on days of alcohol consumption. *Journal of Consulting and Clinical Psychology, 71*(2), 41–52.

Feder, L., & Dugan, L. (2002). A test of the efficacy of court mandated counseling for domestic violence offenders: The Broward experiment. *Justice Quarterly, 19*(2), 343–375.

Finkelhor, D., & Browne, A. (1985). The traumatic impact of CSA: A conceptualization. *American Journal of Orthopsychiatry, 55,* 530–541.

Fritzler, R. B., & Simon, L. M. J. (2000). Creating a domestic violence court: Combat in the trenches. *Court Review, 37*(1), 28–39.

Goldkamp, J. S., & Irons-Guynn, C. (2000). *Emerging judicial strategies for the mentally ill in the criminal caseload: Mental health courts in Fort Lauderdale, Seattle, San Bernardino, and Anchorage* (NCJ 182504). Washington: U.S. Department of Justice.

Goldkamp, J., Weiland, D., Collins, M., & White, M (1996). *The role of drug and alcohol abuse in domestic violence and its treatment: Court experiment* (Final report for the National Institute of Justice). Washington: National Institute of Justice.

Gondolf, E. W. (2011). The weak evidence for batterer program alternatives. *Aggression and Violent Behavior, 16,* 347–353.

Goodman, L. A., Salyers, M. P., Mueser, K. T., Rosenberg, S. D., Swartz, M., Essock, S. M., Swanson, J. (2001). Recent victimization in women and men with severe mental illness: Prevalence and correlates. *Journal of Traumatic Stress, 14*(4), 615–632. doi:10.1023/A:1013026318450.

Gortner, E. T., Gollan, J. K., & Jacobson, N. S. (1997). Couples therapy. In A. Tasman, J. Kay, & J. A. Lieberman (Eds.), *Psychiatry* (pp. 1452–1479). Philadelphia: WB Saunders Company.

Gover, A. A., MacDonald, J. M., & Alpert, G. P. (2003). Combating domestic violence: Findings from an evaluation of a local domestic violence court. *Criminology & Public Policy, 3,* 109–132.

Hamberger, L. K., & Hastings, J. E. (1986). Personality correlates of men who abuse their partners: A cross-validation study. *Journal of Family Violence, 1*(4), 323–341.

Hamberger, L. K., & Hastings, J. E. (1991). Personality correlates of men who batter and nonviolent men: Some continuities and discontinuities. *Journal of Family Violence, 6*(2), 131–147.

Harrell, A., Schaffer, M., DeStefano, C., & Castro, J. (2006). *Evaluation of Milwaukee's judicial oversight demonstration.* Washington: Urban Institute (NCJ 215349).

Harrell, A., Castro, J., Newmark, L., & Visher, C. (2007a). *Final report on the evaluation of the judicial oversight demonstration: Executive summary* (Final report for National Institute of Justice). Washington: U.S. Department of Justice, National Institute of Justice, and The Urban Institute, NCJ 219386.

Harrell, A., Newmark, L., & Visher, C. (2007b). *Final report on the evaluation of the judicial oversight demonstration, vol. 2: Findings and lessons on implementation* (Final report for the National Institute for Justice). Washington: National Institute of Justice.

Healey, K. M., & Smith, C. (1998). *Batterer programs: What criminal justice agencies need to know. Research in Action.* Washington: National Institute of Justice. Retrieved from http://www.ncjrs.gov/pdffiles/171683.pdf. Accessed 1 May 2013.

Healey, K. M., Smith, C., & O'Sullivan, C. (1998). *Batterer interventions: Program approaches and criminal justice strategies. Issues and practices in criminal justice.* Washington: U.S. Department of Justice. Retrieved from http://www.ncjrs.gov/pdffiles/168638.pdf. Accessed 1 May 2013.

Heckert, D. A., & Gondolf, E. W. (2000). The effect of perceptions of sanctions on batterer program outcomes. *Journal of Research in Crime & Delinquency, 37*(4), 369–391.

Heckert, A., & Gondolf, E. W. (2005). Do multiple outcomes and conditional factors improve prediction of domestic violence? *Violence and Victims, 20,* 3–24.

Hegarty, K., Gunn, J., Chondros, P., & Small, R. (2004). Association between depression and abuse by partners of women attending general practice: Descriptive, cross sectional survey. *British Medical Journal, 328,* 621–624.

Henning, K., & Klesges, L. M. (1999). *Evaluation of the Shelby county domestic violence court* (Final report). Shelby County: TN.

Hirschel, D., Buzawa, E., Pattavina, A., Faggiani, D. (2008). Domestic violence and mandatory arrest laws: To what extent do they influence police arrest decisions? *The Journal of Criminal Law and Criminology, 98*(1), 255–298.

Holtzworth-Munroe, A., & Meehan, J. C. (2004). Typologies of men who are martially violent: Scientific and clinical implications. *Journal of Interpersonal Violence, 19,* 1369–1389.

Holtzworth-Munroe, A., Meehan, J. C., Herron, K., Rehman, U., & Stuart, G. (2000). Testing the Holtzworth-Munroe and Stuart (1994) batterer typology. *Journal of Consulting and Clinical Psychology, 68*(6), 1000–1019.

Horvath, A. O., & Symonds, B. D. (1991). Relation between working alliance and outcome in psychotherapy: A meta-analysis. *Journal of Counseling Psychology, 38,* 139–149. doi:10.1037/0022-0167.38.2.139.

Howells, K., & Day, A. (2002). Grasping the nettle: Treating and rehabilitating the violent offender. *Australian Journal of Psychology, 37*(3), 222–228.

Ireland, T., & Widom, C. S. (1994). Childhood victimization and risk for alcohol and drug arrests. *International Journal of Addiction, 29,* 235–274.

Jackson, S., Feder, L., Forde, D. R., Davis, R. C., Maxwell, C. D., & Taylor, B. G. (2003). *Batterer intervention programs: Where do we go from here?* (National Institute of Justice Special Report). Washington: U.S. Department of Justice. Retrieved from http://www.ncjrs.gov/pdffiles1/nij/195079.pdf. Accessed 1 May 2013.

Jacobsen, L. K., Southwick, S. M., & Kosten, T. R. (2001). Substance use disorders in patients with posttraumatic stress disorder: A review of the literature. *American Journal of Psychiatry, 158,* 1184–1190.

Jasinski, J. L., & Williams, L. M. (1998). *Partner violence: A comprehensive review of 20 years of research.* Thousand Oaks: Sage.

Karan, A., Keilitz, S., & Denaro, S. (1999). Domestic violence courts: What are they and how should we manage them? *Juvenile and Family Court Journal, 2,* 75–86.

Kaufman Kantor, G., & Jasinski, J. (1998). Dynamics and risk factors in partner violence. In J. L. Jasinski & L. M. Williams (Eds.), *Partner violence: A comprehensive review of 20 years of research* (pp. 1–43). Thousand Oaks: Sage.

Kaye, J. S. (2002). The changing face of justice: Keynote address. *Fordham Urban Law Journal, 29,* 1925–1928.
Keilitz, S. (2004). Specialization of domestic violence case management in the courts: A national survey. Retrieved from http://www.ncjrs.gov/pdffiles1/nij/grants/186192.pdf. Accessed 1 May 2013.
Kendall-Tackett, K. A., Williams, L. M., & Finkelhor, D. (1993). Impact of sexual abuse on children: A review and synthesis of recent empirical studies. *Psychological Bulletin, 113*(1), 164–180.
Kessler, R. C., Sonnega, A., Bromet, E., Hughes, M., & Nelson, C. B. (1995). Posttraumatic stress disorder in the national comorbidity survey. *Archives of General Psychiatry, 52,* 1048–1060.
Kramer, A., Lorenzon, D., & Mueller, G. (2004). Prevalence of intimate partner violence and health implications for women using emergency departments and primary care clinics. *Women's Health Issues, 14,* 19–29.
Labriola, M., Rempel, M., & David, R. C. (2005). *Testing the effectiveness of batterer programs and judicial monitoring. Results from a randomized trial at the Bronx misdemeanor domestic violence court.* New York: Center for Court Innovation.
Labriola, M., Bradley, S., O'Sullivan, C. S., Rempel, M., & Moore, S. (2009). *A national portrait of domestic violence courts.* New York: Center for Court Innovation. Retrieved from http://www.courtinnovation.org/_uploads/documents/national_portrait.pdf. Accessed 1 May 2013.
Levesque, D. A., Ciavatta, M. M., Castle, P. H., Prochaska, J. M., & Prochaska, J. O. (2012). Evaluation of stage-based, computer-tailored adjunct to usual care for domestic violence offenders. *Psychology of Violence.* doi:10.1037/a0027501.
Little, L., & Kaufman Kantor, G. (2002). Using ecological theory to understand intimate partner violence and child maltreatment. *Journal of Community Health Nursing, 19*(3), 133–145.
Magdol, L., Moffitt, T. E., Caspi, A., & Silva, P. (1998). Developmental antecedents of partner abuse: A prospective-longitudinal study. *Journal of Abnormal Psychology, 107,* 375–389.
Malinosky-Rummell, R., & Hansen, D. J. (1993). Long-term consequences of childhood physical abuse. *Psychological Bulletin, 114,* 68–79.
Martin, D. J., Garske, J. P., & Davis, M. K. (2000). Relation of the therapeutic alliance with outcome and other variables: A meta-analytic review. *Journal of Consulting and Clinical Psychology, 68*(3), 438–450. doi:10.1037/0022-006X.68.3.438.
Mauricio, A. M., Tein, J. Y., & Lopez, F. G. (2007). Borderline and antisocial personality scores as mediators between attachment and intimate partner violence. *Violence and Victims, 22,* 139–157.
Mazur, R., & Aldrich, L. (2003). What makes a domestic violence court work? Lessons from New York. *Judges' Journal, 42*(5–9), 41–42.
McClellan, D. S., Farabee, D., & Crouch, B. M. (1997). Early victimization, drug use, and criminality: A comparison of male and female prisoners. *Criminal Justice Behavior, 24,* 455–467.
McGuire, J. (2002). Explanations of criminal behaviour. In J. McGuire, T. Mason, & A. O'Kane (Eds.), *Behaviour, crime, and legal processes: A guidebook for practitioners* (pp. 135–160). Chichester: Wiley.
Messman-Moore, T. L., & Long, P. J. (2000). Child sexual abuse and revictimization in the form of adult sexual abuse, adult physical abuse, and adult psychological maltreatment. *Journal of Interpersonal Violence, 15,* 489–502.
Miller, W. R. (1983). Motivational interviewing with problem drinkers. *Behavioural Psychotherapy, 11*(2),147–172.
Millon, T. (1997). *Million clinical multiaxial inventory-III.* Minneapolis: Pearson Assessments.
Moore, S. (2009). *Two decades of specialized domestic violence courts: A review of the literature.* The Center for Court Innovation. Retrieved from http://www.courtinnovation.org/_uploads/documents/DV_Court_Lit_Review.pdf. Accessed 1 May 2013.
Murphy, C., & Ting, L. (2010). Interventions for perpetrators of intimate partner violence: A review of efficacy research and recent trends. *Partner Abuse, 1,* 26–44.
National Center for Injury Prevention and Control. (2003). *Costs of intimate partner violence against women in the United States.* Atlanta: Centers for Disease Control and Prevention.

Newmark, L., Rempel, M., Diffily, K., & Kane, K. M. (2001). *Specialized felony domestic violence courts: Lessons on implementation and impact from the Kings County experience*. Washington: Urban Institute.

Noar, S. M., Benac, C. N., & Harris, M. S. (2007). Does tailoring matter? Meta-analytic review of tailored print health behavior change interventions. *Psychological Bulletin, 133*(4), 673–693.

Nolan, J. L. (2001). *Reinventing justice: The American drug court movement*. Princeton: Princeton University Press.

Office of Justice Programs. (1997). Defining drug courts: The key components. U.S. Department of Justice. http://www.ndci.org/sites/default/files/ndci/KeyComponents.pdf. Accessed 1 May 2013.

O'Leary, D. K. (1993). Through a psychological lens: Personality traits, personality disorders, and levels of violence. In R. J. Gelles & D. R. Loseke (Eds.), *Current controversies on family violence* (1st ed., pp. 7–30). Newbury Park: Sage.

Olson, D. H., Portner, J., & Lavee, Y. (1985). *FACES III. Family social science*. St. Paul: University of Minnesota.

Peterson, R. R. (2004). Reducing intimate partner violence: Moving beyond criminal justice interventions. *Criminology & Public Policy, 7*(4), 537–545.

Prochaska, J. O., & DiClemente, C. C. (1983). Stages and processes of self-change of smoking: Toward and integrative model of change. *Journal of Consulting and Clinical Psychology, 51*, 390–395.

Prochaska, J. O., DiClemente, C. C., & Norquist, J. C. (1992). In search of how people change: Applications to addictive behaviors. *American Psychologist, 47*, 1102–1114.

Quann, N. (2007). *Offender profile and recidivism among domestic violence offenders in Ontario, Canada, Ottawa*. Canada: Department of Justice, Research and Statistics Division.

Rennison, D. M. (2003). *Intimate partner violence, 1993–2001*. Washington: Bureau of Justice Statistics. Retrieved from http://bjs.ojp.usdoj.gov/content/pub/pdf/ipv01.pdf. Accessed 1 May 2013.

Rondeau, G., Brodeur, N., Brochu, S., & Lemire, G. (2001). Dropout and completion of treatment among spouse abusers. *Violence and Victims, 16*, 127–143.

Rosenbaum, A., & O'Leary, D. K. (1981). Children: The unintended victims of marital violence. *American Journal of Orthopsychiatry, 51*, 692–699.

Saunders, D. G. (2008). Group interventions for men who batter: A summary of program descriptions and research. *Violence and Victims, 23*(2), 156–172.

Scott, K., King, C., McGinn, H., & Hosseini, N. (2011). Effects of motivational enhancement on immediate outcomes of batterer intervention. *Journal of Family Violence, 26*, 139–149.

Shelton, D. E. (2007). *The current state of domestic violence courts in the United States, 2007* (National Center for State Courts White Paper Series). Ypsilanti: Eastern Michigan University. Retrieved from http://ssrn.com/abstract=1163228. Accessed 1 May 2013.

Siegel, J. A., & Williams, L. M. (2003). The relationship between child sexual abuse and female delinquency and crime: A prospective study. *Journal of Research in Crime and Delinquency, 40*, 71–94.

Simon, L. M. J. (1995). A therapeutic jurisprudence approach to the legal processing of domestic violence cases. *Psychology, Public Policy, and Law, 1*(1), 43–79.

Simon, L. M. J. (1997). Do criminal offenders specialize in crime types? *Applied & Preventive Psychology, 6*, 35–53.

Smith, C., & Thornberry, T. P. (1995). The relationship between childhood maltreatment and adolescent involvement in delinquency. *Criminology, 33*, 451–481.

Stover, C. S., Meadows, A. L., & Kaufman, J. (2009). Interventions for intimate partner violence: Review and implications for evidence-based practice. *Professional Psychology: Research and Practice, 40*(3), 223–233.

Straus, M. A. (1979). Measuring family conflict and violence: The conflict tactics scale. *Journal of Marriage in the Family, 41*, 75–88.

Stuart, G. L., Moore, T. M., Kahler, C. W., & Ramsey, S. E. (2007a). Substance abuse and relationship violence among men court-referred to batterer intervention programs. *Substance Abuse, 24*(2), 107–122.

Stuart, G. L., Temple, J. R., & Moore, T. M. (2007b). Improving batterer intervention programs through theory-based research. *Journal of the American Medical Association, 298*(5), 560–562.

Tjaden, P., & Thoennes, N. (2000). *Full report of the prevalence, incidence, and consequences of violence against women: Findings from the national violence against women survey* (Research in Brief). Washington: National Institute of Justice. Retrieved from https://www.ncjrs.gov/pdffiles1/nij/183781.pdf. Accessed 1 May 2013.

Tolman, R. M., & Bennett, L. W. (1990). A review of quantitative research on men who batter. *Journal of Interpersonal Violence, 5*, 87–118.

Turgeon, C. (2008). Bridging theory and practice: A Roundtable on court responses to domestic violence. *Journal of Court Innovation, 1*(2), 345–370.

Violence Women Act of 1994. (1994). Pub. L. No. 103-322, Title IV, 108 Stat. 1902-55.

Visher, C., Harrell, A., Newmark, L. & Yahner, J. (2008). Reducing intimate partner violence: An evaluation of a comprehensive justice system-community collaboration. *Criminology & Public Policy, 7*(4), 495–523.

Walker, L. E. (2001). Battering in adult relations. *Encyclopedia of Women and Gender, 1*, 169–187.

Waltz, J., Babcock, J. C., Jacobson, N. S., & Gottman, J. M. (2000). Testing a typology of batterers. *Journal of Consulting and Clinical Psychology, 68*(4), 669–685.

Weber, J. (2000). Domestic violence courts: Components and considerations. *Journal of the Center for Families, Children & the Courts, 2*, 23–36.

Wexler, D. B. (1991). Putting mental health into mental health law: Therapeutic jurisprudence. In D. B. Wexler & B. Winick (Eds.), *Essays in therapeutic jurisprudence* (pp. 3–15). Durham: Carolina Academic Press.

Wexler, D. B., & Winick, B. J. (1991). *Essays in therapeutic jurisprudence*. Durham: Carolina Academic Press.

Wexler, D. B., & Winick, B. J. (Eds.). (1996). *Law in a therapeutic key: Developments in therapeutic jurisprudence*. Durham: Carolina Academic Press.

Widom, C. S. (1989a). *The intergenerational transmission of violence*. New York: Harry Frank Guggenheim Foundation.

Widom, C. S. (1989b). Child abuse, neglect, and violent criminal behavior. *Criminology, 27*, 251–271.

Widom, C. S., & Maxfield, M. G. (2001). *An update on the "cycle of violence", 2001*. Washington: National Institute of Justice. Retrieved from www.ncjrs.gov/pdffiles1/nij/184894.pdf. Accessed 1 May 2013.

Widom, C. S., & White, H. R. (1997). Problem behaviors in abused and neglected children grown up: Prevalence and co-occurrence of substance abuse, crime and violence. *Criminal Behavior and Mental Health, 7*, 287–310.

Widom, C. S., DuMont, K., & Czaja, S. (2007). A prospective investigation of major depressive disorder and comorbidity in abused and neglected children grown up. *Archives of General Psychiatry, 64*, 49–56.

Wilt, S., & Olson, S. (1996). Prevalence of domestic violence in the United States. *Journal of the American Medical Women's Association, 51*, 77–82.

Wolff, N. (2000). Using randomized controlled trials to evaluate socially complex services: Problems, challenges, and recommendations. *Journal of Mental Health Policy and Economics, 3*, 97–109.

Wolff, N. (2001). Randomized trials of socially complex interventions: Promise or peril? *Journal of Health Services Research and Policy, 6*(2), 123–126.

Wulfert, E., Blanchard, E. B., Freidenberg, B. M., & Martell, R. S. (2006). Retaining pathological gamblers in cognitive behavior therapy through motivational enhancement—A pilot study. *Behavior Modification, 30*, 315–340.

Zorza, J. (1992). The criminal law of misdemeanor domestic violence, 1970–1990. *Journal of Criminal Law and Criminology, 8*, 240–279.

Chapter 7
Gender Issues in Problem-Solving Courts

Anna Williams Shavers

Introduction

> Gender-based violence is one of the most extreme and pervasive forms of discrimination, severely impairing and nullifying the enforcement of women's rights [and there is a] strong connection between the problems of discrimination and violence against women.[1]

Professors Barbara Babb and Nancy Wolff describe, endorse, and make a compelling case for the use of unified family court systems (UFCs) and specialty problem-solving court systems (PSCs) respectively, to handle family law cases that include allegations of domestic violence. This comment briefly explores their recommendations and examines the unique aspects of gender issues and domestic violence cases in the context of Therapeutic Jurisprudence[2] and problem-solving courts. *Domestic Violence and the Legal System* is a brief examination of the history of addressing domestic violence in the legal system. Here I start with the discussion of a recent much publicized domestic violence case that was heard by the Supreme Court. In *Proposals for Specialty Family Law Courts and Domestic Violence Courts*, I discuss the Babb and Wolff proposals in the context of the basic arguments for including

Cline Williams Professor of Citizenship Law, University of Nebraska College of Law. This comment is based upon remarks made at the Problem-Solving Courts Symposium, January 2010, at the University of Nebraska, Lincoln, Nebraska, in response to the presentations by Barbara Babb and Nancy Wolff.

[1] Jessica Lenahan (Gonzalez) et al. v. United States, Case 12.626, Report No. 80/11, Inter-Am. C.H.R., Para. 110 (July 21, 2011) (released publicly on August 17, 2011) [Lenahan Final Report].
[2] See David B. Wexler & Bruce J. Winick, Law in a therapeutic key: developments in therapeutic jurisprudence (1996).

A. W. Shavers (✉)
University of Nebraska–Lincoln College of Law, Lincoln, NE, USA
e-mail: ashavers@unl.edu

R. L. Wiener, E. M. Brank (eds.), *Problem Solving Courts*,
DOI 10.1007/978-1-4614-7403-6_7, © Springer Science+Business Media, LLC 2013

Therapeutic Jurisprudence in the legal system. Finally, I end in *Proceed with Caution in the Use of Special Courts for Domestic Violence Matters* with a cautionary note based upon the unique issues involved with domestic violence cases.

Domestic Violence and the Legal System

Jessica Gonzales was in divorce proceedings with her estranged husband, Simon Gonzales, in Douglas County, Colorado, in 1999.[3] In connection with the proceedings, she obtained a temporary restraining order (TRO). The TRO ordered Simon Gonzales not to molest or disturb the peace of Jessica or the three children, three girls (ages 10, 9, and 7 years), of the marriage. The TRO was subsequently made permanent, but it allowed Simon some "parenting time" with the girls even though he had a history of suicidal threats and attempts as well as abusive erratic behavior. Colorado's mandatory enforcement law requires police officers to use "every reasonable means" to enforce restraining orders.[4] The brutal and tragic facts of what happened to this family are the subject matter of *Town of Castle Rock v. Gonzales*,[5] which was decided by the Supreme Court in June 2005.

In June 1999, Simon abducted the three girls while they were apparently riding their bicycles near their home. That evening for approximately 5 hours, Jessica attempted to obtain help from the police in having her daughters returned to her. Despite showing the police the restraining order, making numerous telephone calls to the police, and informing the police of the location where Simon was likely holding the girls, she ultimately had to go to the police station before the officers actually took an incident report from her. A little over 3 hours later, at about 3:20 A.M. Simon Gonzales drove to the police station, got out of his truck, and opened fire on the station with a semiautomatic handgun. He was shot dead by police officers on the scene. The three girls (ages 10, 9 and 7 years), were found by the police in the cab of Simon's truck, where apparently they had been murdered by Simon earlier that evening. Simon Gonzales had purchased his gun earlier that evening, shortly after he abducted the three girls.[6] Jessica filed a lawsuit against the City of Castle

---

[3] The Gonzales' divorce proceeding was apparently filed in district court in Castle Rock, Colorado, where at that time, the district court was a court of general jurisdiction that handled family law cases. Colorado decided not to adopt the unified family court, but some areas of the state have established family courts. *See* Nancy Thoennes, Family Court Pilot in Colorado's 17th Judicial District. Denver, Colorado: Center for Policy Research (2001), http://www.centerforpolicyresearch.org/Publications/tabid/233/id/468/Default.aspx.

[4] *See* Colo. Rev. Stat. §§ 18-6-803.5(3) (a).

[5] Town of Castle Rock v. Gonzales, 545 U.S. 748 (2005).

[6] These facts are based upon the description of the facts in Town of Castle Rock v. Gonzales. The facts were never fully developed because the case was dismissed before trial. There is some dispute of the facts. *See* Jessica Gonzales v. United States, Petition No. 1490–05, IACHR Report No. 52/07, OEA/Ser.L./V/II.128, doc. 19, Para. 1 (July 24, 2007) [Gonzales, admissibility report].

Rock, Colorado, and three police officers, alleging that they violated her constitutional rights when they did not enforce the restraining order.[7] The Supreme Court ultimately dismissed Jessica's case and held that there was no basis in law to uphold her claims against either the individual police officers involved or the town of Castle Rock, Colorado, because she did not have an enforceable property interest in the restraining order.[8] The majority concluded that the government had not created a property interest protected under the Fourteenth Amendment when it issued a restraining order. Therefore, there was no property right that had been violated.

This decision reminds us that domestic violence has historically gone unprotected. Domestic violence and many issues that disproportionately affect women were viewed as belonging to the private sphere of our lives and are matters that the public sphere cannot and perhaps should not adequately address. The public sphere includes the court system that is used to punish and provide relief. Historically, domestic violence was a private matter, unworthy of relief from the courts or of proper police protection. Social as well as legal support for victims was virtually nonexistent. Even after the recognition of domestic violence as a crime, the legal system has struggled with developing an appropriate method for handling these disputes.[9] One reform that has been recognized nationwide is mandatory arrest laws for protective order violations.[10] As it has been noted, however, "[w]hen protective orders have been available, their enforcement has been weak."[11] The *Gonzales* case supports this conclusion and presents a crucial question: what is the responsibility of the legal system and law enforcement in particular, when a victim has accessed the court system and is determined to be in need of protection?

In December 2005, after her case was dismissed by the U.S. Supreme Court, Jessica submitted her petition to the Inter-American Commission on Human Rights

---

[7] Jessica Gonzales filed a claim under 42 U.S.C. § 1983, which provides a remedy for deprivation of rights secured by the Constitution of the United States when that deprivation takes place "under color of any statute, ordinance, regulation, custom, or usage, of any State or Territory. . . ." She claimed that her procedural due process rights under the Due Process Clause of the Fourteenth Amendment were violated when the police failed to provide protection pursuant to a validly obtained protective order. Town of Castle Rock v. Gonzales, 545 U.S. 748, 754 (2005)

[8] Section 1983 authorizes a cause of action for the violation of any constitutional right, including substantive due process and equal protection violations. *See, e.g.*, Deshaney v. Winnebago Cty. Soc. Servs. Dept., 489 U.S. 189 (1989) (failure to provide petitioner with adequate protection against his father's violence did not violate his rights under the substantive component of the Due Process Clause).

[9] *See generally*, Karen Czapanskiy, Domestic Violence, the Family and the Lawyering Process: Lessons from Studies on Gender Bias in the Courts, 27 Fam. L. Q. 247 (1993).

[10] *See* Arthur L. Rizer III, Mandatory Arrest: Do We Need to Take a Closer Look?, 36 UWLA L. Rev. 1, 9 (2005) (noting that 15 states that have enacted mandatory arrest statutes and 24 states that have enacted a mandatory arrest statute requiring arrest when a protective order has been violated).

[11] Randal B. Fritzler & Leonore M. J. Simon, *Creating a Domestic Violence Court: Combat in the Trenches*, 37 CT. REV. 28, 29 (2000)

(IACHR)[12] to try and obtain an answer to this question.[13] She asserted that the U.S. Supreme Court and the Castle Rock Police Department violated her human rights. She first appeared before the Commission in March 2007 on a hearing regarding the admissibility of the matter before the IACHR. After having determined that the matter was admissible[14] and considering the position of the Petitioner and the response of the State and the United States, the IACHR issued its final report in Jessica *Lenahan (Gonzales) v. United States of America*, concluding that the United States violated her human rights and those of her children.[15]

In its report on admissibility, the IACHR acknowledged the history of the treatment of domestic violence in the U.S. court system and the allegations in the petition that:

> [P]olice authorities engage in a systematic and widespread practice of treating domestic violence as a low-priority crime, *belonging to the private sphere*, as a result of discriminatory stereotypes about the victims. These stereotypes influence negatively the police response to the implementation of restraining orders. The failures in the police response affect women disproportionately since they constitute the majority of victims of domestic violence. The deficiencies in the state response allegedly have a particularly alarming effect on women that pertain to racial and ethnic minorities, and lower-income groups.[16]

The *Gonzales* case and the IACHR report emphasizes the fact that domestic violence continues to be a serious problem in the U.S.[17] as it is around the world.[18] Domestic violence is generally defined to occur among cohabitants or former cohabitants and the cases can either be felonies or misdemeanors. It includes sexual abuse; emotional

---

[12] The Inter-American Commission of Human Rights (IACHR) is the principal body of the inter-American system charged with human rights protection. The commission investigates petitions of alleged violations of human rights by the member nations of the Organization of American States (OAS). The United States is one of the 35 members of OAS.

[13] *See* Gonzales, admissibility report, *supra* note 6 at Para. 1.

[14] Gonzales, admissibility report, *supra* note 6 at Para. 1. doc. 22, rev. 1 (2007).

[15] Lenahan Final Report, *supra* note 1.

[16] Jessica Gonzales v. United States, Petition No. 1490–05, IACHR Report No. 52/07, OEA/Ser.L./V/II.128, Gonzales, admissibility report, *supra* note 6 at doc.19, Para. 58] (rejecting the U.S. position that the OAS American Declaration on the Rights and Duties of Man did not impose positive governmental obligations).

[17] *See, e.g.*, Michael Rand and Callie Rennison, "How Much Violence Against Women Is There?" in Violence Against Women and Family Violence: Developments in Research, Practice, and Policy, Edited by Bonnie S. Fisher U.S. Department of Justice: National Institute of Justice. (2004) NCJ 199701 at I-1–5 (noting that in 1998, about 1 million violent crimes were committed against persons by their current or former spouses, boyfriends, or girlfriends; violent crimes included murder, rape, sexual assault, robbery, aggravated assault, and simple assault); National Center for Injury Prevention and Control, Centers for Disease Control and Prevention, Costs of Intimate Partner Violence Against Women in the United States 1–4 (2003), *available at* http://www.cdc.gov/ncipc/pub-res/ipv_cost/IPVBook-Final-Feb18.pdf; Patricia Tjaden and Nancy Thoennes, U.S. Department of Justice, Extent, Nature and Consequences of Intimate Partner Violence: Findings from the National Violence Against Women Study 9–11 (2000), *available at* http://www.ncjrs.gov/pdffiles1/nij/181867.pdf.

[18] *See* United Nations Centre for Social Development and Humanitarian Affairs, Violence Against Women in the Family, U.N. Doc. ST/CSDHA/2 (1989).

abuse; physical behavior involving infrequent slaps, pushes, grabs, or shoves to frequent and severe life-threatening assaults; and threat of violence. Intimate partner violence is committed primarily against women.[19] Women are at an increased risk of harm shortly after separation from an abusive partner.[20] Often children are abducted as a means for the offender to gain control over the victim.[21] Nearly one in four adult women is a victim of domestic violence in her lifetime.[22] The IACHR noted that the Petitioner stated that "in the United States between one and five million women suffer nonfatal violence at the hands of an intimate partner each year,"[23] and "[t]he United States Government characterizes the problem as 'acute' and 'significant,' and acknowledges that there were at least 3.5 million incidents of domestic violence in a four-year period, contemporary with the facts pertaining to this case."[24] While all domestic violence cases or incidents will not have the same tragic end as the *Gonzales* case, there is this possibility. As the IACHR further noted, "women were still very unlikely to gain protection in the United States because of law enforcement's widespread under-enforcement of domestic violence laws."[25] All of the possible consequences need to be considered when trying to decide an appropriate method to address and respond to domestic violence situations presented to the court either between two intimate partners or in connection with abuse in a broader family unit.

---

[19] U.S. Department of Justice, Bureau of Justice Statistics, Family Violence Statistics, Mathew Durose and Others (June 2005).

[20] Ronet Bachman and Linda E. Salzman, L., Bureau of Justice Statistics, Violence Against Women: Estimates From the Redesigned Survey 1 (January 2000); *See generally*, Barbara J. Hart, Minnesota Center Against Violence and Abuse, *Battered Women and the Criminal Justice System* (1992), http://www.mincava.umn.edu/documents/hart/hart.html.

[21] *See generally*, Barbara J. Hart, Minnesota Center Against Violence and Abuse, *Parental Abduction and Domestic Violence* (1992), http://www.mincava.umn.edu/documents/hart/hart.html.

[22] See The Centers for Disease Control and Prevention and The National Institute of Justice, Extent, Nature, and Consequences of Intimate Partner Violence, July 2000. The Commonwealth Fund, Health Concerns Across a Woman's Lifespan: 1998 Survey of Women's Health, 1999.

[23] Lenahan Final Report, *supra* note 1, Para. 93, *citing* Petitioners' petition dated December 27, 2005 and Final Observations Regarding the Merits of the Case submitted by the petitioners, March 24, 2008, citing statistics from Center for Disease Control and Prevention, Costs of Intimate Partner Violence against Women in the United States 18 (2003) (estimating 5.3 million intimate partner assaults against women in the United States each year); Patricia Tjaden and Nancy Thoennes, U.S. Department of Justice, Office of Justice Programs, National Institute of Justice, Extent, Nature and Consequences of Intimate Partner Violence, July 2000.

[24] *Id.* Para. 94 *citing* U.S. Response to the Petition Alleging Violations of the Human Rights of Jessica Gonzales by the United States of America and the State of Colorado, September 22, 2006, p. 12.

[25] *Id.* Para. 96 citing as an example *Thurman v. City of Torrington*, 595 F. Supp. 1521 (D. Conn. 1984).

Proposals for Specialty Family Law Courts and Domestic Violence Courts

The movement for court reform as well as the1970s feminist movement goal to increase the awareness of the subordination of women and to improve all facets of women's lives drew attention to the handling of domestic violence cases in court as well as by law enforcement officers. Actions of abusers came to be defined as crimes and support was provided to victims in various forms including the availability of restraining orders. This was a convergence of social and legal strategies that eventually led to consideration of the need to apply principles of Therapeutic Jurisprudence to family law matters generally and domestic violence more specifically.

Specialty/Specialized and Therapeutic Courts

UFCs and other therapeutic courts are often discussed under the general category of "problem-solving" courts.[26] These courts are typically seen as using unconventional action-oriented methods in the way the legal system handles offenders.[27] Although drug treatment courts began appearing in the 1980s, the drug treatment court established in Dade County, Florida, is often cited as the first modern "problem-solving court."[28] While the early drug treatment courts can be viewed as a tool of judicial efficiency designed to handle the load of drug offense cases appearing on the courts' dockets, the modern drug treatment courts focused on the therapeutic aspects of the drug offender. The perceived success of drug treatment courts[29] has led to the creation of and advocacy for a number of other "problem-solving courts,"[30] including

[26] *See generally*, Richard Boldt & Jana Singer, Juristocracy in the Trenches: Problem-Solving Judges and Therapeutic Jurisprudence in Drug Treatment Courts and Unified Family Courts, 65 Md. L. Rev. 82, 83 (2006); James L. Nolan, Jr., Redefining Criminal Courts: Problem-Solving and the Meaning of Justice, 40 Am. Crim. L. Rev. 1541, 1541 (2003) ("problem-solving courts 'involve principles and methods grounded in Therapeutic Jurisprudence' ").

[27] *See, e.g.,* Boldt and Singer, *supra* note 26 at 83 ("[T]he judges who serve on these 'problem-solving' courts have largely repudiated the classical virtues of restraint, disinterest, and modesty, replacing these features of the traditional judicial role with bold, engaged, action-oriented norms." quoting Mary Ann Glendon, A Nation Under Lawyers 4–5 (1994)).

[28] Boldt and Singer, *supra* note 26 at 84.

[29] *See generally*, Boldt and Singer, *supra* note 26 at 83.

[30] *See* Judging in a Therapeutic Key: Therapeutic Jurisprudence and the Courts (Bruce J. Winick & David B. Wexler eds., 2003) [hereinafter Judging in a Therapeutic Key] and David B. Wexler & Bruce J. Winick, Law in a Therapeutic Key: Developments in Therapeutic Jurisprudence (1996) [hereinafter Law in a Therapeutic Key].

mental health courts,[31] domestic violence courts,[32] veterans' courts,[33] and community courts.[34] These developments tend to occur in existing courts with specialized dockets or when there is a realization that specialized dockets should be created. It is reported that by 2007, over 2,500 problem-solving courts existed in the U.S.[35] A major influence on the creation of these courts has been the development of the concept of "Therapeutic Jurisprudence" (TJ), which was originated by David Wexler and Bruce Winick.[36] Bruce Winick describes Therapeutic Jurisprudence as "the study of law's healing potential. TJ originated as a means to assess the impact of the legal system on mentally disabled individuals."[37] As Robert Schopp has noted, TJ was originally proposed "as a research agenda intended to broaden a recurring pattern of relatively narrow discussion in mental health law scholarship."[38] TJ recognizes that the application of law and the agents of the legal system to an individual can have either therapeutic or counter-therapeutic consequences and questions whether such rules, procedures, and roles can or should be reshaped so as to enhance their therapeutic potential, while not subordinating due process principles. TJ reforms generally envision the judge as performing a therapeutic function.

Wexler and Winick have offered this definition of TJ in its broader application to law and its healing potential:

> Therapeutic jurisprudence is the "study of the role of the law as a therapeutic agent." It focuses on the law's impact on emotional life and on psychological well-being. These are areas that have not received very much attention in the law until now. Therapeutic jurisprudence focuses our attention on this previously underappreciated aspect, humanizing the law and concerning itself with the human, emotional, psychological side of law and the legal process. Basically, therapeutic jurisprudence is a perspective that regards the law as a social force that produces behaviors and consequences. Sometimes these consequences fall within the realm of what

---

[31] *See generally*, Sarah L. Miller & Abigayl M. Perelman, Mental Health Courts: An Overview and Redefinition of Tasks and Goals, 33 Law & Psychol. Rev. 113, 113 (2009).

[32] *See generally*, Hon. Catherine Shaffer, *Therapeutic Domestic Violence Courts: An Efficient Approach to Adjudication?*, 27 Seattle U. L. Rev. 981 (2004).

[33] *See generally*, Hon. Robert T. Russell, *Veterans Treatment Courts Developing Throughout the Nation*, in Future Trends in State Courts (2009) http://www.vis-res.com/pdf/Trends2009.pdf.

[34] *See generally*, Thomas J. Scheff, *Community Conferences: Shame and Anger in Therapeutic Jurisprudence,* 67 Rev. Jur. U.P.R. 95 (1998).

[35] Robert V. Wolf, "Principles of Problem-Solving Justice" (Center for Court Innovation, n.d.), http://www.courtinnovation.org/topic/problem-solving-justice.

[36] *See* David Wexler, Therapeutic Jurisprudence: The Law as a Therapeutic Agent (1990); Bruce J. Winick, *Therapeutic Jurisprudence and Problem Solving Courts*, 30 Fordham Urb. L.J. 1055 (2003). *See generally*, Winick and Wexler, Judging in a Therapeutic Key, *supra* note 30 (collection of essays and edited versions of republished articles in the area).

[37] Bruce Winick, *Applying the Law Therapeutically in Domestic Violence Cases,* 69 UMKC L. Rev. 33 (2000) [hereinafter *Applying the Law*] *citing* David B. Wexler & Bruce J. Winick, Law in a Therapeutic Key: Developments in Therapeutic Jurisprudence (1996); Bruce J. Winick, *The Jurisprudence of Therapeutic Jurisprudence*, 3 Psychol. Pub. Pol'y & L. 184 (1997).

[38] Schopp, Robert F., "Integrating Restorative Justice And Therapeutic Jurisprudence," 67 Revista Jurídica Universidad de Puerto Rico 665 (1990) *citing* David Wexler, Therapeutic Jurisprudence: The Law as a Therapeutic Agent 3–22 (1998).

> we call therapeutic; other times antitherapeutic consequences are produced. Therapeutic jurisprudence wants us to be aware of this and wants us to see whether the law can be made or applied in a more therapeutic way so long as other values, such as justice and due process, can be fully respected.[39]

Problem-solving courts utilize TJ principles and focus on having a positive outcome on the offender in lieu of or in addition to punishment. In order to accomplish these goals, judges and other court personnel must often assume nontraditional, less adversarial based roles. One commentator summarizes the goals of the early problem-solving courts: "At their core was the idea that it was no longer enough just to arrest, process, and adjudicate an offender, but law enforcement officers, prosecutors, judges, and probation officers also needed to try to reduce recidivism, improve public confidence in justice, and prevent crime down the road."[40]

Richard Boldt and Jana Singer have described the successful use of TJ principles in drug treatment courts to produce desired "behaviors and consequences" as including four key components: " the referral of defendants to substance abuse treatment facilities in the community; the use of the threat of traditional criminal penalties as leverage to retain defendants in treatment; judicial monitoring of defendants' progress in treatment through the use of regular urinalysis testing and periodic 'status hearings' in open court; and the imposition of increasingly severe 'graduated sanctions,' in instances of noncompliance with the treatment regime, and graduated rewards for successes."[41] A recent report of the National Drug Court Institute concludes that the success of drug courts is closely correlated with the extent to which the program adhered to the core ingredients identified in the "10 Key Components" drafted by drug court professionals in 1996.[42] Is it possible to develop similar standards for courts handling domestic violence matters? If not, should we have domestic violence courts?

Specialty Courts and Domestic Violence

In the past two decades, there has been a trend toward establishing UFCs and domestic violence specialty courts. They have taken various forms.[43] UFCs can be all encompassing and are sometimes referred to as Integrated Domestic Violence

---

[39] David B. Wexler & Bruce J. Winick, *Law in Therapeutic Key: Developments in Therapeutic Jurisprudence* xvii (1996).

[40] Wolf, *supra* note 5 at 1.

[41] Boldt and Singer, *supra note* 26 at 84–85 (2006), *citing* Steven Belenko, Research on Drug Courts 6–7 (1998) and Drug Court Standards Committee, National Association of Drug Court Professionals, Defining Drug Courts: The Key Components (1997) (listing 10 key components).

[42] West Huddleston & Douglas B. Marlowe, Painting the Current Picture: A National Report on Drug Courts and Other Problem-Solving Court Programs in the United States 14–15, National Drug Court Institute and United States Department of Justice Bureau of Justice Assistance, (July 2011).

[43] *See generally*, Emily Sack, Creating a Domestic Violence Court: Guidelines and Best Practices 2, Family Violence Prevention Fund (2002).

("IDV") courts if domestic violence is present in the family. IDVs typically use the "one-family-one judge" model and have one judge assigned to handle all criminal and civil matters relating to a family.[44] There are some specialized domestic violence courts that exist outside of the UFCs. These would typically be criminal domestic violence courts.[45] The varied treatment of domestic violence in family law specialty courts suggests that it is not yet possible to develop a structure for guiding principles or key components involved in the utilization of Therapeutic Jurisprudence in domestic violence cases.

Barbara Babb in her article, "Unified Family Courts: An Interdisciplinary Framework and a Problem-Solving Approach,"[46] is a strong advocate for UFCs as specialty problem-solving courts.[47] She includes domestic violence matters in the list of disputes that can be handled in UFCs. Nancy Wolff focuses specifically on domestic violence courts in her article, "Domestic violence courts: The case of Lady Justice meets the Serpents of the Caduceus: Has the lady's each yielded promise or peril?"[48] In each case, the task presented is to make the case that the treatment of domestic violence cases is appropriate for the application of Therapeutic Jurisprudence in a specialty court.[49]

The endorsement of UFCs is based upon the need to resolve disputes that involve families and may benefit from a holistic approach rather than a traditional adversarial one. This has been made possible in part by the development of modern doctrines in family law matters such as no-fault divorces and various court-approved shared custody arrangements. As one commentator had noted, a unified family court goes

---

[44] *See, e.g.*, Problem-Solving Courts, New York (described as handling all criminal, family and matrimonial matters with domestic violence being the threshold requirement for entry into the IDV). https://www.nycourts.gov/courts/problem_solving/idv/home.shtml; Unified Family Court Pilot Project (seeking the adoption of authorizing legislation by the Tennessee legislature) http://www.shelbycountychildren.org/what-we-do/initiatives/unified-family-court.html.

[45] *See* Anne H. Geraghty & Wallace J. Mlyniec, *Tempering Enthusiasm with Caution*, 40 FAM. CT. R. 435, 437 (2002).

[46] Barbara Babb, *Unified Family Courts: An Interdisciplinary Framework and a Problem-Solving Approach*, in Wiener, R., & Brank, E. (eds.) Problem Solving Courts: Social Science and Legal Perspectives, Springer, 2012 [hereinafter Unified Family Courts]. Citations herein are based on a draft copy of the article.

[47] *See also* Barbara A. Babb, University of Baltimore Law School, Remarks at the Eleventh Annual Symposium on Contemporary Urban Challenges (March 1, 2002), *Problem Solving Courts: From Adversarial Litigation to Innovative Jurisprudence,* 29 FORDHAM URB. L.J. 1929, 1944 (2002); Barbara A. Babb, *Where We Stand: An Analysis of America's Family Law Adjudicatory Systems and the Mandate to Establish Unified Family Courts,* 32 FAM. L.Q. 31, 35–36 (1998) (discussing the historical development of family courts).

[48] Nancy Wolff, *Domestic violence courts: The case of Lady Justice meets the Serpents of the Caduceus: Has the lady's reach yielded promise or peril*? In Wiener, R., & Brank, E. (eds.) Problem-Solving Courts: Social Science and Legal Perspectives, Springer, 2012. Citations herein are based on a draft copy of the article.

[49] Bruce Winick has argued that specialty courts are better-suited to handle domestic violence cases than conventional courts if they are properly structured. *See* Winick, *Applying the Law, supra* note 37.

beyond dispute resolution, but should fulfill both the social and legal needs of families, including providing families with the skills necessary to avoid the need for legal intervention in the future.[50] The American Bar Association (ABA) has played a leading role in the creation and strengthening of unified family courts.[51] A 1993 ABA report stated: "We need to reorganize the way courts work with families and children so that judges and court personnel can give each child's case the attention it demands...."[52] One recommendation of the report was that all matters involving families and children should be consolidated into a unified one court system with a one-judge–one-family concept. A unified family court has been defined as a single court system with specially trained judges that address legal, social, and emotional issues in a holistic way with linkage to social services and resources from a case management team, to provide a user-friendly environment that addresses the needs of families in a comprehensive manner.[53] These courts typically have jurisdiction over domestic violence cases.[54] Some of the courts either do not exercise jurisdiction over criminal domestic abuse matters or exercise jurisdiction only over misdemeanors.[55]

Babb does not single out domestic violence as a special case for justifying the use of specialty courts nor does she suggest its exclusion; rather, she includes it in a list of difficult issues that family court judges must confront in UFCs when fashioning effective therapeutic outcomes for families. This list includes "domestic violence, mental illness, [and] substance abuse."[56]

As Babb and others have recognized, the increasing number of family law cases and the complexity of family structure and legal issues have driven the need for family law court reform.[57] The establishment of UFCs is intended to address some of these challenges. Social science research supports this development and the use

---

[50] Paul A. Williams, *A Unified Family Court for Missouri,* 63 Umkc L. Rev. 383, 396–97 (1994).

[51] *See* Adopted Resolution 117 (Coalition for Justice; Committee on State Justice Initiatives) August 2001 http://www.americanbar.org/groups/criminal_justice/policy/index_aba_criminal_justice_policies_by_meeting.html. *See generally*, Herbert Belgrad, *An Introduction to Unified Family Courts from the American Bar Association's Perspective*, 37 Fam. L.Q. 329, 329 (2003) (describing the American Bar Association's endorsement UFCs).adopted resolution 117 August 2001.

[52] ABA, America's children at risk: a national agenda for legal action 53, 54 (1993).

[53] *See generally*, Symposium, *What Works and What Does Not*, 29 Fordham Urb. L.J. 1929, 1944 (2002); ABA, America's Children at Risk: A National Agenda for Legal Action. 53, 54 (1993).

[54] *See generally*, Andrew Schepard & James W. Bozzomo, *Efficiency, Therapeutic Justice, Mediation and Evaluation: Reflections on a Survey of Unified Family Courts*, 37 Fam. L.Q. 333, 335 (2003) (reporting that 94 % of the jurisdictions in their survey had jurisdiction over domestic violence cases).

[55] *Id.* at 344.

[56] Babb, *Unified Family Courts, supra* note 46 at 17.

[57] *See* Babb, *Unified Family Courts, supra* note 46 at 2. *See also* Deborah J. Chase, *Pro Se Justice And Unified Family Courts*, 37 Fam. L.Q. 403 (2003); Barbara A. Babb & Judith D. Moran, *Substance Abuse, Families, and Unified Family Courts: The Creation of a Caring Justice System,* 3 J. Health Care L. & Pol'y 1 (1999); Jessica Pearson, *Court Services: Meeting the Needs of Twenty-First Century Families*, 33 Fam. L.Q. 617 (1999).

of Therapeutic Jurisprudence. The research emphasizes the need for effective social service interventions in family law matters.[58] Thus, as Babb has suggested, the judges can make multidisciplinary decisions informed by court support staff with backgrounds in mental health and social work.[59] These decisions include legal and nonlegal matters. Babb's development of an ecological approach to family law matters based upon the social science research of Urie Bronfenbrenner,[60] "the ecology of human development," helps demonstrate that the establishment of UFCs with their underlying Therapeutic Jurisprudence basis is supported by social science research and reinforces the idea that the handling of all cases involving children and families is appropriate. This ecological approach provides a research paradigm, which offers to those involved with UFCs "an analytical tool to account for the many factors affecting parties' lives."[61] This approach requires consideration of the total environment of the family and the competing influences on their lives.[62] This analysis leads to the conclusion that UFCs must have comprehensive subject matter jurisdiction. As noted above, this includes domestic violence cases. She does, however, recognize that there is disagreement over the inclusion of criminal matters, such as child abuse and domestic violence in the jurisdiction of UFCs.[63] By remarking that the aim of the all-inclusive IDVs is to "protect and assist victims" as well as "to promote defendant accountability,"[64] she seems to conclude that UFCs can adequately handle domestic violence matters and in fact that this may result in a positive outcome in an ecological approach to the family. For example, elsewhere, she has noted that the ecological holistic approach has led some jurisdictions to include domestic violence as a factor in deciding child custody issues.[65]

There are some extremely positive and compelling reasons for establishing UFCs, but few that deal specifically with the question of whether the holistic approach is

---

[58] *See generally*, Nancy Ver Steegh, *Book Review, The Unfinished Business of Modern Court Reform: Reflections on Children, Courts, and Custody by Andrew I. Schepard*, 38 Fam. L.Q. 449 (2004); Catherine J. Ross, *The Failure of Fragmentation: The Promise of a System of Unified Family Courts*, 32 Fam. L.Q. 3, 7 (1998).

[59] *See* Barbara A. Babb, *Fashioning an Interdisciplinary Framework for Court Reform in Family Law: A Blueprint to Construct a Unified Family Court*, 71 S. Cal. L. Rev. 469, 475 (1998) (describing a multidisciplinary team approach to family law decision-making).

[60] Urie Bronfenbrenner, The Ecology Of Human Development (1979).

[61] Babb, *Unified Family Courts*, *supra* note 46 at 7.

[62] *Id* at 11–14.

[63] *Id.* at 19 *citing* Sanford N. Katz & Jeffrey A. Kuhn, Recommendations for a Model Family Court 8–9 (1991) (due process and other concerns regarding the treatment of the offender) and Linda Szymanski, Theresa Homisak, & E. Hunter Hurst, III, Policy Alternatives and Current Court Practice in the Special Problem Areas of Jurisdiction over the Family 8–9 (1993) (noting significant concerns unless confined to misdemeanors).

[64] *Id.* at 20 *citing* Judith S. Kaye, *Delivering Justice Today: A Problem-Solving Approach*, 22 Yale L. & Pol'y Rev. 125, 143 (2004).

[65] See Barbara A. Babb, An Interdisciplinary Approach to Family Law Jurisprudence: Application of an Ecological and Therapeutic Perspective, 72 Ind. L.J. 775, 787 n. 76 (1997) citing Joan S. Meier, Notes from the Underground: Integrating Psychological and Legal Perspectives on Domestic Violence in Theory and Practice, 21 Hofstra L. Rev. 1295, 1308–09 (1993).

appropriate for cases involving domestic abuse allegations. Most family law matters will not involve domestic violence, and the families may benefit greatly from the use of UFCs. It may be necessary, however, to consider whether domestic violence cases should be screened out or assigned to a different path. This may be necessary to protect the victim as well as preserve the offender's due process rights.

As Robert W. Wolf has noted, in a study published by the Center for Court Innovation, the subject matter of problem-solving courts often have different goals for success or rehabilitation. As he notes, drug courts focus on the offender and may view a successful outcome as rehabilitation of the offender, whereas domestic violence courts must view a success as having dual goals: a need to hold offenders accountable while keeping victims safe.[66] There is not only a need to recognize the difference in the various types of problem-solving courts but also a need to question whether certain types of problems are suitable for these methods. While it can be argued that like drug courts, "deterring recidivism" in domestic violence cases is an extremely important goal, and the two goals in domestic violence can be accommodated by viewing a lack of recidivism as an indicator of victim safety, thus achieving the desired therapeutic outcome,[67] this approach could lead to the victim perceiving the focus of the process to be on the offender. In addition, unlike domestic violence offenders, in drug courts, the offender is typically nonviolent.

Nancy Wolff tackles the issue of Therapeutic Jurisprudence and domestic violence in problem-solving courts head-on.[68] She first describes the creation of state and local responses to domestic violence in the 1970s, which included law enforcement training as well as legislation that criminalized domestic violence and in some cases mandated prosecution. Sentences often included treatment for the batterers.[69] Then she focuses on the creation of specialized domestic violence courts. By 2009, there were over 200 specialized courts.[70] These courts attempted to address accountability for the offenders as well as protection for the victims. A primary goal was to include punishment as a means of holding the offender accountable. She concludes that although these specialized courts are often categorized as problem-solving courts, they are mistakenly included alongside drug courts and mental health courts that usually have as their goal the decriminalization of the offender's behavior.[71] Therefore, she asserts that "[i]n theory and practice, domestic violence courts focus primarily on victim safety and, as such, appeal to principles of restorative justice, the need to repair or heal the victim rather than principles of Therapeutic Jurisprudence, the need to treat the offender."[72] She argues that domestic violence courts should embrace

---

[66] Wolf, *supra* note 35 at 2.

[67] *See generally*, Melissa Labriola, Sarah Bradley, Chris S. O'Sullivan, Michael Rempel, Samantha Moore, A National Portrait of Domestic Violence Courts 80. Report submitted to the National Institute of Justice, New York, NY: Center for Court Innovation (2009).

[68] Wolff, *supra* note 48.

[69] *Id.* at 4.

[70] *Id.* at 5 *citing* Labriola, Bradley, O'Sullivan, Rempel, & Moore, *supra* note 67.

[71] *Id.* at 6.

[72] *Id.* at 6 (citations omitted).

Therapeutic Jurisprudence principles to address the situation of both the offender and the victim. Her arguments in support of this position, although in different words, closely parallel those of Babb with respect to the need to rely on social science research and ecological theory to develop a holistic approach to address intimate partner violence. Wolff also opposes a fragmented court system to deal with domestic matters and concludes that such a system "is liability for the victim and an asset for the batterer."[73] She argues that the ineffectiveness of domestic violence courts can be attributed in large part to their failure to appropriately apply Therapeutic Jurisprudence. The concentration only on the batterer for therapeutic intervention is driven by the dichotomization of domestic violence into the batterer (man) harming the victim (woman). This view has developed, she asserts, because of the assumptions that domestic violence derives from the patriarchal subordination of women: "(1) batterer behavior is caused by socio-cultural factors that condition men to use their power against and over women; (2) batterers bear the full responsibility for domestic violence; (3) any remedial or rehabilitative intervention should focus on the batterer; (4) all batterers are equal in motivation, pathology, and behavior; and (5) batterers are rational decision-makers and will stop behaviors in which their costs exceed their benefits."[74] Arguably then, if adhering to the premise of Winick and Wexler that the "people appearing in problem-solving courts ... are there because they have problems that they have not recognized or had the ability to deal with effectively,"[75] in domestic violence courts, this would include both the offender and the victim.

The use of specialty courts in domestic violence matters differs from drug courts or mental health courts because it is not only the accused or perpetrator who must be the focus of the court in determining the appropriate contours of therapeutic responses. The determination of appropriate therapeutic responses or interventions must also focus on the victim and often the children of the relationship. Wolff suggests that this means that the court must focus on the dysfunction within the family unit and not just the offender. This could reveal that the principals in the relationship, both the offender-man and the victim-woman, may have "behaviors that contribute to [the] dynamic elements" of the domestic violence incidence.[76] Further, such an approach can take account of the fact that victims seek help to stop the violence but not necessarily to end the relationship. Wolff cautions that court personnel will need to have sufficient training to use gender-sensitive approaches and develop therapeutic responses that focus on both parties.

Wolff's approach holds much merit, but without the necessary training and consideration of all relevant factors in the relationship, the courts may develop remedies that have a detrimental effect on the victim. For example, if an offender is offered a diversion program, and the victim is offered counseling, the victim may view the process as failing to meet her needs, i.e., to see the offender punished, thus having a

---

[73] *Id.* at 9.

[74] *Id.* at 12.

[75] Winick and Wexler, Judging in a Therapeutic Key, *supra* note 30 at 8.

[76] Wolff, *supra* note 48 at 19.

therapeutic effect for the offender and an antitherapeutic effect for the victim. Wolff outlines a strategy to avoid such results. This strategy includes (1) holistic therapeutic orientation for the principals and their children, (2) an assessment of the family unit and profiling of the principals, (3) targeted interventions for the principals, and (4) coordinated and continuous intervention to develop and sustain the appropriate balance of treatment.[77] Wolff concludes by suggesting a research agenda to explore the effectiveness of domestic violence courts.

The use of Therapeutic Jurisprudence in domestic violence cases as urged by Babb and Wolff presents a number of questions that they recognize, but remain to be explored. One primary basis for these questions is how the appropriate balance can be achieved between "principles of restorative justice, the need to repair or heal the victim ... principles of therapeutic jurisprudence, the need to treat the offender"[78] and principles of retributive justice, the need for punishment of the offender. In the next section, I explore issues raised in trying to achieve this balance.

Proceed with Caution in the Use of Special Courts for Domestic Violence Matters

If it is a basic feature of problem-solving courts that "people appearing in problem-solving courts ... are there because they have problems that they have not recognized or had the ability to deal with effectively,"[79] is it appropriate to label the victim in intimate partner violence, most often a woman, as a person having a problem that can be addressed by Therapeutic Jurisprudence? Drug courts and mental health courts would seem to dictate no as the answer. The conduct of the offender in those courts, may have affected others, but those affected are not the subject of the therapeutic actions and typically had no prior relationship with the nonviolent offender.[80] The question here is what type of problem is Therapeutic Jurisprudence best at addressing.

Professors Babb and Wolff make a strong case for including domestic violence issues in unified family courts and specialty domestic violence courts. I simply want to join with others in advising that this be approached with extreme caution and reflection.[81] As Bruce Winick cautioned, TJ is appropriate "when consistent with other important legal values."[82]

The historical gendered exclusion of domestic violence cases from the legal system raises a question as to whether the legal system has sufficiently evolved to deal

[77] *Id.* at 25–28.

[78] *Id.* at 6 (citations omitted).

[79] Winick and Wexler, Judging in a Therapeutic Key, *supra* note 30 at 8.

[80] *See generally*, Julie Stubbs, *Domestic Violence and Women's Safety: Feminist Challenges to Restorative Justice*, in Restorative Justice and Family Violence, 42, 43 (Heather Strang & John Braithwaite eds., 2002).

[81] *See, e.g.*, Geraghty & Mlyniec, *supra* note 45.

[82] Winick, *Applying the Law, supra* note 37 at 33.

with both the offender and victim on an equal basis. The argument by some commentators that domestic violence is unsuitable for restorative justice practices because of the inherent power imbalances and ongoing entanglements of domestic relationships[83] also seems applicable to special courts that apply Therapeutic Jurisprudence to victims.[84] This is especially true if the court seeks "reconciliation rather than punishment, healing rather than retribution."[85] Julia Weber, for example, recognizes that "the danger lies in the possible minimization of the need for a strong law enforcement response in domestic violence cases."[86] As she puts it, the question for domestic violence courts is, "Does a therapeutic approach hold perpetrators accountable for violent crimes?"[87] There are some aspects of "blaming the victim" in approaches that would make both parties equally responsible for the domestic violence incidence. In its development of standards to address the treatment of the offender in family violence cases, the National Council of Juvenile and Family Court Judges included as possible unsuitable approaches "those which orient themselves toward the couple before dealing with the offender's criminal behavior" and those which may "put the victim at substantial risk of revictimization."[88] Weber also notes that if domestic violence courts require victims who come to court seeking protection to participate in [therapeutic] programs, they run the risk of triggering the "unintended effect of reinforcing the batterer's belief that the victim is responsible for the violence and that his role is relatively inconsequential, or that if they are both ordered into counseling, they are equally culpable."[89] There has been some opposition by courts to including domestic violence criminal cases in the UFC because it has the effect of essentially decriminalizing violent criminal actions.[90] The fear that a rehabilitative model will

---

[83] *See, e.g.*, Katherine Van Wormer, *Restorative Justice as Social Justice for Victims of Gendered Violence: A Standpoint Feminist Perspective*, 54 Soc. Work 107 (2009).

[84] *See, e.g.*, John E. Cummings, *Comment, The Cost of Crazy: How Therapeutic Jurisprudence and Mental Health Courts Lower Incarceration Costs, Reduce Recidivism, and Improve Public Safety*, 56 Loy. L. Rev. 279, 281 (2010) (noting that although problem-solving courts have their origins in therapeutic jurisprudence, all problem-solving courts are rooted in the legal theories of therapeutic jurisprudence and restorative justice).

[85] *Id.*

[86] Julia Weber, *Domestic Violence Courts: Components and Considerations*, 2 J. Ctr. Fams. Child & Cts., 23, 27 (2000).

[87] *Id.* at 34.

[88] National Council of Juvenile and Family Court Judges, Family Violence: Improving Court Practice 49 (1990).

[89] Weber, *supra* note 86 at 32.

[90] *See generally*, Nancy Thoennes, Integrated Approaches to Manage Multi-Case Families in the Justice System V: Center for Police Research (2007) (e.g., Maricopa County); Susan Keilitz, Specialization of Domestic Violence Case Management in the Courts: A National Survey, National Institute of Justice, Office of Justice Programs, U.S. Department of Justice (2004) *citing* Deborah Epstein, *Effective Intervention in Domestic Violence Cases: Rethinking the Roles of Prosecutors, Judges, and the Court System,* 11 Yale J.L. & Feminism 3 (1999).

result in leniency being shown to the offender has caused domestic violence advocates to reject that approach.[91] The UFC would need extremely qualified personnel to assess the voluntariness of the victim when selecting the option of utilizing available services to keep the family together and not pursue criminal charges against the offender.

One restorative justice practice that has been strongly endorsed for use in UFCs is mediation. Mediation has been called a vital function of a UFC.[92] Although some scholars and advocates have endorsed the use of mediation even in cases of domestic violence, many others continue to argue against the use of mediation and other alternative dispute techniques when domestic violence is involved in a family law matter.[93] Babb has noted elsewhere that "judges must understand the social science research documenting the coercive and antitherapeutic nature of alternative dispute resolution techniques in some circumstances, such as actions involving victims of domestic violence and their abusers."[94]

Justice Stevens in his dissent in *Town of Castle Rock v. Gonzales*,[95] commented on an experiment by the Minneapolis, Minnesota police department in which randomly assigned domestic violence offenders were handled by using one of three different responses: (1) arresting the offender, (2) mediating the dispute, or (3) requiring the offender to leave the house for 8 hours. The study concluded that mediating the dispute or requiring the offender to leave for 8 hours were both less effective means of reducing domestic violence recidivism than arresting the offender.[96]

As Deborah Chase has cautioned with respect to problem-solving courts generally, "the vulnerability of these courts to well-intended disregard of the legal rights of the litigants must be acknowledged and clearly identified."[97] Along these lines,

---

[91] *See, e.g.*, Geraghty & Mlyniec, *supra* note 45 at 443 *citing* Victor Eugene Flango, Creating Family Friendly Courts: Lessons from Two Oregon Counties, 34 FAM. L.Q. 115, 120 (Spring 2000).

[92] *See* Schepard & Bozzomo, *supra* note 54 at 345.

[93] *See generally*, Nancy Ver Steegh, Yes, No, and Maybe: Informed Decision Making About Divorce Mediation in the Presence of Domestic Violence, 9 WM. & Mary J. Women & L. 145, 147 n.2 (2003) ("Compare Carrie-Anne Tondo, et al., Mediation Trends, 39 Fam. Ct. Rev. 431 (2001) (arguing that mediation is never appropriate), with Penelope E. Bryan, Reclaiming Professionalism: The Lawyer's Role in Divorce Mediation, 28 Fam. L. Q. 177, 203–05 (1994)"); Aimee Davis, *Mediating Cases Involving Domestic Violence: Solution or Setback?*, 8 Cardozo J. Conflict Resol. 253, 268 (2006); Leigh Goodmark, *Law is the Answer? Do We Know That for Sure*?: Questioning the Efficacy of Legal Interventions for Battered Women, 23 ST. LOUIS U. PUB. L. REV. 7, 11 (2004); Laurie S. Kohn, *What's So Funny About Peace, Love, and Understanding? Restorative Justice as a New Paradigm for Domestic Violence Intervention*, 40 Seton Hall l. Rev. 517, 527 (2010); Tom Lininger, *Bearing the Cross*, 74 Fordham L. Rev. 1353, 1361 (2005).

[94] Barbara A. Babb, *An Interdisciplinary Approach to Family Law Jurisprudence: Application of an Ecological and Therapeutic Perspective*, 72 Ind. L.J. 775, 803 n.179 (1997).

[95] 545 U.S. 748, 772.

[96] *Id.* at 780 n.8 *citing* Sack, Battered Women and the State: The Struggle for the Future of Domestic Violence Policy, 2004 Wis. L. Rev. 1657.

[97] Deborah J. Chase, *Pro Se Justice And Unified Family Courts*, 37 FAM. L.Q. 403 (2003) *citing* Anne H. Geraghty & Wallace J. Mlyniec, *Unified Family Courts: Tempering Enthusiasm with Caution*, 40 FAM. CT. R. 435 (2002).

commentators have also argued that the rights of offenders as well as victims may be compromised. These arguments are largely based upon a possible denial of due process[98] and the need to preserve the rights of offenders. This has been addressed in part by some courts that require domestic violence cases which proceed to trial to be placed on the criminal court calendar.[99] More generally, some have argued that handing domestic violence either in a UFC or a specialized court should be discouraged because of the benefits of a pluralist court system.[100] The *Gonzales* case makes it clear there remains a need for law reform and otherwise determine how best to handle domestic violence issues. It does not yet appear that the case has been made for the uniform adoption of domestic violence problem-solving courts as currently proposed.[101]

Along with the research that Nancy Wolff suggests is necessary, empirical legal research is needed to evaluate the establishment of problem-solving courts for domestic violence cases. Are the victims experiencing more safety? Does a power imbalance continue to exist? How can we determine whether the use of various Therapeutic Jurisprudence techniques is effective?[102]

Although the IACHR decision in the *Gonzales* case is nonbinding, some guidance may be found in the IACHR ruling which sets forth comprehensive recommendations for changes to U.S. law and policy pertaining to domestic violence. They include the recommendation that the United States:

> [C]ontinue adopting public policies and institutional programs aimed at restructuring the stereotypes of domestic violence victims, and to promote the eradication of discriminatory socio-cultural patterns that impede women and children's full protection from domestic violence acts, including programs to train public officials in all branches of the administration of justice and police, and comprehensive prevention programs.[103]

In view of the fact that it was the result of feminist efforts that domestic violence claims became recognized in the courts and law enforcement systems, perhaps one

---

[98] *See, e.g.*, Gloria Danziger, *Delinquency Jurisdiction in a Unified Family Court: Balancing Intervention, Prevention, and Adjudication,* 37 FAM. L.Q. 381, 394–397 (2003) (discussing the role of the judge and due process in unified family court) *citing* Anne H. Geraghty & Wallace J. Mlyniec, *Unified Family Courts: Tempering Enthusiasm with Caution*, 40 FAM. CT. REV. 435, 437 (2002).

[99] *See, e.g.*, Minnesota Judicial Branch, Fourth District, *Problem-Solving & Specialty Courts, Domestic Violence Court*, http://www.mncourts.gov/district/4/?page=2004.

[100] *See generally*, Elizabeth L. MacDowell, When Courts Collide: Integrated Domestic Violence Courts and Court Pluralism, 20 Tex. J. Women & L. 95 (2010–2011); Tamar M. Meekins, *Specialized Justice: "The Over-Emergence of Specialty Courts and the Threat of a New Criminal Defense Paradigm*", 40 Suffolk U. L. Rev. 1, 6–7(2006).

[101] *See generally*, Samantha Moore, Two decades of specialized domestic violence courts: A review of the literature 2, New York, NY: Center for Court Innovation (November 2009) (noting that domestic violence courts lack an established set of principles).

[102] *See e.g.*, Steve Leben, *Book Review*, 26 Justice System Journal 109 (reviewing Judging in a Therapeutic Key: Therapeutic Jurisprudence and the Courts, Bruce J. Winick and David B. Wexler., eds. (2003)) (noting that the book lacks "data to support the effectiveness of TJ over alternative procedures and concepts, as well as discussion of several conceptual challenges to TJ"). Available at http://www.ncsconline.org/wc/publications/kis_prosoljudgingjsjv26no1.pdf.

[103] Lenahan Final Report, *supra* note 1 at Para. 201.

of the most essential questions for assessing the effectiveness of problem-solving courts to address domestic violence is to view it from a feminist perspective and as Katherine Bartlett suggests: "Ask the woman question." As she describes it, "[i]n law, asking the woman question means examining how the law fails to take into account the experiences and values that seem more typical of women than of men, for whatever reason, or how existing legal standards and concepts might disadvantage women."[104] Therefore, as we assess the Babb and Wolff proposals, we must ask and assess whether the use of Therapeutic Jurisprudence to structure unified family courts or special domestic violence courts disadvantage women in their attempts to obtain justice.

[104] Katharine T. Bartlett, Feminist Legal Methods, 103 Harv. L. Rev. 829, 837 (1990). *See also* Katharine T. Bartlett, Gender and Law: Theory, Doctrine, Commentary 634 (1993) (a feminist analysis "take[s] greater account of how legal rules often invisibly represent the partial perspectives of those who are dominant in society and ignore the perspectives of others").

Part III
Mental Health Courts, Global and Philosophic View of Problem Solving Courts

Chapter 8
Mental Health Courts May Work, But Does It Matter If They Do?

John Petrila

Introduction

Mental health courts (MHC) have become increasingly popular in the last 15 years. They first appeared in contemporary form in 1997, in Broward County, Florida and Marion County, Indiana (Petrila and Redlich 2008). Today, there are more than 250 MHCs. Most are adult courts, but juvenile MHCs have emerged as well (Cocozza and Shufelt 2006). The courts were created to help address the needs of the growing number of people with mental illnesses entering the criminal justice system. Based philosophically on therapeutic justice (Winick and Wexler 2003), the courts are nonadversarial in nature and attempt to meet social and treatment needs that often go beyond judicial notice in traditional criminal proceedings. Their characteristics are described in more detail in Chap 12.

Like many policy innovations, MHCs emerged and began proliferating without any evidence that they worked (Redlich et al. 2006). As courts were created, single site studies of a number of jurisdictions emerged suggesting that MHCs improved access to services, reduced recidivism, led to better mental health outcomes, and did so in an economically efficient manner (for an excellent overview of this research, see Almquist and Dodd 2009; also Chap. 9).

More recently, results are becoming available from the first multisite MHC study (Steadman et al. 2011; also Chap. 9). The findings are consistent with those of the single-site studies. In the 18-month period following enrollment in the MHC, the MHC group had fewer arrests, a lower annualized arrest rate and fewer days incarcerated than the treatment as usual group, that is, individuals who would have been eligible for the MHC but who were neither referred nor admitted to the MHC.

These results, from both single site and the multisite study, are encouraging. While the evidence that MHCs "work" may not be as robust as that for drug courts (see Chap. 1 for a discussion of the effectiveness of drug courts, including both

J. Petrila (✉)
College of Public Health, Department of Health Policy & Management, CPH 2139
13201 Bruce Downs Blvd
University of South Florida
Tampa, FL 33612 USA
e-mail: jpetril1@health.usf.edu

R. L. Wiener, E. M. Brank (eds.), *Problem Solving Courts*,
DOI 10.1007/978-1-4614-7403-6_8, © Springer Science+Business Media, LLC 2013

strengths and weaknesses), the fact that the evidence from these disparate studies points in the same direction suggests that MHCs *can* meet goals of improved public safety and better access to treatment. However, simply because something works does not mean that it should be sustained. The rest of this chapter is devoted to a discussion of whether it matters that MHCs appear to work. While I conclude that the courts' success matters in some essential ways, the courts also present substantive and procedural issues that warrant continuing examination, and the chapter concludes with a discussion of the most important of these.

Does it Matter Whether the Courts "Work"?

The available evidence suggests that MHCs can be successful in important ways. However, an initiative should not necessarily be sustained simply because it is successful. It is also important to ask whether the success of MHCs matters in the larger context of developments in the criminal justice system. There are at least three arguments that MHCs do not matter in this larger sense, including diminishing judicial budgets, the boutique nature of MHCs, and the fact that other forms of diversion may reach people much more quickly. Each of these arguments is discussed in turn.

The Impact of Greatly Reduced Judicial Budgets

The "great recession" has left few public or private entities in the United States untouched. The courts have been no exception. A newspaper story in 2010 reported that courtroom closings and layoffs had become routine in many states (Welch 2010). In some states, the cuts have been extraordinarily deep. For example, in California, state general revenue funding for the judicial system has been reduced by more than 30 % since 2008, with the 2011 budget eliminating $ 350 million from an overall budget of $ 3.5 billion (Dolan and Kim 2011; see also, Legislative Analyst's Office 2012; Moyer 2012). Many legal commentators have discussed the dilemmas created for judicial systems implementing these reductions (Shepard 2011; Dooley 2008/2009; White 2009). Justice Dooley of the Vermont Supreme Court put it this way:

> ...we can cut our expenditures for alternative dispute resolution, particularly mediation, and guardian ad litem support, but cutting the former will mean a significant increase in caseloads and cutting the latter will significantly impair the quality of parental rights and responsibility decisions, perhaps our most important determinations (Dooley 2008/2009; p. 35).

As Justice Dooley suggests, reductions in judicial budgets have an impact on programs, and such cuts may affect specialty courts in some jurisdictions. For example, as a result of California's fiscal situation, Governor Jerry Brown vetoed legislation that would have encouraged superior courts to create veterans' courts (Glantz

2011). Nevada has considered closing its MHCs (Doughman 2011) as did Michigan (Weatherhead 2009). Therapeutic and other specialty courts exist in part to achieve judicial efficiencies in managing certain types of cases (Petrila 2003). MHCs appear to achieve those efficiencies for a small group of cases involving mental illnesses. However, as criminal and civil dockets continue to grow while the number of available court personnel diminishes, court systems may be increasingly unwilling to tolerate the allocation of resources necessary to administer a specialty court for a comparative handful of people.

At the same time, if evaluations can show that the courts are cost-effective (particularly within the confines of the criminal justice system), then advocates for MHCs might be able to use this as an argument to maintain such courts even in the face of the ongoing erosion of financial support to many state judicial systems. This makes the RAND Institute study of the Allegheny MHC worth noting, given that the study concludes that the Allegheny court is cost-efficient, primarily because reduced jail expenditures offset increased treatment costs incurred because of the court's success in gaining access to services for enrollees (Ridgely et al. 2007).

Mental Health Courts are Boutique Courts That Have Little Impact on Overall Need

Mental health court caseloads are usually not very large. Juvenile MHC caseloads reportedly range from fewer than 10 to 75 (OJJDP 2011), a handful of cases given that juvenile courts processed approximately 1.5 million cases in 2009 (OJJDP 2012). Caseloads in adult MHCs tend to fall into the same range and may be limited for a number of reasons, for example, staff capacity (Almquist and Dodd 2009). Many MHCs do not have independent budgets for a judge, prosecutor, or defense attorney and therefore rely on "donations" from those offices, effectively limiting the amount of time that can be devoted to the MHC docket. In addition, if a caseworker is assigned to a court, for example by a local treatment provider, the court docket can be limited by the number of cases that can be handled by the caseworker.

The most recent study of the prevalence of serious mental illnesses among jailed individuals found that 14.5 % of males and 31 % of females had a serious mental illness, defined as major depressive disorder, depressive disorder not otherwise specified, bipolar disorder, and various psychotic disorders such as schizophrenia spectrum disorder, schizoaffective disorder, and delusional disorder (Steadman et al. 2009). Given the 13 million annual jail admissions in 2007, the authors concluded that more than 2 million (2,161,705) individuals with serious mental illnesses were booked into jail in a year. There are now approximately 250 MHCs in the United States (Steadman et al. 2011). If one assumes that all MHCs have active caseloads of 100 clients (in fact, most have smaller caseloads) that would mean that 25,000 people would be enrolled at any one time. While this is not an insignificant number, it is only 0.01 % of people booked into jail with serious mental illnesses. Therefore, it is difficult to argue that MHCs are reaching a high percentage of people who might arguably meet their eligibility criteria. On the one hand, this might argue for expanding court caseloads; on the other hand, in many jurisdictions that rely on borrowed time from a judge and others, this will not be a realistic option.

Other Diversion Efforts Work More Quickly Than Mental Health Courts

Many jurisdictions have initiated programs to divert people with mental illnesses from the criminal justice system. Some programs are designed to divert people prior to arrest and booking, while others divert after arrest. In 1992, a national survey estimated that 52 United States jails had diversion programs, but by 2005 that number had grown to more than 300 (Steadman and Naples 2005). There is some evidence that cohorts of individuals diverted through prebooking programs differ in some respects from those diverted postbooking, with those in prebooking programs more educated, more involved with employment, and generally more satisfied with their lives than those in postbooking (Lattimore et al. 2003). While a number of important research questions have gone unaddressed, such as the systemic impact of diversion programs (Ryan et al. 2010), various studies have reported favorable outcomes for diversion programs in access to service, reduced use of jail, and improved access to entitlements (Case et al. 2009; Tyuse 2005).

While MHCs may achieve similar outcomes, research suggests that at least in some jurisdictions a considerable period of time elapses before an arrestee actually is accepted into the court. The Council of State Governments has created a guide titled *Essential Elements of a Mental Health Court* (Thompson et al. 2008). This guide (Element 3) describes as essential that the MHC process identify, refer and accept clients "as quickly as possible". This is consistent with one of the primary goals of diversion programs generally (Steadman et al. 1995). However, in the most thorough study of the "quickness in processing" issue to date, Redlich et al. found that mental health court clients had significantly increased median and mean times from referral to admission to the court. In one comparison of MHC clients with offenders with mental illness *not* referred to MHC, median time elapsed for MHC clients was 70 days versus 37 days for those processed in the ordinary manner. They conclude "Thus, we did not find diversion to be swift; indeed, we found diversion to take about twice as long in comparison to traditional processing of offenders with mental illness from the same jurisdictions" (Redlich et al. 2012).

In short, one may argue that it is not enough that MHCs appear to "work". Rather, their apparent success obscures their comparatively marginal impact on the lives of most people with mental illnesses in the criminal justice system, their boutique status, and the fact that at least some courts prolong the exposure of their clients to the criminal justice system, particularly in the case of misdemeanor courts.

Given these issues, are MHCs worth preserving? In my opinion, they are, for three primary reasons.

Mental Health Court Processes Provide the Individual with Voice and a Sense of Fairness Largely Missing From the Criminal Justice System

The impact of large caseloads on the administration of justice is not a new issue (Levin 1975). However, for a variety of reasons, both federal and state court caseloads have expanded dramatically in the last three decades (for a review, see Diamond and Bina 2004). More than 90 % of all criminal adjudications in US courts are by plea bargain (Fisher 2003). In many instances, plea bargaining is a cursory process with little regard for the defendant's individual issues and constitutional rights beyond surface adherence to constitutional norms (Bowers 2007). More broadly, despite constitutional guarantees of due process, legal scholars have concluded that for many, especially those charged with low-level offenses, "the experience of being arrested, incarcerated, and processed through pretrial court procedures is the primary form of punishment administered by the lower criminal courts, rendering the ultimate adjudication and sentencing essentially irrelevant" (Blackwell and Cunningham 2004, p. 61, discussing Feely 1992).

Mental health courts, in contrast, put the individual at the center of the court process. In contrast to the experience of most arrestees, an individual who potentially meets MHC eligibility standards typically may be referred for screening soon after arrest. In addition, MHC judges generally take pains to involve the defendant in the court process, rather than relying on defense or prosecution counsel. This is based on the notion of "procedural justice", which asserts that the legal decision-making process and the interpersonal treatment of the defendant in that process are essential to achieve therapeutic outcomes and that a defendant who believes she has voice in a fair process is more likely to agree to treatment and other court-ordered conditions (Tyler and Blader 2003). At least two studies examining the issue of procedural justice in an MHC concluded that defendants in those courts in fact reported that they had "voice" in decision making (Wales et al. 2010; Poythress et al. 2002). These same studies found that defendants reported low levels of perceived coercion. Poythress et al. also found that the procedural justice and perceived coercion scores of the MHC clients were significantly lower than item scores from a matched comparison group whose cases were adjudicated by a traditional criminal court. In addition, in contrast to traditional court, the defendant spoke much more frequently than either defense or state lawyer, providing literal voice in a venue in which the defendant is more often silent except for responses to the judge when entering a plea (Boothroyd et al. 2003).

One reason MHCs have remained boutique courts is their small caseloads. However, those small caseloads provide an opportunity for the judge to engage in an ongoing dialogue with the defendant. From the results available to date, that dialogue appears to have a positive effect on the defendant's perception of the court proceeding, something that at least in theory may make the individual more receptive to treatment because of a sense of greater control over his or her life (Tyler 2005).

Mental Health Court Processes are Consistent with Recovery and Self-determination Principles at the Heart of Mental Health Treatment

"Recovery" from mental illness has become the cornerstone of contemporary mental health treatment. The President's New Freedom Commission, in its final report, wrote

> First, services and treatment must be consumer and family center, geared to give consumers real and meaningful choices about treatment options and providers... Second, care must focus on increasing consumers' ability to successfully cope with life's challenges, on facilitating recovery, and on building resilience—not just managing symptoms (President's New Freedom Commission 2003, p. 5).

This is a statement of two principles, the first that care must be patient centered, the second that recovery is the essential goal, building on the patient's strengths and helping to ameliorate and protect against deficits caused by the illness.

As discussed above, one of the things that MHCs appear to do best is to put the defendant at the center of the court process. The dialogue between court and defendant, the lack of formal lawyering, and the continuing discussion between judge and defendant through status hearings, all emphasize the defendant's role in taking control of his or her life. This "defendant-centered" style of judging also attempts to maximize autonomy, within limits established by the court, and a sense of control is essential to recovery-oriented treatment. As one commentator recently wrote,

> A central tenet of the recovery model is that empowerment of the user is important in achieving good outcome in serious mental illness. To understand why this may be so, it is important to appreciate that people with mental illness may feel disempowered, not only as a result of involuntary confinement or paternalistic treatment, but also by their own acceptance of the stereotype of a person with mental illness... those who accept that they are mentally ill and have a sense of mastery over their lives (an internal locus of control) have the best outcomes (Warner 2010, p. 8).

Many individuals in the criminal justice system are literally silent; their voices simply not heard other than in the most perfunctory manner from the beginning to the end of the criminal justice process (Natapoff 2005). One advocate of restorative justice asserts that the status quo in criminal justice "silences, marginalises, and disempowers" the victim, offender, and surrounding community (Barton 2000).

Mental health courts attempt to address these issues. In doing so, they align themselves with the central philosophy of mental health treatment. While MHCs may impose limits on individual autonomy case disposition, they attempt to create outcomes that maximize the defendant's autonomy and control in ways quite at variance with ordinary criminal procedure while fitting comfortably within the dominant treatment paradigm. There is insufficient empirical evidence to demonstrate that a commitment to procedural justice causes "better" outcomes (Hollander-Blumoff 2011) but recovery-oriented treatment can have a salutary effect on the individual (President's New Freedom Commission 2003). Therefore, efforts to bring a recovery model to bear in therapeutically oriented legal proceedings appear worth pursuing, recognizing that this is a hypothesis about the potential impact of such proceedings that warrants further testing.

Mental Health Courts and Other Therapeutic Courts Keep a Rehabilitative Model Alive in a Punitive Era

The United States criminal justice and juvenile justice systems have become increasingly punitive and retributive in the last 30 years. In the juvenile system, waiver to adult court has become easier, children are often tried as adults, and the process has become more adversarial in response. In the adult system, prosecutorial discretion has been expanded, judicial discretion at sentencing has been reduced through the use of sentencing guidelines, and the number of people arrested and incarcerated has increased dramatically.

The numbers are startling in many respects. Between 1980 and 2003, the number of individuals convicted for drug offenses increased by 1,100 %; there were 41,000 incarcerated drug offenders in 1980 and 493,800 in 2003 (Tonry, 1996). In 2007, 751 people from every 100,000 were in jail or prisons in the United States, dwarfing rates in other countries; Russia was second with 627 incarcerated for every 100,000 while England incarcerated 151, Germany 88, and Japan 62. One of every 100 adults in the United States was incarcerated (Tonry 2008).

These punitive policies were abetted by the belief among academicians and policy makers that criminals had changed and that correctional rehabilitative policies simply did not work. Dilulio (1995) coined the term "super-predator" as a descriptor for what he believed were intrinsically dangerous, violent youth whose growing numbers (in his view) were exposing communities to increasing risk of violence. A philosophic commitment to rehabilitation as a core goal of correctional policy gave way to changing social attitudes, a spike in violent crime, and empirical research suggesting that rehabilitation did not reduce future offending (for a review see Cullen and Gendreau 2000).

Drug courts developed in response to the impact of the "war on drugs" and the exponential growth of drug-related cases. They exist in large part "to re-institutionalize the penological goals of diversion and rehabilitation" (Miller 2004, p. 1481). MHCs developed in part for the same reasons. While therapeutic courts initially served as a counter-weight to generally punitive national and state correctional policies, their commitment to rehabilitation may become more congruent with emerging criminal justice policies. The economic duress to state budgets caused in no small measure by punitive policies is now forcing states and the federal government to assess the negative impact of a nearly exclusive reliance on incarceration and arrest (though as noted above, these economic stressors have cut deeply into judicial budgets in some jurisdictions potentially eroding support for "boutique" courts). Many states have taken steps to reduce their correctional budgets and the number of people who are incarcerated; these efforts have led to an examination of diversion and community supervision strategies as a partial remedy (Kircchoff 2010). MHCs, while not yet attaining the mainstream status of drug courts, have been important in bringing rehabilitative ideals to bear for a very disenfranchised group of defendants. They have been able to do this in part because of their small caseloads and commitment to procedural justice; in courts with overcrowded dockets where time per case is at a premium, "voice" and fashioning extralegal outcomes for more than a few defendants may be virtually impossible. MHCs, in this sense, provide an alternative manner of judging that is more individualized, more responsive to individual defendant needs, and more likely to go beyond traditional judicial bounds in case disposition.

The Future of Mental Health Courts: The Case for Changed Practice

Mental health courts have accomplished a good deal beyond the number adjudicated cases. They have provided voice to defendants in a judicial system that rarely does so, aligned themselves with the core principle of recovery, and kept alive a commitment to rehabilitation in an era devoted primarily to punishment. Given these accomplishments, what improvements might MHCs make consistent with these ideals? One is jurisdictional, a second procedural, and a third, philosophical.

Mental Health Courts Should Rarely If Ever Assume Jurisdiction Over Misdemeanor Cases

The Bazelon Center has recommended that MHCs be reserved for cases in which the person faces significant jail or prison time and then only as part of broader system reform (Bazelon Center, http://www.bazelon.org/Where-We-Stand/Access-to-Services/Diversion-from-Incarceration-and-Reentry-/Mental-Health-Courts.aspx), recommendations that appear increasingly sound. Early MHCs were almost exclusively misdemeanor courts (Griffin et al. 2002). However, since then, many new courts have adopted felony or mixed misdemeanor/felony dockets (Redlich et al. 2005).

It is understandable that the first generation of MHCs were misdemeanor courts. They were designed to divert defendants with mental illnesses whose frequent arrests were often for public nuisance misdemeanors. In addition, MHCs were experiments and the misdemeanor cases were considered to be safer than felony cases in terms of public risk. Today, however, there is enough evidence about MHCs to suggest that a focus on misdemeanor cases is problematic for several reasons.

First, as Redlich et al. (2012) illustrate, the MHCs they examined often did not provide quick case processing. Rather, individuals referred to MHCs often experienced delays in case adjudication that exceeded traditional court processing. Individuals with mental illnesses already often are jailed on average 3 or 4 times longer than other arrestees. As noted earlier, subjecting such individuals to even longer delays in court processing runs counter to the spirit of diversion, and may leave the defendant in a judicial and clinical limbo.

Second, other forms of diversion may work much more quickly for individuals at risk for misdemeanor arrest. For example, Lee County Florida has created a prebooking triage center, designed to offer law enforcement a speedy alternative to arrest and booking. From April 2008 through April 2010, police brought 684 individuals voluntarily to the triage center, where they received a place to sleep and referrals to treatment and human services providers (Haynes et al. 2011). For the individuals who completed the program, recidivism and time spent in jail were reduced and the intervening law enforcement officers reported that in more than ½ of the cases, they would have arrested the person had the triage center not been available. In addition, law enforcement spent less than 10 min in more than 95 % of the cases in dropping the person at the triage center. This is not to suggest that a prebooking triage center makes sense for every community. However, it does suggest that other diversion strategies may be more effective at keeping cases out of the criminal justice system, maximizing time spent by law enforcement on their primary responsibilities, and enabling individuals with mental illnesses to avoid long waiting periods while their cases are processed by the judicial system.

Mental Health Courts Can Become More Recovery-Oriented by Re-Examining Procedural Issues

Mental health courts are aligned to important values in treatment based on recovery, in their emphasis on defendant voice and placing the defendant at the center of court process. At the same time, the courts operate in ways that may impede the defendant's recovery. This is true particularly of the reliance on status hearings.

One of the "essential elements" of an MHC is monitoring adherence to court requirements (Thompson et al. 2008; Essential Element 9). Additionally, one way that therapeutic courts routinely monitor adherence is through status hearings. At a status hearing, the judge reviews the individual's progress or lack of progress with the plan developed by the MHC team. Courts hold status hearings with varying degrees of frequency, some as often as weekly initially. These hearings invariably require the defendant's presence, and this requirement may impose significant barriers to recovery.

Employment is an essential part of recovery. It is important not only because it provides wages. Self-reports by people with serious mental illnesses also emphasize that working can provide coping strategies for psychiatric symptoms, foster self-esteem and autonomy, and hasten the recovery process (Dunn et al. 2008). In the current recession, finding employment is difficult for anyone. Unemployment among people with serious mental illnesses historically runs to 90 % and higher (Frese 2009). One difficulty with status hearings is that the requirement that the individual appear personally before the court on a regular basis may create an additional, significant barrier to holding a job. The person has to request time off (which may not be available to a new employee), presumably reveal why the time is necessary, and in doing so may have to reveal the fact that he or she is under the continuing supervision of a criminal court and that one of the reasons is ongoing treatment for mental illness.

Neither disclosure will carry favor with most employers, and absence from work for court appearances will reduce income as well.

There is nothing objectionable about any court wishing to monitor compliance with its conditions. However, the requirement of routine physical presence by the defendant at status hearings may create significant barriers to an essential element of recovery, which is employment. To date, no one has systematically studied the impact of status hearings on outcomes in MHCs. However, in a very well-designed, randomized study, Marlowe et al. found that the frequency of contact between defendant and judge was *not* associated with better outcomes (Marlowe et al. 2005). Judges in therapeutic courts often consider that their interaction with the defendant is crucial to the success of the court, that the relationship formed between judge and defendant is essentially therapeutic. However, it is fair to consider whether less frequent hearings, videoconferencing (used increasingly in judicial proceedings), phone calls, or reports from probation officers or clinicians can substitute for the routine status hearing that is a feature of many MHCs.

Mental health courts run a risk of becoming overly paternalistic

Treatment courts are based on principles of therapeutic justice and restorative justice. The judge, by definition, assumes a more active role, and defense counsel assumes a team-oriented rather than adversarial role. Justice Kaye, when Chief of the New York Court of Appeals, put it most clearly when she wrote that in therapeutic courts

> the lawyers also have new roles. The prosecution and defense are not sparring champions, they are members of a team with a common goal: Getting the defendant off drugs. When this goal is attained, everyone wins. Defendants win dismissal of their charges... the public wins safer streets and reduced recidivism (Kaye 1998, p. 5).

The assumption that all parties in a therapeutic court are operating with benevolent motives is a fair one. The point, after all, is to place the person in treatment, provide support necessary to achieve good clinical outcomes, and break the cycle of repeated arrests.

However, it is worth asking if this has a cost, whether certain elements of the process that seem positive may have negative impact in some situations. For example, I have noted above that the frequent interactions between judge and defendant are a means of giving the individual "voice" and that MHC defendants report very low levels of perceived coercion and report that they believe the proceedings are fair and that they are given voice. At the same time, there is another view. A public defender who appears frequently in therapeutic courts writes

> There is frequent interaction between the judge and the defendant in specialty courts, since hearings are scheduled so the judge may determine the effectiveness of the defendant's treatment or the extent of compliance with the imposed conditions. The judge often inquires of the defendant in open court about particular aspects of the defendant's life and compliance with treatment, including asking questions that, if truthfully answered, may inculpate the defendant in criminal activity. In other circumstances, the judge may make statements to

> the defendant which tend to shame, coerce, chastise, or belittle the defendant for a certain behavior. At times, the judge will publicly chastise the defendant, in very harsh tones, for his or her failure to move through the treatment process or to follow through with other aspects of the program. The defense attorney is expected to stand idly by while this interaction takes place (Meekins 2006/2007).

Others argue that therapeutic courts lack true legitimacy, in part because they erode the role of defense counsel and in part, because coercion is often intertwined with treatment (Casey 2004; Miller 2004). Others suggest that in the interest of minimizing coercion, therapeutic courts should move from "problem-solving" to identifying the individual's capacity and interest in change and supporting self-efficacy (King 2010).

These issues get at the heart of the potential tension between honoring the defendant's due process rights and acting in a therapeutic manner. The issue is particularly acute for defense counsel, who as Meekins notes above may be "standing idly" in open court while the judge causes the defendant to disclose private matters regarding mental health status and treatment, potentially incriminate herself, and listen to public criticism about failure to comply with the court's directives. This ethical conflict, of course, is not new. It arose as mental health law emerged, with lawyers struggling in involuntary civil commitment hearings over whether to adopt an adversarial role or act in what he or she perceived was the client's interest (Ferris 2008). This is not to say that MHCs create negative outcomes, nor is it to say that the therapeutic, less adversarial approach should be abandoned in favor of restoring a traditional approach that did little good for many people with serious mental illnesses. However, benevolent philosophies and practices can give way to paternalism and the exercise of more control than necessary. For this reason, it is important to keep these issues in the forefront as MHCs expand in both the adult and juvenile justice systems. In the end, MHCs are still criminal courts and so due process rights cannot simply be abandoned. Having said that, it is difficult to say as a practical matter how such rights can best be preserved in a therapeutic court. Minimally, as Professor Redlich argues (see Chapter 9), it suggests that it is extremely important to assure that the defendant is well and truly informed about options at each point in the process, from initial referral for eligibility screening, to the decision to accept admission to the MHC, to disposition. This is particularly true when the time under supervision of the MHC will significantly exceed the time the person would be involved with the criminal justice system after a traditional disposition, for example in misdemeanor cases.

Summary

Mental health courts appear to "work" in creating access to service and in reducing recidivism compared to traditional criminal courts, at least based on the handful of courts that have been examined to date. MHCs also align themselves in important ways with current treatment philosophies, and do their share in keeping a rehabilitative focus alive in a criminal justice system that has been primarily punitive for more than three decades. At the same time, MHC judges and team members should continue to examine whether certain practices may impede recovery and take care *not* to assume that everything such a court does has merit because it is based on therapeutic intentions. Finally, policy makers and community leaders should always ask whether there are alternative strategies for addressing the needs of individuals with mental illnesses involved or at risk of becoming involved with the criminal justice system, primarily by examining diversion strategies that occur *prior* to formal court involvement. This is particularly the case for individuals who might be charged with misdemeanors.

References

Almquist, L., & Dodd, E. (2009). *Mental health courts: A guide to research-informed policy and practice*. New York: Council of State Governments Justice Center. http://www.consensusproject.org/jc_publications/mental-health-courts-a-guide-to-research-informed-policy-and-practice/Mental_Health_Court_Research_Guide.pdf.

Blackwell, B., & Cunningham, C. (2004). Taking the punishment out of the process: From substantive criminal justice through procedural justice to restorative justice. *Law and Contemporary Justice, 67,* 59–86.

Barton, C. (2000). Restorative justice empowerment. *Australian Journal of Professional and Applied Ethics, 2,* 16–31.

Boothroyd, R., Poythress, N., McGaha, A., & Petrila, J. (2003). The Broward mental health court: Process, outcomes, and service utilization. *International Journal of Law and Psychiatry, 26,* 55–71.

Bowers, J. (2007). Grassroots plea bargaining. *Marquette Law Review, 91,* 85.

Case, B., Steadman, H., Dupuis, S., & Morris, L. (2009). Who succeeds in jail diversion programs for persons with mental illness? A multi-site study. *Behavioral Sciences and the Law, 27,* 661–674.

Casey, T. (2004). When good intentions are not enough: Problem-solving courts and the impending crisis of legitimacy. *Southern Methodist University Law Review, 57,* 1459–1519.

Cocozza, J., & Shufelt, J. (2006). Juvenile mental health courts: An emerging strategy. *National Center for Mental Health and Juvenile Justice: Research and program brief.* Available at http://www.ncmhjj.com/pdfs/publications/JuvenileMentalHealthCourts.pdf.

Cullen, F. T., & Gendreau, P. (2000). Assessing correctional rehabilitation: Policy, practice, and prospects. *Criminal Justice, 3,* 109–174.

Diamond, S., & Bina, J. (2004). Puzzles about supply-side explanations for vanishing trials: A new look at fundamentals. *Journal of Empirical Legal Studies, 1,* 637–658.

Dilulio, J. (27. Nov 1995). The coming of the super-predator. *Weekly Standard,* 23–28.

Dolan, M., & Kim, V. (20 July 2011). Budget cuts to worsen California court delays, officials say. *Los Angeles Times.*

Dooley, J. (2008/2009). Judicial funding in times of budget crisis. *Vermont Bar Journal, 34,* 34–36.

Doughman, A. (1. Feb 2011). Long-term costs to state could outweigh budget savings in mental health funding. *Nevada News Bureau.*

Dunn, E., Wewiorski, N., & Rogers, E. (2008). The meaning and importance of employment to people in recovery from serious mental illness: Results of a qualitative study. *Journal of Psychiatric Rehabilitation, 32,* 59–62.

Feely, M. (1992). The process is the punishment: Handling cases in a lower criminal court (2nd edition). New York: Russell Sage Foundation.

Ferris, C. E. (2008). The search for due process in civil commitment hearings: How procedural realities have altered substantive standards. *Vanderbilt Law Review, 61,* 3–983.

Fisher, G. (2003). Dickering for justice: Power, interests, and the plea bargaining juggernaut. Stanford: Stanford University Press.
Frese, F. (2009). Coming out of the shadows. *Health Affairs, 28,* 880–886.
Glantz, A. (8. Aug 2011). Brown nixes special veterans' courts, citing costs. *The Bay Citizen.*
Griffin, P., Steadman, H., & Petrila, J. (2002). The use of criminal charges and sanctions in mental health courts. *Psychiatric Services, 53,* 1285–1289.
Haynes, D., Petrila, J., Arnall, A., & Pateidl, E. (2011). Lee County Triage Center; phase II report. The Criminal Justice, Mental Health, and Substance Abuse Technical Assistance Center. Tampa, FL: University of South Florida, Louie de la Parte Florida Mental Health Institute, Mental Health Law & Policy.
Hollander-Blumoff, R. (2011). The psychology of procedural justice in the federal courts. *Hastings Law Journal, 63,* 127–178.
Kaye, J. (1998). Lawyering for a new age. *Fordham Law Review, 67,* 1–12.
King, M. (2010). Should problem solving courts be solution-focused courts? *Monash University Faculty of Law Legal Research Paper No. 2010/03.* Available at http://papers.ssrn.com/sol3/papers.cfm?abstract_id – 1725022.
Kircchoff, S. (2010). *Economic impacts of prison growth.* Washington DC: Congressional Research Service (available at http://www.fas.org/sgp/crs/misc/R41177.pdf).
Lattimore, P., Broner, N., Sherman, R., Frisman, L., & Shafer, M. (2003). A comparison of prebooking and postbooking diversion programs for mentally ill substance-using individuals with justice involvement. *Journal of Contemporary Criminal Justice, 19,* 30–64.
Legislative Analyst's Office. (2012). *The 2012–12 Budget: Managing Ongoing Reductions to the Judicial Branch.* Sacramento: Legislative Analyst's Office (available at http://www.lao.ca.gov/analysis/2012/crim_justice/managing-ongoing-reductions-041312.pdf).
Levin, M. A. (1975). Delay in five criminal courts. *The Journal of Legal Studies, 4,* 83–131.
Office of Juvenile Justice and Delinquency Prevention. (2011). OJJDP model programs guide: Mental health court. Available at http://www.ojjdp.gov/mpg/progTypesMentalHealthCourt.aspx.
Marlowe, D., Festinger, D., Dugosh, K., & Lee, P. (2005). Are judicial status hearings a "key component" of drug court? Six and twelve month outcomes. *Drug and Alcohol Dependence, 79,* 145–155.
Meekins, T. (2006/2007). "Specialized justice": The over-emergence of specialty courts and the threat of a new criminal defense paradigm. *Suffolk University Law Review, 40,* 1–59.
Miller, E. (2004). Embracing addiction: Drug courts and the false promise of judicial interventionism. *Ohio State Law Journal, 65,* 1479–1576.
Moyer, B. (2012). Automatic cuts would cripple the courts. Federal Bar association: *Washington Watch,* March 2012. Available at http://fedbar.org/Advocacy/Washington-Watch/WW-Archives/2012/March-2012-Automatic-Cuts-Would-Cripple-the-Courts.aspx.
Natapoff, A. (2005). Speechless: The silencing of criminal defendants. *New York Law Review, 80,* 1449–1504.
Office of Justice Programs, Office of Juvenile Justice and Delinquency Prevention (2012). *Juveniles in court: Delinquency cases by manner of handling, 1985–2009. Statistical Briefing Book.* Washington DC: United States Department of Justice (available at http://www.ojjdp.gov/ojstatbb/court/qa06401.asp?qaDate=2009).
Petrila, J. (2003). An introduction to special jurisdiction courts. *International Journal of Law and Psychiatry, 26,* 3–12.
Petrila, J., & Redlich, A. (2008). Mental illness and the courts: Some reflections on judges as innovators. *Court Review, 43,* 164–176.
Poythress, N., Petrila, J., McGaha, A., & Boothroyd, R. (2002). Perceived coercion and procedural justice in the Broward mental health court. *International Journal of Law and Psychiatry, 25,* 517–533.
President's New Freedom Commission (2003). *Achieving the Promise: Transforming Mental Health Care in America. Final Report.* DHHS Pub. No. SMA-03–3832. Rockville, MD.

Redlich, A., Liu, S., Steadman, H., Callahan, L., & Robbins, P. (2012). Is diversion swift? Comparing mental health court and traditional criminal processing. *Criminal Justice and Behavior, 39*(4), 420–433. Available at: http://works.bepress.com/allison_redlich/9.
Redlich, A., Steadman, H., Monahan, J., Petrila, J., & Griffin, P. (2005). The second generation of mental health courts. *Psychology, Public Policy, and Law, 11,* 527–538.
Redlich, A., Steadman, H., Monahan, J., Robbins, P., & Petrila, J. (2006). Patterns of practice in mental health courts: A national survey. *Law & Human Behavior, 30,* 347–362.
Ridgely, M. S., Greenberg, M. D., DeMartini, C., Dembosky, J. W. (2007). *Justice, treatment, and cost: An evaluation of the fiscal impact of Allegheny county mental health court.* Santa Monica: RAND Corporation.
Ryan, S., Brown, C., & Watanabe-Galloway, S. (2010). Toward successful postbooking diversion: What are the next steps? *Psychiatric Services, 61,* 469–477.
Shepard, J. (2011). Four big, dumb trends affecting state courts. *Indiana Law Review, 43,* 533–540.
Steadman, H. J., Morris, S. M., & Dennis, D. L. (1995). The diversion of mentally ill persons from jails to community-based services. *American Journal of Public Health, 85,* 1630–1635.
Steadman, H., & Naples, M. (2005). Assessing the effectiveness of jail diversion programs for persons with serious mental illness and co-occurring substance abuse disorders. *Behavioral Sciences and the Law, 23,* 163–170.
Steadman, H., Osher, F., Robbins, P., Case, B., & Samuels, S. (2009). Prevalence of serious mental illness among jail inmates. *Psychiatric Services, 60,* 761–765.
Steadman, H., Redlich, A., Callahan, L., Robbins, P., Vesselinov, R. (2011). Effect of mental health courts on arrests and jail days. *Archives of General Psychiatry, 68,* 167–172.
Thompson, M., Osher, F., & Tomasini-Joshi, D. (2008). *Improving responses to people with mental illnesses: The essential elements of a mental health court.* New York: Council of State Governments Justice Center.
Tonry, M. (2008). *Crime, punishment, and politics in comparative perspective.* Chicago: University of Chicago Press.
Tonry, M. (1996). *Malign neglect: race, crime, and punishment in America.* New York: Oxford.
Tyler, T. (Ed.). (2005). *Procedural justice Vol. 1.* New York: Ashgate.
Tyler, T., & Blader, S. L. (2003). The group engagement model: Procedural justice, social identity, and cooperative behavior. *Personalities and Social Psychology Review, 7,* 349–361.
Tyuse, S. (2005). The effectiveness of a jail diversion program in linking participants to federal entitlements and stable housing. *Californian Journal of Health Promotion, 3,* 84–98.
Weatherhead, T. (20. Feb 2009). Mental health services stressed by high demand, budget cuts. *Capital News Service.*
Wales, H., Hiday, V., & Ray, B. (2010). Procedural justice and the mental health court judge's role in reducing recidivism. *International Journal of Law and Psychiatry, 33,* 265–271.
Warner, R. (2010). Does the scientific evidence support the recovery model? *The Psychiatrist, 34,* 5–10.
Welch, W. (1. April 2010). Court budget cuts swift hand of justice. *USA Today.*
White, J. (2009). Court funding—a good first step. *Florida Bar Journal, 83,* 6.
Winick, B., & Wexler, D. (Eds.). (2003). *Judging in a therapeutic key: Therapeutic jurisprudence and the courts.* Durham: Carolina Academic Press.

Chapter 9
The Past, Present, and Future of Mental Health Courts

Allison D. Redlich

Mental health courts (MHCs) are an ever-growing popular solution to a well-documented problem—the overabundance of persons with mental illness in the criminal justice system. MHCs are but one of several types of specialty courts designed to improve the practices and effectiveness of criminal justice. The first two MHCs appeared in 1997 in Marion County, Indiana, and Broward County, Florida. In 2010, there were estimated to be more than 200 adult MHCs in the USA (as well as nearly two dozen juvenile MHCs; Cocozza and Shufelt 2006). As with any new intervention, changes associated with growth, controversy, improvement, funding, and local policies are inevitable.

Several years ago, my colleagues and I (Redlich et al. 2005, 2006) examined the characteristics of what we called first- and second-generation MHCs. Here, I revisit this work by noting continuing trends in yesterday's and today's courts, trends that may portend tomorrow's courts. First, to describe MHCs and the research that has been done on them, I use the Council of State Governments' (CSG) Ten Essential Elements of a Mental Health Court as a guiding framework (Thompson et al. 2008). Second, I forecast what the next generation of MHCs may look like on the basis of the trends, research, and ongoing controversies surrounding these specialty courts.

Yesterday's and Today's Mental Health Courts

Among those interested in MHCs, there is a saying that aptly describes the courts' tendency toward idiosyncrasy, "If you've seen one mental health court . . . you've seen one mental health court" (Council of State Governments 2008, p. 7). Nevertheless, there are several defining features of the courts. Generally, an MHC is a criminal court for offenders with mental health problems. The courts aim to divert eligible persons (typically defined by criminal charge and clinical criteria) from jail or prison into community-based mental health and substance use treatment. The ultimate goal

A. D. Redlich (✉)
State University of New York at Albany, Albany, USA
e-mail: aredlich@albany.edu

R. L. Wiener, E. M. Brank (eds.), *Problem Solving Courts*,
DOI 10.1007/978-1-4614-7403-6_9, © Springer Science+Business Media, LLC 2013

is to reduce the repeated cycling of offenders with mental illness through the criminal justice system. Often, a therapeutic jurisprudence approach is the means to achieve this end (Winick and Wexler 2003). Judges and other court personnel may receive training on mental illness and may self-select themselves to be part of this specialized court. The courts have been described as being less formal and less adversarial than traditional courts (Petrila 2003).

Although voluntary for defendants to enroll, once individuals are in the court, they are mandated to comply with court orders, which can include taking one's prescribed medications, attending treatment appointments and AA/NA meetings, and checking in with the court on a regular basis (i.e., periodic status review hearings before the judge). Noncompliance can result in sanctions, including increased judicial and community supervision, community service, and the controversial use of short jail stays. Compliance with orders can lead to graduation from the court and pre-stipulated conditions, such as removing the charges/conviction from one's record. Some courts offer incentives for compliance, such as phase completion certificates and gift cards (Fisler 2005).

In an effort to reduce the idiosyncrasies of MHCs, the Council of State Governments (CSG) developed the Ten Essential Elements of a Mental Health Court (Thompson et al. 2008). These 10 elements can be divided into three topic areas: planning and sustainability (Elements 1 and 10), pre-court enrollment considerations (Elements 2–5) and in-court considerations (Elements 6–9). Below, these important features of MHCs are reviewed in terms of what the extant research indicates and areas in which more research is needed.

Planning and Sustainability

Element 1, Planning and Administration "A broad-based group of stakeholders representing the criminal justice, mental health, substance abuse treatment, and related systems and the community guides the planning and administration of the court."

Element 10, Sustainability "Data are collected and analyzed to demonstrate the impact of the mental health court, its performance is assessed periodically (and procedures are modified accordingly), court processes are institutionalized, and support for the court in the community is cultivated and expanded."

Mental health courts can arise for a variety of reasons, ranging from the successful implementation of other specialty courts in the jurisdiction (e.g., Drug Treatment Courts), to a highly visible tragedy involving an offender with mental illness, to other reasons idiosyncratic to the community. Fisler (2005) provides an excellent overview of the planning and thinking that went into establishing the Brooklyn Mental Health Court, including their decision to focus exclusively on felony offenders. The collaboration and involvement of multiple systems, including but not limited to, the criminal justice (and all its actors), the mental health, and the substance systems, are typically emphasized as being "core elements" to the development of these and other formal diversion programs (see Steadman et al. 2001). Additionally, as noted by Petrila and Redlich (2008), many MHCs began from in-kind resources, often with judges taking on the MHC caseload in addition to their other dockets.

Despite a reliance on existing resources, obtaining funding and sustainability is an ongoing struggle for the courts. However, federal funds from agencies such as the Bureau of Justice Assistance and the Substance Abuse and Mental Health Association have been made available. Nevertheless, some MHCs simply do not sustain, although precise numbers are not known. As found by Redlich et al. (2006), 14 % of existing MHCs did not think or were unsure whether their court would sustain beyond the next 3 years. The authors also describe an anecdotal example of a court that had closed its door, returning the clients back to traditional court processing by alphabetical assignment. Given that some proportion of MHCs will cease to exist, an interesting question for future research is to determine the effect, if any, this has on the clients who were participating in the court. Within this Essential Element of sustainability, the CSG (i.e., Thompson et al. 2008) stresses the importance of programmatic research and evaluation components to assess performance and influence funders and community policymakers. For example, Steadman (2005) states, "Mental health courts usually receive initial funding based on their potential for positive impacts. They are funded (or not) in subsequent years based on their ability to demonstrate results" (p. 1).

Pre-Court Enrollment Considerations

CSG delineates four elements of MHCs they deem essential to the fair and equitable enrollment of clients.

Element 2, Target Population "Eligibility criteria address public safety, consider the availability of other alternatives for defendants with mental illness, and appreciate a community's treatment capacity. Eligibility criteria also take into account the relationship between mental illness and a defendant's offenses, while allowing the individual circumstances of each case to be considered."

Typically, an MHC's target population is defined by two gross eligibility criteria: criminal charges and clinical diagnoses/problems. Over time, MHCs have grown more willing to accept defendants charged with felony offenses compared with misdemeanor offenses. In the first generation of MHCs, most only accepted defendants with misdemeanor charges. Now, about one in ten courts only accept defendants charged with felonies (Almquist and Dodd 2009; Redlich et al. 2006). Some courts, on a case-by-case basis, are even willing to take in offenders charged with violent felonies, such as arson and sex offenses. For example, a recent research study on four MHCs revealed that up to 54 % of the offenders' target arrest charges were for person crimes, including those mentioned earlier (Steadman et al. 2011). As noted by Moore and Hiday (2006) for the Orange County, NC MHC, "[A] violent offense in and of itself is not cause for exclusion; rather the degree and circumstances of the violence determine exclusion" (p. 662).

Does this trend mean MHCs have become less concerned with public safety? The answer to this question is most likely "no." Rather, after demonstrating success with misdemeanant offenders, the courts have come to recognize the lack of a consistent (and predictive) relation between charges and future violence and/or were able to convince stakeholders that some offenders charged with felonies can be trusted to reside in the community (Almquist and Dodd 2009). In addition, controversy exists about whether misdemeanants are an appropriate target population for MHCs, as participation necessarily entails criminal justice involvement. Seltzer (2005) argues that MHCs should be reserved for eligible individuals charged with more serious crimes, and individuals charged with less serious crimes should be diverted from the criminal justice system entirely. Because MHCs are necessarily deeper into the criminal justice processing pipeline, it has been argued that when feasible, discretion in charging and adjudicating should be practiced via diversion programs available earlier in the pipeline, such as police-based Crisis Intervention Teams or even pre-booking jail-based programs. Finally, another reason for an increased focus on felons relates to cost-saving. If MHCs are intended to reduce the costs associated with processing offenders with mental health problems through the system, diverting felons (whose jail stays are longer) rather than misdemeanants is more cost-effective.

In terms of clinical criteria, a survey by the CSG (2006) revealed that 26 % of the courts had no specific mental health eligibility restrictions. In contrast, 37 % required an Axis I diagnosis and an additional 21 % required a diagnosis of "serious mental illness" (typically defined as schizo-spectrum, bipolar, and major depressive disorders). The remaining 16 % focused on specific diagnoses, such as schizophrenia. Thus, slightly more than one-quarter of the courts may take in persons who are not seriously mentally ill, who may have only personality disorder, or who may not even have a mental health problem. As described in Redlich et al. (2005), one MHC judge claimed to accept persons whose only problems were medical (hepatitis and AIDS).

A related issue to defining the target population is ensuring that referrals and those accepted into the court are representative of the larger eligible population. Research has consistently demonstrated that diversion programs, including MHCs, have an overrepresentation of older, white woman compared to the larger criminal justice population (e.g., Naples et al. 2007; Steadman et al. 2005) and perhaps even compared with the mentally ill criminal justice population. For example, in a large-scale prevalence study, Steadman et al. (2009) found the rate of serious mental illness to be 31 % among female jail inmates (which is quite high compared with previously reported prevalence rates). However, many MHCs report having rates of females that approach or exceed 50 % (e.g., Cosden et al. 2005; Henrickx et al. 2005; Steadman et al. 2005). If MHCs are indeed a "better" alternative to traditional court processing, inequitable referral and disposition decision practices are problematic and perhaps even unconstitutional. More research is needed to conclusively determine (1) if and why certain subsets of offenders with mental illness are more apt to be referred and/or accepted and (2) if indeed MHCs are more effective than traditional processing, and thus raise constitutional issues of equity.

Element 3, Timely Participant Identification and Linkage to Services "Participants are identified, referred, and accepted into mental health court, and linked to community-based service providers, as quickly as possible."

A main goal of diversion is to divert eligible individuals swiftly (Steadman et al. 1995). If people are languishing in the criminal justice system, particularly in jail, diversion is arguably not occurring. In a study on seven MHCs, Steadman et al. (2005) investigated the time from MHC referral until MHC disposition (decision to accept or reject referred person). The median length of time was 20 days. However, the total time from (1) arrest to (2) referral to (3) MHC disposition to (4) MHC enrollment was not captured. It may be that while the courts have implemented successful procedures to refer potentially eligible persons and then make decisions in a short span of time, the length of time before referral and after the decision may take much longer. It is this entire period—from initial arrest to eventual enrollment—that is important in determining whether diversion is swift.

Redlich et al. (2012) examined the median number of days from target arrest to MHC enrollment for 311 MHC clients (from three courts). Overall, the median number of days was 70. However, whether the person had been detained the entire period or had been released played an important role. For those detained the entire time, the median length was 42 days; for those released at any point, the median length was about 2.8 times longer, at 119 days.

In interpreting these data, it is important to establish the median length of traditional criminal processing. Redlich et al. (2012) thus compared the time from arrest with adjudication for two traditionally processed samples, one with and one without mental health problems. (Adjudication is a comparable endpoint to MHC enrollment because, as we discuss below, the majority of MHCs require guilty pleas as a condition of enrollment, which is the endpoint of adjudication for most defendants.) First, using data collected by the Bureau of Justice Statistics (Cohen and Reaves 2006), for 13,018 felony defendants from the 75 largest urban counties, Redlich et al. found that time from arrest to adjudication was a median of 76 days, which is quite similar to the 70 days reported for MHC clients. Second, using a comparison sample with known mental health problems ($n = 336$) matched to the MHC sample (who came from the same three jurisdictions), the median time between arrest and adjudication was 37 days. Overall, MHC processing was found to take twice as long as traditional court processing for offenders with mental health problems from the same jurisdictions.

Element 4, Terms of Participation "Terms of participation promote public safety, and are clear, individualized, and the least restrictive necessary to ensure treatment engagement. They also strive to minimize the impact of the charges on the participants' criminal records, and they support a positive legal outcome for participants who successfully complete the program."

In part due to the rapid growth of MHCs, some courts started without having set finalized terms of participation and/or did not anticipate potential issues. For example, CSG recommends that the length of MHC participation not exceed the length of criminal justice involvement if the offender had not enrolled in the court (e.g., the length of time in jail or on probation). In making a fully informed decision about whether to enroll in the court, participants should know the length of involvement—and factors that can extend or abbreviate involvement—before opting in. Several courts have developed contractual agreements for offenders to sign. For example, the Washoe County, NV MHC adopted a "Mental Health Court Agreement" that stipulates 15 conditions, including "I will sign any releases of information as required in order for the court to obtain information needed for my participation," "I will take medications for my psychiatric condition as prescribed by a doctor," and "I understand that should I fail to comply with these conditions, I will be subject to sanctions, including jail, community service, or any other sanction the court deems appropriate" (see Redlich et al. 2010a).

Similarly, offenders, especially first-time offenders, should be made aware of possible collateral consequences of pleading guilty (e.g., restrictions on housing, possibility of deportation) and the final outcome upon successful or unsuccessful participation. Most MHCs (67 %) require that clients plead guilty as a condition of enrollment. An additional 16 % requires this for some of their clients (CSG 2006). One study of two MHCs found that between 55 and 73 % of defendants claimed not to know that pleading guilty was a condition of their MHC enrollment (Redlich et al. 2010a). In this same study, most but not all (77–89 %) understood that if they complied with the conditions of the court, they could have the relevant arrest or conviction dropped from their record. The results of this study and others (e.g., Poythress et al. 2002) suggest some potential MHC participants are not being informed of MHC procedures and requirements, or if they are being informed, do not fully appreciate the information.

Element 5, Informed Consent "Defendants fully understand the program requirements before agreeing to participate in the mental health court. They are provided legal counsel to inform this decision, and subsequent decisions about program involvement. Procedures exist in the mental health court to address, in a timely fashion, concerns about a defendant's competency whenever they arise."

In theory, MHC clients are legally required to make knowing, intelligent, and voluntary decisions to enter the court, but do they? (see Redlich 2005). MHC clients should hold specific knowledge about the court's rules and procedures, as well as general legal knowledge. Given that competence is a threshold issue in that persons are presumed competent to stand trial unless the question is raised, in theory, MHC participants processed post-adjudication should meet these requirements (i.e., the requirements set in *Dusky v. U.S.* 1960). Moreover, mental illness is the primary reason to question competence (Pinals 2005). In a court in which many clients have (serious) mental health problems, it stands to reason that some will not be considered competent to proceed.

To address these issues, colleagues and I (Redlich et al. 2010a) surveyed 200 newly enrolled clients at two courts about their understanding and appreciation of MHC procedures and regulations and the voluntary nature of the courts (see previous text) and assessed adjudicative competence. We found that although most clients (69 %) claimed that they chose to enroll in the court, at the same time, most (60 %)

claimed not to have been told that it was voluntary to enroll. In both courts, the majority claimed not to have been told about MHC requirements prior to entering, did not appreciate that they could stop participating, or have the ability to cite disadvantages to being in the court (e.g., having to comply with judicial and treatment orders, possible stigma associated with the MHC). As to adjudicative competence, at one court, approximately 17 % of newly enrolled clients demonstrated either mild or significant impairments in adjudicative competence, and at the other court, about 39 % showed similar impairments. Given that, in theory, all MHC clients are presumed competent, these rates of individuals with deficient knowledge are of concern.

In sum, Essential Elements 2 through 5 (Thompson et al. 2008) strive to ensure that potential MHC clients are appropriate candidates who are diverted in a timely manner and who are able to make informed and voluntary decisions to enter. The reviewed research raises several questions about fairness and equity in who is referred and accepted into MHCs, whether diversion does indeed occur in a timely manner, and whether defendants are given and appreciate the information necessary to make a competent and voluntary decision to enroll. The next set of essential elements focus on ensuring fair and effective participation once participation has begun.

In-Court Considerations

Element 6, Treatment Support and Services "Mental health courts connect participants to comprehensive and individualized treatment supports and services in the community. They strive to use—and increase the availability of—treatment and services that are evidence-based."

Although research on whether MHCs "work" has advanced significantly in the past few years, much of the focus has been on whether MHC participation influences recidivism (e.g., McNiel and Binder 2007; Moore and Hiday 2006). In contrast, less research has focused on the effectiveness of MHCs linking clients with community treatment, and to my knowledge, no research has examined the receipt of treatment services that are evidence-based. In studying the Broward County, FL MHC, Boothroyd et al. (2003) compared the receipt of treatment of MHC clients and a comparison sample within an 8-month period. They found that the percentage of MHC clients receiving treatment from baseline to the 8-month follow-up rose significantly from 36 to 53 %. In contrast, treatment receipt for the comparison sample remained the same (28–29 %) during this period. Additionally, of the clients who received treatment, the MHC sample received significantly more than the comparison sample. Similar findings were reported for the Clark County, OR MHC (Henrickx et al. 2005; see also Almquist and Dodd 2009). Specifically, compared with the year before enrolling, in the 1 year post-enrollment, Clark County MHC clients had significantly more hours of case management, medication monitoring, and days of outpatient service, and significantly fewer hours of crisis intervention and inpatient days. Thus, although more research is needed, to date studies have shown that MHCs do indeed facilitate treatment access. Whether MHCs increase treatment *engagement* and access to evidence-based services needs more attention. Further, the link between treatment utilization and improved outcomes is wholly unclear. Whether reduced recidivism among MHC clients, for example, is attributable to increased access to treatment, to simply being in the court, to a combination of treatment and court involvement, or to some other unidentified set of factors (e.g., self-selection enrollment bias) is not yet well understood.

Element 7, Confidentiality "Health and legal information should be shared in a way that protects potential participants' confidentiality rights as consumers and their constitutional rights as defendants. Information gathered as part of the participants' court mandated program should be safeguarded in the event that participants are returned to traditional court processing."

Mental health courts face a difficult challenge in re: confidentiality. On the one hand, adult criminal court proceedings are usually public. On the other hand, mental health issues and accompanying health records are usually private. Within this element, Thompson et al. (2008) recommend obtaining signed release-of-information forms (that clearly specify who does and does not have access to records) and avoiding discussion of clinical issues in open court. As described by Linhorst et al. (2010), the St. Louis County Municipal MHC utilizes Health Insurance Portability and Accountability Act (HIPAA)- compliant release forms, as well as maintaining separate court and treatment files. In addition, about 1.5 years into the court's operation, the MHC changed locations to afford more privacy. To my knowledge, a systematic study on whether and how existing MHCs attend to issues of confidentiality has not yet been conducted.

Another aspect related to confidentiality concerns the sharing of data across systems. Petrila (2006) refers to the 1996 HIPAA act as "the most misunderstood law in the country" as it actually does not present a barrier to cross-systems collaboration but has been interpreted to be and in practice has become a major barrier. As applied to MHCs, cross-system professionals may misinterpret the law, fear harsh consequences, and be unwilling to share information believed to be protected by HIPAA. For example, mental health professionals may be reticent to share private health information with the MHC; however, judicial order is one of the many permitted disclosures of such information (Petrila 2006). According to Petrila, it is a myth that HIPAA applies to all persons. In fact, courts are not entities covered under the act.

Element 8, Court Team "A team of criminal justice staff, mental health staff, and service and treatment providers, which receives special, ongoing training, helps mental health court participants achieve treatment and criminal justice goals by regularly reviewing and revising the court process."

An integrated court team is a defining feature of MHCs. Notwithstanding descriptions of individual courts (e.g., Fisler 2005), there has not been much attention placed on the workings of these teams. Often the teams are composed of the MHC judge, the defense and prosecuting attorneys, community treatment providers, probation officers, and possibly others (e.g., vocational specialists, a consumer representative). Of course, there are exceptions. For example, the district attorney's office was initially unsupportive of the Washoe County, NV MHC and has not been involved in its operation (or represented on the team). Nevertheless, the Washoe County court has been quite effective and has sustained since 2001.

Training of court team members has also not been a main topic of research. Whether and how often judges and other court personnel receive training, to my knowledge, has not been established. Also, the content of training is unknown (see, Chap. 13, this volume). As a companion effort to the Essential Elements, the CSG has developed MHC learning sites. Five well-established MHCs were chosen as sites that other developing or operational MHCs could learn from and ask questions of. In part, these five courts were selected on their adherence to the Essential Elements. The National GAINS Center and the CSG's Consensus Criminal Justice/Mental Health project are also excellent sources of information for the courts. But again, the degree to which training occurs, who gets trained and how often, and what are the elements of training are sorely in need of research. This is important as there can be quite a bit of staff turnover in MHCs. In a recently completed comprehensive study of four MHCs (Steadman et al. 2011), within approximately a 3-year period, two judges and two MHC coordinators turned over. Whether this is a common occurrence or a rarity is unknown. In addition, attorney turnover and idiosyncratic judicial styles can be problematic.

Element 9, Monitoring Adherence to Court Requirements "Criminal justice and mental health staff collaboratively monitor participants' adherence to court conditions, offer individualized graduated incentives and sanctions, and modify treatment as necessary to promote public safety and participants' recovery."

Like several of the other elements, monitoring compliance with court and treatment orders is a mainstay of MHCs. Rewarding or punishing compliance/noncompliance is also central. Research has shown that the courts vary quite a bit in the frequency of judicial and community supervision. At the onset of participation, courts require newly enrolled clients to return before the judge as often as a few times a week to as infrequently as a few times a year (Redlich et al. 2006). Additionally, most MHCs (71 %) utilize a combination of criminal justice (e.g., probation officers) and mental health professionals (e.g., case managers) to supervise clients in the community, which serves to increase the intensity.

The use of jail as a sanction for noncompliance has also been a controversial issue. Because a main goal of MHCs is to divert persons from jail, to some, jail as a sanction for noncompliance is not appropriate nor effective toward gaining compliance. As reported in Redlich et al. (2006), about 41 % of the courts were categorized as using jail as a sanction rarely (5 % of the time or less) to never. Twenty percent reported using it for a fifth or more of their cases. Interestingly, there was also a significant correlation between frequency of judicial supervision and jail sanction use, such that those courts who required more frequent hearings reported higher use of jail sanctions.

In newer research, we have taken a closer look at the use of court hearings as supervision across four MHCs (Redlich et al. 2010b). One aspect we investigated was whether MHC clients appeared before the judge from in-custody or from the community. We found the rate of in-custody appearances to depend on completion

Table 9.1 Characteristics of first, second, and future generation mental health courts

	Eight first-generation MHCs (%)	Seven second-generation MHCs (%)	Ninety second-generation MHCs (%)	*Proposed next-generation MHCs*
Post-adjudication	50	86	83	*Increase*
Misdemeanor-exclusive	75	0	40	*Decrease*
Rare use of jail as a sanction	75	29	41	*Decrease*
Mental health-only supervision	50	14	14	*Decrease*

status and court. On average, terminated clients attended 36 % of their hearings incarcerated, compared with 15–24 % of hearings of clients who were either still in the court or who graduated. Moreover, in one of the courts, 45 % of all clients (regardless of completion status) made half to all of their appearances from jail, whereas in another court, participants rarely made appearances while in custody. Thus, although it is often assumed that MHC clients appear before the judge on their own volition, some clients have no choice but to appear.

To summarize, Elements 6 through 9 focus on standardizing procedures and requirements for MHC clients once they are enrolled in the court. Although some of these procedures and requirements have been the subject of research, others, such as confidentiality regulations, training, and receipt of evidence-based treatment, need to be examined. The research that has been done has highlighted the successes of the courts, as well as areas in need of refinement.

Tomorrow's Mental Health Courts

Mental health courts have been in existence for more than a decade. Since their inception, they have been critiqued (e.g., Seltzer 2005) and have most certainly evolved. In this section, I revisit and elaborate on first- and second-generation MHCs and speculate about what the next generation may look like.

My colleagues and I (Redlich et al. 2005) compared early and later MHCs on four dimensions: (1) case processing (pre- vs. post-adjudication), (2) criminal charges (misdemeanor vs. felony), (3) use of jail as a sanction, and (4) community supervision (mental health vs. criminal court). First, we (Redlich et al. 2005) compared eight early MHCs (i.e., the "first generation of MHCs") described in the literature (Goldkamp and Irons-Guynn 2000; Griffin et al. 2002) with seven later MHCs (i.e, the "second generation of MHCs"). As shown in Table 9.1, in comparison with first-generation courts, we found that second-generation courts were more likely to process cases post-adjudication (i.e., require guilty pleas), to include more felony charges in their eligibility criteria, to use jail as a sanction, and were less likely to use mental health professionals as the only means of community supervision.

Next, we surveyed the then population of adult MHCs ($n = 90$) (Redlich et al. 2006) on many characteristics, including the four dimensions. As seen in Table 9.1, we found that for two of the four dimensions (processing cases post-adjudication and only using mental health professionals to supervise clients in the community), proportions of courts did not appreciably change from the initial examination of seven second-generation MHCs to the larger population of 90 second-generation MHCs. In contrast, the remaining two dimensions did show divergent results. The proportion of misdemeanor-exclusive courts was 40 %, compared with 75 % for first-generation courts and 0 % for the seven second-generation courts. A trend we noted in the larger survey was that courts from the same state tended to mimic one another. Florida and Ohio, two states with a relatively larger number of MHCs (in 2005), accounted for the majority of misdemeanor-only courts. In addition, the surveys revealed there to be MHCs that were felony-exclusive.

The reported use of jail as a sanction was also somewhat different than found for the first generation. A possible reason for this discrepancy relates to the number of misdemeanor-exclusive courts. Specifically, the percentage of felons that MHCs accept significantly predicts the use of jail as a sanction ($r = .39$, $p < .01$; see Table 4, Redlich et al. 2006). Thus, because the sample of 90 MHCs included more misdemeanor-exclusive courts, the frequency of jail sanction use dropped, although less than one would expect. Overall, we also found that 92 % of the courts reported using jail as a sanction at least some of the time.

What can we anticipate for the next generation of MHCs? As noted in the last column of Table 9.1, I believe we will see a continued *increase* in the number of courts that process cases post-adjudication and a continued *decrease* in the number of courts that process only misdemeanants, that rarely use jail as a sanction, and that utilize mental health professionals as the only means of supervising clients in the community. As discussed in Redlich et al. (2005) and supported empirically in Redlich et al. (2006), these four dimensions are interrelated: MHCs that process more felons are more likely to require guilty pleas, to use jail as a sanction, and to have criminal justice professionals in conjunction with mental health professionals supervise clients.

But why will courts continue to take in more felons to begin with? As discussed previously, two potential reasons relate to the controversy over the most appropriate target population (i.e., felons vs. misdemeanants, Seltzer 2005) and cost-savings. A third potential reason relates to what I label, "regression to the mean." Regression to the mean is a statistical phenomenon in which data points gravitate toward the average. The quintessential example is of a child who has very tall parents. The child is likely to be shorter than his parents because of this tendency, or in this case, regressing toward the average height. Related to MHCs, the "mean" is the traditional criminal justice system method of adjudication.

Mental health courts are criminal justice inventions for the most part. They were devised by judges and other criminal justice personnel who (1) were aware of drug treatment and other specialty courts and/or (2) recognized that the traditional adversarial system was ineffective in dealing with the large number of repeat offenders with mental health problems (Kaye 2004). Most MHCs operating today were initiated by a judge or a defense attorney. Even if there are specific MHCs that were initiated by a local chapter of an advocacy organization for persons with mental illness, for instance, the courts are undeniably criminal justice entities. MHCs are part of the community's criminal court system: hearings are held in the courthouse, the administrative judge oversees the court, judges and lawyers are paid by the county legal system, etc. MHCs are not part of the mental health or human services system.

Because MHCs are criminal justice inventions and entities, I believe more "criminal justice-like" practices will follow, which is consistent with the trend noted from the first- to second-generation courts. These practices will manifest in the four dimensions already noted, as well as in other ways. One other way relates to formality. MHCs and other specialty courts have been described as less formal than traditional courts and as involving less "lawyering" (Petrila 2003). Motions are rarely filed and due process rights can be suspended in favor of a more paternalistic approach. As the courts continue to evolve, I believe we will see an increase in the number and type of formal rules and regulations. Many of the early courts (and perhaps some courts still today) did not specify the circumstances under which court information was to be kept confidential, which prompted some of the Essential Elements mentioned in previous text. The nation's first specialty court, the juvenile court, followed a similar path. In 1967, in the landmark Supreme Court case, *In re Gault*, the juvenile court was lambasted for being too informal and even referred to as a "kangaroo court." For MHCs not to follow suit, they must too adopt a more legalistic due process framework if they have not done so already.

Another possible manifestation of MHCs inching back toward traditional criminal court practices relates to who the courts allow in. We have already seen and discussed the trend toward allowing more felons charged with serious and violent crimes in, but we may also see expansion of mental health eligibility criteria. As found in the CSG (2006) survey, about a quarter of the courts do not specify restrictions about clinical problems. Across the seven courts examined in Redlich et al. (2005) and Steadman et al. (2005), 38 % of the persons *accepted* for the courts did not have a serious mental illness. Indeed, 5 % did not have a mental illness at all.

An overarching emphasis of the criminal justice system is equality, the notion of a blind Lady Justice. MHCs have been criticized for trying to create "separate but equal" (Stefan and Winick 2005) courtrooms that make divisive lines between offenders with and without mental health problems (see Chap. 10, this volume). Because of concerns of fairness and equity in MHC diversion practices and because of the emphasis placed on these constructs in the criminal justice system as a whole, will MHCs continue to be exclusively for offenders with mental illness? One active MHC judge took pride in the fact that he was willing to accept in clients to the MHC that other judges did not want to deal with, regardless of whether they had mental illnesses (Redlich et al. 2005).

In conclusion, the criminal justice system inherited the problem of the overabundance of persons with mental illness repeatedly cycling through their doors. Although it was not a problem of their creation, it became apparent that they had no choice but to deal with it. In response, the criminal justice system created MHCs, in part based on the successes of other problem-solving courts. Given that MHCs are criminal justice inventions and entities, regressing back toward a more traditional and even adversarial approach is arguably a reasonable expectation. The question that remains for the future is whether MHCs and other specialty courts will continue to be "special." How will they distinguish themselves from traditional courts? As the courts adopt a more legalistic and due process orientation, the challenge will be to retain the features that set them apart from treatment-as-usual in the criminal justice system, features that were created in response to the perceived ineffectiveness of said traditional treatment.

References

Almquist, L., & Dodd, E. (2009). *Mental health courts: A guide to research-informed policy and practice*. New York: Council of State Governments Justice Center. http://www.consensusproject.org/jc_publications/mental-health-courts-a-guide-to-research-informed-policy-and-practice/Mental_Health_Court_Research_Guide.pdf.

Boothroyd, R., Poythress, N., McGaha, A., & Petrila, J. (2003). The Broward Mental Health Court: Process, outcomes and service utilization. *International Journal of Law and Psychiatry, 26,* 55–71.

Cocazza, J., & Shufelt, J. (2006). *Juvenile mental health courts: An emerging strategy*. Delmar, NY: Research and Program Brief, National Center for Mental Health and Juvenile Justice.

Cohen, T. H., & Reaves, B. A. (2006). *Felony defendants in large urban counties, 2002*. Washington, DC: U.S. Department of Justice, Office of Justice Programs, Bureau of Justice Statistics.

Cosden, M., Ellens, J., Schnell, J., & Yamini-Diouf, Y. (2005). Efficacy of a mental health treatment court with assertive community treatment. *Behavioral Sciences and the Law, 23,* 199–214.

Council of State Governments. (2006). *Mental health courts: A national snapshot*. New York: Council of State Governments Justice Center.

Council of State Governments. (2008). *Mental health courts: A primer for policymakers and practitioners*. New York: Council of State Governments Justice Center.

Dusky v. U.S., 362 U.S. 402 (1960).

Fisler, C. (2005). Building true and managing risk: A look at a felony mental health court. *Psychology, Public Policy, and Law, 11,* 587–604.

Goldkamp, J. D., & Irons-Guynn, C. (2000). *Emerging judicial strategies for the mentally ill in the criminal caseload: Mental health courts in Fort Lauderdale, Seattle, San Bernardino, and Anchorage*. Washington DC, US Department of Justice, Office of Justice Programs, Bureau of Justice Assistance Monograph, pub. No. NCJ 182504.

Griffin, P., Steadman, H. J., & Petrila, J. (2002). The use of criminal charges and sanctions in mental health courts. *Psychiatric Services, 53,* 1285–1289.

Henrickx, H. A., Swart, S. C., Ama, S. M., Dolezal, C. D., & King, S. (2005). Rearrest and linkage to mental health services among clients of the Clark County mental health court program. *Psychiatric Services, 56,* 853–857.

Kaye, J. S. (2004). Delivering justice today: A problem-solving approach. *Yale Law and Policy Review, 22,* 125–151.

Linhorst, D. M., Dirks-Linhorst, P. A., Stiffelman, S., Gianino, J., Bernsen, H. L., & Kelley, B. J. (2010). Implementing the essential elements of a mental health court: The experiences of a large multijurisdictional suburban county. *Journal of Behavioral Health Services and Research, 37,* 427–442. Published online October, 1, 2009.

McNiel, D. E., & Binder, R. L. (2007). Effectiveness of a mental health court in reducing criminal recidivism and violence. *American Journal of Psychiatry, 164,* 1395–1403.

Moore, M. E., & Hiday, V. A. (2006). Mental health court outcomes: A comparison of re-arrest and re-arrest severity between mental health court and traditional court participants. *Law and Human Behavior, 30,* 659–674.

Naples, M., Morris, L. S., & Steadman, H. J. (2007). Factors in disproportionate representation among persons recommended by programs accepted by courts for jail diversion. *Psychiatric Services, 58,* 1095–1101.

Petrila, J. (2003). An introduction to special jurisdiction courts. *International Journal of Law and Psychiatry, 26,* 3–12.

Petrila, J. (2006). *Dispelling the myths about sharing data between mental health and criminal justice systems.* TAPA Center for Jail Diversion Easy Access Net Teleconference, Delmar, NY. Available at http://www.gainscenter.samhsa.gov/html/resources/presentation_materials/pdfs/Myths_11_13_06.pdf.

Petrila, J., & Redlich, A. D. (2008). Options for diverting persons with mental illness from the criminal justice system. *Court Review, 43,* 164–173.

Pinals, D. A. (2005). Where two road meet: Restoration of competence to stand trial from a clinical perspective. *New England School of Law, 31*(1), 81–108.

Poythress, N. G., Petrila, J., McGaha, A., & Boothroyd, R. (2002). Perceived coercion and procedural justice in the Broward County Mental Health Court. *International Journal of Law and Psychiatry, 25,* 517–533. doi:10.1016/S0160-2527(01)00110-8.

Redlich, A. D. (2005). Voluntary, but knowing and intelligent? Comprehension in mental health courts. *Psychology, Public Policy, and the Law, 11,* 605–619.

Redlich, A. D., Steadman, H. J., Monahan, J., Petrila, J., & Griffin, P. (2005). The second generation of mental health courts. *Psychology, Public Policy, and the Law, 11,* 527–538.

Redlich, A. D., Steadman, H. J., Robbins, P. C., Monahan, J., & Petrila, J. (2006). Patterns of practice in mental health courts: A national survey. *Law and Human Behavior, 30,* 347–362.

Redlich, A. D., Hoover, S., Summers, A., & Steadman, H. J. (2010a). Enrollment in mental health courts: Voluntariness, knowingness, and adjudicative competence. *Law and Human Behavior, 31,* 91–104.

Redlich, A. D., Steadman, H. J., Callahan, L., Robbins, P. C., Vessilinov, R., & Ozdogru, A. A. (2010b). The use of mental health court appearances in supervision. *International Journal of Law and Psychiatry, 33,* 272–277.

Redlich, A. D., Liu, S., Steadman, H. J., Callahan, L., & Robbins, P. C. (2012). Is diversion swift? Comparing mental health court and traditional criminal justice processing. *Criminal Justice and Behavior, 39,* 420–433.

Seltzer, T. (2005). Mental health courts: A misguided attempt to address the criminal justice system's unfair treatment of people with mental illnesses. *Psychology, Public Policy, and Law, 11,* 570–586.

Steadman, H. J. (2005). *A guide to collecting mental health outcome data.* A publication of the Council of State Government, prepared for the Bureau of Justice Assistance. http://www.consensusproject.org/jc_publications/guide-to-collecting-mental-health-court-outcome-data/MHC-Outcome-Data.pdf.

Steadman, H. J., Morris, S. M., & Dennis, D. L. (1995). The diversion of mentally ill persons from jails to community-based services. *American Journal of Public Health, 85,* 1630–1635.

Steadman, H. J., Stainbrook., K. A.,, Griffin, P., Draine, J., Dupont, R., & Horey, C. (2001). A specialized crisis response as a core element of police-based diversion programs. *Psychiatric Services, 52,* 219–222.

Steadman, H. J., Redlich, A. D., Griffin, P., Petrila, J., & Monahan, J. (2005). From referral to disposition: Case processing in seven mental health courts. *Behavioral Sciences and the Law, 23,* 1–12.

Steadman, H. J., Osher, F. C., Robbins, P. C., Case, B., & Samuels, S. (2009). Prevalence of serious mental illness among jail inmates. *Psychiatric Services, 60,* 761–765.

Steadman, H. J., Redlich, A. D., Callahan, L., Robbins, P. C., & Vesselinov, R. (2011). Assessing the effectiveness of mental health courts: A multi-site study. *Archives of General Psychiatry, 68,* 167–172.

Stefan, S., & Winick, B. J. (2005). A dialogue on mental health courts. *Psychology, Public Policy, and Law, 11,* 507–526.

Thompson, M., Osher, F., & Tomasini-Joshi, D. (2008). *Improving responses to people with mental illnesses: The essential elements of a mental health court.* New York: Council of State Governments Justice Center.

Winick, B. J., & Wexler, D. B. (2003). *Judging in a therapeutic key: Therapeutic jurisprudence and the courts*. Durham, NC: Carolina Academic Press.

Chapter 10
Mental Health Courts: Competence, Responsibility, and Proportionality

Robert F. Schopp

Introduction

As generally discussed, mental health courts (MHCs) function as a component in the criminal justice system designed to reduce recidivism by promoting effective treatment for offenders who commit offenses due to the effects of their mental illness. A primary purpose of MHCs, as with criminal justice system generally, is to reduce crime. Specifically, MHCs are designed to reduce recidivism by offenders whose crimes are "more a product of mental illness than of criminality."[1] MHCs can vary in their specific applications and procedures. As described in the prior chapters, they frequently require guilty pleas from mentally ill offenders, place those offenders on probation, and require as a condition of probation that those offenders participate in treatment intended to ameliorate the disorders that increase their propensity to commit crimes. If the offenders do not participate in the treatment required as a condition of probation, incarceration for brief periods is applied to enforce treatment participation. The criminal records can be expunged for those offenders who complete their conditions of probation.[2]

MHCs are designed to promote the well-being of the mentally ill offenders by providing treatment that improves their clinical conditions in a manner that decreases risk of recidivism and punishment. Decreasing the risk of recidivism also promotes the well-being of society. What could be objectionable or questionable about a problem solving court that promotes the well-being of mentally ill offenders and of society generally? Consider the following concerns. First, do MHCs actually decrease recidivism more effectively than available alternatives? This is essentially an empirical inquiry requiring ongoing collection of relevant evidence regarding recidivism rates

[1] Susan Stefan & Bruce J. Winick, *A Dialogue on Mental Health Courts*, 11 Psychol., Pub., Pol., & L 507 (2005).

[2] *See generally*, Petrilla and Redlich, this volume.

R. F. Schopp (✉)
College of Law, University of Nebraska, Lincoln, Nebraska, USA
e-mail: rschopp1@unl.edu

R. L. Wiener, E. M. Brank (eds.), *Problem Solving Courts*,
DOI 10.1007/978-1-4614-7403-6_10, © Springer Science+Business Media, LLC 2013

of offenders who have been addressed through MHCs as compared with relevantly similar offenders who have been addressed through the available alternatives.

Second, what are the alternatives and what considerations other than comparative rates of recidivism are relevant to identifying the most appropriate legal institution to apply in attempting to reduce recidivism among offenders with mental illness? Consider, for example, civil commitment. State statutes ordinarily authorize civil commitment of individuals who fulfill the criteria of mental illness and dangerousness to others.[3] If an offender presents a risk of harm to others due to mental illness, what justifies the state in applying the police power through civil commitment or through an MHC within the criminal justice system? Alternately, consider a criminal trial with a defense of not guilty by reason of insanity followed by post-acquittal commitment. [4] What type and degree of psychological impairment justifies the state in accepting a guilty plea and requiring treatment as a condition of probation, rather than finding the offender not guilty by reason of insanity and applying treatment through post-acquittal commitment?

MHCs are often described as applying a framework grounded in Therapeutic Jurisprudence. That framework pursues the development of legal rules, procedures, and roles that promote the well-being of those involved in a manner that recognizes and protects other important values embodied in law.[5] In order to advance this project, MHCs must decrease recidivism without causing disproportionate harm to the well-being of some participants or seriously undermining other important values embodied in the relevant law. Thus, justifying MHCs requires that we identify the full range of relevant values and examine the ways in which MHCs may advance or undermine them under various conditions.

The analysis proceeds in the following manner. Section "Relevant Values Embodied in Law" identifies some important values embodied in the criminal law and examines some potential concerns regarding the compatibility of MHCs with these values. Section "MHCs and Legal Mental Illness" examines the appropriate conception and scope of psychological impairment that is compatible with the functions of the MHCs as components in the more comprehensive criminal justice system. Section "Conclusion" concludes the analysis.

Relevant Values Embodied in Law

Prevention

It is not controversial that prevention of crime through a variety of processes including deterrence, incapacitation, reform, rehabilitation, and the expressive function of

[3] Michael L. Perlin, Mental Disability Law § 2A (2nd ed. 1998).

[4] *Id.* at §§ 9B-1, 2.

[5] David B. Wexler,. (1996) Justice, Mental Health, and Therapeutic Jurisprudence, in *Law in a Therapeutic Key* 713 (David B. Wexler & Bruce J. Winick, eds. 1996).

criminal punishment constitutes an important purpose of the criminal law. What approach would best advance the goal of prevention by minimizing recidivism among offenders with mental illness? Arguably, early English common law provided an effective approach. It applied capital punishment for a broad range of offenses against persons and property shortly after conviction of the offenders.[6] Such a practice would virtually eliminate recidivism by those offenders through incapacitation, and it would promote the general deterrence function with an emphatic demonstration to the general public that legitimate or deceptive claims of mental illness would not enable offenders to avoid punishment.

Set aside the question regarding the general justification of capital punishment. Even if one assumes that capital punishment is justified in principle, it would be grossly disproportionate to the offenses and offenders addressed in MHCs. Supreme Court decisions have precluded capital punishment of juvenile and mentally retarded offenders, partially on the basis that these offenders are significantly less culpable or blameworthy than ordinary offenders who commit similar offenses.[7] The Court has applied a similar rationale in precluding a sentence of life in prison without the possibility of parole for juvenile offenders who are convicted of crimes that do not include homicide.[8] According to a narrow contemporary interpretation, "culpability elements" are the mental states required by the definitions of specific offenses. These may include, for example, purpose or knowledge regarding the causation of death in a statute defining the offense of murder.[9] In a more general sense, a person is culpable to the degree that he is blameworthy or deserving of disapproval or censure.[10] The Supreme Court opinions referring to punishment in proportion to culpability or blameworthiness apply the term "culpability" in this more general sense because they preclude capital punishment for categories of offenders who have fulfilled the required offense elements for capital offenses. Thus, these opinions identify these categories of offenders as insufficiently culpable in the more general sense of blameworthiness sufficient to deserve capital punishment despite their having fulfilled the offense elements, including the culpability elements in the more specific sense.

Although the cases cited have specifically addressed capital punishment or life sentences without the possibility of parole, the widely accepted principle of proportionality in the application of criminal punishment prescribes punishment severity in proportion to the culpability or blameworthiness of the offender for the offense. MHCs are generally designed to address offenders whose crimes are "more a product of mental illness than of criminality."[11] The application of probation with conditions that promote treatment would be consistent with the premise that offenders addressed

---

[6] Nina Rivkind & Steven F. Shatz, The Death Penalty 20 (3rd ed. 2009).

[7] Roper vs. Simmons, 125 S.Ct. 1183, 1194–96 (2005); Atkins vs. Virginia 536 U.S. 304, 319 (2002).

[8] Graham vs. Florida, 2010 WL 1946731 (U.S.).

[9] American Law Institute, Model Penal Code §§ 2.02, 210.1, 210.2 (Proposed Official Draft, 1962).

[10] Black's Law Dictionary 193 (9th ed., 2009); I Newer Shorter Oxford English Dictionary 568 (Lesley Brown, ed., 1993).

[11] Stefan & Winick, *supra*, note 1, at 507.

by MHCs resemble the juvenile or mentally retarded offenders addressed by these Supreme Court cases in that they should be punished less severely than ordinary offenders who commit similar offenses because they are less culpable than ordinary offenders.

Supreme Court decisions have also precluded capital punishment as excessive for crimes that are serious wrongs but do not take the lives of the victims.[12] Although MHCs are apparently becoming more inclusive of felonies, as well as misdemeanors, the crimes addressed by MHCs are ordinarily misdemeanors or relatively less severe felonies, rather than the extremely severe murders that ordinarily qualify the offender for capital punishment.[13] The mental illness manifested by the offenders addressed in MHCs is understood to render them less culpable and more amenable to prevention through treatment than ordinary offenders who commit similar crimes. Thus, the principle of proportionality would prescribe punishment that is less severe than that applied to unimpaired offenders who commit similar offenses.

In short, frequent executions immediately following conviction may minimize recidivism by these offenders and perhaps by others, but it would violate other important values that are central to the justification of criminal punishment. Careful consideration of the most defensible role of MHCs requires explicit identification of the other important values implicated by the functions and practices of these courts. This chapter does not purport to provide a comprehensive review of the values relevant to the functions of MHCs and of the criminal justice system more generally. The next three sections identify three relevant values and provide preliminary analyses of some relevant concerns raised by MHCs regarding these values.

Retributive Justice

As ordinarily understood, justice requires that each individual is treated as that person is due according to the applicable principles. Retributive justice requires that each offender receive the punishment that is consistent with the applicable principles of justified punishment.[14] The Supreme Court's cases do not provide a single consistent theory of justified punishment under the Eighth Amendment, but several of those opinions identify retribution as an important purpose or limit of punishment.[15] A retributive justification of punishment prescribes punishment in proportion to the desert of the offender.[16] Supreme Court opinions apply the retributive purpose of punishment as addressing punishment in proportion to the severity of the offense and the culpability or blameworthiness of the offender. The Eighth Amendment

---

[12] Kennedy vs. Louisiana, 128 S.Ct. 2641 (2008); Coker vs. Georgia, 433 U.S. 584 (1977).

[13] Petrilla, *supra* note 2; Redlich, *supra* note 2.

[14] The Cambridge Dictionary of Philosophy 759 (Robert Audi ed., 2nd ed. 1999).

[15] Roper vs. Simmons, 125 S.Ct. 1183, 1194–96 (2005); Atkins vs. Virginia 536 U.S. 304, 319 (2002); Gregg vs. Georgia, 428 U.S. 153, 183–84 (1976).

[16] The Cambridge Dictionary of Philosophy, *supra* note 14, at 759.

proscribes excessive punishment, rather than prescribing specific punishments. Thus, these opinions discuss retributive limits on the severity of punishment.[17]

MHCs ordinarily address offenders who have committed misdemeanors or felonies of relatively low severity as compared with the severe offenses and sentences addressed by these Supreme Court opinions.[18] The range of impairment addressed by these courts varies in that some specifically address offenders with "serious mental illness" or an Axis I diagnosis, but others do not specify criteria of mental illness.[19] Consider an offender who commits a felony that does not involve violence against persons. Anderson manifests a chronic schizophrenic disorder that varies in severity across time.[20] He voluntarily participates in treatment when his impairment is relatively less severe, but when the severity exacerbates, his capacities to accurately perceive reality, to reason coherently, and to make reasoned judgments deteriorate. He then obeys the orders of the hallucinatory voice of God to stop taking the medication because Satan's agents are using the medication to prevent him from doing God's work. His cognitive deterioration exacerbates and in response to hallucinatory orders from God, he breaks into the neighbor's house in order to destroy the evil device that the neighbor is using to beam Satan's mind waves into his brain. He destroys the neighbor's furnace.

Arguably, Anderson's crime is primarily a function of his mental illness, rather than of his criminality in the sense that his inclination to engage in criminal conduct is a response to psychological impairment that distorts his ability to recognize and adaptively respond to reality. He has not engaged in any criminal conduct during the periods when his schizophrenic disorder has been in remission. During those periods, his neighbors describe him as "odd" or "idiosyncratic," but he does not engage in criminal or otherwise dangerous behavior. Monitored treatment is likely to promote his well-being and the well-being of society by reducing the severity of his impairment and the risk of further offenses associated with his disorder. Consider, however, some questions regarding the justification for applying the reported MHC process to Anderson. What would justify an MHC in requiring a guilty plea for Anderson in a jurisdiction that has an insanity defense that authorizes a verdict of not guilty by reason of insanity for those who manifest a disorder that rendered them unable to know that their conduct was wrongful? The insanity defense reflects the principle that those who meet this standard are not responsible for their offenses, but requiring a guilty plea apparently reflects the premise that Anderson is responsible for his offense and thus merits the condemnation inherent in criminal conviction and punishment.

---

[17] Roper vs. Simmons, 125 S.Ct. 1183, 1194–96 (2005); Atkins vs. Virginia 536 U.S. 304, 319 (2002); Gregg vs. Georgia, 428 U.S. 153, 183–84 (1976).

[18] Petrilla, *supra* note 2; Redlich, *supra* note 2.

[19] Petrilla, *supra* note 2; Redlich, *supra* note 2. American Psychiatric Association, Diagnostic and Statistical Manual of Mental Disorders 27–28 (4th ed. Text Revision, 2000) (Axis I disorders include a broad range of clinical disorders other than personality disorders and mental retardation.).

[20] American Psychiatric Association, *id.* at 298–313.

Insofar as the court uses the threat of jail or actual applications of short periods of incarceration to promote compliance with the treatment required as a condition of probation, it apparently applies the judgment that Anderson merits condemnation for his culpable criminal conduct and for his failure to comply with the conditions of probation, although his disorder renders him not culpable for his offense. In short, the MHC appears to violate the principle of retributive justice by expressing condemnation of Anderson, who does not merit that condemnation, by requiring a guilty plea from an offender who is not guilty because of his impairment, and by applying punishment through incarceration for noncompliance to an offender who does not deserve that punishment because his failure to comply is a result of his serious impairment.

Consider currently available alternative forms of state intervention. Civil commitment of mentally ill individuals most often requires findings that the individual is mentally ill and dangerous to himself or to others. Specific provisions vary across states, with most explicitly applying commitment under the police power to those who endanger other persons, while some may include those who endanger the property of others.[21] Anderson does not present a clear danger to himself or to other persons, although one may reasonably argue that by breaking and entering the dwelling of others, he places himself in danger of serious harm by the occupants of that dwelling who may exercise defensive force in the belief that they are threatened by someone who is forcefully entering their home.

Alternately, one may argue that by breaking into a home and destroying the furnace in response to his hallucinatory directives, he demonstrates that his psychosis presents a risk to others. Destroying the furnace may have endangered the residents of the house by causing a fire or by releasing toxic fumes. Furthermore, by acting in compliance with the unpredictable content of his delusions and hallucinations in a manner that violates law and the protected interests of others, he provides evidence that suggests that he presents a risk of violence against other persons if his hallucinations and delusions promote such conduct. Thus, Anderson may, or may not, be considered appropriate for civil commitment, depending upon the specific statutory criteria, the accepted interpretations of those criteria, and the specific description of his impairment and behavior at the time of the commitment hearing.

Insofar as civil commitment is applicable to Anderson under the relevant state law, he may be subject to involuntary inpatient or outpatient monitoring and treatment. Alternately, particularly in states with commitment criteria that require overt conduct demonstrating imminent danger to other persons, Anderson could be subject to criminal charges, acquittal as not guilty by reason of insanity, and post-acquittal commitment. Arguably, either civil commitment or post-acquittal commitment would be more consistent with the principle of retributive justice than a guilty plea and suspended sentence in MHC. Neither form of commitment requires a guilty plea or authorizes the use of jail as a means of enforcing participation in clinically appropriate treatment for an individual who manifests mental disorder of a type and degree

[21] Perlin, *supra* note 3, at § 2A–4.8.

that renders him inappropriate for the condemnation inherent in criminal conviction and punishment.

Compare Anderson to Baker, who suffers from chronic, serious but not psychotic depression involving severe sadness, fatigue, pessimism, and anhedonia.[22] He spent extended periods lying dormant in bed—"I'm hopeless, I'm worthless." He has lost his apartment because he has been unable to work with minimum adequacy during the worst periods of depression. He spends extended periods lying in homeless shelters, under highway overpasses, and in alleys. When he is hungry and unable to secure food from assistance agencies, he sometimes steals food from stores. One night when he has not eaten for several days, he breaks into a neighbor's basement to steal food. He is arrested and agrees in the local MHC to plead guilty and participate in a required treatment plan designed to ameliorate his depressive disorder.

His crime is a felony but he did not harm or endanger any person.[23] He would not qualify for civil commitment in jurisdictions that require imminent danger to other persons because he did not engage in any conduct that directly created risk to other persons. As discussed previously regarding Anderson, some courts may interpret this conduct as indicative of danger to self, to others, or to property, but in some jurisdictions, he does not present a clear case for commitment.[24] He would not qualify for the insanity defense because he knew his conduct was contrary to law and to socially accepted morality. He believed his conduct was wrong, and by engaging in that conduct, he deepened his depression by reinforcing his belief that he is worthless. Although his depression includes severe pessimism, it does not distort his ability to comprehend the criminal charges against him or to communicate with his attorney. Thus, he is competent to plead guilty and waive his right to trial.[25]

Although Baker's depressive disorder does not render him not guilty by reason of insanity, it substantially mitigates his culpability. He refrained from criminal conduct until he became desperate for food, and his clear sense of guilt and shame supports the interpretation that he engaged in criminal conduct only when it seemed to him that there was no alternative. Thus, a suspended sentence with participation in treatment as a condition of probation would be proportionate to his culpability for this offense by ordinary standards of retributive proportionality. Treatment as a condition of probation is reasonably related to the offense and to the preventive purpose of the criminal law in that it would be reasonably expected to ameliorate his impairment in a manner that would improve his adaptive capacity and his ability to obtain employment. Thus, it is reasonably designed to reduce the risk that he would commit similar offenses in the future. An MHC would provide an institutional structure that could facilitate and enforce treatment as a condition of probation that would be reasonably expected to promote Baker's treatment interests and society's

---

[22] American Psychiatric Association, *supra* note 19, at 349–52, 371–82. (Anhedonia refers to the inability to experience pleasure in activities that are normally pleasurable.)

[23] Model Penal Code § 221.1 (Proposed Official Draft 1962).

[24] *See supra*, text accompanying note 21.

[25] Godinez vs. Moran, 509 U.S. 389 (1993); Dusky vs. United States, 362 U.S. 402 (1960).

preventive interests through established coordination between the court and mental health treatment providers.

It remains unclear, however, whether this process justifies expunging Baker's record of the crime and conviction. Baker was criminally responsible for his offense and competent to participate in the criminal justice process. Determining whether successful participation in the treatment process as a condition of probation justifies expunging the record requires clarification of the boundaries of expungement. According to one definition, expungement of a person's record involves, "removal of a conviction … from a person's criminal record."[26] This definition appears to indicate that the court's record of the conviction is destroyed or deleted in a manner that renders it no longer accessible to the courts, law enforcement, or the public. One state statute indexed as an expungement provision, in contrast, provides a more limited approach. That provision authorizes the court to set aside a conviction for an offense when the sentence involved only probation or probation and a fine, and the offender has fulfilled the conditions of probation.[27] By setting aside the conviction, the court removes "civil disabilities and disqualifications imposed as a result of the conviction."[28] The record of the offense remains available, however, for a variety of purposes, such as sentencing the same offender for a subsequent offense, impeaching the offender as a witness, or evaluating the offender's application for a license or certificate.[29]

Insofar as expungement is understood as deleting the record of the conviction or as rendering that record unavailable in the manner of ordinary criminal records, it raises serious questions regarding the ability of the courts and law enforcement to consistently enforce the criminal law, the integrity of the criminal justice process, and the ability of the citizenry to monitor and discipline that process. Insofar as it refers only to relieving Baker of some disabilities ordinarily associated with prior convictions, however, there may be persuasive arguments that such a process is consistent with the application of the principles of retributive justice to an offender whose impairment substantially reduces his culpability as compared with ordinary offenders who commit similar offenses. Expungement in this sense would not distort the record of the criminal justice process. Rather, it would provide one process for reducing the severity of the criminal punishment. Insofar as the offender's impairment rendered him less culpable than ordinary offenders who committed similar offenses, this reduction in severity in response to treatment participation would render his punishment proportionate to his limited culpability. It would also promote the societal interest in promoting participation in treatment expected to ameliorate his disorder and reduce the risk of recidivism by promoting rehabilitation and reintegration.

In short, civil commitment and post-insanity acquittal commitment constitute established institutions designed to serve the preventive purpose by providing treatment designed to ameliorate Anderson's impairment and reduce the risk of recidivism in a

---

[26] Black's Law Dictionary 662 (9th ed. 2009).

[27] Neb. Rev. Stat. § 29–2264 (Reissue of 2008).

[28] *Id.* at § 29–2264(4)(b).

[29] *Id.* at § 29–2264(5).

manner that conforms to the principles of retributive justice that are fundamental to the criminal justice process. Accepting a guilty plea from Anderson and subjecting him to jail for the purpose of enforcing treatment requirements of probation raises serious concerns regarding those principles and thus regarding the integrity of the criminal justice process.

A guilty plea with required treatment as a condition of probation for Baker, in contrast, could conform to those principles of retributive justice and reduce the risk of recidivism by advancing Baker's treatment interests. The factors that render Baker appropriate for MHC include the nature and severity of the offense, the type and severity of his impairment, and the relationship between his impairment and his offense. His offense is a serious but nonviolent felony that renders probation at least arguably within a defensible range of sentencing. His depressive disorder does not involve psychotic impairment that would render him appropriate for an insanity defense. Neither does it render him incompetent to plead guilty. Thus, his disorder does not undermine the legitimacy of his guilty plea. It is sufficiently severe, however, to significantly reduce his culpability for his crime. Thus, it provides a basis to justify a relatively less severe sentence of probation for the offense and it provides reason to think that the treatment conditions of probation will promote his treatment interests as well as the public interest in reducing the risk of recidivism.

Comparative Justice

The principle of comparative justice requires that the criminal justice process treat like cases alike and relevantly different cases differently in proportion to the relevant differences.[30] Insofar as the courts addressing criminal cases consistently apply defensible principles of retributive justice, they conform to the requirement of comparative justice. Consistent application of applicable principles of retributive justice would result in similar sentences for offenders who commit offenses of similar severity with similar degrees of culpability. Consistent application of those principles would generate differences in severity of punishment, however, when offenders differed in the severity of their offenses or in the circumstances relevant to their degree of culpability. Such differences would reflect differences in the degree of punishment that was proportionate to these offenders and offenses, rather than arbitrary or discriminatory departures from the principled application of punishment. Several concurring opinions in Furman vs. Georgia represent the importance of comparative justice in Eighth Amendment doctrine by emphasizing the significance of arbitrary or discriminatory variations in capital sentencing as a justification for their reversal of three capital sentences brought through sentencing procedures that allowed the sentencers unguided discretion in applying or withholding capital punishment.[31]

---

[30] Joel Feinberg, Rights, Justice, and the Bounds of Liberty 265–87 (1980).

[31] Furman vs. Georgia, 408 U.S. 238, 242–57 (Douglas, J., concurring), 274–77 (Brennan, J., concurring), 308–10 (Stewart, J., concurring), 364–66 (Marshall, J., concurring).

Upon initial review, MHCs raise two interrelated concerns regarding the pursuit of comparative justice. First, insofar as these courts accept guilty pleas and apply jail as a means of enforcing conditions of probation, do they violate principles of comparative justice by subjecting some offenders who commit offenses due to their mental illness to sanctions and condemnation more severe than those applied to similarly impaired people who engage in similarly harmful or dangerous conduct but are subject to civil commitment or to post-insanity acquittal commitment? Second, insofar as these offenders are competent to plead guilty and criminally responsible for their offenses, do MHCs violate the requirements of comparative justice by subjecting these individuals to less severe punishment than that applied to other offenders who commit similar offenses in circumstances that render them comparably less culpable for reasons other than mental illness?

MHCs can provide reasonable responses to these questions insofar as they apply standards that reflect relevant differences among offenders resulting from the type and severity of impairment they manifest. Insofar as MHCs accept guilty pleas and apply suspended sentences with requirements of participation in treatment enforced by periods of incarceration to offenders who manifest impairment that does not preclude competence to proceed or criminal responsibility but that reduces their culpability as compared with unimpaired offenders who commit similar offenses, these MHCs can respond to these questions in a manner that conforms to the principles of comparative justice. Some of the practices attributed to MHCs raise questions regarding the ability of MHCs to function in a manner that conforms to this response and thus to the requirement of comparative justice. Consider, for example, the following questions.

What type and degree of impairment justifies treating some offenders as competent to proceed and criminally responsible but subjecting them to less severe punishment than that applied to other offenders who commit similar offenses? If an offender is sufficiently impaired to render that offender not responsible for the criminal conduct, what justifies accepting the guilty plea, rather than applying civil commitment or post-insanity acquittal commitment? Alternately, if that offender is not sufficiently impaired to render him not responsible, what justifies punishing him less severely than other offenders who commit similar offenses or expunging his record but not the records of other offenders who commit similar offenses?

Consider Cook who consistently scored between 75 and 80 on intelligence tests when he was in school. He consistently performed poorly in school and dropped out of high school when he became old enough to find a job doing unskilled work. When the economy encountered a downturn, he lost his job and was unable to find any other work. He has been unable to pay rent, and he has been spending nights in homeless shelters or under highway overpasses. When he was unable to find any food for several days, he broke into a house to steal some food. He was arrested and charged with burglary. In contrast to Baker, Cook suffers no diagnosable psychological disorder, but his limited intelligence, skills, and resources render it very difficult for him to respond adaptively to the situational stress, hunger, and fear. This severe stress and his limited capacities do not prevent him from fulfilling the culpability elements required by the offense definition, but they mitigate his blameworthiness as compared with ordinary offenders who commit similar offenses.

Thus, he resembles Baker in that he is criminally responsible for his offense but deserving of less severe punishment than ordinary offenders who commit similar offenses in a system of retributive justice that prescribes punishment in proportion to the severity of the offense and the blameworthiness of the offender. Is there any defensible justification for punishing Cook more severely than Baker by placing Baker but not Cook on probation?

Assume that Baker and Cook are similar in the degree to which they are reasonably considered less culpable than ordinary offenders who commit similar offenses, although both are criminally responsible. Comparative justice would require that they receive similar sentences and that they receive less severe sentences than ordinary offenders who commit similar offenses in the absence of comparable mitigating circumstances. If MHCs provided treatment, rather than punishment, for all and only offenders with mental disorders, regardless of the type and degree of impairment, then those MHCs would violate the principle of comparative justice because they would allow mentally ill offenders to avoid punishment, with its inherent expression of condemnation, regardless of the degree to which their impairment justified differential punishment as compared with ordinary offenders and as compared with offenders, such as Cook, who were less culpable than ordinary offenders for reasons other than mental disorder.

MHCs would facilitate comparative justice, however, insofar as they met two conditions. First, these courts would apply alternative dispositions to mentally impaired offenders in a manner that reflected the degree to which those offenders' impairment rendered them less culpable than ordinary offenders. That is, they would not apply a general approach to all offenders with psychological impairment. Rather, they would carefully assess the manner and degree to which each individual's impairment rendered that offender less blameworthy than ordinary offenders and they would suspend criminal sentences on the condition of participation in treatment for those whose impairment reduced their culpability to a degree comparable with that of other offenders who qualify for suspended sentences with appropriate conditions of probation. Thus, they would promote treatment designed to reduce recidivism while addressing these offenders in a manner consistent with the suspended sentences and required conditions of probation applied to other similarly blameworthy offenders by other problem-solving courts or by the court of general jurisdiction. Offenders such as Cook, for example, may receive a similar suspended sentence with conditions of probation that required basic training in vocational and adaptive skills.

One potential strength of an identified MHC is that a regular pattern of interaction between the court and the available clinical resources would promote the abilities of the court and of the clinicians to communicate effectively with one another and thus to accurately identify offenders appropriate for clinical interventions and to provide appropriate treatment plans designed to ameliorate their disorders and to reduce the risk of disorder-related recidivism. Clinicians can apply relevant expertise in the form of descriptive and explanatory assessment that informs the court regarding the type and degree of the offender's impairment and the manner in which that impairment contributed to the criminal conduct. Such expertise may enable the MHC to more accurately understand the similarities and differences among Anderson, Baker, Cook, and the more general population of offenders. The court can apply this understanding in assessing the relative degrees of culpability among these offenders and for each of these individuals as compared with ordinary offenders. Similarly, such clinical expertise can provide relevant information regarding available treatment alternatives that can inform the court in developing conditions of probation that are consistent with each offender's degree of culpability as well as with the societal interest in reducing the risk of recidivism.

The second condition that would facilitate comparative justice would involve an integrated criminal justice system that would include other problem-solving courts designed to provide suspended sentences and conditions of probation for offenders like Cook who resemble mentally impaired offenders insofar as they commit their offenses in circumstances that justify less severe sentences than ordinary offenders but for reasons that are primarily attributable to factors other than psychological impairment. Insofar as MHCs function as the only alternative to the primary criminal courts, they arguably raise concerns regarding comparative justice because they provide an alternative that is available only to those who are less culpable than most offenders because of mental illness. Insofar as MHCs function within a more comprehensive institutional structure that can provide appropriate alternative dispositions for those offenders who manifest lesser culpability for a variety of reasons, they promote comparative justice by providing different dispositions that reflect relevant differences in culpability.

A comprehensive institutional structure may include primary criminal courts and a number of problem-solving courts directed toward specific populations or concerns. These may include, for example, MHCs and drug courts. Such a complex structure may well constitute a two-edged sword for the purpose of pursuing comparative justice. As discussed, courts prepared to address offenders with mental illness or with other conditions or circumstances that mitigate their culpability and render them appropriate for various preventive interventions as conditions of probation could promote comparative justice insofar as they provide dispositions that reflect relevant differences and similarities. To the degree that the more comprehensive criminal justice system becomes fragmented into a variety of different courts designed to address a variety of offenders and circumstance, however, it seems likely that it will be very difficult to coordinate the courts in a manner that will enable them to consistently apply a principled approach to the application of criminal sanctions. This concern arises again in the next section addressing the integrity of the process.

One additional concern regarding comparative justice involves the distribution of treatment resources. Insofar as MHCs interact with the available treatment providers in such a way as to effectively give some impaired offenders priority for access to treatment over similarly impaired offenders who appear in other courts or over other comparably impaired individuals who do not commit crimes, that priority creates concerns regarding preferential treatment for those who commit crimes and are channeled into MHCs. This concern reflects a more general problem regarding access to treatment for impaired individuals, but in the context of MHCs, it also undermines comparative retributive justice insofar as the involvement of these courts provides a benefit of enhanced access to treatment for some impaired offenders who commit offenses as compared with those who experience similar treatment needs but are channeled to other courts or those who refrain from crime.

Integrity of the Process

Criminal punishment constitutes a severe government intrusion into ordinarily protected liberties. Thus, it is limited by a variety of substantive and procedural rules designed to discipline the exercise of this form of coercion upon individuals. Rigorous enforcement of these rules, and of the principles that underlie the rules, protects individual defendants and the citizens generally from abusive application of coercive force in the form of criminal punishment.

Consider, for example, Anderson who committed his crime in response to hallucinatory orders from God during a period of psychotic decompensation. If he remains psychotically impaired when appearing in the MHC, his competence to plead guilty and to waive the right to a trial on the question of guilt and insanity is highly questionable. The requirement of competence to proceed, including the capacities to comprehend the process and to communicate with his attorney, is central to protecting his right to a fair trial and to maintaining a disciplined criminal justice process.[32] Thus, if MHCs allowed some defendants, such as Anderson, to plead guilty when they were in a psychotic state that impaired their ability to comprehend and reason regarding the decision to plead guilty, they would distort the integrity of the process in a manner that undermines the protections from unjustified convictions and punishment for Anderson and for the citizenry more generally.

If Anderson has received treatment and regained competence to proceed before pleading guilty, he may competently decide that he would prefer a guilty plea in an MHC to pursuing an insanity defense in a criminal trial. He may prefer this because doing so will facilitate ongoing treatment without subjecting him to post-acquittal commitment and because the MHC may expunge his record upon completion of the required treatment. Although this decision may well promote Anderson's treatment interests and his comprehensive interests, it raises important concerns regarding the integrity of the process that protects the citizenry more generally. Applying a guilty verdict to a defendant who clearly appears to qualify for a not guilty by reason of insanity verdict undermines the integrity of the process. Insofar as the MHC applies incarceration as a means of enforcing the required participation in treatment, it violates the obligation of society to apply coercive force in the form of criminal punishment only to those who merit that punishment according to the standards of the applicable law because of their culpable criminal conduct.

Criminal punishment expresses societal condemnation of the criminal conduct as wrong and of the offender as a culpable wrongdoer by the standards of the conventional public morality embodied in law.[33] A verdict of guilty and the application of

---

[32] Perlin, *supra* note 3, at § 8A-2.1.

[33] Robert F. Schopp, Justification Defenses and Just Convictions 22–26 (1998).

a criminal sentence to an offender, such as Anderson, who lacked the capacities of criminal responsibility at the time of the crime violates the applicable principles of retributive justice and undermines the integrity of the process. It does so by applying the condemnation applicable to culpable wrongdoers to an individual who does not qualify as culpable. It may seem plausible to respond that limiting the punishment to probation with conditions requiring treatment compliance ameliorates this concern because the minimal application of punishment renders negligible the harshness of the punishment and of the condemnation expressed. This response encounters the following dilemma.

Either the sentence is within the range that is proportionate to the offense or it is not. If it is within that range, then it expresses condemnation of the offender as a culpable wrongdoer who deserves punishment that is in the ordinary range of proportionality to this offense, and thus, it reaffirms the condemnation of the offender expressed by the conviction. If an offender, such as Anderson, lacks the capacities required for criminal responsibility, this condemnation of an offender who does not merit such condemnation violates the principles of retributive justice and undermines the integrity of the process. Alternately, if it is sufficiently mild to be clearly disproportionate to the severity of the offense, it expresses the proposition that this offender is not sufficiently culpable to be subject to the punishment prescribed as proportionate to this offense. Then, the conviction and sentence jointly express the incoherent proposition that this offender is, and is not, culpable for this offense. Allowing courts to engage in such incoherent decision-making undermines the discipline of law on the courts. Insofar as this incoherence is visible to the public, it undermines the public trust in the courts. Insofar as it is not visible to the public, in contrast, it undermines the discipline of transparency on the judicial process.

The potential to expunge the record at a later point may appeal to Anderson, but it exacerbates the risk to the citizenry generally insofar as it encourages the courts to consider it legitimate to apply punishment for instrumental purposes to those who do not merit condemnation. Similarly, it undermines the integrity of the process insofar as it allows the courts to conceal the apparently inconsistent interpretation and application of law. Insofar as expungement is limited to relieving the offender of specific disabilities associated with the conviction, it does not distort the record. Insofar as expungement allows revision of the record or limitation of access to the record that would ordinarily be accessible, however, it dilutes the discipline of the criminal process.[34] Expungement also has the potential to undermine the integrity of the process if it encourages judges to interpret and apply substantive and procedural standards loosely because they think of the process as promoting, rather than harming, the interests of the individual defendant. Insofar as it has this effect, it may encourage judges to undermine the institutional structure by considering it appropriate to depart from the applicable standards and practices when doing so appears to serve the interests of those immediately affected.

A similar concern arises regarding the use of jail to enforce conformity to the conditions of probation. Insofar as an offender competently pleads guilty to a crime

---

[34] *See supra*, notes 26–29 and accompanying text.

for which he is responsible and probation is an appropriate disposition, the use of jail to enforce the conditions of probation falls within the legitimate range of coercive force applied by the courts. If the defendant lacked competence to wave the right to trial and plead guilty, however, incarceration for failing to conform to conditions of a plea agreement to which he was unable to competently consent raises concerns regarding the legitimacy of the incarceration and of the plea agreement on which it is based. Similarly, if the defendant's impairment was sufficient to undermine his responsibility for the initial crime, then incarceration to enforce conditions of probation as a sentence for that crime raises serious questions regarding the intrusion into ordinarily protected liberty ostensibly justified as punishment for a crime for which he is not responsible.

Baker, in contrast to Anderson, manifests a type and severity of impairment that does not render him incompetent to plead guilty and waive the right to a trial. Insofar as his offense falls within the range of offenses for which a suspended sentence with conditions of probation is consistent with the applicable principles of retributive and comparative justice, the court can accept his guilty plea and suspend his sentence on condition that he fulfills the required conditions of probation. Furthermore, the enforcement of the conditions of probation with brief periods of incarceration would be consistent with the requirements of competence, retributive justice, and comparative justice insofar as similar practices are applied to other offenders with suspended sentences and Baker has not deteriorated into a more severe state of impairment that would undermine his responsibility for his failure to conform. Finally, if expungement consists only of the removal of some disabilities ordinarily associated with conviction, it can be consistent with the principles of retributive and comparative justice, as well as with the integrity of the process.

Insofar as expungement involves deletion of the record of conviction or removal of the record from the ordinary range of accessibility, however, the expungement of Baker's record can raise serious concerns regarding the effectiveness and the integrity of the process. Regarding effectiveness, to the degree that expungement deletes the conviction from the record or reduces access to the record, it undermines the opportunity to accurately review the offender's history with the criminal justice system. Alternately, to the degree that expungement leaves the record intact but limits access to that record, it reduces the transparency of the criminal process and the effectiveness of the record as a means to monitor and discipline the application of coercive force through the criminal justice system. Although a particular offender, such as Baker, may prefer to have his record expunged, allowing expungement has the potential to dilute the ability of the citizenry to monitor the courts in their application of the principles of retributive and comparative justice. It may also be expected to encourage courts to apply the coercive force of the criminal law in a less disciplined manner because it may seem that unjustified convictions can be corrected in retrospect. Insofar as expunging the record reduces the degree to which the courts or others have access to accurate accounts of the process, it may undermine the ability of the courts or other actors to monitor the consistent application of these principles by preventing full awareness of prior applications to relevantly similar or relevantly different offenders. Thus, it has the potential to undermine the principles of retributive and comparative justice.[35] These concerns regarding the potential of expungement to dilute the integrity of the process remain speculative. Thus, the most defensible response to these concerns may involve awareness and careful monitoring in developing the procedures applied by MHCs.

Assume that Cook's limited intelligence, education, occupational skills, and social skills reduce his culpability level to a degree similar to that to which Baker's depression reduces his culpability. Thus, Baker and Cook remain criminally responsible for similar crimes, but both are less culpable than unimpaired offenders who commit similar crimes. If this assumption is accurate, comparative justice should require similar punishment expressing similar degrees of condemnation. Insofar as MHCs are limited to individuals whose crimes are understood as reflecting decreased culpability due to mental illness, they undermine comparative justice by providing an alternative institutional structure that will reduce Baker's punishment in a manner that reflects his reduced culpability but will not reduce Cook's punishment in a manner that reflects his comparably reduced culpability. Such a disparity due to the presence of an MHC in a system with no corresponding problem-solving court for offenders like Cook undermines the integrity of the process because it is not merely a function of unavoidable variations of judgment by different individual judges. Rather, it reflects a disparity in the institutional structure that undermines the comparative justice function of the institution.

MHCs would be consistent with the integrity of the process regarding this concern, however, if the more comprehensive criminal justice system included MHCs designed to address the specific concerns regarding retributive and comparative justice that arise with impaired offenders like Baker as well as alternative structures and processes that accurately applied the general principles of criminal justice to other offenders. These may include, for example, problem-solving courts prepared to address offenders such as Cook and criminal courts prepared to competently address concerns regarding criminal competence and responsibility raised by offenders such as Anderson. In short, specialty courts could reasonably be expected to promote the well-being of those affected and the more general set of relevant values insofar as they developed specialized expertise and functioned effectively as components in an integrated institutional structure designed to implement these values.

MHCs and Legal Mental Illness

Offenders such as Anderson, Baker, and Cook reveal an underlying question that is central to the legitimacy of MHCs. What type and degree of impairment justifies practices of the MHCs that appear to deviate from more general practices that the criminal justice system applies to the broad range of ordinary offenders? As indicated

[35] *See supra*, [Sections titled] "Retributive Justice" and "Comparative Justice" regarding retributive and comparative justice.

in section "Relevant Values Embodied in Law," the point here is not that MHCs necessarily deviate from defensible standards of criminal punishment. Rather, MHCs function as components in a more comprehensive criminal justice system. MHCs can facilitate societal interests in reducing recidivism without violating other important societal values insofar as they pursue the preventive function in a manner consistent with the complex set of purposes and principles that govern that system. Thus, they present a particular context in which it is important to address two questions that permeate mental health law. First, what type and degree of impairment should qualify as "mental illness" for this specific legal purpose? Second, how does that type and degree of impairment justify differential treatment of individuals with that impairment for this particular legal purpose? That is, what integrated set of purposes and principles justify us in treating individuals who manifest that impairment differently than non-mentally ill people who commit similar offenses?[36]

At first glance, it may seem reasonable to suggest that specialized MHCs within the criminal justice system would be appropriate for addressing criminal behavior by individuals who manifest severe impairment that renders them incompetent to proceed in the ordinary process of criminal adjudication and inappropriate for criminal punishment with its inherent expression of condemnation. The prior discussion of Anderson and Baker suggests, however, that this interpretation would be misguided as applied to MHCs as they are frequently designed and applied. Insofar as MHCs require that defendants plead guilty and apply periods of incarceration as methods of enforcing the requirements of probation, the integrity of the process requires that the individuals are competent to plead guilty and sufficiently responsible for their conduct to justify guilty verdicts and the application of incarceration for failure to conform to the required conditions of probation.

These requirements and the discussion of Anderson and Baker may suggest that MHCs should be limited to individuals, such as Baker, who do not fall within specified diagnostic categories. Those who qualify for psychotic diagnoses manifest distortions of their ability to recognize and reason about reality, as well as distortions in their ability to reason about their relationship to reality.[37] Thus, these individuals will often lack the capacities required to qualify as competent to proceed or to plead guilty. Anderson provides an example of one whose psychotic disorder precludes competence to plead guilty and prevents him from meeting minimal requirements of responsibility for his initial crime and for his failure to fulfill conditions of probation. Thus, his impairment undermines the justification for subjecting him to incarceration as punishment for the crime or for the failure to fulfill the conditions of probation.

Consider Davis who suffers from a chronic schizophrenic disorder that includes serious but encapsulated distortion of his ability to recognize and reason about reality. This distortion includes persecutory delusions and hallucinations that he experiences as threats to kill him by agents of a secret criminal conspiracy.[38] Due to his disorder, he hides for days at a time to avoid being killed by the conspirators. This pattern of

[36] Robert F. Schopp, Competence, Condemnation, and Commitment 41–49 (2001).

[37] American Psychiatric Association, *supra* note 19, at 297–98.

[38] *Id.* at 297–302.

hiding for unpredictable periods of time prevents him from holding a job. He has had several jobs, but he has been fired from each when he failed to attend work without notice during his periods of hiding. Thus, he sometimes lacks food for several days. At one point, following several days of hiding without food, he broke into a house in order to steal food. He was fully aware that this was a violation of law and accepted morality. He agreed at the time of the offense that it was wrong to steal from this family because he did not believe that they were part of the conspiracy. He selected their house partially because he believed that they were not part of the conspiracy and, thus, that they were not watching him. He broke into this family's house because after several days without eating, he was desperate to secure food, and he had no income or alternative source of food. Although he suffers from a psychotic disorder, he resembles Baker in that he does not qualify for acquittal under common standards for insanity because he understood that his conduct was wrong. He is competent to plead guilty and waive his right to a jury trial because he can understand the process and communicate with his attorney.

Davis is guilty by common legal standards. Some readers may conclude that Davis illustrates the inadequacy of common legal standards for the insanity defense. Others may agree that Davis should be held responsible because he was aware that he was committing a crime against innocent persons. Most would probably agree, however, that his disorder renders him substantially less culpable than most criminals who commit similar crimes of burglary. A sentence of probation with required participation in treatment for his disorder would reasonably be expected to reduce the risk that he would commit further crimes, promote his treatment interests, and be proportionate to his reduced degree of culpability. Thus, the guilty verdict, suspended sentence, and required treatment would plausibly be consistent with the principles of retributive and comparative justice. By conforming to these principles and the standard of competence to plead, the court would maintain the integrity of the criminal justice process.

If Davis failed to conform to the treatment process because he disliked the relatively minor side-effects of the treatment or because he found it embarrassing to be required to participate in that treatment, brief periods of incarceration to motivate compliance would be consistent with his conditions of probation and with his impairment which is serious but does not render him incompetent to plead guilty or preclude responsibility for this conduct. In contrast, if he ceased participating in the treatment because his delusions and hallucinations exacerbated and caused him to believe that the judge and treatment providers had joined the conspiracy to kill him by requiring that he ingest poison disguised as medication, then incarceration for his failure to conform to the conditions of probation would undermine the integrity of the process by applying criminal punishment that did not conform to the principles of retributive justice because Davis' impairment would be sufficient to render him not responsible for his failure to fulfill the conditions of probation.

The examples of Anderson, Baker, and Davis arguably illustrate a more general point about the significance of psychological impairment for various legal purposes. The significance of an individual's impairment for a particular legal purpose cannot be determined merely by diagnostic category. Rather, one must describe the functional impairment manifested by this individual and the manner in which that impairment affects this person's ability to perform the psychological processes that are relevant to the specific legal status at issue. The court must determine whether that functional impairment and the resulting distortion of the relevant psychological operations are sufficient to render that person ineligible for the legal status at issue.[39] Participation in MHCs as discussed in this chapter requires competence to plead guilty as well as responsibility for the crimes that justify the guilty finding and for the failure to conform to the conditions of probation that justify the application of incarceration.

In appropriate cases, clinicians can evaluate the offenders' impairment and provide relevant testimony that describes this impairment and explains the manner in which that impairment influences the criminal conduct and the capacities relevant to judicial determinations of competence, responsibility, and sentence severity. That testimony can also include advice regarding available treatment that can reasonably be expected to ameliorate the impairment and, thus, to promote the offender's treatment interests as well as societal interests in reducing recidivism. Insofar as a particular offender is at least minimally competent and responsible, he can plead guilty and be placed on probation with conditions that fall within the range that is consistent with his degree of culpability and that promote participation in treatment expected to improve his well-being and to promote the societal interest in preventing recidivism.

Conclusion

MHCs draw attention to several important components of the criminal law as well as to concerns that are central to mental health law more generally. Various components of criminal and civil law treat some individuals differently than they treat people generally because those individuals are identified as manifesting mental illness. In order to justify differential treatment of these individuals, respect the standing of these individuals, and maintain the integrity of these specific legal institutions, as well as the integrity of the process of self-government through law, we must clearly identify the type and degree of impairment that constitutes mental illness for each specific legal purpose because it justifies differential treatment for those who manifest that impairment. In addition, we must explain the justification for treating individuals with that impairment differently than we treat most individuals in relevantly similar circumstances.

The harsh sanctions and expression of condemnation inherent in criminal punishment require careful attention to the requirements of competence, responsibility, and proportionality. Thus, identifying the type and degree of psychological impairment that justifies treating some offenders differently than we treat most ordinary offenders who commit similar offenses requires that we examine carefully the significance of various types and degrees of impairment for the appropriate attributions of competence, responsibility, and proportionality. This requirement takes on particular significance in context of criminal punishment because criminal punishment

---

[39] Schopp, *supra* note 36, at 44–49.

involves the intentional infliction of harsh sanctions and potentially severe intrusions into protected liberties. The analysis in this chapter advances an initial interpretation of some of the important considerations that must be addressed if MHCs are to pursue societal interests in reducing recidivism in a manner that conforms to the more general principles of criminal competence, responsibility, and proportionality that discipline the infliction of coercive force on individuals by the state in the form of criminal punishment.

One important aspect of this analysis addresses the integration of the legitimate functions of MHCs with related institutions, including general criminal courts and those that apply civil commitment or alternative forms of mental health intervention. Maintaining discipline on the functions of each of these institutions requires integration of the legitimate functions of each with the legitimate functions of the other institutions and with the principles that justify these various functions. In ideal circumstances, a defensible set of coercive state institutions would cohere with the complex set of purposes and justifications that provide the foundation in principle for this integrated institutional structure. In such an ideal world, a single criminal court would have the ability to understand and give justified mitigating effect to all relevant mitigating circumstances. A court with comprehensive understanding of the full range of relevant sentencing factors would be able to weigh them against each other and recognize the net aggravating and mitigating effects of all relevant considerations. In addition, that comprehensive understanding of the full range of sentencing considerations, in conjunction with full understanding of all the available rehabilitative alternatives, would enable the court to attain retributive justice and comparative justice while maximizing the rehabilitative function that would minimize recidivism.

In our world, however, it is not realistic to expect that any human institutions will fully conform in practice to the relevant purposes and justifications in principle. Thus, specific variations of these institutions must be assessed and pursued, or rejected, in context of the realistically available alternatives. In this world, a series of factors impair the ability of criminal courts to attain the ideal. These factors include, for example, a very heavy caseload that prevents courts from expending extended periods of inquiry regarding the most effective disposition for each offender; a lack of clarity regarding the most justifiable integration of various sentencing considerations such as retribution, rehabilitation, deterrence, and comparative justice; and the ongoing difficulties that arise when legal actors and clinicians attempt to communicate and interact with each other. Thus, in our world, a variety of problem-solving courts that focus their attention on specific categories of offenders, such as drug courts and MHCs, may reasonably be expected to advance the preventive functions of the criminal law in a manner that approximates the requirements of retributive and comparative justice more effectively than the realistically available alternatives. Ongoing critical review and revision constitutes one aspect of a responsible attempt to conform as closely as possible to the justifications in principle.

Acknowledgments I am grateful to Eve Brank, Mike Quattrocchi, Barb Sturgis, and Richard Wiener for helpful comments on prior drafts.

Appendix: Relevant Offenders

Anderson:

1. Destroys neighbors furnace.
2. Chronic schizophrenic disorder; hallucinatory orders from God.
3. Lacks competence to proceed, criminal responsibility.

Baker:

1. Breaks into neighbor's basement to steal food.
2. Chronic major but not psychotic depressive disorder.
3. Competent to proceed, criminally responsible.

Cook:

1. Breaks into house to steal food.
2. No clinical diagnosis, limited intelligence and employment skills.
3. Competent to proceed, criminally responsible.

Davis:

1. Breaks into house to steal food.
2. Chronic schizophrenic disorder, hallucinatory threats to kill him.
3. Competent to proceed, knew the burglary was wrong.

Chapter 11
The Evolution of Problem-Solving Courts in Australia and New Zealand: A Trans-Tasman Comparative Perspective

Elizabeth Richardson, Katey Thom and Brian McKenna

Introduction

There has been a continual yet gradual expansion of problem-solving courts in Australia since these courts were first imported from the USA in the late 1990s. Australian states and territories have embraced the concept of problem-solving courts, albeit with some caution and deliberation, adapting the problem-solving court model to suit the local circumstances of each jurisdiction (Nolan 2009). Although many Australian problem-solving courts have come about through grassroots judicial innovation, increasingly, the expansion of these initiatives is being driven by governments.

As Nolan (2009) found, the cultural and structural differences between the USA and Australia have led to quite different problem-solving court practices in each country. There has been a tendency by those working in Australian courts to critically reflect on innovative practices and a preference that problem-solving courts be supported by legislation (Nolan 2009; Popovic 2003). Australian problem-solving court magistrates are also less emotive and expressive; they are also more concerned about ensuring procedural rights are protected and that principles of open justice are observed (Nolan 2009). The approach in Australian courts has been described as "problem-oriented" (Freiberg 2001, 2005) or "solution-focused" (King 2009, 2010).[1] These terms reflect the belief that courts should not be seen to be "solving" a person's problems for them. Rather, courts should assist the person to address the factors

[1] The Law Reform Commission of Western Australia (2008, 2009) has used the term "court intervention programs," whereas Payne (2005) preferred the use of the term "specialty courts."

E. Richardson (✉)
Australian Centre for Justice Innovation, Faculty of Law, Monash University, Monash University Law Chambers, Level 1/555 Lonsdale Street, Melbourne 3000, Australia
e-mail: liz.richardson@monash.edu

K. Thom
Centre for Mental Health Research, University of Auckland, Auckland, New Zealand

B. McKenna
Australian Catholic University and North Western Mental Health, Melbourne, Australia

R. L. Wiener, E. M. Brank (eds.), *Problem Solving Courts*,
DOI 10.1007/978-1-4614-7403-6_11,

relating to their offending behavior themselves via an individualized treatment or intervention plan monitored by the court (King 2009, 2010).

In contrast to Australia, the problem-solving court movement in New Zealand is much less developed but is beginning to gather momentum. There are a number of projects currently operating and more courts planned. The introduction of two pilot alcohol and drug courts in 2012 is the first of these initiatives that has been driven by government. However, there has been limited discussion to date regarding the problem-solving court movement in New Zealand.

The purposes of this chapter are twofold. First, we will provide an overview of problem-solving courts currently operating in Australia and New Zealand. Many Australian jurisdictions are planning new problem-solving courts or adapting the practices of the courts already in operation. With over a decade of experience with drug courts and mental health courts, there is recognition that many people coming before court do not have a single problem that can be neatly separated out and identified as the sole cause of offending (King et al. 2009). Gradually more courts are seeking ways to address high rates of coexisting mental health and addiction problems (also known as coexisting disorders, co-occurring disorders, dual diagnosis, and comorbidity), in addition to high rates in offender populations of intellectual disability, acquired brain injury, homelessness, and other psychosocial needs. This has led some Australian states, and New Zealand, to develop integrated programs that address multiple and complex problems more holistically.

The second key aim of this chapter is to explore the complex issue of collaboration. Collaboration is a multifaceted concept that is integral to the successful operation of problem-solving courts, but it is a concept that has not yet adequately been explored in the literature or in practice of these courts in Australia. It is an important issue for both "single-issue" problem-solving courts, which process many offenders with coexisting mental health and addiction problems and those courts that have already developed integrated or holistic programs addressing multiple problems. We will examine the ways in which problem-solving courts can bring about meaningful and effective interdisciplinary collaboration between the legal, health, and welfare sectors beyond paying lip service to the concept.

The Australian and New Zealand Problem-Solving Court Movements

Drug courts, family violence courts, mental health courts and, to a lesser extent, community justice courts, have become regular fixtures across Australia.[2] However, these courts have been established in an incremental fashion rather than through an

[2] Australian problem-solving courts have been comprehensively reviewed elsewhere (Freiberg 2001, 2005; King et al. 2009; Law Reform Commission of Western Australia 2008, 2009; Payne 2005; Richardson and McSherry 2010).

integrated strategy (King 2006).[3] Magistrates' Courts have generally been the sites for the establishment of problem-solving courts due, largely, to the broader adaptability of the lower courts to economic, political, and social change (Freiberg 2001; Roach Anleu and Mack 2007).[4] In many instances, these courts have come about because innovative magistrates have been willing to experiment and find effective, more humane ways of dealing with offenders who have significant psychosocial problems. Most problem-solving courts in Australia are underpinned by the concept of therapeutic jurisprudence.[5] Therapeutic jurisprudence refers to the meta-theory developed by Wexler and Winick (1991) that advocates studying, and is the study of, the therapeutic and antitherapeutic impact of the law in practice. Freiberg (2011b) summarizes the concept as "an approach to the study of the law as a therapeutic agent, focusing upon the impact of the law on the emotional life and psychological well-being of not only offenders but of all of the participants in a justice system: judicial officers, victims, offenders, plaintiffs, defendants and others" (p. 300).

Problem-solving courts currently in operation in New Zealand have predominantly been grassroots judicial initiatives in reaction to perceived ineffective responses to core social issues. Therefore, they largely function by drawing on existing resources available to the judiciary and have not received national recognition (Recordon 2005). Although problem-solving courts are a relatively recent development in New Zealand—beginning with the establishment of family violence courts in 2001—there are now a number of problem-solving courts for youth, and one for persons who are experiencing homelessness. The establishment of adult drug courts has been approached cautiously in New Zealand. Following support from some judicial officers (Cheng 2011; TVNZ 2010) and a report from the New Zealand Law Commission, which recommended that the government establish these courts (New Zealand Law Commission 2011), two alcohol and drug courts are currently being piloted in the Auckland region. A mental health court has also not yet been established in New Zealand, although the idea has been mooted in academic circles (Brookbanks 2006; Toki 2010). A community court project has also commenced in Porirua District Court building on principles used in other community courts internationally.

---

[3] Although King's comments pertained to drug courts, this is true generally of other types of problem-solving courts, however, the broader drug diversion system has become more structured in Australia over recent years as a result of national campaigns to target illicit drug use such as the National Illicit Drugs Strategy and the Illicit Drug Diversion Initiative (Hughes and Ritter 2008; Law Reform Commission of Western Australia 2008).

[4] King and Auty (2005) have noted that Magistrates' Courts have not traditionally been the site of innovation. The pressure of onerous lists, multiple jurisdictions, and circuit requirements meant that magistrates had little time to consider different ways of administering justice, but it is these same pressures that have driven the push towards problem-solving courts. Freiberg (2001) has also discussed the factors behind the adoption of problem-solving courts in Australia in more detail.

[5] As Nolan (2009) highlighted, this is not the case in England, Scotland, and Ireland, where therapeutic jurisprudence has not generally been embraced.

Australian Drug Courts, Mental Health Courts, and Community Courts

Most Australian jurisdictions have established drug courts and these sit within the broader scheme of drug diversion programs operating in each state (Hughes and Ritter 2008; King et al. 2009). These drug courts have been positively evaluated, and amongst other outcomes, generally have shown reductions in recidivism while participants are on the drug court program and after the program has been completed (King et al. 2009; Law Reform Commission of Western Australia 2008).[6] It can be said that drug courts have become an established part of the legal landscape in Australia. However, it has also become clear that these courts are not immune from economic or political pressures in Australia. In 2012, New South Wales closed the Youth Drug Court, which had operated since 2000, and the Queensland government moved, despite positive evaluations of these courts, to close the five drug courts operating in that state and the special circumstances court list for people who are homeless and have mental illnesses, as cost cutting measures.

In Australia, drug courts are often centralized to a particular court location rather than being available throughout each State. In New South Wales, a Drug Court pilot was established in 1998 in Parramatta, a region of Sydney. However, it was not until March 2011 that a second Drug Court was established in the Hunter Region of New South Wales; it accepts referrals from a number of courts in the area. In Victoria, the only drug court operates from the Dandenong Magistrates' Court, an outer suburb of metropolitan Melbourne. This means that participants generally have to commit an offence or reside in a particular location in order to access the drug court, which raises some issues regarding inequity of access. This situation has been termed "justice by geography" (Clancey and Howard 2006) or "postcode justice" (Coverdale 2011; Ross 2009). Coverdale (2011) notes that problem-solving courts, while progressive, rely "on a level of court based programs, and local support and rehabilitation services, often not available to smaller rural centres" and "limited and inconsistent roll-out of programs... is likely to result in inequitable outcomes for court participants in regional centres not covered by the program" (p. 9). "Postcode justice" has additional implications for indigenous offenders living in remote rural communities and areas who are likely to receive inferior services when compared to urban areas (Blagg 2009, p. 24).

Currently, in Australia, mental health courts based on the problem-solving court model[7] operate in four states: in South Australia, the Magistrates' Court Diversion Program was established in 1999, in Tasmania, the Mental Health Diversion List

---

[6] Studies of Australian drug courts have generally used experimental or quasiexperimental design: for an overview of Australian drug court evaluations see Indermaur and Roberts (2003) and Jones (2011).

[7] These courts can be contrasted to the Queensland Mental Health Court, which sits in the Supreme Court of Queensland and primarily determines legal issues of fitness to plead and criminal responsibility. For a more comprehensive overview of Australian mental health courts see Richardson and McSherry (2010).

commenced in 2007, in Victoria, the Assessment and Referral Court List was established in 2010, and a mental health court list was established in Western Australia in 2012.[8] As with drug courts, mental health courts sit alongside other court diversion schemes that target individuals with mental illnesses such as forensic mental health court liaison services and legislative powers of diversion in New South Wales (Richardson and McSherry 2010). There are various other single-issue problem-solving courts such as the intellectual disability diversion program in Western Australia.

The Neighborhood Justice Centre (NJC) is the sole community court currently operating in Australia.[9] This court commenced in 2007 in Collingwood, an inner-city suburb of Melbourne, Victoria and is underpinned by both therapeutic jurisprudence and restorative justice principles.[10] The NJC has been modeled on the Red Hook Community Justice Center and the Midtown Community Court operating in New York, USA and the North Liverpool Community Justice Centre in the UK. Like its counterparts, the NJC consists of a court housed in the same building (a former school) along with a wide range of community services and treatment providers that assist offenders and victims involved in the court but also any member of the local community. The NJC has sought to develop strong connections with the community and has been positively evaluated.[11]

In 2005, Freiberg suggested that there are two ways in which problem-solving courts might develop: governments could create more specialized courts that deal with more problems or establish more courts in places where they do not currently exist (p. 214). Alternatively, governments could integrate problem-solving approaches into the broader criminal justice system (Freiberg 2005). What is currently happening in Australia appears to be a combination of these two approaches. More courts are gradually being established (and as noted above, some have also been closed), but are not focused on different or new problems. Rather, as we will discuss later in

[8] Other states considering establishing mental health courts include New South Wales, where a symposium was held by the Law Reform Commission of New South Wales on 1 April 2011 to consider "Should NSW have a Mental Health Court?" See, http://sydney.edu.au/news/law/457.html?eventcategoryid=35&eventid=7386 and http://www.abc.net.au/rn/allinthemind/stories/2011/3189078.htm. Retrieved 15 June 2011. The Law Reform Commission of New South Wales subsequently made recommendations that a mental health court be established in that state: New South Wales Law Reform Commission (2012).

[9] A Community Court in Northern Territory also exists, however, this is a indigenous sentencing court. See below for further discussion of these types of courts.

[10] Restorative justice has been described as "the restoration of victims, offenders and communities primarily through mediated encounters between victims and offenders—and in some cases their supporters—where they discuss what happened, in relation to harmful behavior, and why it happened, and determine what offenders will do to make amends" (King et al. 2009, p. 39).

[11] More information on the Neighbourhood Justice Centre can be found at http://www.neighbourhoodjustice.vic.gov.au/site/page.cfm.

this chapter, the approach seems to indicate a move toward dealing better with coexisting or multiple and complex problems, and the provision of holistic or integrated services, both in problem-solving courts and in the mainstream court systems.[12]

New Zealand's Problem-Solving Courts for Young Offenders

Although New Zealand has only recently established a drug court for adult offenders, there are two courts operating within the youth justice system of New Zealand that focus on drug-related issues. The first is a drug specific court instigated in Christchurch in 2002, which focuses on enhancing the treatment of offenders who have a serious drug dependency that has contributed to their repeat offending (Becroft 2010). In 2007, a second court commenced in Auckland for "at-risk" youth with mental health and/or drug and alcohol issues called the Intensive Monitoring Group (IMG) (Mooney 2010). The development of the Christchurch youth drug court was influenced by youth drug court initiatives in Sydney.

Both the Christchurch youth drug court and the IMG accept young people onto their list based on recommendations from family group conferences.[13] These drug courts have a dual focus on holding the young person accountable for his or her actions while also ensuring the victim's issues and interests are addressed. To be eligible, the young person must be a repeat offender and have a moderate-to-serious drug dependency. Although the IMG was modeled heavily on the Christchurch youth drug court, it seeks to address both drug dependency and mental health issues (Becroft 2010). In addition to reliance on restorative justice principles, both courts utilize the common elements of problem-solving courts including the development of a treatment plan that focuses on outcomes for the victim, society, and the offender; collaboration between stakeholders (police, child welfare agencies, court staff, etc.); the use of screening and assessment tools; and consistent monitoring of the offender's progress while on the court program (Becroft 2010).

Therapeutic jurisprudence principles incorporated into these courts include consistency of judges and professionals (that is, the same judge regularly reviews the case

[12] Examples of holistic approaches to dealing with an individual with multiple problems can be found in Michael King's *Solution-Focused Judging Bench Book* (2009) at p. 40–41. King (2009) states that "problem-solving programs that take this approach seek to provide assistance to participants where needed and appropriate in major life domains, such as health (addressing substance abuse and other problems), employment and training, accommodation, financial planning, other life skills, recreation and relationships" (p. 40–41).

[13] Family group conferences are used both as a precharge mechanism to determine whether prosecution can be avoided and also to determine how to process cases admitted or proved in the youth court (Ministry of Justice 2011). Family group conferences involve the young offender, the victim, and their families with the aim to reach a group consensus on a "just" outcome (Ministry of Justice 2011). The conferences results in a family group conference plan, which includes methods of addressing the victim's needs and concerns, accountability issues, the young person's treatment plan, and other relevant issues such as education and cultural reports (Court in the Act 2008, October).

and develops a rapport with the young person), immediacy of treatment, and a physical court layout that fosters communication (Becroft 2010). Collaborative teams in both courts represent major stakeholder interests in the proceedings. Court officials facilitate the nonadversarial approach to youth justice in New Zealand and consist of the court clerk, the police prosecutor, and youth justice coordinators. Representatives from social care and health agencies are also part of the collaborative team and include social workers, education advisors, and regional youth forensic mental health service staff. Specialist youth advocates also represent the young person's interests within the collaborative team endeavor.

Evaluations of the youth drug court and the IMG have generated mixed results. An initial mixed-method, process evaluation of the pilot Christchurch youth drug court indicated positive results in terms of early identification and reduction of alcohol or drug dependency in young people through treatment delivery, ongoing monitoring, and successful interagency co-ordination (Carswell 2004). A later study by Searle and Spier (2006), however, indicated that members of the youth drug court pilot sample were as likely to reoffend as a national and partially matched sample of youth in regular Youth Court at 6- and 12-month follow-up periods. A preliminary evaluation of the IMG, which partially matched 11 IMG participants with 22 young people who met the IMG criteria but were dealt with by standard youth court practice, found no differences in self-reported recidivism after a 6-month follow-up period. The IMG participants were significantly more likely to access clinical services to address their identified needs than the control group and the risk of recidivism was also reduced compared to the control group. Both mixed-method evaluations, however, were plagued by many of the methodological problems related to sample sizes, matched-comparison studies, and generalizability (Mooney 2010; Searle and Spier 2006) that have been extensively detailed in the wider literature on problem-solving court evaluations (for example, see Roberts and Indermaur 2007; Steadman 2005; Steadman et al. 2001; Wolff and Pogorzelski 2005).

In addition to these youth drug courts, there are now ten courts specifically for young Māori and two Pasifika youth court in New Zealand (Becroft 2011). The Rangatahi Courts represent a community-based response to the current over-representation of young Māori offenders. Founded on the original Poho o Rawiri Rangatahi Court (Marae Monitoring Court) in Gisborne, these are the newest New Zealand youth problem-solving courts. Although their practices are similar to those of the IMG in Auckland, the Rangatahi courts use Māori language, culture, and protocols as part of the court process (Becroft 2010). They sit in marae (tribal specific settings) in order to help young Māori to "face up to their offending in the gaze of their elders and ancestors" (Court in the Act 2010, July, p. 1). As Judge Bidois has explained, the Rangatahi courts are not just a youth court being held on a marae, instead these courts engage meaningfully with the elders and the community, promote offender accountability, and seek solutions through the tikanga (protocols) that connect youth with "their marae and learning their whakapapa (genealogy) so that they know who they are and can take some pride in that" (Keith 2010). Insights into the process of these courts and their impact should be gained through a yet-to-be-released evaluation of the courts presently being undertaken by the Ministry of Justice.

Pacific island ethnic communities, arising from migration patterns in the 1960s, are part of the New Zealand social fabric. Two Pasifika (Pacific Island) youth courts have also commenced. This court enlists the appropriate elders from the young person's community to support and guide them in seeking meaningful solutions and accountability for their actions (Becroft 2011; Court in the Act 2010, July). Eligibility for the Rangatahi and Pasifika youth courts are determined via family group conferences and rely on victim approval. Similar principles used in these youth courts are also being implemented in a newly developed pilot program for adult Māori offenders known as the Matariki Court.

The Rangatahi and Pasifika youth courts are similar in many ways to indigenous sentencing courts that operate in most Australian states and territories (King et al. 2009).[14] There has been some debate in Australia over whether indigenous sentencing courts are in fact problem-solving courts (Freiberg 2001; King and Auty 2005; King et al. 2009). Indigenous sentencing courts are perhaps better described as specialist courts that incorporate some problem-solving, restorative, and therapeutic practices (Freiberg 2004; King et al. 2009). The New Zealand Rangatahi and Pasifika youth courts similarly seem to combine elements of problem-solving, restorative, and therapeutic practices and are referred to as specialist courts (Court in the Act 2010). However, Australian indigenous sentencing courts do not involve consistent oversight by the court, which is a key feature of the Rangatahi and Pasifika youth courts.

Regardless of whether these courts are correctly described as problem-solving courts, Nolan (2009) has highlighted that a key feature of the Australian "legal accent"[15] is the influence of issues relating to indigenous offenders (p. 108). Although indigenous people are disproportionately represented in Australian criminal justice systems, there have historically been low rates of participation of indigenous offenders in diversion programs, which is an issue that many jurisdictions are seeking to address by developing culturally appropriate diversionary responses (Joudo 2008; National Justice CEOs Group and the Victorian Government Department of Justice 2010; Richardson and McSherry 2010). The Rangatahi and Pasifika youth courts and the Matariki Court for adult offenders operating in New Zealand indicate that

[14] Indigenous sentencing courts have emerged as a result of the over-representation of indigenous offenders in the criminal justice system and a recognition that there is a more appropriate way of delivering justice to indigenous offenders such as the use of more informal and flexible processes (King et al. 2009). A key feature of Indigenous sentencing courts is that the magistrate is usually "assisted or advised by one or more respected persons from the offender's community" (King et al. 2009).

[15] Nolan (2009) uses the term "legal accents" to denote that, just as countries have different accents in terms of language and speech, so too do countries have different legal accents as a result of the particular legal culture reflected in the different ways in which these countries have developed problem-solving courts.

the need to address issues relating to indigenous offenders is also part of the legal accent of problem-solving courts in that country (Becroft 2011).

Family Violence Courts—Offender Treatment, Judicial Monitoring, and the Role of Therapeutic Jurisprudence

Family violence courts in New Zealand hear criminal cases in eight district courts across the North Island and have a dual focus on both the victim and offender. Specifically, they aim to respond quickly to cases of family violence, while ensuring victims' safety and encouraging offenders to take responsibility for their actions in a coordinated way. The family violence courts take place at a regular time and place and involve judges, police prosecutors, community probation officers, victim advisors, court staff, and a variety of community support services working collaboratively. Defendants are encouraged to take part in a government-funded domestic violence program and/or drug and alcohol counseling. Victims are assisted by a victim advisor who puts forward their views to the court and who also applies for protection orders and facilitates assistance from other government or community support services (Ministry of Justice 2008).

It appears there are regional differences in the operation of family violence courts. The Waitakere family violence court in Auckland, for instance, has been described as being underpinned by therapeutic jurisprudence principles (Morgan et al. 2008) and many aspects of traditional problem-solving courts have been incorporated into its processes, such as voluntary participation, coordinated approaches to domestic violence (for both victims and defendants), judicial monitoring, involvement of community, and nonadversarial approaches (Ministry of Justice 2008). In contrast, other domestic violence courts include minimal problem-solving features. Rather, they appear to incorporate a restorative justice focus and have been described as more "pragmatic" and "less touchy-feely" by some commentators (Mansfield 2008). Although the recent introduction of national guidelines for family violence courts acknowledge these regional variations (Ministry of Justice 2008), they stipulate all courts should aim to operate under the principles of consistency, collaboration, communication, and community involvement[16]—principles which sit well with problem-solving courts underpinned by therapeutic jurisprudence.

There are mixed results from two research projects on the family violence courts operating in the Auckland region. One study is an evaluation research project involving interpretative phenomenological analysis of the interviews of people working in agencies interfacing with the courts, with victims and with victims' advocates (Morgan et al. 2008). The other is a mixed method evaluation combining interviews

[16] Regardless, questions over whether a national model for domestic violence courts should be implemented (Mansfield 2008) at the expense of localized need (Ministry of Justice 2008) remain.

with government and nongovernment agencies interfacing with the courts and a statistical analysis of the court outcomes, sentencing, and reconviction rates (Knaggs et al. 2008).

Although these studies describe promising outcomes that are afforded through continual information sharing and collaboration between stakeholders (Morgan et al. 2008), they have also questioned the ability of the courts to speed up processes and ensure victim safety (Knaggs et al. 2008). Victim safety was reported to have been put at risk by the significant decrease in the number of protection orders being filed and concern was raised as to the lack of close monitoring of offenders following widespread use by the court of Section 106 of the *Sentencing Act 2002* (NZ), which enables discharge without conviction. The studies reported that there was the potential for offenders to be left with the impression that family violence is not serious and that their accountability was diminished because of Section 106 discharges (Knaggs et al. 2008; Morgan et al. 2008). In the study, examining the Waitakere and Manukau Family Violence Courts, other significant findings included the fact that in one court reoffending rates were shown not to have decreased 1 year after sentence and the other court had difficulties dealing with high volumes of cases (Knaggs et al. 2008).

Since these evaluations, the two Auckland courts have addressed many of these concerns including imposing a daily cap on the numbers of cases allowed to come before judges (Collins 2008). However, concern still continues over whether a "therapeutic" approach to deal with family violence is appropriate, with some commentators citing their opposition to the notion of keeping families together after violent episodes and with others arguing that the therapeutic jurisprudence approach is too generous to offenders (Collins 2008; Mansfield 2008).

Similar concerns have also been raised in relation to Australian family violence courts which operate in most states and territories (King et al. 2009). Generally, the focus in Australian family violence courts has been on seeking to improve the court process, access to services, advice, and support to victims of family violence (King et al. 2009). Although family violence courts primarily center on the nature of the offence and on the victim (King et al. 2009), increasingly these courts are also likely to order an offender to participate in an offender treatment program (King and Batagol 2010). Judicial monitoring is a common feature in family violence courts operating in the USA, yet in Australia, judicial monitoring is used in Western Australia and South Australia only (King and Batagol 2010). Rempel et al. (2008) found in their study of family violence courts that judicial monitoring had no impact on the rates of reoffending for domestic violence offences or other offences. King (2009) has noted that family violence courts have not been widely evaluated and the extent to which these courts have successfully reduced the rates of family violence is unknown (p. 20).

Stewart (2005, 2011) has raised concerns about the growing trend towards the use of offender treatment. Treatment options have been found to be resource-intensive and of limited effect (Stewart 2011). In addition, the potential for the focus on offender treatment to mislead victims that an offender is nonviolent or can be "cured" has been noted (Day et al. 2009; Gondolf 2002; Stewart 2011, p. 14). As noted above, the use of offender treatment programs and reliance on therapeutic jurisprudence principles have also been criticized for being unduly focused on the rehabilitation of the offender as opposed to the protection of the victim (Stewart 2005, 2011). In light of this research, some family violence courts are now moving to emphasize offender accountability and deterrence from offending rather than rehabilitation of offenders (King and Batagol, 2010). However, limited detail is available regarding the ways in which the principles of offender accountability and victim safety are playing out in practice (Stewart 2011).

Stewart (2011) has also argued against the "uncritical acceptance of the appropriateness of therapeutic jurisprudence and restorative justice as judicial responses to domestic violence" (p. 2). Others have suggested that a therapeutic jurisprudence approach should not solely focus on the offender, but instead examine the effect of the law on both the victim and the perpetrator of the violence (King and Batagol 2010). King and Batagol (2010) contend that judicial monitoring, using judicial techniques appropriately tailored for the context of a family violence court, can be used to enhance offender accountability and bring about positive behavioral change in a manner that observes therapeutic jurisprudence principles but also sits well with feminist approaches to family violence. They propose "judicial monitoring can have different goals depending on the context, including achieving enforcement, ensuring victim safety, promoting offender accountability and/or promoting offender motivation to engage in positive behavioral change while supporting them through the process" (King and Batagol 2010, p. 406). We note that judicial officers are likely to need training to enable this nuanced type of judicial monitoring to occur.

Integrated Court Programs Dealing with Multiple and Complex Problems

An important trend in the Australian and New Zealand problem-solving court movement is the development of programs that seek to address multiple problems in a holistic way. There is rarely one cause of crime but originally problem-solving courts often presupposed one main problem was the cause of the offending (Freiberg 2001). In practice, these courts, whether called drug courts or mental health courts, for example, are arguably required to deal with a range of problems, and do not limit themselves to just dealing with a single problem. Problem-solving courts (and the criminal justice and health systems more broadly) are increasingly required to manage people with coexisting mental health and addiction problems as well as those with multiple and complex health and social care needs.

A recent Australian study of prisoners in New South Wales found that the rates of a coexisting mental health and addiction problems in the preceding 12-month period was 29 % and were higher than similar rates in the community (Butler et al. 2011). Further, offenders who have coexisting conditions are more likely to reoffend after release from prison compared to offenders who have only a substance disorder, or only a mental illness, or offenders who have neither (Smith and Trimboli 2010). As has recently been stated, coexisting mental health and addiction problems are "the rule or expectation rather than the exception, and [have] significant economic and human costs" (Canaway and Merkes 2010, p. 262).

The success of problem-solving courts is dependent on adequate resourcing; that is, problem-solving courts will only be effective if adequate treatment and services are available in the community (Richardson and McSherry 2010).[17] In order for courts to address coexisting mental health and addiction problems adequately, it is necessary to have access to integrated services. However, these services are not always widely available. There are a number of barriers to the provision of services addressing coexisting mental health and addiction problems. These include the fact that:

- the mental health sectors and drug and alcohol sectors have traditionally operated separate from one another (commonly referred to as "silos" and the associated "silo mentality");
- the problem that the notion of "coexisting mental health and addiction problems" (and the other terms commonly used) is not a homogenous concept;
- the lack of consistent definitions; and
- treatment philosophies, ideologies, institutional cultures, and attitudes differ between the sectors (Canaway and Merkes 2010).

In short, the service delivery area for coexisting mental health and addiction problem is very complex and diverse. Overcoming these barriers is complicated by the large number of stakeholders and the lack of a consistent conceptual model (Canaway and Merkes 2010).[18] The problems faced by the legal, health, and social service systems are also compounded by the over-representation of offenders with intellectual disability and acquired brain injury in the criminal justice system (Hamilton 2010; Holland et al. 2007; Jackson et al. 2011).

There have been a number of initiatives that seek to move beyond programs and approaches that are based on the notion that there is "one" cause of criminal behavior (King 2009; Hamilton 2010) and which attempt to address health and social complexity in an integrated way.[19] A holistic approach combating multiple issues has

---

[17] Although Richardson and McSherry (2010) were commenting on the need for adequate resources in mental health courts, these comments apply equally to other problem-solving courts.

[18] There has been considerable attention focused on this issue at a National and State level in Australia, New Zealand, the USA, and the UK to the extent that there are now numerous government initiatives, policy documents, and guides to best practice regarding coexisting mental health and addiction problems.

[19] One significant initiative that has now ceased operation, and although not targeting criminal offenders, was the Multiple and Complex Needs Panel (the Panel) a statutory body that operated as part of the Multiple and Complex Needs Initiative (MACNI) in Victoria from 2004–2009. Although the Panel was not a problem-solving court and operated in the civil justice system, it sought to improve service provision to those people with multiple needs, who often became involved with the criminal justice system (Hamilton 2010). MACNI involved work at many levels in order to gain the cooperation of the different service sectors (Hamilton 2010, p. 316). The Panel ceased operation in 2009 due to legislative changes to the MACNI, which saw many of the functions of the Panel devolved to Department of Human Service regions. However, the model continues to influence policy as there is much to be learned from the experiences of this program. It is described in

also been used in the former Geraldton Sentencing Regime in Western Australia and the Court Integrated Services Program (CISP) currently operating in the Magistrates' Court of Victoria (King 2009). The CISP is a diversion program that operates in the mainstream court system but feeds into problem-solving courts where appropriate. It provides a general intervention program not based on a specific "problem." It uses a multidisciplinary team from a range of sectors to address the problems that each offender may have through "assessment and referral to treatment, case management, brokered treatment and referral to outreach services" (King et al. 2009, p. 141). CISP has been positively evaluated, indicating the program has successfully reduced recidivism and participants showed improvements in health and well-being while on the program (Ross 2009).[20]

In New Zealand, a pilot "special circumstances" court known as "Te Kooti o Timatanga Hou—The court of new beginnings" was established in 2010. This court, modeled on the now defunct Queensland Special Circumstances Court Diversion Program (formerly known as the Homeless Persons Court Diversion Program), is a problem-solving court that attempts to deal with multiple issues of homelessness, mental impairment, and drug dependency. The special circumstances court in New Zealand sits one half day per month in the Auckland District Court and was the result of a collaborative initiative between the judiciary, social support agencies, and health services. The court draws largely on existing resources of the judiciary and other services and functions by facilitating focused coordination between the judiciary, charitable social services, the police, alcohol and drug treatment providers, mental health services, housing New Zealand, and the Ministry of Health. It aims to find solutions to low-level persistent offending by homeless people in the inner city who also have ongoing or untreated mental health and/or drug dependency. Offenders are not eligible if they have committed serious offences. A dedicated coordinator, a social worker, is responsible for formulating and implementing a treatment plan for the offender who is then monitored by the court (Sisterson 2010).

In the USA, the issues of coexisting mental health and addiction problems have been addressed in some states through the development of problem-solving courts called Co-occurring Disorder Courts (Peters and Osher 2004) and hybrid problem-solving courts address other coexisting conditions or issues (Winick et al. 2010). South Australia is also moving in the same direction. Difficulties with recidivism for offenders with coexisting substance abuse and mental illness in the Magistrates' Court Diversion Program has led to the development of a Treatment Intervention Program that seeks to address the needs of this group of offenders. This program, which has replaced the Magistrates' Court Diversion Program in many of the court locations, involves a holistic assessment of needs, the brokering of services to address these needs, drug testing of offenders, and referral for pharmacotherapy (King 2011).

---

detail at http://www.dhs.vic.gov.au/operations/multiple-and-complex-needs-unit/how-macni-was-developed. Retrieved 10 July 2011.

[20] The evaluation of outcomes from CISP by Ross (2009) "involved comparing the post-court records of 200 persons who had completed CISP in 2007 with a sample of 200 persons sentenced in other Magistrates' Court venues in the same period" (p. 111).

The high rates of offenders with coexisting or multiple problems, coupled with the problems of "postcode justice" discussed above, has led to some calls for the "mainstreaming" of problem-solving approaches to all courts. Problem-solving courts often can only deal with a small number of the large proportion of offenders appearing before the courts with coexisting conditions and multiple problems (Bartels 2009). It has been argued that all courts are problem-solving courts and should have the same resources available in all courts to address the underlying causes of offending (King et al. 2009). However, there are barriers to this, both philosophically and also due to the resource intensive nature of such programs (Bartels 2009, King et al. 2009). As King et al. (2009) have stated "it is probably unrealistic to expect that all courts can be provided with the resources necessary to implement a true problem-oriented system" (p. 165). However, there are undoubtedly ways in which courts can better address the causes of offending outside, or in addition to, the problem-solving court model (King 2009, 2010; King et al. 2009; Bartels 2009).[21] Regardless of the way in which each jurisdiction chooses to go with problem-solving approaches to justice, all options rest on the ability of the legal, health, and welfare sectors to collaborate effectively. It is to this complex issue that we now turn.

Achieving Effective Collaboration Between the Legal, Health, and Welfare Sectors

One of the key common elements of problem-solving courts is the use of a "collaborative approach, relying on both government and nonprofit partners (i.e., criminal justice agencies, social service providers, community groups, and others) to help achieve their goals" (Berman and Feinblatt 2001, p. 131). Freiberg (2003) has stated that problem-solving courts require "a range of disparate groups with often conflicting interests to work together" (p. 14). Collaboration is a concept integral to the effective operation of problem-solving courts that requires focused consideration in order to overcome "poor intersectoral collaboration" (Carney 2000, p. 324).

Collaboration, partnership, "joined-up," or multiagency approaches are not new concepts in criminal justice (Blagg 2008; Gilling 1994) and there is a breadth of literature on collaboration and how to achieve it in a range of settings (Burnett and Appleton 2004; Fletcher et al. 2009; Harvie and Manzi 2011; Morrissey et al. 2009). Blagg (2008) has highlighted that the view in contemporary justice policy is that

---

[21] In Australia, the Victorian Government is currently exploring the mainstreaming of problem-solving and therapeutic approaches through the Integrating Court Programs (ICP) project. See http://www.courts.vic.gov.au/Integrating-Court-Programs. Retrieved 15 July 2011. The project website states "The challenge at the heart of the Integrating Court Programs (ICP) project is to take the lessons learned from Victoria's local court initiatives—both the well-publicized and the little-known—and consider how they can be applied across the court system, beginning with the Magistrates' Court. The overall aim is to develop a more holistic response to court users that embeds the successful processes and outcomes of problem-oriented approaches to justice within the day-to-day business of the courts."

"complex problems require a joint approach that harnesses the skills and resources of agencies (welfare, policing, judicial, treatment) on a collaborative basis" (p. 4). However, a joint approach is not always easy to achieve in practice (Blagg 2008; Rosenbaum 2002; Sandfort 1999).

Collaboration has been described as a "mutually beneficial and well-defined relationship entered into by two or more organizations to achieve common goals" (Mattessich et al. 2001, p. 4). However, in the context of problem-solving courts, and notably those that have arisen in an ad hoc, grassroots manner, the collaborative relationship between the court, health, and social services may not be underpinned by well-defined, mutually agreed common goals. Rather, the courts may rely on the good will of personnel and agencies (Carswell 2004), which may not be long-lasting or reliable. Collaboration arises in problem-solving courts in a number of ways. However, our main focus is on collaboration between the court and external agencies providing treatment and support services that underpin the intervention by the problem-solving court. It is in this context that we believe effective collaboration is harder to achieve largely due to the complexities of the wider health and social service systems. Manasse (2009) has noted in the context of one mental health court that collaboration can be thwarted by "system incompatibility, goal/role conflict, and communication failures" (p. 164).

Collaboration is integral to problem-solving courts in the following ways. First, it is relevant to the relationship between the defendant and court. King (2009, 2010) has highlighted this in the solution-focused approach that he advocates for problem-solving courts. He gives numerous examples of the ways in which the magistrate, in particular, should collaborate with the participant regarding how he or she will bring about behavioral change and steps the court can take to support that change (King 2009, 2010).

Secondly, collaboration is vital to the interdisciplinary court team that supports problem-solving courts. Much has been written in the wider problem-solving court literature about the changing roles of the judge, prosecutor, defense counsel, case workers, and court clinicians and the need for these groups to all work together in relation to each participant (see for example Freiberg 2001, 2005, 2011a; Law Reform Commission of Western Australia 2008; Thompson et al. 2007). Generally speaking, anecdotally in Australia and New Zealand, collaboration appears to be working well in the context of court teams (Carswell 2004; Dive 2009), possibly due to the small number of professionals involved in the teams, the closer connection with the court and magistrate, and a shared vision and commitment to the goals of the court.

The third way in which collaboration is relevant is between the court and external service providers. Problem-solving courts generally seek to use the authority of the court to "leverage services," to improve accountability for service provision (Blagg 2008) and provide a single system experience for participants by minimizing process duplication between the legal, health, and social service sectors (National Justice CEOs Group and the Victorian Government Department of Justice 2010). These goals are generally achieved by way of individualized intervention plans developed by the court team or a court order whereby participants are connected with a range of treatment and support services relevant to their circumstances. Clinical or case worker members of the court team liaise with treatment and service providers in the community with regards to the entry of participants into treatment or provision of other supports, and monitor their ongoing progress.

Problem-solving courts such as drug courts and mental health courts (and other like courts) are showing some potential with regards to reducing rates of recidivism and other positive outcomes. However, the degree to which any success is occurring because the courts have been successful in bringing about effective collaboration between the legal, health, and social service sectors (or the extent to which concerted focus on collaboration might bring about more improvements in recidivism and other measures) is unclear.[22]

The dynamics of the collaborative process has rarely been examined in the evaluations that have been conducted of Australian and New Zealand problem-solving courts. In an evaluation of the Mental Health Diversion List in Tasmania, care and service providers were surveyed as to their opinions and perceptions of the mental health court (Newitt and Stojcevski 2009). However the complexities of the collaborative processes were not explored. The evaluation found that service providers largely had positive perceptions of the program but had limited understanding of the operation of the program or its functions (Newitt and Stojcevski 2009). Similar results were found in a process evaluation of the Christchurch Youth Drug Court (Carswell 2004). Most people surveyed in the Tasmanian evaluation believed that the mental health court was helping to improve coordination between justice agencies and health service providers (Newitt and Stojcevski 2009). The Tasmanian List is different from other Australian mental health courts because the court liaison officers responsible for liaising with service providers are employees of the Department of Health and Human Services and are perceived to have more influence with service providers and access to treatment because they are positioned within the health sector (Newitt and Stojcevski 2009).[23]

The court liaison officers in problem-solving courts are generally at the forefront of the collaboration process. As the "boundary spanners" (Steadman 1992), they are the lynchpins in the process of sourcing appropriate treatment and services to incorporate into individualized treatment plans for problem-solving court participants.

---

[22] Conversely, in the evaluations conducted of the Christchurch Youth Drug Court, Carswell (2004) found amongst other outcomes, that interagency co-ordination was working well. However, a later study found that the Youth Drug Court was not reducing reoffending (Searle and Spiers 2006). Although it is not possible to say why that was, and numerous factors were undoubtedly involved, successful interagency coordination was not seemingly having a significant impact on reoffending in this court.

[23] This arrangement is uncommon in Australia and reflects the way in which this program was established using only the existing resources available to the Court with no additional funding or resources available to commence the pilot. Thus, the existing forensic mental health liaison workers who, prior to the commencement of the Mental Health Diversion List, provided forensic mental health assessments to the Magistrates Court of Tasmania agreed to become involved in the new List as part of their current work with the Court. The provision of these services continues to be provided by the Department of Health even though the List has become an established program in the Magistrates Court.

The degree of difficulty that court liaison officers face in liaising on behalf of the court with agencies in the health and social service sector is likely to be high, particularly for those who are court employees and not members of the health sector, as is the situation in Tasmania. Some courts may be assisted by Steering Committees and service provider operations groups (such as the South Australian Magistrates Court Diversion Program and the Treatment Intervention Program).[24] However, again there is no indication regarding the success that such groups have had in influencing the broader sectors within which they work.[25] Memorandums of understanding may be used in some circumstances but the extent to which these documents flow down to operational practices is not known (Fletcher et al. 2009, p. 555).

Anecdotally, it is becoming clear in some Australian and New Zealand problem-solving courts (and like initiatives) that effective collaboration between legal, health, and social service sectors is not easy to achieve (Hamilton 2010; Stewart 2011; King 2011). A greater awareness of the difficulties of collaboration and knowledge of principles of effective collaboration are needed to give courts the tools to enable successful collaboration to occur or to improve the processes they already use. It may take the courts years to develop good relationships with treatment and service providers.

Difficulties arise because of the fragmented and segregated manner in which the different health and social service sectors often operate. Manasse (2009) highlights, for example, that mental health courts, which seek to connect the criminal justice system and the mental health system, are attempting to bring two generally "inflexible government bureaucrac(ies)" together (p. 165–166). This is likely to give rise to problems when these courts are trying to work within the rigid constraints of both systems and further, deal with the "ever-changing political environment" of the criminal justice and mental health systems (Manasse 2009 p. 167). Given the different philosophies and cultures of external agencies it may be unrealistic to expect that a problem-solving court alone (via the court liaison officers or other boundary spanners) will be able to influence the broader health and welfare system to achieve long-lasting change. Hamilton (2010) has highlighted many challenges

[24] These groups may also play a role in selecting service providers and which treatment and services will be utilized by the problem-solving court program. In Australia, the way in which service providers for problem-solving courts are selected and paid for differs in each jurisdiction. Generally, most problem-solving courts only have access to the treatment and service providers available in the community. Many grassroots programs, such as the Tasmanian Mental Health Diversion List start with no additional funds to purchase services. However, in some states interdepartmental agreements between government departments to make services available for these programs are used. Programs which have been established as government funded pilots may have brokerage funds available to purchase designated funds for purchasing services or goods to address a participant's specific needs and to assist in his or her engagement with the program (Trimboli 2012, 22; see Tasmania Law Reform Institute 2006).

[25] Nor do we have any indication of the reciprocal impact that problem-solving courts are having on health and social services, for example, are these courts stretching services in the community and resulting in rationing of services for other users who are not accessing these services through the criminal justice system.

posed by system silos, complex service contracts, quality assurance, and accreditation of services. She suggests that the necessary service cooperation and coordination needed to meet the goal of service integration remains elusive (p. 316). The legal, health, and social service sectors do not often have common purposes, there are differences in professional values, and these different purposes are often competing, so reaching agreement or achieving homogeneity of purpose and principles may be difficult. As Gilling (1994) has said "the multi-agency approach seeks to force these discourses together, but the context of collaboration is such that certain discourses find themselves in a more privileged position, and others find it difficult to establish themselves" (p. 246). As Freiberg (2011b) has argued, interdisciplinarity assumes a degree of synthesis between different disciplines, but it can also be threatening to existing bodies of knowledge and power because of the way in which it challenges structures, boundaries, and practices of the fields, which it seeks to bring together (p. 298).

The many problems that may arise from intersectoral collaboration may be overcome with "thoughtful implementation," yet there will undoubtedly be unforeseen obstacles (Manasse 2009, p. 188). The literature on building partnerships and collaboration suggests that the process of collaboration is a continuous one that requires ongoing attention, commitment, and work (Mattessich et al. 2001). Further, Freiberg (2011b) contends interdisciplinary collaboration in and of itself may be insufficient to bring about broad institutional change. In addition to collaboration and partnerships there must be an integrative theory. That is, "either a coherent intellectual framework or theory or meta-narrative that will fundamentally change the way that the justice system is perceived and operates" (p. 299). Freiberg suggests that therapeutic jurisprudence, due to its "intensely interdisciplinary" (p. 301) nature, and nonadversarial justice (which includes therapeutic jurisprudence), has this potential to transform the justice system in this way. Both therapeutic jurisprudence and nonadversarial justice have already been embraced by many working in problem-solving courts, and the legal system more broadly, but the extent to which these concepts are well understood by those working within, and in partnership with, these courts is unclear. These fields of inquiry are not yet fully fledged theories but Freiberg contends that they have already demonstrated their potential to transform the justice system. Considerable work is now required to develop these areas of knowledge so that they can fulfill this transformative role more fully.

In addition to developing a cohesive underlying theory, collaboration within problem-solving courts, and between the court and external agencies, needs to be addressed in Australia and New Zealand in a number of other ways. One way may be through the use of formal agreements and memorandum of understanding (MOU). There are examples of problem-solving courts working to consolidate strong working relationships with external service providers through the use of more formal arrangements. The Drug Court in New South Wales for example, has joined partnership with Housing NSW[26] via an Operating Agreement formalizing collaboration

[26] Housing NSW is an agency of the NSW Department of Family and Community Services responsible for social housing in that state.

between the Drug Court of New South Wales and Housing NSW to "provide housing and support to clients with complex housing needs in order to assist them to sustain their tenancies" (Housing NSW 2011). Such agreements may represent a future trend as problem-solving courts seek to improve relationships with external providers, although any agreement or MOU must be implemented in such a way that the principles flow down to practices at all levels of operation of programs.

Presently, in Australia, there are few national or state guidelines that set out the key elements or principles of the various types of problem-solving courts. Such guidelines could bring clarity to the role, purpose, and principles of problem-solving courts, and amongst other things, assist the collaboration process by aiding external agencies to gain a better understanding of the role and operations of problem-solving courts along these lines. The Family Violence Courts National Operating Guidelines in New Zealand (Ministry of Justice 2008) provide an example of the type of document that could be developed. In Australia, *Guidelines for Best Practice for the Diversion and Support of Offenders with a Mental Illness* (the "Diversion Guidelines") published by the National Justice CEO's Group and the Victorian Government Department of Justice (2010) may also be a useful starting point for developing a key elements document. The numerous "essential elements" and "key component" documents that have been developed in the USA (as discussed in Hora 2011) and that are now providing measurement tools for evaluation of problem-solving courts (Hiller et al. 2010; Linhorst et al. 2009; Newitt and Stojcevski 2009) will be useful resources as Australia and New Zealand seek to develop similar tools.

Effective collaboration between the legal, health, and social service sectors may be best achieved by legislation supporting the work of each problem-solving court. Although most drug courts in Australia are underpinned by legislation, many other problem-solving courts in Australia and New Zealand are not.[27] Given the numerous jurisdictions and the types of problem-solving courts operating, we propose that model legislation could be developed so that each jurisdiction has a template from which to work from in developing the legislation appropriate to the individual state or territory or country. Legislation may add to the legitimacy of a problem-solving court and provide the statutory leverage required to bring about long-lasting change to the way in which the courts, health, and social service systems work together to respond to the needs of people participating in problem-solving courts (Hamilton 2010; Popovic 2003). The disadvantage of legislation is that it may hinder flexibility in the way in which problem-solving court programs run, although in Australia often the legislation is not overly detailed and a certain amount of flexibility is possible.

At the same time, courts need to ensure that collaboration practices are monitored and, if possible, evaluated to some extent, either as part of process or outcome evaluations. There are a number of studies that have analyzed interagency collaboration, which identify a range of informal and formal collaboration activities (Fletcher et al. 2009; Konrad 1996; Lehman et al. 2009; Wenzel et al. 2004). Wenzel et al.

[27] The debate regarding whether to underpin problem-solving courts with legislation is not a straightforward one, however, and requires future consideration as to the advantages and disadvantages of such an approach.

(2004) found there were generally strong linkages between drug courts and treatment providers and barriers included funding limitations, data systems, data sharing, and staffing shortages. Service providers emphasized a need for greater and more frequent communication between drug courts and providers and more education about the roles of each party, in order to bring about greater respect and trust (Wenzel et al. 2004).[28] A similar analysis of problem-solving courts in Australia and New Zealand would be useful to gain an understanding of the situation in these countries.

Conclusion

Nolan (2009) argued that adopted legal programs act as "legal irritants" on the culture in which they operate (p. 37). That is, the legal program can bring about changes to the community and culture in which it is situated (or in his words "transplanted"). It follows that the adoption of problem-solving courts is not the end of the story; rather the relevant program will continue to evolve and influence the legal "space" around it (Nolan 2009). In this way, "judging and legal processes, like other social processes [are] not static... [t]hey adapt to the need of a particular society and time" (King 2007, p. 19).

Problem-solving courts are continuing to evolve in Australia and are now growing in New Zealand. In both countries, we have a dynamic academic, legal, and professional culture contributing to the development of theory and practice. The longer these courts operate the more embedded in the local legal systems they become and the need to look at overseas practices for inspiration lessens. It is important to appreciate that problem-solving courts, at least in Australia, have been fitted into existing systems of diversion programs operating in the criminal justice system, as well as the local health and social service systems, and, it is within these systems that they continue to be largely contextualized.

As we have highlighted, an issue integral to the longevity of problem-solving courts is the ability of the legal, health, and social services sectors to better address issues of coexisting mental health and addiction problems, develop integrated services, and achieve effective collaboration between the various sectors. Australia and New Zealand are not alone in tackling these issues.

Nolan (2009) has argued that those involved in the American problem-solving court movement have not taken an interest in what is happening overseas nor are they likely to look outside its borders to see how other countries are doing things. We believe that this is gradually changing. As the lines of communication between judges,

[28] Wenzel et al. (2004) conducted a study of collaboration practices in 14 drug courts in the USA and examined the following factors: "(1) The extent to which drug courts and providers accommodate each other's practice standards; (2) the availability and extent of case management services; (3) cross training of staff; (4) documentation of relationships (e.g., written agreements); (5) resource sharing; (6) joint assessment of clients; (7) joint planning of client service goals; (8) client referrals; (9) mutual sensitivity to concerns of the other agency or program; (10) sharing of information about clients; and (11) staff meetings" (Wenzel et al. 2004, p. 256).

court practitioners, and academics from different countries become more open, the dialogue regarding ways to tackle the common issues facing many problem-solving courts will surely become more of a two-way conversation. As Wexler has also recognized, "increasingly the development of therapeutic jurisprudence is an international enterprise" (King 2006, p. 139) and it is one which Australia and New Zealand are actively contributing to in terms of academic discourse, practical research, and evaluation. We believe a detailed examination of how to achieve effective collaboration between the legal, health, and social service sectors in Australian and New Zealand problem-solving courts should be part of this cross-jurisdictional dialogue.

Acknowledgments The authors thank Bernadette McSherry and Arie Freiberg for comments on earlier drafts of this chapter.

References

Bartels, L. (2009). *Challenges in mainstreaming specialty courts. Trends & issues in crime and criminal justice, no. 383*. Canberra: Australian Institute of Criminology.

Becroft, A. (2010). *Problem solving and therapeutic youth courts in New Zealand—restoring cultural links*. Paper presented at the annual meeting of the South Pacific Council of Youth and Children's Courts, Sydney, Australia.

Becroft, A. (2011). *2011, a big year for youth justice: 21 years old and challenging youth advocates in court and beyond!* Paper presented at the National Youth Advocates' Conference, Te Papa Tongarewa, Wellington.

Berman, G., & Feinblatt, J. (2001). Problem-solving courts: A brief primer. *Law and Policy, 23*(2), 125–140. doi:10.1111/1467-9930.00107.

Blagg, H. (2008). *Problem-oriented courts*. A research paper prepared for the Law Reform Commission of Western Australia Project 96. Perth: Law Reform Commission of Western Australia. http://www.lrc.justice.wa.gov.au/_files/P96-BlaggRP.pdf. Accessed 30 Apr 2013.

Blagg, H. (2009). *Youth Justice in Western Australia*. Prepared for the Commissioner of Children and Young People, WA. http://www.ccyp.wa.gov.au/files/article/Harry%20Blagg%20report%20-%20Youth%20Justice%20in%20Western%20Australia%20-%20FINAL.pdf. Accessed 30 Apr 2013.

Brookbanks, W. (2006). *Making a case for a mental health court in New Zealand*. Paper presented at the 3rd International Conference on Therapeutic Jurisprudence, Perth, Western Australia.

Burnett, R., & Appleton, C. (2004). *Joined up youth justice: Tackling youth crime in partnership*. London: Russell House Publishing Ltd.

Butler, T., Indig, D., Allnutt, S., & Mamoon, H. (2011). Co-occurring mental illness and substance use disorder among Australian prisoners. *Drug and Alcohol Review, 30*, 188–194. doi:10.1111/j.1465-3362.2010.00216.x.

Canaway, R., & Merkes, M. (2010). Barriers to comorbidity service delivery: The complexities of dual diagnosis and the need to agree on terminology and conceptual frameworks. *Australian Health Review, 34*, 262–268. doi:10.1071/AH08723.

Carney, T. (2000). New configurations of justice and services for the vulnerable: Panacea or panegyric? *Australian and New Zealand Journal of Criminology, 33*(3), 318–340.

Carswell, S. (2004). *Process evaluation of the Christchurch Youth Drug Court Pilot*. Wellington: Ministry of Justice. http://www.justice.govt.nz/publications/global-publications/p/process-evaluation-of-the-christchurch-youth-drug-court-pilot/publication. Accessed 29 Apr 2013.

Cheng, D. (4 May 2011). Specialised drug courts aim to cut reoffending. *New Zealand Herald Online*. http://www.nzherald.co.nz. Accessed 29 Apr 2013.

Clancey, G., & Howard, J. (2006). Diversion and criminal justice drug treatment: Mechanism of emancipation or social control? *Drug and Alcohol Review, 25,* 377–385. doi:10.1080/09595230600741388.

Collins, S. (13 August 2008). Specialist family violence courts fail. *New Zealand Herald Online*. http://www.nzherald.co.nz. Accessed 29 Apr 2013.

Court in the Act. (October 2008). Specialist youth courts. *Court in the Act, Newsletter of the Youth Court of New Zealand*, Issue 39. http://www.courts.govt.nz/courts/youth/documents/publications-and-media/newsletters/court-in-act-issue-39.pdf. Accessed 30 Apr 2013.

Court in the Act. (July 2010). Te Kooti Rangatahi ki Orakei, the Pasifika Youth Court, and Te Kooti Rangatahi ki Owae - three inspiring community initiatives opened in the same week. *Court in the Act, Newsletter of the Youth Court of New Zealand,* Issue 47. http://www.courts.govt.nz/courts/youth/documents/publications-and-media/newsletters/Issue%2047.pdf. Accessed 30 Apr 2013.

Coverdale, R. (July 2011). Postcode justice - *rural and regional disadvantage in the administration of the law in Victoria*. (Deakin University School of Law) http://www.deakin.edu.au/buslaw/law/news/docs/postcodejus-rpt.pdf. Accessed 30 Apr 2013.

Day, A., Chung, D., O'Leary, P., & Carson, E. (2009). Programs for men who perpetrate domestic violence: An examination of the issues underlying the effectiveness of intervention programs. *Journal of Family Violence, 24*(3), 203–212. doi:10.1007/s10896-008-9221-4.

Dive, R. (2009). *Drug Court of NSW 2009 review*. http://www.drugcourt.lawlink.nsw.gov.au/agdbasev7wr/_assets/drgcrt/m40700112/2009review.pdf. Accessed 30 Apr 2013.

Fletcher, B. W., Lehman, W. E. K., Wexler, H. K., Melnick, G., Taxman, F., & Young, D. W. (2009). Measuring collaboration and integration activities in criminal justice and substance abuse treatment agencies. *Drug and Alcohol Dependence, 1035,* 554–564. doi:10.1016/j.drugalcdep.2009.01.001.

Freiberg, A. (2001). Problem-oriented courts: Innovative solutions to intractable problems? *Journal of Judicial Administration, 11,* 8–27.

Freiberg, A. (2003). Therapeutic jurisprudence in Australia: Paradigm shift or pragmatic incrementalism? *Law in Context, 20*(2), 6–23.

Freiberg, A. (2004, November). *Innovations in the court system.* Paper presented at the Crime in Australia: International Connections Conference, Australian Institute of Criminology, Melbourne.

Freiberg, A. (2005). Problem-oriented courts: An update. *Journal of Judicial Administration, 14,* 196–219.

Freiberg, A. (2011a). Post-adversarial and post-inquisitorial justice: Transcending traditional penological paradigms. *European Journal of Criminology, 8,* 82–101. doi:10.1177/1477370810385434.

Freiberg, A. (2011b). Psychiatry, psychology and non-adversarial justice: From integration to transformation. *Psychiatry, Psychology and Law, 18*(2), 297–314. doi:10.1080/13218719.2010.543755.

Gilling, D. (1994). Multi-agency crime prevention: Some barriers to collaboration. *The Howard Journal of Criminal Justice, 33*(3), 246–257. doi:10.1111/j.1468-2311.1994.tb00810.x.

Gondolf, E. W. (2002). *Batterer intervention systems: Issues, outcomes and recommendations.* Thousand Oaks: Sage Publications.

Harvie, P., & Manzi, T. (2011). Interpreting multi-agency partnerships: Ideology, discourse and domestic violence. *Social and Legal Studies, 20*(1), 79–95. doi:10.1177/0964663910384907.

Hamilton, M. (2010). People with Complex Needs and the Criminal Justice System. *Current Issues in Criminal Justice, 22*(2), 307-324.

Hiller, M., Belenko, S., Taxman, F., Young, D., Perdoni, M., & Saum, C. (2010). Measuring drug court structure and operations: Key components and beyond. *Criminal Justice and Behaviour, 37*(9), 933–950. doi:10.1177/0093854810373727.

Holland, S. Persson, P. McClelland, M., & Berends, R. (2 September 2007). *Intellectual disability in the Victorian prison system: Characteristics of prisoners with an intellectual disability released from prison in 2003-2006*. Corrections research paper series, paper No. 2, Department of Justice of Victoria. http://www.justice.vic.gov.au/resources/f2a52573-4686-46a5-9069-73a622395be8/intellectual_disability_in_the_victorian_prison_system.pdf. Accessed 30 Apr 2013.

Hora, P. (2011). Courting new solutions using problem-solving justice: Key components, guiding principles, strategies, responses, models, approaches, blueprints and tool kits. *Chapman Journal of Criminal Justice, 2*(1), 7-52. http://ssrn.com/abstract=1801315. Accessed 30 Apr 2013.

Housing NSW (18 February 2011). *Operating agreementc – Drug Court partnership between Housing NSW and Drug Court NSW*. NSW Housing and Human Services Accord.

Hughes, C., & Ritter, A., (2008). *Monograph No. 16: A summary of diversion programs for drug and drug-related offenders in Australia*. DPMP Monograph Series. Sydney: National Drug and Alcohol Research Centre. http://www.dpmp.unsw.edu.au/DPMPWeb.nsf/resources/Monograph+16.pdf/$file/DPMP+MONO+16.pdf. Accessed 30 Apr 2013.

Indermaur, D., & Roberts, L. (2003). Drug courts in Australia: The first generation. *Current Issues in Criminal Justice, 15*(2), 136–154.

Jackson, M. Hardy, G. Persson, P., & Holland, S. (2011). *Acquired brain injury in the victorian prison system*. Corrections research paper series, paper No. 04 April 2011, Department of Justice of Victoria. http://www.justice.vic.gov.au/resources/70313138-7b11-4652-a6c2-c98c02cb3ad6/acquired_brain_injury_in_the_victorian_prison_system.pdf. Accessed 30 Apr 2013.

Jones, C. (November 2011). Intensive judicial supervision and drug court outcomes: Interim findings from a randomized controlled trial. *Crime and Justice Bulletin, Contemporary Issues in Crime and Justice*, no. 152. NSW Bureau of Crime Statistics and Research. http://www.bocsar.nsw.gov.au/lawlink/bocsar/ll_bocsar.nsf/vwFiles/CJB152.pdf/$file/CJB152.pdf. Accessed 30 Apr 2013.

Joudo, J. (2008). *Responding to substance abuse and offending in Indigenous communities: review of diversion programs*. Research and public policy series, no. 88. Canberra: Australian Institute of Criminology. http://www.aic.gov.au/documents/1/8/0/%7B1807C117-551B-4D5A-B30C-CF07EF532F7D%7Drpp88.pdf. Accessed 30 Apr 2013.

Keith, L. (17 June 2010). Court will help 'lost' Maori youth. *Taranaki Daily News Online*. http://www.stuff.co.nz/taranaki-daily-news. Accessed 29 Apr 2013.

King, M. S. (2006). *Challenges facing Australian court drug diversion initiatives*. Paper presented at the Court Drug Diversion Initiatives Conference, Brisbane, Australia.

King, M. S. (2007). Therapeutic jurisprudence and criminal law practice: A judicial perspective. *Criminal Law Journal, 31*, 12–19.

King, M. S. (2009). *Solution-focused judging bench book*. Melbourne: Australasian Institute of Judicial Administration and the Legal Services Board of Victoria.

King, M. S. (2010). *Should problem-solving courts be solution-focused courts? Revista Juridica Universidad de Puerto Rico, Forthcoming; Monash University Faculty of Law Legal Studies*. Research paper no. 2010/03. http://ssrn.com/abstract=1725022. Accessed 30 Apr 2013.

King, S. (8 April 2011). *Next generation treatment courts. Paper presented at Mental Health Diversion* List (MHDL) Integration and Collaboration: Building capacity and engagement for the provision of criminal justice services to Tasmania's mentally ill workshop. The Tasmanian Institute of Law Enforcement Studies (TILES), University of Tasmania, Hobart. http://www.utas.edu.au/tiles/events/workshops/workshop_pdf/mhdl_workshop_SKing.ppt.pdf. Accessed 30 Apr 2013.

King, M. S., & Auty, K. (2005). Therapeutic jurisprudence: An emerging trend in courts of summary jurisdiction. *Alternative Law Journal, 30*(2), 69–74.

King, M., & Batagol, B. (2010). Enforcer, manager or leader? The judicial role in family violence courts. *International Journal of Law and Psychiatry, 33*, 406–416. doi:10.1016/j.ijlp.2010.09.011.

King, M., Freiberg, A., Batagol, B., & Hyams, R. (2009). *Non-adversarial justice*. Sydney: Federation Press.

Knaggs, T., Leahy, F., Soboleva, N., & Ong, S. (2008). *The Waitakere and Manukau Family Violence Courts: An evaluation study*. Wellington: Ministry of Justice of New Zealand.

Konrad, E. L. (1996). A multidimensional framework for conceptualizing human services integration initiatives. *New Directions for Evaluation, 69*, 5-19.

Law Reform Commission of Western Australia. (2008). *Project No. 96: Court intervention programs: Consultation paper*. Perth: Quality Press. http://www.lrc.justice.wa.gov.au/P/project_96.aspx. Accessed 30 Apr 2013.

Law Reform Commission of Western Australia. (2009). *Project No. 96: Court intervention programs - Final report*. Perth: Quality Press. http://www.lrc.justice.wa.gov.au/_files/P96-FR.pdf. Accessed 30 Apr 2013.

Lehman, W. E. K., Fletcher, B. W., Wexler, H. K., & Melnick, G. (2009). Organizational factors and collaboration and integration activities in criminal justice and drug abuse treatment agencies. *Drug and Alcohol Dependence, 1035*, 565–572. doi:10.1016/j.drugalcdep.2009.01.004.

Linhorst, D. M., Dirks-Linhorst, P. A., Stiffelman, S., Gianino, J., Bernsen, H. L., & Kelley, B. J. (2009). Implementing the essential elements of a mental health court: The experiences of a large multijurisdictional suburban county. *Journal of Behavioral Health Services & Research, 37*(4), 427–442. doi:10.1007/s11414-009-9193-z.

Manasse, M. (2009). The dilemmas and opportunities of collaboration: Drawing lessons from one mental health court. *Journal of Court Innovation, 2*(1), 157–190.

Mansfield, A. (2008). Carrots, sticks, and family violence courts. *New Zealand Lawyer Magazine*, 82. http://www.nzlawyermagazine.co.nz/Archives/Issue82/F3/tabid/733/Default.aspx. Accessed 29 Apr 2013.

Mattessich, P., Monsey, B., & Murray-Close, M. (2001). *Collaboration: What makes it work* (2nd ed.). St. Paul: Fieldstone Alliance.

Ministry of Justice. (2011). Family group conference [Fact sheet]. http://www2.justice.govt.nz/youth/about-youth/family-group-conference.asp. Accessed 10 Mar 2011.

Ministry of Justice. (2008). *Family violence courts national operating guidelines*. Wellington: Ministry of Justice. http://www.justice.govt.nz/publications/global-publications/f/family-violence-courts-2013-national-operating-guidelines. Accessed 29 Apr 2013.

Mooney, N. (2010). Predicting offending within the New Zealand youth justice system: Evaluating measures of risk, need and psychopathy. (Unpublished Doctor of Clinical Psychology thesis). Massey University, Wellington.

Morgan, M., Coombes, L., Te Hiwi, E., & McGray, S. (2008). *Responding together: An integrated report evaluating the aims of the waitakere family violence court protocols*. Wellington: Ministry of Justice.

Morrissey, J. P., Fagan, J. A., & Cocozza, J. J. (2009). New models of collaboration between criminal justice and mental health systems. *American Journal of Psychiatry, 166*(11), 1211–1214. doi:10.1176/appi.ajp.2009.09050670.

National Justice CEOs Group and the Victorian Government Department of Justice. (2010). *Diversion and support of people with mental illness: Guidelines for best practice*. Melbourne: Justice Health, Victorian Government Department of Justice and the National Justice Chief Executive Officers' Group. http://www.aic.gov.au/crime_community/communitycrime/mental%20health%20and%20crime/~/media/aic/njceo/diversion_support.pdf.

New South Wales Law Reform Commission. (2012). *People with cognitive and mental health impairments in the criminal justice system: Diversion*. Report no. 135. Sydney: Author. http://www.lawlink.nsw.gov.au/lawlink/lrc/ll_lrc.nsf/vwFiles/r135.pdf/$file/r135.pdf. Accessed 30 Apr 2013.

New Zealand Law Commission. (2011). *Controlling and regulating drugs: A review of the Misuse of Drugs Act 1975*. Law commission report no. 122. Wellington: Author. http://www.lawcom.govt.nz/sites/default/files/publications/2011/05/part_1_report_-_controlling_and_regulating_drugs.pdf. Accessed 30 Apr 2013.

Newitt, E., & Stojcevski, V. (2009). *Mental health diversion list evaluation report*. Hobart: Magistrates Court of Tasmania. http://www.magistratescourt.tas.gov.au/_data/assets/pdf_file/0003/

127029/Mental_Health_Diversion_List_-_Evaluation_Report_-_May_2009.pdf. Accessed 30 Apr 2013.
Nolan, J. L. (2009). *Legal accents, legal borrowing: The international problem-solving court movement*. New Jersey: Princeton University Press.
Payne, J. (2005). *Specialty courts in Australia: Report to the Criminology Research Council*. Canberra: Australian Institute of Criminology.
Peters, R. H., & Osher, F. C. (2004). *Co-occurring disorders and specialty courts*. (2nd ed.). Delmar: The National Gains Center.
Popovic, J. (2003). Judicial officers: Complementing conventional law and changing the culture of the judiciary. *Law in Context, 20*(3), 121–136.
Recordon, P. (2005, October). *The family violence specialist court*. Paper presented at the Towards a Restorative Society Symposium, Victoria University, Wellington.
Rempel, M., Labriola, M., & Davis, R. C. (2008). Does judicial monitoring deter domestic violence recidivism? Results of a quasi-experimental comparison in the Bronx. *Violence Against Women, 14*(2), 185–207. doi:10.1177/1077801207312535.
Richardson, E., & McSherry, B. (2010). Diversion down under – Programs for offenders with mental illnesses in Australia. *International Journal of Law and Psychiatry, 33*(4), 249–257. doi:10.1016/j.ijlp.2010.06.007.
Roach Anleu, S., & Mack, K. (2007). Magistrates, magistrates courts, and social change. *Law and Policy, 29*(2), 183–209. doi:10.1111/j.1467-9930.2007.00252.x.
Roberts, L., & Indermaur, D. (2007). Key challenges in evaluating therapeutic jurisprudence initiatives. *Journal of Judicial Administration, 17*, 60–70.
Rosenbaum, D. P. (2002). Evaluating multi-agency anti-crime partnerships: Theory, design, and measurement issues. *Crime Prevention Studies, 14*, 171–225.
Ross, S. (2009). *Evaluation of the court integrated services program: Final report*. Melbourne: University of Melbourne. http://www.justice.vic.gov.au/resources/9931fe61-ca5e-4c54-a118-597fe9a7363c/cisp_evaluation_report.pdf. Accessed 30 Apr 2013.
Sandfort, J. (1999). The structural impediments to human service collaboration: Examining welfare reform at the front lines. *Social Service Review, 73*(3), 314-339. http://www.hhh.umn.edu/people/jsandfort/pubs/peer_reviewed/examine_welfare_reform.pdf. Accessed 30 Apr 2013.
Searle, W., & Spier, P. (2006). *Christchurch Youth Drug Court Pilot: One year follow-up study*. http://www.justice.govt.nz/publications/global-publications/c/christchurch-youth-drug-court-pilot-one-year-follow-up-study-february-2006. Accessed 30 Apr 2013.
Sisterson, C. (2010, August 6). New Special Circumstances Court to open its doors next month. *New Zealand Lawyer Magazine*, 142. http://www.nzlawyermagazine.co.nz/Archives/Issue142/142N5/tabid/2508/Default.aspx. Accessed 30 Apr 2013.
Smith, N., & Trimboli, L. (2010). Comorbid substance and non-substance mental health disorders and re-offending among NSW prisoners. *Crime and Justice Bulletin, Contemporary Issues in Crime and Justice*, no. 140. NSW Bureau of Crime Statistics and Research. http://www.bocsar.nsw.gov.au/lawlink/bocsar/ll_bocsar.nsf/vwFiles/CJB140.pdf/$file/CJB140.pdf. Accessed 30 Apr 2013.
Steadman, H. (1992). Boundary spanners: A key component for the effective interactions of the justice and mental health systems. *Law and Human Behavior, 16*(1), 75–87. doi:10.1007/BF02351050.
Steadman, H. (2005). *A guide to collecting mental health court outcome data*. New York: Council of State Governments. http://consensusproject.org/jc_publications/guide-to-collecting-mental-health-court-outcome-data/MHC-Outcome-Data.pdf. Accessed 30 Apr 2013.
Steadman, H. J., Davidson, S., & Brown, C. (2001). Mental health courts: Their promise and unanswered questions. *Psychiatric Services, 52*, 457–458.
Stewart, J. (2005). *Specialist domestic/family violence courts within the Australian context*. Australian Domestic & Family Violence Clearinghouse. Issues paper no. 10. http://www.austdvclearinghouse.unsw.edu.au/documents/Issuespaper_10.pdf. Accessed 30 Apr 2013.

Stewart, J. (2011). *Specialist domestic courts: What we know now - how far have Australian jurisdictions progressed?* Australian Domestic & Family Violence Clearinghouse. Topic paper 20: 2011. http://www.austdvclearinghouse.unsw.edu.au/PDF%20files/Topic%20Paper%2020.pdf. Accessed 30 Apr 2013.

Tasmania Law Reform Institute. (2006). The establishment of a drug court pilot in Tasmania research paper no. 2. Tasmania Law Reform Institute. http://www.utas.edu.au/_data/assets/pdf_file/0003/283818/Drug_Court_17nov06_A4_Final.pdf. Accessed 30 Apr 2013.

Thompson, M., Osher, F., & Tomasini-Joshi, D. (2007). *Improving responses to people with mental illnesses: The essential elements of a mental health court.* New York: Council of State Governments Justice Center.

Toki, V. (2010). Therapeutic jurisprudence and mental health courts for Maori. *International Journal of Law and Psychiatry, 33,* 440–447. doi:10.1016/j.ijlp.2010.09.014.

Trimboli, L. (2012). NSW Court Referral of Eligible Defendants into Treatment (CREDIT) pilot program: An evaluation. *Crime and Justice Bulletin Contemporary Issues in Criminal Justice Number 159.* NSW Bureau of Crime Statistics and Research. http://www.lawlink.nsw.gov.au/Lawlink/bocsar/ll_bocsar.nsf/vwFiles/cjb159.pdf/$file/cjb159.pdf. Accessed 30 Apr 2013.

TVNZ. (6 December 2010). Govt's 'head in the sand' over drug courts. http://tvnz.co.nz/national-news/govt-s-head-in-sand-over-drug-courts-3948847. Accessed 30 Apr 2013.

Wenzel, S. L., Turner, S. F., & Ridgely, M. S. (2004). Collaborations between drug courts and service providers: Characteristics and challenges. *Journal of Criminal Justice, 32*(3), 253–263. doi: 10.1016/j.jcrimjus.2004.02.005.

Wexler, D. B., & Winick, B. J. (Eds.). (1991). *Essays in therapeutic jurisprudence.* Durham: Carolina Academic Press.

Winick, B. J., Wiener, R., Castro, A., Emmert, A., & Skovran, L. C. (2010). Dealing with mentally ill domestic violence perpetrators: A therapeutic jurisprudence judicial model. *International Journal of Law and Psychiatry, 33*(5–6), 428–439. doi:10.1016/j.ijlp.2010.09.013.

Wolff, N., & Pogorzelski, W. (2005). Measuring the effectiveness of mental health courts: Challenges and recommendations. *Psychology, Public Policy, and Law, 11*(4), 539–569. doi:10.1037/1076-8971.11.4.539.

Chapter 12
Problem Solving Courts: Therapeutic Jurisprudence in Practice

Bruce J. Winick

Problem-Solving Courts: A Judicial Revolution

A remarkable transformation in the judiciary has occurred over the past 20 years (Winick and Wexler 2003). The traditional role of the courts has been to adjudicate disputed issues of fact in civil and criminal cases. Traditionally, judges were neutral arbiters considering conflicting evidence and rendering a decision based on the law and the facts. Recently, however, the kinds of cases that come to court have changed. We still have civil and criminal disputes, for which the traditional judicial role is appropriate, but many new types of cases do not involve factual disputes. A variety of social and psychological problems have found their way to the courts, and as a result, a metamorphosis has occurred in the judicial role. Indeed, these courts, collectively often referred to as "problem-solving courts," have different jurisdiction than traditional courts and separate judges who preside in them (Conference of Chief Justices and Conference of State Courts Administrators 2000; Winick and Wexler 2003; Winick 2003). Problems such as drug addiction, alcoholism, domestic violence, untreated mental illness, and prisoner reentry into society have taken up more and more judicial time, and the judiciary has responded by establishing a variety of specialty courts to deal with these problems.

Although traditional courts focus exclusively on the narrow dispute in controversy, problem-solving courts attempt to understand and address the underlying problem that is responsible for the immediate dispute, and to help the individuals before the

This chapter was prepared for a conference at the University of Nebraska Lincoln in January of 2010. Professor Winick participated in this conference with a video link. He was ill at the time of the conference. At the time near the end of his life, Professor Winick was engaged in some empirical work with Richard Wiener, the editor of this book. Bruce nearly completed this chapter before his untimely passing. Margot Winick, daughter of Professor Winick gave permission for us to include this chapter in the current book. Dr. Wiener completed some sections and did some light editing of the manuscript. As was always the case, little work was required to prepare Professor Winick's paper for publication.

B. J. Winick (✉)
University of Miami, Coral Gables, FL, USA

R. L. Wiener, E. M. Brank (eds.), *Problem Solving Courts*,
DOI 10.1007/978-1-4614-7403-6_12, © Springer Science+Business Media, LLC 2013

court to effectively deal with the problem in ways that will prevent recurring court involvement. These courts are voluntary (Winick 2003). The individuals who choose to go to them have social, mental health, or substance abuse problems. These newer courts also include criminal cases involving individuals with drug or alcoholism problems, mental health problems, or problems of family and domestic violence. The juvenile court, pioneered in Chicago in 1899, is the forerunner of these specialized courts. It represented an attempt to provide a rehabilitative approach to the problem of juvenile delinquency, rather than the punitive approach of the adult criminal court. The modern antecedent of these courts is the drug treatment court, founded in Miami in 1989 (Hora 2002).

In many ways, the problem-solving court judge functions as a social worker. Judges may not be the best professionals to play this role as they will not have received clinical training in psychology or social work. However, these problems confront the judge because our society often fails to adequately deal with the problem of substance abuse and other psychosocial problems, with the result that the individual often winds up in jail and the court.

Drug Treatment Court

This court was a response to the recognition by Miami judges and prosecutors that the drug problem had overrun the courts with more cases than could be handled, and that a new model was needed. The Miami drug treatment court soon adopted a treatment orientation. Processing nonviolent drug possession charges in the criminal courts and sentencing the offenders to prison had not succeeded in changing their addictive behavior. Instead of the traditional criminal court's retributivist intervention, which did little to avoid repetition of the underlying problem, the drug court sought to provide a judicially supervised treatment experience. The aim was to help the addicts and end the revolving door problem. Rehabilitation was the hallmark, and the drug court judge was cast as a member of the treatment team.

Drug offenders who chose not to contest their charges were given a new option. A pretrial diversion program existed in Miami and included drug treatment, but prosecutors did not agree to divert all drug possession offenses, and there existed uncertainty about the efficacy of traditional community drug treatment. The new option created by drug treatment court was designed for drug offenders who wished to deal seriously with their substance abuse problem. They could voluntarily elect to enter drug court and accept several conditions. They would agree to remain drug-free, to participate in a court-approved drug treatment program, to submit to periodic urine analysis drug testing in order to monitor their compliance with the treatment plan, and to report periodically to court for judicial supervision of their progress (Winick 2000). The drug courts and the other problem-solving courts that evolved from them, although often differing substantially, seem to have the following common elements: (1) immediate intervention, (2) a nonadversarial process, (3) intensive judge–offender interaction, (4) an interdisciplinary team approach, and (5) clearly defined rules and goals, often specified in a behavioral contract (Watson et al. 2001; Winick 2000).

A defendant choosing to participate in drug treatment court enters into a behavioral contract with a court in which he agrees to remain drug-free, to attend a community treatment program, to submit to periodic drug testing, and to report to court every 10–14 days. At each report date, the defendant's progress is monitored. The defendant appears at court along with all other defendants in a proceeding that may last several hours. The treatment staff discusses each defendant in open court. The court learns immediately whether the defendant is complying with the condition that he or she remains drug-free.

If the results of a drug test are negative, the judge publicly praises the individual and the other participants and their lawyers, including the state prosecutor, join in a round of applause. This praise can be a significant positive reinforcement for the individual who has accepted treatment, helping to build self-esteem and ensure continued compliance. If the drug test is positive, however, the judge will apply a sanction that has been previously agreed to. The sanctions range from judicial scolding to requiring the defendant to spend several hours in the jury box, to a night in the county jail. Subsequent failures result in increasingly more severe sanctions designed to increase compliance. If the individual remains drug-free for a specified period of time, the judge will dismiss his charges and give him a "graduation" ceremony. This ceremony celebrates the defendant's accomplishments and is attended by other successful graduates and their friends and families. The judge gives a speech and calls individuals up to the microphone to give their reactions. The officer presents a diploma, and everyone claps and congratulates the defendant (Belenko 2001). These positive rituals help not only the targeted defendants, but also the other program participants who witness them (Bandura 1986). There are now 2,300 such courts across the country (National Drug Court Institute 2009).

Domestic Violence Court

Based on the drug treatment court model, domestic violence court is designed to deal with the specialized problems of domestic violence. Its aim is to protect the victims of domestic violence, to motivate perpetrators of domestic violence to attend batterers' intervention programs, and to monitor compliance with court orders and treatment progress. Currently, there are over 300 domestic violence courts (Littel 2003). Domestic violence is between intimates rather than strangers, and the violence is typically progressive (Conference of Chief Justices and Conference of State Courts Administrators 2000; Littel 2003; Winick 2000).

Domestic violence was once considered a private issue, and the police and the courts intervened only in cases of serious harm (Mazur and Aldrich 2003). Most victims chose not to prosecute or to cooperate with the prosecution when the police filed criminal charges. The police, probably based on sexist traditions, failed to take domestic violence seriously, and would rarely intervene. Awareness of the extent and seriousness of domestic violence increased in the 1990s. More than 1 million women are battered by an intimate partner annually (Kaye and Knipps 2000). Domestic violence is responsible for almost one-third of all female homicide victims (Catalano 2007; Winick 2003; Winick et al. 2010).

In response to the emerging awareness of the seriousness of domestic violence, jurisdiction over these cases was placed in a specialized court—the domestic violence court. These courts combine criminal and civil jurisdiction, allowing both adjudication and punishment of offenders and the issuance of civil restraining orders designed to prevent future violence. They also provide services to victims and their families. They seek to both, punish the batterer and to encourage behavior change through batterers' intervention programs that offenders are mandated or encouraged to participate in as a result of conditions of bail, pretrial diversion, or probation (Winick 2000). The domestic violence court seeks to increase coordination and continuity of case processing (Sack 2002). It increases the consistency of judicial monitoring of perpetrators. Like drug treatment court, these courts represent a new judicial model distinct from the traditional criminal court. The judges, court officers, and prosecutors develop a special expertise in issues raised by domestic violence. As with the drug court, these courts involve extensive judicial collaboration with governmental agencies and community-based organizations. Domestic violence courts combine criminal and civil jurisdiction, allowing both punishment of offenders and civil protection orders mandating that the batterer does not contact the victim. The civil orders are enforced through the court's contempt powers, and violation of such an order is often itself a separate offense.

Although in some states, domestic violence courts possess only criminal jurisdiction over the offender, an integrated criminal/civil model is increasingly used. In some courts, the judge can also deal with child support and divorce issues arising in the case. A variation is the Unified Family Court, where the judge can handle all legal issues relating to the same family, including domestic violence, divorce and child support, delinquency, and dependency issues (Babb 1998; Littel 2003; Winick and Wexler 2003).

Domestic violence court, like other problem-solving courts, uses an interdisciplinary team effort in which judges, attorneys, resource coordination staff, and treatment staff work together. Like other problem-solving judicial models, they seek to motivate offenders to accept rehabilitation, participate in treatment programs, and monitor their compliance. They differ from other problem-solving courts, however, because domestic violence courts exist to prevent serious violence by the perpetrator. As avoiding recidivism is an important mission of the domestic violence court, these courts are considerably more adversarial in nature than other problem-solving courts.

Mental Health Court

A recently emerging problem-solving court model is mental health court, which began in 1997 in Broward County, Florida (Erickson et al. 2006; Petrila et al. 2001;

Stefan and Winick 2005). More than 110 such courts now exist in the USA (Erickson et al. 2006; Stefan and Winick 2005). The mental health court started off as a misdemeanor criminal court designed to deal with people arrested for minor offenses whose major problem is mental illness rather than criminality (Petrila et al. 2001). Some jurisdictions have extended the model to include felony cases (Fisler 2005). Like drug offenders and domestic violence perpetrators, mental health court deals with a recurring criminal offender pattern. The individuals opting to participate in mental health court are a revolving door category of patients who are periodically committed to mental hospitals, where they are treated with psychotropic medication (Goldkamp and Irons-Guynn 2000; Winick 2003). When functioning is restored, they are discharged to the community where many exercise their right to refuse to continue to take psychotropic medication (Winick 2003). As a result, they frequently decompensate, sometimes committing minor offenses that result in their arrest. Mental health courts seek to divert these patients from the criminal justice system and to motivate them to voluntarily accept treatment while in the community. In addition, they link them with treatment resources, and provide social service support and judicial monitoring to ensure treatment compliance (Winick 2003).

The aim of these courts is to stabilize their mental conditions by persuading offenders to take medication and by monitoring their compliance with treatment. Diversion from their criminal charges provides an incentive for offenders to participate in mental health court. As with drug court, if they succeed in the treatment program, the court drops their criminal charges. Similar to other problem-solving courts, they are generally informal and nonadversarial in nature. Like other problem-solving courts, participation is voluntary and treatment compliance is judicially monitored. The criminal justice system has replaced the mental hospital as the principal way of dealing with mentally ill individuals. Increasing numbers of offenders suffer from mental illness even though the jails and prisons have few resources to address their clinical needs (Erickson et al. 2006). This phenomenon is due to the tightening of civil commitment criteria, the declining public hospital census, limited access to community services, and the increased likelihood of arrest for minor nuisance offenses by those with mental illness (Watson et al. 2001; Stefan and Winick 2005).

Police are increasingly taught to apply the Memphis model in which these mentally ill offenders are diverted from the criminal justice system directly into treatment (Steadman et al. 2000). However, not all jurisdictions have adopted this model, with the result that many of these defendants still wind up in the criminal justice system. As their offenses are often more of a product of their untreated mental illness than criminality, the mental health court model can be a helpful way of diverting them from the jails that are highly antitherapeutic, motivating them to accept needed treatment, and facilitating their receiving it in the community (Winick et al. 2010).

Other Problem-Solving Court Models

In addition to the problem-solving courts discussed above, several other models have emerged in recent years. These include reentry court, dependency court, teen court, veteran court, and various hybrid models.

Reentry courts help offenders who are on judicially supervised parole after they have been released from prison. Their goal is to ensure a successful transition for the offender back into the community. Some might view this model as a "rear door" treatment court facilitating a successful reintegration of ex-offenders into the community. In this sense, the drug treatment court is a "front door" model, diverting drug offenders from the judicial and correctional process. Many offenders at the end of their prison terms will still need help with their addiction problems, and this type of court can offer judicially supervised treatment to discharged prisoners who choose to participate. In addition, a reentry court for sex offenders has been proposed. This model would attempt to monitor the risk of reoffending through close supervision and polygraph examinations.

Dependency court is a branch of family court that handles allegations of child abuse and neglect. It is a civil, rather than criminal court that determines whether child abuse or neglect has occurred and provides services in order to stabilize the families involved. The court also has the power to terminate parental rights and place children in foster care if parental abuse continues. As much of child abuse and neglect co-occurs with substance abuse, the dependency court has adapted the drug court model in an effort to assist interested parents to end their addictions.

Another type of problem-solving court is the teen court, also known as youth court. This court deals with juveniles who the state has charged with minor offenses. It utilizes juveniles who have been through the teen court process and have received training to play the role of members of the court—prosecutor, defense attorney, and jury. This model provides the young people involved, with a measure of empathy training and gives them the opportunity to view their behavior through the eyes of other parties involved.

Most recently, we have witnessed the development of veterans' courts charged with the responsibility of assisting soldiers returning to the community after serving in the military. Veteran participants are primarily those the state has charged with nonviolent misdemeanor offenses (Hawkins 2010). Typically, the court negotiates a treatment plan for the defendant, which can include drug, alcohol, and mental health services. After the parties agree to the treatment plan, the court officers arrange a plea agreement in which the defendants agree to comply in exchange for reduction or dismissal of charges at the end of the process. As with the case of mental health courts and drug courts, the judge carefully monitors the veterans' progress through a series of appearances and hearings (Hawkins 2010). Veterans' courts sometimes also order financial education, parental training, and other social services to assist the returning soldiers to readjust to community life.

In addition to the problem-solving court models discussed previously, some jurisdictions have created hybrid models to deal with more specific, overlapping problems. These courts combine the techniques of drug, domestic violence, and mental health court. For instance, dependency drug treatment courts deal with the substance abuse problems of parents whose children are in the abuse and neglect systems (Winick and Wexler 2003; Wyatt 2001; Winick et al. 2010). Juvenile drug treatment court deals with juveniles in the delinquency system that have addiction problems. Miami has pioneered a domestic violence mental health court that seeks to deal with individuals with untreated mental illness who engage in domestic violence (Winick et al. 2010).

The Value of Problem-Solving Courts

All the problem-solving courts were created as a result of the realization that traditional court interventions had failed in certain areas, including substance abuse, domestic violence, certain kinds of criminality, child abuse and neglect, and mental illness. These problems are all repetitive in nature and were not being solved by traditional courts, which treated the symptoms rather than the underlying problem. Instead, such traditional approaches led to a continued need for judicial intervention when the underlying problem produced additional criminal behavior. Moreover, courts of general jurisdiction generally lack both expertise in specialized problems of this nature, as well as the tools, such as treatment and social services, to effectively deal with these problems.

As a response to these failures, courts created new approaches that were collaborative and interdisciplinary and involved an active, leading role for the judge. In these new courts, the judge coordinates many of the parties involved, motivates the offender, and monitors compliance and progress. In addition, the judge's role extends beyond the courtroom. These judges are tasked not only with resolving the court case, but also with educating the public and preventing the antisocial behavior in question. As a result of this expanded role, problem-solving courts have begun generating information on the problems dealt with in these courts that is better in both quality and quantity than before. They help to raise awareness in the community about the problems they deal with, including causes, resources, and potential solutions. Moreover, their expertise advocates for increased funding for community resources. In addition, they can help to monitor and improve the effectiveness of treatment providers and other community agencies (Winick 2003).

Problem-solving courts represent a new role for the judge. Judges in these courts take a holistic approach to the offender and help to solve his underlying problem by providing motivation, compliance monitoring, and connection to appropriate services. These courts intervene in social and behavioral problems that are caused by chronic, underlying issues that can seriously impair both the individual's and the community's quality of life. As such, the judge plays an important public health function. The techniques and approaches of the problem-solving courts have also begun to appear in some courts of general jurisdiction (Schma 2003).

Are these courts successful? Many program studies and anecdotal evidence of drug treatment court suggest yes. They seem to reduce recidivism and drug use and other criminal behavior during and well after participation in the court program (Belenko 1998; United States Government Accountability Office 2005). They also serve as a highly cost effective alternative to criminal court because they decrease crime rates, criminal justice costs, and costs to victims (Quinn 2009 -citing West Huddleston). However, the lack of control groups and other methodological problems suggests that we may not yet know how successful these programs are on a scientific basis (Belenko 1998; King et al. 2009; Wiener et al. 2010). Similarly, although the effectiveness of mental health courts have not received empirical verification, preliminary outcome data and anecdotal reports indicate that they are somewhat successful in engaging participants in treatment and reducing recidivism (Boothroyd et al. 2003; Cosden et al. 2003; Redlich 2005; Trupin and Richards 2003). One multisite study (Steadman et al. 2010) did report better public safety outcomes for mental health courts.

Considerably more research is needed on the functioning of problem-solving courts and their effectiveness in rehabilitating offenders and avoiding recidivism. To the extent that these courts are successful, as the preliminary research and many anecdotal reports suggest, there is considerable need to understand why they work and more research is needed on this question. The interaction between the problem-solving court judge and the individual seems to be an important ingredient in program success, and more empirical work should probe how this occurs (Petrucci 2002; Wiener et al. 2010).

This chapter suggests how judges in problem-solving courts should act to increase their effectiveness. These suggestions come from psychological literature in other contexts. Therefore, there is a great need for further analytical analysis and empirical research concerning the application of these principles in the problem-solving court arena.

The problem-solving court model presents some potential risks that are worthy of comment. Problem-solving courts constitute an effective means of treating those with psychosocial problems who resist treatment in the community. If applied to those who otherwise would not have been involved in the criminal justice system, this would constitute an abuse of the model. The risk is that the police, in order to get them into treatment may arrest people with these problems for offenses for which they may not have otherwise arrested them. Such a widening of the social net would be inappropriate. There is no evidence that these courts have been used in this way, however. There are much better ways of getting needed treatment to those suffering from these problems than through the stigmatizing and unpleasant means of arrest. The police should be taught methods of diverting minor offenders by bringing them to appropriate community treatment facilities. Police arrest practices should not change in response to problem-solving courts.

An additional concern is the risk that these courts could lead to a fragmentation in the service delivery system. All who voluntarily seek these treatment services should have easy access to them in the community. Given the serious social problems like untreated substance abuse, domestic violence, and mental health problems, treatment services should be available on demand for all who desire them and outreach services should be increased to reach out to all who are in need. We should have more of a preventative approach designed to avoid the problem of arrest. If these needed services are provided, problem-solving courts will not result in affording those in the criminal justice system a superior access to needed services.

Therapeutic Jurisprudence as the Foundation for Problem-Solving Courts

Therapeutic jurisprudence can be regarded as the "philosophic foundation" for the hundreds of problem-solving courts that have emerged since the early 1990s (King et al. 2009; Petrila 2007; Redlich et al. 2005; Winick and Wexler 2003; Winick 2003). The problem-solving courts' revolution can be best understood by situating it within the scholarly and law reform approach known as therapeutic jurisprudence (Wexler and Winick 1991; Winick 2005). Therapeutic jurisprudence is an interdisciplinary perspective that can provide grounding for the new judicial movement, because therapeutic jurisprudence specifically asks what legal arrangements work and why. The field began in the late 1980's as an interdisciplinary scholarly approach in the area of mental health law. It criticized various aspects of mental health law for producing antitherapeutic consequences for the people that the law was designed to help. Although it originated in the area of mental health law, therapeutic jurisprudence soon found easy application to other areas of the law—criminal law, juvenile law, family law, personal injury law—and has now emerged as a therapeutic approach to the law generally (Wexler and Winick 2003).

Legal rules and the way they are applied are social forces. Sometimes they impose negative consequences. Therapeutic jurisprudence's basic insight is that scholars should study those consequences, reshape, and then redesign law in order to accomplish the goal of minimizing antitherapeutic effects. When it is consistent with other legal goals, therapeutic jurisprudence aims to increase law's therapeutic potential. Therapeutic jurisprudence is an interdisciplinary approach to legal scholarship that has a law reform agenda.

Therapeutic jurisprudence is not only concerned with measuring the therapeutic impact of legal rules and procedures, but also about the way they are applied by various legal actors—judges, lawyers, police officers, and expert witnesses testifying in court, among others (Winick 1999, 2000, 2003, 2005). Whether they are conscious of this aspect of the consequences of their behavior, these legal actors are therapeutic agents, affecting the mental health and psychological well-being of the people they encounter in the legal setting. For example, how lawyers deal with their clients in the law office and the courtroom can have a significant impact on a client's emotional well-being, and therapeutic jurisprudence has spawned a growing literature concerning how attorneys should act in this regard (Stolle et al. 2000).

Similarly, in the way they function on the bench, judges are therapeutic agents. The explicit purpose of problem-solving courts is the rehabilitation of offenders through a team approach that casts the judge in a leading role. The essential function of a problem-solving court judge is therefore as a behavior change agent. Therapeutic jurisprudence has much to offer judges concerning how they should deal with the people appearing before them. It also provides suggestions as to how these courts can be structured and administered to maximize their therapeutic potential.

Therapeutic jurisprudence is one of the major "vectors" of a growing movement in the law toward a common goal of a more comprehensive, humane, and psychologically optimal way of handling legal matters (Daicoff 2000). Problem-solving courts are also one of these "vectors," and thus, share many common aims with therapeutic jurisprudence (Casey and Rottman 2000; Rottman and Casey 1999). Problem-solving courts are thus related to therapeutic jurisprudence, but are not identical with the concept. Problem-solving courts often use principles of therapeutic jurisprudence to enhance their functioning. Indeed, the Conference of Chief Justices and the Conference of State Court Administrators, following a joint task force analysis, approved a resolution of the growing movement in the direction of problem-solving courts, and their use of principles of therapeutic jurisprudence in performing their functions (Conference of Chief Justices and Conference of State Courts Administrators 2000; Winick et al. 2010). These principles include "integration of treatment services with judicial case processing, ongoing judicial intervention, close monitoring of an immediate response to behavior, multidisciplinary involvement, and collaboration with community-based and governmental organizations" (Conference of Chief Justices and Conference of State Courts Administrators 2000). Therapeutic jurisprudence can thus provide principles or what Professor Robert Schopp has called "instrumental prescriptions" for how courts might perform their problem-solving functions (Schopp 1999; Winick and Wexler 2003).

Although problem-solving courts developed separately from therapeutic jurisprudence, their development occurred at the same time, and they share similar aims. Drug treatment courts, domestic violence courts, and mental health courts, for example, can be seen as taking a therapeutic jurisprudence approach to the processing of cases, inasmuch as their goal is the rehabilitation of the offender and their use of the legal process, in particular, the role of the judge, to accomplish this goal (Winick 2003). All of these courts seek to deal with the offender's underlying problem, and emphasize on its resolution through the provision of treatment and rehabilitative services where the judge is an important member of the treatment team. Judges in these specialized courts receive special training in the nature and treatment of drug addiction, domestic violence, and mental illness, and themselves function as therapeutic agents through their supervision and monitoring of the offender's treatment progress (Hora et al. 1999; Winick 2000, 2003). Unlike traditional judges functioning in traditional courts, judges in problem-solving courts consciously view themselves as therapeutic agents, and, therefore, one can see them as playing a therapeutic jurisprudence function in their dealings with the individuals who appear before them.

Moreover, principles of therapeutic jurisprudence can help problem-solving court judges play this function well. Therapeutic jurisprudence has already produced a large body of interdisciplinary scholarship analyzing principles of psychology and the behavioral sciences, and probing the ways in which they can be used in legal contexts to improve mental health and emotional well-being (Winick and Wexler 2003; Winick 2003). A growing body of therapeutic jurisprudence scholarship has also addressed how judges in specialized problem-solving courts can apply principles of therapeutic jurisprudence in their work (Casey and Rottman 2000; Fritzler and Simon 2000; Hora 2002; Hora et al. 1999; Petrucci 2002; Shiff and Wexler 1996; Winick 2003). For instance, an edited book by Winick and Wexler and a symposium issue of Court Review, the official publication of the American Judges Association, were devoted entirely to therapeutic jurisprudence and its application to judging

(Winick 2000). An understanding of therapeutic jurisprudence's approach and of the psychological and social work principles it uses can thus provide considerable help in the structuring of problem-solving courts and in defining the role played by judges functioning within them.

Just as judges dealing with antitrust cases need to understand basic principles of economics, and judges dealing with patent cases need to understand basic principles of engineering, judges performing in a problem-solving capacity, dealing as they do with human problems, need to understand some principles of psychology, the science of human behavior. They must be aware that they are functioning as therapeutic agents, and that how they interact with the individuals appearing before them will have inevitable consequences for the ability of those individuals to achieve rehabilitation or otherwise to deal with their underlying problems.

The people appearing in problem-solving courts—and often in general criminal, civil, and family courts—are there because they have problems that they have not recognized or had the ability to deal with, effectively. They may suffer from alcoholism or substance abuse problems, and these may contribute to repetitive criminality, domestic violence, or child abuse and neglect. They may be repetitive perpetrators of domestic violence or child abuse because of cognitive distortions concerning their relationships with their spouses or children or because they lack the social skills to manage their anger or to resolve problems other than through violence. Some will suffer from mental illness that impairs their judgment about the desirability of their continuing to take needed medication. Various psychological defense mechanisms may make it hard for them to recognize and deal with their problems. They are in denial about the wrongfulness of their conduct, or they may rationalize it and minimize its impact on themselves and others. Effective treatment exists for many, if not all of these problems, but only if the individual recognizes the existence of a problem and is motivated to deal with it.

Instrumental Prescriptions for Problems Solving Court Judges

Judges in problem-solving courts need to understand how to deal with the psychological defense mechanisms. Therapeutic jurisprudence is a law and psychology based field of study that incorporates insights and approaches from psychology in analyzing how the law functions and how we can improve it. For example, an existing body of therapeutic jurisprudence scholarship deals with these defense mechanisms (Winick 1998, 2000; Winick and Perez 2010). Emerging principles of therapeutic jurisprudence shed light on how court structures and the conduct of individual judges can help people recognize and solve crucial life problems.

Motivation for change is an essential ingredient in treatment success. The individual himself is approaching the realization that he should change his course of behavior, but has not yet undertaken change. The judge in the court process can help to provide motivation for the individual to reach that conclusion. The arrest and court involvement can function as a real catalyst for change, as a therapeutic opportunity for the individual. The individual can plead guilty or not guilty, but the problem-solving court gives him an additional option of choosing to deal with his problem. If he does so successfully, the judge may dismiss or modify the charges. The judge discusses these issues with the individual using a form of motivational interviewing (Winick 2003; Winick and Perez 2010). The judge can, through dialogue, allow the individual to see that his substance abuse or behavioral problem is responsible for his failure to attain a variety of short- and long-term goals. Once the individual sees this connection, he may be ready to deal with his problems. Although we call them problem-solving courts, the court cannot solve the individual's problems. Only the individual can do so. However, the court can provide substantial assistance through structured treatment, periodic reporting, and compliance monitoring. The individual will not undertake change, however, if he believes that real change is outside his ability. The judge uses strength-based approaches to bolster the individual's sense of self-esteem and self-efficacy. Therapeutic jurisprudence adapts these techniques for judicial use. These techniques, combining motivational interviewing with the literature on stages of change were originally developed in the context of substance abuse treatment, where the treatment professional tries to motivate the patient (Miller and Rollnick 2002; Birgden 2002). These techniques can be adapted for use by problem-solving court judges to encourage offenders to confront and face their problems and begin to deal with them through a structured treatment program that, as an essential feature, includes judicial monitoring and compliance checking.

Interpersonal Skills

Judges functioning in these ways need to develop enhanced interpersonal skills, to understand the psychology of procedural justice, to acquire the ability to serve as effective risk managers, and to learn about the other approaches that therapeutic jurisprudence has to offer. To succeed, a genuine treatment alliance needs to be forged.

The judge needs to develop refined interviewing, counseling, and interpersonal skills. The individual may have engaged in wrongdoing, but a special sensitivity to his pain and shame is called for. Judges may strongly disapprove of the individual's conduct, but must strive in the judge–offender dialogue to be supportive, empathic, warm, and good listeners. They should shame and criticize not the individual, but his conduct (Braithwaite 1989). If the individual perceives the judge to be cold, insensitive, or judgmental, the creation of a treatment alliance will be frustrated. Once the individual enters the program, thereby recognizing that his prior behavior has been inappropriate, the judge and treatment staff should shift to a future-focused orientation that concentrates on the steps needed to solve the problem. Focusing upon past failures produces demoralization and resignation. To be an effective change-agent, the judge should display empathy to the individual, even if not to his act.

Empathy involves the ability to experience another person's feelings and to see the world through that person's eyes (Winick 1998). Empathy has both cognitive and affective components. The judge should convey both an intellectual response to the individual, communicating that she understands the individual's predicament, and an emotional response, communicating that she shares the individual's feelings. The judge must remember that the individual is a fellow human being whom she is helping. The judge should communicate a sense of caring, sympathy, genuineness, and understanding (Goleman 1995; Shuman 1993). Just as physicians need to develop their "bedside manner," judges need to develop what can be termed their "benchside manner". The objective is to create a comfortable space in which offenders can feel free to express their emotions about their problems and deal effectively, with them.

In helping offenders in their courts to deal with their problems, problem-solving court judges need to be good listeners. The judge should seek to promote dialogue rather than giving the offender a speech. The judges must communicate to the offenders that he really wishes to hear them and is interested in their problems, and in helping to solve them. Active listening and passive listening techniques may be helpful in this connection (Binder et al. 1991; Winick 1998). Problem-solving court judges need to be alert to the individual's nonverbal forms of communication. Nonverbal forms of communication, such as facial expression, body language, and tone of voice, can be extremely helpful in understanding the individual's emotions and how the judge should respond to them.

Problem-solving courts are animated by the therapeutic jurisprudence vision that the law is an instrument for helping people, particularly those with a variety of psychological and emotional problems. Society neglects many of our serious social problems. Treatment resources are scarce and preventive services almost nonexistent. Courts that take on the task of dealing with the difficult problems of drug addiction, alcoholism, domestic violence, mental illness, child abuse and neglect, and juvenile delinquency function, in part, act as psychosocial agencies. To succeed in this role, the judges in these courts need to be aware of some basic principles of psychology and social work. Thus, therapeutic jurisprudence can provide a theoretical foundation for much of the problem-solving court movement, and a variety of principles that can help judges play this new and exciting role.

Autonomy Versus Paternalism

Too often, problem-solving court judges are paternalistic in their approach. Indeed, some regard what they do as a form of benign paternalism. This is inappropriate. No one likes to be treated paternalistically, and program participants will find a paternalistic attitude to be offensive. Paternalism may create resentment and possibly backfire by producing a psychological reactance to the advice offered that might be counterproductive (Brehm and Brehm 1981). Many offenders will be in denial about their underlying problems, and paternalism is unlikely to succeed in allowing them to deal with such denial (Winick 1998). Instead, it may produce anxiety and other psychological distress that will make it harder for them to do so.

People respond better when others respect their autonomy and they are free to make choices for themselves. The judge should avoid pressuring the individual to elect to participate in a problem-solving court program. The judge should remind an individual charged with a drug offense that he is free to deal with the charges in criminal court and accept a sentence to prison if found guilty. Drug treatment court is not required, but is only an alternative option. Hence, the judge should remind the offender that the choice is theirs, and that they should not elect the drug treatment court unless they are prepared to admit the existence of a problem and express a willingness to deal with it. This approach can be empowering to such individuals who often feel powerless and helpless.

Judge as Motivator

Individuals should see the role of the problem-solving court judge in discussing rehabilitation with the offender as one of persuasion rather than of coercion. Judges should be aware of the psychological value of choice (Winick 1992, 2005). Self-determination is an essential aspect of psychological health. Moreover, if individuals who make their own choices perceive them as noncoerced, they will function more effectively and with greater satisfaction. People who feel coerced, by contrast, may respond with a negative psychological reaction (Brehm and Brehm 1981), and may experience various other psychological difficulties (Winick 1995). In appropriate circumstances, judges should communicate their own views concerning the individual's best interests to the individual, but should ultimately cede the choice to the individual. To succeed, treatment or rehabilitation will require a degree of intrinsic motivation on the part of the individual (Bandura 1986; Winick 1991; Deci 1975). If offenders participate in the program only because of extrinsic motivation, then it will be less likely that they will internalize the program goals and genuinely change their attitudes and behaviors.

The individual should be afforded a choice not only in deciding whether to elect to participate in a problem-solving court, but also in the design of the rehabilitative plan, when feasible. Typically, there may be many options available in fashioning such a plan, including variations in rehabilitative techniques and service providers (Babb and Moran 1999; Brown 2001). The problem-solving court judge can lay the options out for the individual, who can then exercise choice. The individual's choice concerning the various issues that arise in the design of the treatment plan can be empowering, and can influence the likelihood of success.

Some problem-solving court judges describe what they do as "benevolent coercion," and extol the virtues of judicial coercion as an essential ingredient in the rehabilitative enterprise (Tauber 2002). Although many of the individuals in drug treatment or other problem-solving courts who agree to participate in a course of treatment or rehabilitation will benefit from the structure, supervision, and compliance monitoring that they provide, it is neither appropriate nor desirable to regard this as coercion (Winick and Wexler 2003; Winick 2003). Individuals who decide to accept diversion to a drug treatment or other problem-solving court, or to plead guilty and accept treatment in a problem-solving court program as a condition of probation, are making legally voluntary choices as long as they are not subjected to duress, force, fraud, or a form of improper inducement (Wertheimer 1987). Individuals making such choices may be functioning within a coercive context. Although they may face hard choices, none of which may be agreeable, they are in these difficult situations because of their own actions. For example, the arrest was not a vehicle forcing them into treatment, instead they possessed drugs or committed some other crime for which they could benefit from treatment. Moreover, they are free to either plead not guilty and face trial, or plead guilty and receive an appropriate sentence. Therefore, extending to them the additional option of accepting a rehabilitative alternative does not make the choice that they will then face, a coercive one.

An analogy to plea-bargaining is appropriate. Although offenders who have been offered plea deals may feel that the choice they are required to make is coercive, as long as the prosecutor's offer was not illegal, unauthorized, unethical, or otherwise inappropriate, the courts have held that it does not constitute legal coercion (Wertheimer 1987; Winick 1991, 2005). Accordingly, if an individual's decision about whether to accept a guilty plea is not coerced, then his or her decision as to whether to accept diversion to a problem-solving court, or to plead guilty and accept treatment through the auspices of such a court as a condition for probation also would not constitute coercion in a legal sense. Plea-bargaining is an example in which individuals face hard choices, but where, an offer that is improper, illegal, or unethical is absent, the courts will not consider the choice coercive.

Parole from prison presents another example. The criminal justice system may release an individual on parole before the expiration of his prison term, if he accepts certain conditions of parole. These conditions may include, for example, an undertaking that the individual not use alcoholic beverages or associate with other individuals who have a criminal record. Unless the conditions of parole are improper or illegal, we would consider the individual's choice to accept these conditions as voluntary, rather than coerced (Wertheimer 1987). Even though the individual's desire to be released from prison might be so powerful that he may feel that he has no real choice other than to accept the conditions of parole, it would be absurd for the law to invalidate his choice on grounds of coercion. As long as the conditions of parole are not unlawful, improper, or unreasonable, parole accords the individual an opportunity that he may find more desirable than serving the remainder of his sentence in prison.

Opportunities for diversion from the criminal process are essentially similar. An individual charged with a crime that must decide between facing his charges or accepting diversion into a rehabilitative program may be facing a hard choice. It is a fair and reasonable choice, however, and is not one that the law will invalidate on grounds of coercion (McKune v. Lile 2002; Winick 2005).

The sanctions concerning whether to enter the program do not constitute coercion in a legal sense. Indeed, if properly applied, the individual may not even experience it as psychologically coercive. Therapeutic jurisprudence scholarship has examined what makes people feel coerced and feel that they have acted voluntarily and refers to this issue as the psychological perception of coercion. It builds on the work by MacArthur Research Network on mental health and the law. The foundation conducted research to explore the causes and correlates of what makes people feel coerced. Researchers examined the context of mental patients facing involuntary hospitalization. They concluded that even though patients were subjected to legal compulsion through involuntary civil commitment, they did not feel coerced when treated with dignity and respect by people who they perceived as acting with genuine benevolence, and as providing them with a sense of "voice" (the ability to have their say), and with "validation" (the impression that what they said was taken seriously) (Monahan et al. 1995). The degree of perceived coercion correlated with and the kinds of pressures that doctors, families, and friends placed upon the patient (Monahan et al. 1995). Negative pressures, such as threats and force, tend to make individuals feel coerced, whereas positive pressures, such as persuasion and inducement, do not (Monahan et al. 1995). Even though courts subject these individuals to the legal compulsion of civil commitment, if treated in these ways, they tend to not feel coerced.

Problem-solving court judges should apply the lessons of the MacArthur research on coercion, treating all individuals with respect, and according them with voice and validation (Winick 2005). They should avoid negative pressures and threats, relying instead on positive pressures like persuasion and inducement. This is more likely to result in the individual experiencing the problem-solving court as voluntary, rather than coerced. If experienced as voluntary, the psychological benefits of choice will be achieved and the negative psychological effects of coercion can be avoided (Winick 1999, 2003, 2005). As long as individuals experience their decisions to participate in problem-solving court treatment or rehabilitative program as voluntary, those perceptions can have significant positive effects on treatment outcomes (Cascardi et al. 2000; Winick 2000). They can engage individuals' intrinsic motivation, whereas coercion is more likely to produce the feeling that they will perform in the program only as a result of extrinsic motivation. Real and lasting behavior change will occur only if the individuals see for themselves the point of participating in the program and exercise autonomy in making their decisions. Judges, therefore, should use techniques of persuasion, motivation, and inducement, but avoid a heavy-handed approach, strong negative pressure, and coercion.

Treating individuals with dignity and respect and respecting their autonomy can also have the added dividend of increasing self-esteem and self-efficacy. People may otherwise feel that they cannot succeed, and either will reject the program as a result or will succumb to the pressures, reinforced by their environment to return to substance abuse or antisocial patterns. Feeling that they have made a voluntary choice in favor of treatment can increase commitment to achieving the treatment goal, and set in motion a variety of psychological mechanisms that can help to bring it about.

In a dialogue that treats the individual with dignity and respect, problem-solving court judges should present to those considering whether to enter the program, information concerning the rehabilitative alternatives to criminal court that they present. They should also mention the positive consequences for successfully completing the program, including the dismissal of charges. Then, judges should leave offenders free to engage in instrumental thinking concerning the value of electing these rehabilitative alternatives. Judges should also give these individuals the opportunity to ask questions about their options, the freedom to engage in their own processing of the information, and the freedom to reach their own decisions. The judge should avoid pressuring the individual to make a decision.

The line between coercion and choice can be a narrow one. Moreover, the concept of legal coercion does not necessarily coincide with the psychological perception of coercion. When judges, attorneys, and other court personnel help individuals to consider whether to opt for a problem-solving court rehabilitative alternative instead of criminal court, they should rely on persuasion or inducement, and avoid coercion and negative forms of pressure. Of course, once the individual chooses the treatment option, his future actions are constrained by the choice the client has voluntarily entered into. Thus, the individual, as a condition for accepting the drug treatment court, may agree to attend a drug treatment program, to remain drug-free, and to submit to periodic drug testing. The individual knows that if he or she fails to comply, the court can apply sanctions (typically graduated sanctions) agreed to, in advance by the individual (Hora 2002; Hora et al. 1999). Moreover, the individual knows that repeated noncompliance can result in expulsion from the program and return to criminal court, or a violation of probation if the individual had pled guilty (Hora 2002; Hora et al. 1999).

These approaches fit well with the technique of motivational interviewing mentioned above. Five basic principles underlie this technique (Miller and Rollnick 2002). First, the interviewer needs to express empathy (Clark 2001). This involves understanding the individual's feelings and perspectives without judging, criticizing, or blaming (Birgden 2002). Second, the interviewer, in a nonconfrontational way, should seek to develop discrepancies between the individual's present behavior and important personal goals (Miller and Rollnick 2002). Applying this approach, the judge should attempt to elicit the individual's underlying goals and objectives (Miller and Rollnick 2002). In addition, the judge should attempt to get the individual to recognize the existence of a problem through the use of interviewing techniques, such as open-ended questioning, reflective listening, providing frequent statements of affirmation and support, and eliciting self-motivational statements (Miller and Rollnick 2002). For example, if the individual wishes to obtain or keep a particular job, the judge can ask questions designed to probe the relationship between drinking or substance abuse and poor performance in previous employment that may have resulted in dismissal. An interviewer will create motivation for change only when individuals perceive the discrepancy between how they are behaving achieving their personal goals.

Third, the interviewer should avoid arguing with the individual, which can be counterproductive and create defensiveness (Miller and Rollnick 2002). Fourth, when interviewers encounter resistance, they should attempt to roll with the resistance, rather than becoming confrontational (Miller and Rollnick 2002). This requires listening with empathy and providing feedback to what the individual is saying by introducing new information, which also allows the individual to remain in control, to make his or her own decisions, and to create solutions to his or her own problems.

Fifth, it is important for the interviewer to foster self-efficacy in the individual. The individual will not attempt change unless he feels that he can reach the goal, overcome barriers and obstacles to its achievement, and succeed in effectuating change (Miller and Rollnick 2002).

Motivational interviewing can be particularly effective when people find themselves at the point in which they are contemplating change (Birgden 2002). The individuals' arrest and court involvement may function as a wake-up call, giving them the message that it is time to confront their behavior patterns and consider making a genuine commitment to rehabilitation. The problem-solving court provides the client with such an opportunity, and through judicial monitoring, compliance checking, and treatment, offers a feasible way of undertaking and achieving behavior change.

Compliance

Insuring compliance with requirements of the treatment program is an essential component of all problem-solving courts. The unique feature of these courts is the role the judge plays by monitoring and assuring compliance. Therapeutic jurisprudence scholarship has addressed the problem of increasing compliance in a variety of legal contexts (Wexler and Winick 1991). It analyzes how health care compliance principles and methods of behavioral or contingency contracting can be adapted in the legal context. Therapeutic jurisprudence work has also explored the implications of the psychology of procedural justice for improving compliance with judicial orders. This work provides instrumental prescriptions for how problem-solving court judges can function.

Health Care Compliance Principles

Compliance is a significant issue in the context of medical practice as many patients fail to heed the doctor's treatment recommendations (Meichenbaum and Turk 1987). How can physicians and other healers convince their patients to comply with their medical advice? Patient noncompliance is a significant problem that the medical literature has addressed extensively. The behavioral medicine literature, which uses principles of behavioral psychology, deals with compliance with medical treatment. For example, the work of psychologists Donald Meichenbaum and Donald Turk sets forth a number of health care compliance principles, and shows how health care professionals can apply them to increase the likelihood that their patients will follow their treatment recommendations.

Several factors increase patient noncompliance. Sometimes the physician fails to instruct the patient adequately. The interaction between physician and patient during the time when the physician recommends the treatment can be most significant. Compliance will be less likely if the physician appears to be distant, distracted, reads case notes, uses professional jargon, asks questions calling for brief "yes" or "no" answers, fails to allow the patient the opportunity to tell her story in her own words, describes the treatment plan imprecisely or in technical terms, acts paternalistically, or is abrupt with the patient.

Meichenbaum and Turk recommend that health care providers can increase compliance when they introduce themselves to the patient, avoid jargon, and elicit the patient's views, preferences, and active involvement in designing the treatment plan. Providing choice, even over minor details of treatment, can be significant. Compliance is furthered when the physician is perceived as prestigious, competent, caring, and motivated by the patient's best interests. Involvement of family members can also increase compliance. Family members and friends can provide encouragement and reminders to the patient and can help the physician access information about compliance. A public commitment to the family and significant others also enhances compliance. Patient compliance is augmented when the patient anticipates disapproval of the physician and of the patient's family members. Furthermore, the individual patient can be significant in increasing compliance with the treatment program.

Judges in problem-solving courts should understand and apply the insights of this literature. Judges, court personnel, treatment providers, and defense attorneys, should carefully and understandably instruct the problem-solving court participant concerning his obligations to participate in the treatment program and to report periodically to the court. The judge should have a dialogue with the participant in which he is encouraged to express concerns. The judge should listen carefully and act concerned rather than distant, provide the individual with her undivided attention during conversations, avoid jargon and paternalism, and generally treat the individual with dignity and respect. The judge should encourage the individual's active involvement in both the negotiation and design of the rehabilitative plan, providing as great a degree of choice concerning the details as circumstances permit. Judges should always give the impression that the individual's best interests motivated them. The judge should encourage the involvement of family members and make a commitment to them in a formal and relatively public way.

Behavioral Contracting

These compliance principles are captured by a behavioral psychology technique known as "behavioral contracting" or "contingency management". This technique involves an explicit, formal contract that the individual enters into with the court setting forth specific goals and procedures (Winick 1991). The technique involves both agreed-upon rewards and positive reinforcement for success and aversive conditioners for failure. Behavioral contracting is frequently used in clinical practice, and the combination of positive reinforcement to encourage compliance and aversive conditioning to decrease or extinguish noncompliant behavior can be quite effective. The contract provides rewards and penalties for the achievement and failure to reach intermediate and long-term goals. The contract specifies partial rewards or sanctions that can be provided periodically upon the attainment or nonattainment of intermediate goals, thereby facilitating the progressive shaping of the individual's behavior. Tailoring the rewards and punishments to the individual's incentive preferences, and involving the individual in the process of selecting the goals and reinforcers, when practicable, can significantly increase motivation to comply. Including subgoals will best maintain self-motivation, provide inducements to action, provide guideposts for performance, and, if attained, self-satisfaction needed to sustain effort.

The behavioral contract explicitly records the expectations of the parties making target behaviors objectified, measurable, and well understood by all parties. This is an application of the goal-setting effect, under which the mere setting of a goal produces positive expectancies for its achievement that themselves help to bring about success. Goals serve to structure and guide the individual's performance, providing direction and focusing interest, attention, and personal involvement. The principles of intrinsic motivation, anticipated emotions, cognitive dissonance, and the psychological value of choice explain success.

Many drug court treatment programs explicitly use such behavioral contracts (Burdon et al. 2001). Whether or not formally negotiated and executed, individuals agreeing to participate in treatment or rehabilitation in a variety of problem-solving court contexts are, in effect, engaging in behavioral contracting (Winick 2003). Domestic violence perpetrators who agree to enter a batterer's intervention program as a condition of bail, diversion, or probation are, in effect, engaging in behavioral contracting with the domestic violence court (Winick 2000). Those with mental illness who elect to participate in mental health court similarly engage in behavioral contracting with the mental health court (Winick 2003). Offenders that agree to participate in reentry courts and to submit to the reentry court judge's supervision are also engaging in behavioral contracting (LaFond and Winick 2003). Although some clients do not explicitly enter into these contracts, the parties should negotiate, wire, and formally execute them in a formal and public way.

Problem-solving courts judges should understand the psychology of behavioral contracting, and use it to increase motivation, commitment, compliance, and effective performance. The process through which the behavioral contract is negotiated and entered into can itself provide an important opportunity for minimizing feelings of coercion that might undermine compliance and successful performance. The judge should make it clear that whether or not individuals enter into the behavioral contract is up to them, and should stress that it is a voluntary choice. If individuals feel coerced, they may enter the program because of extrinsic motivation only, and may not achieve lasting behavior change. On the other hand, experiencing choice as voluntary will spark intrinsic motivation and succeed in internalizing treatment goals.

As the MacArthur Research Network on Mental Health and the Law research shows, according individuals with a sense of voice and validation, treating them with dignity and respect, and conveying to them that the court is acting in good faith and in their best interest will diminish the perception of coercion and increase the perception of voluntary choice (Monahan et al. 1995; Winick 2005). The judge should remind individuals opting for a problem-solving court rehabilitative program that the choice is entirely up to them. In addition, they should be given the opportunity, when practicable, to participate in the negotiation of the behavioral contract and the selection of the reinforcers, sanctions, and conditions that will be used and applied. This participation and involvement should occur in ways that respect their need for voice and validation. If handled properly, the negotiation and entry into the behavioral contract can constitute an important opportunity to engage intrinsic motivation and commitment and to establish a mechanism that will help to assure compliance in ways that the individual will regard as fair.

By requiring an individual accepting drug treatment court to agree to periodic drug testing and reporting to court, the drug treatment court is monitoring compliance with the behavioral contract. When the drug test shows the individual to be drug-free, the judge praises the individual, often in the presence of a room full of attorneys, court personnel, and other drug treatment court participants. Such praise is an important form of positive reinforcement that rewards the individual for compliant behavior, helps to shape future behavior, and builds much needed self-esteem and self-efficacy. At the successful completion of the drug treatment court program, the individual is given a graduation ceremony in court where the arresting officer usually presents a "diploma," the judge offers praise, and there is general applause (Belenko et al. 2003). When other program participants observe this "graduation" ritual, they themselves receive a form of vicarious reinforcement (Bandura 1962).

When the individual's drug test is positive, the judge applies an agreed-upon sanction or aversive conditioner, which should deter future noncompliant behavior (Hora 2002). Future incidents of noncompliance are then subjected to graduated sanctions that were agreed to in advance by the individual, as well as verbal disapproval, occurring in the presence of others (Hora 2002). The court maintains close monitoring and supervision of the treatment process by having the individual report to the court every 10–14 days, so that the judge may receive frequent feedback from the treatment team and information concerning whether the individual has remained drug-free (Hora 2002).

The periodic delivery of positive reinforcement or sanctions contingent upon whether the individual has met intermediate goals helps to maintain the individual's commitment and motivation during the one and one-half to two years that drug treatment court typically requires. In this way, what the drug treatment court applies is behavioral contracting or contingency management, a technique, which, if properly applied, can substantially increase the likelihood of treatment success (Burdon et al. 2001). Other problem-solving courts should adapt this approach and all judges in these courts should receive training in its application.

The Psychology of Procedural Justice

Therapeutic jurisprudence scholarship has frequently pointed to the literature on the psychology of procedural justice, suggesting that its application in a variety of contexts can achieve therapeutic benefits for the individuals involved (Lind and Tyler 1988; Tyler 1990). In all of their interactions with the individual, problem-solving court judges should be careful to apply procedures that fully respect the individual's participatory and dignitary interests (Winick 2005). This literature, based on empirical work in a variety of litigation and arbitration contexts, shows that the way in which people are treated at hearings relate closely to whether they experience greater satisfaction and comply more willingly with the ultimate outcome of the proceedings, even if it is adverse to them. These positive results are produced when the individual is given a sense of "voice," (the ability to tell their story) and "validation" (the feeling that what they have said has been taken seriously by the judge or hearing officer), and generally treated in ways that they consider to be fair.

Thus, according individuals in problem-solving court contexts a full measure of procedural justice can help to increase compliance with, and successful participation in a treatment or rehabilitative program (Tyler 1990). For reasons developed earlier, according individuals procedural justice will also diminish their perception of coercion in the judicial process and increase the chances that they will experience the decision to enter into a treatment or rehabilitative program as voluntary. This perception can itself help to increase the likelihood of genuine participation on the part of the individual, intrinsic motivation, program compliance, and treatment success (Winick 2005). These utilitarian reasons for respecting the procedural rights of individuals in problem-solving court contexts coalesce with the historic commitment to fairness embodied in the concept of due process of law (Reisig 2002). Even when functioning as psychosocial agencies, problem-solving courts should accord the individual a full measure of due process.

Conclusion

Problem-solving courts represent a newly broadened conception of the role of the courts, one that is fully consistent with the basic concept of therapeutic jurisprudence. They are a noble undertaking to close the revolving door to certain kinds of repetitive offenses by providing the judicially supervised and monitored treatment to those motivated to undertake it. To perform this new judicial role, judges need to develop and improve their interpersonal, psychological, and social work skills. Therapeutic jurisprudence can help judges in this effort.

Problem-solving courts can become natural laboratories for the development and application of therapeutic jurisprudence principles and for research on what works best in the court-involved treatment and rehabilitative process. Problem-solving courts, applying principles of therapeutic jurisprudence, can become an important force for dealing with a number of the most vexing social and psychological problems that affect our communities. Therapeutic jurisprudence and problem-solving courts share a common mission—how legal rules, judicial practices, and court structures and administration can be redesigned to facilitate the rehabilitative process. Although problem-solving courts are not identical with therapeutic jurisprudence, these two approaches can be seen as having a symbiotic relationship (Winick and Wexler 2003). Together they can do much to transform law into an instrument of healing for both the individual and the community.

References

Babb, B. (1998). Fashioning an interdisciplinary framework for court reform in family law: A blueprint to construct a unified family court. *Southern California Law Review, 71*, 469–545.

Babb, B., & Moran, J. (1999). Substance abuse, families, and unified family courts: The creation of a caring justice system. *Journal of Health Care Law & Policy, 3*(1), 1–43.

Bandura, A. (1962). Social learning through imitation. In M. Jones (Ed.), Nebraska symposium on motivation (pp. 211–274). Symposium conducted in Lincoln, NE: University of Nebraska Press.

Bandura, A. (1986). *Social foundations of thought and action: A social cognitive theory*. Englewood Cliffs: Prentice-Hall.

Belenko, S. R. (1998). Research on drug courts: A critical review. *National Drug Court Institute Review, 1*(1), 1–42.

Belenko, S. R. (2001). *Research on drug courts: A critical review 2001 update*. New York: The National Center on Addiction and Substance Abuse, Columbia University.

Belenko, S., Lang, M., & O'Connor, L. (2003). Self-reported psychiatric treatment needs among felony drug offenders. *Journal of Contemporary Criminal Justice, 19*(1), 9–29.

Binder, D., Bergman, P., & Price, S. (1991). *Lawyers as counselors: A client-centered approach*. St. Paul: West Publishing Company.

Birgden, A. (2002). Dealing with the resistant criminal client: A psychologically-minded strategy for more effective legal counseling. *Criminal Law Bulletin, 38*(2), 225–243.

Boothroyd, R. A., Poythress, N. G., McGaha, A., & Petrila, J. (2003). The Broward mental health court: Process, outcomes, and service utilization. *International Journal of Law and Psychiatry, 26*, 55–71. doi:10.1016/S0160-2527(02)00203-0.

Braithwaite, J. (1989). *Crime, shame and reintegration*. Cambridge: Cambridge University Press.

Brehm, S. S., & Brehm, J. W. (1981). *Psychological reactance: A theory of freedom and control*. New York: Academic Press.

Brown, A. (2001). Drug courts help keep families together. *The Florida Bar*.

Burdon, W. M., Roll, J. M., Prendergast, M. L., & Rawson, R. A. (2001). Drug courts and contingency management. *Journal of Drug Issues, 31*(1), 73–90. doi:10.1177/002204260103100105.

Cascardi, M., Poythress, N. G., & Hall, A. (2000). Procedural justice in the context of civil commitment: An analogue study. *Behavioral Sciences & Law, 18*(6), 731–740. doi:10.1002/bsl.421.

Casey, P. & Rottman, D. (2000). Therapeutic jurisprudence in the courts. *Behavioral Sciences & Law, 18*(4), 445–457. doi:10.1002/1099-0798(2000)18:4<445::AID-BSL371>3.0.CO;2-J.

Catalano, S. (2007). *Intimate partner violence in the United States*. Washington, DC: Bureau of Justice Statistics. http://bjs.ojp.usdoj.gov/index.cfm?ty=pbdetail&iid=1000.

Clark, M. (2001). Change-focused drug courts: Examining the critical ingredients of positive behavior change. *National Drug Court Institute Review, 3*(2), 35–87.

Conference of Chief Justices and Conference of State Courts Administrators (2000). CCJ Resolution 22: COSCA Resolution 4: In support of problem-solving courts. *Journal of the Center for Families, Children, and the Courts, 2*, 1–3.

Cosden, M., Ellens, J., Schnell, J., Yamini-Diouf, Y., & Wolfe, M. (2003). Evaluation of a mental health treatment court with assertive community treatment. *Behavioral Sciences & the Law, 21*, 415–427. doi:10.1002/bsl.542.

Daicoff, S. (2000). The role of therapeutic jurisprudence within the comprehensive law movement. In D. P. Stolle, D. B. Wexler, & B. J. Winick (Eds.), *Practicing therapeutic jurisprudence: Law as a helping profession* (pp. 465–492). Durham: Carolina Academic Press.

Deci, E. (1975). *Intrinsic motivation* (E. Aronson, Ed.). New York: Plenum.

Erickson, S., Campbell, A., & Lamberti, S. (2006). Variations in mental health courts: Challenges, opportunities, and a call for caution. *Community Mental Health Journal, 42*, 335–344. doi:10.1007/s10597-006-9046-7.

Fisler, C. (2005). Building trust and managing risk: A look at a felony mental health court. *Psychology, Public Policy and Law, 11*, 587–604. doi:10.1037/1076-8971.11.4.587.

Fritzler, R., & Simon, L. (2000). The development of a specialized domestic violence court in Vancouver, Washington utilizing innovative judicial paradigms. *University of Missouri at Kansas City Law Review, 69,* 139–177.
Goldkamp, J., & Irons-Guynn, C. (2000). *Emerging judicial strategies for the mentally ill in the criminal caseload: mental health courts in Ft. Lauderdale, Seattle, San Bernardino, and Anchorage.* US Department of Justice, Bureau of Justice Assistance.
Goleman, D. (1995). *Emotional intelligence.* New York: Bantam Books.
Hawkins, M. D. (2010). Coming home: Accommodating the special needs of military veterans to the criminal justice system. *Ohio State Journal of Criminal Law, 7,* 563–572.
Hora, P. F. (2002). A dozen years of drug treatment courts: Uncovering our theoretical foundation and the construction of a mainstream paradigm. *Substance Use & Misuse, 37,* 1469–1488. doi:10.1081/JA-120014419.
Hora, P., Schma, W., & Rosenthal, J. (1999). Therapeutic jurisprudence and the drug court movement: Revolutionizing the criminal justice system's responses to drug abuse and crime in America. *Notre Dame Law Review, 74,* 439–538.
Kaye, J., & Knipps, S. (2000). Judicial responses to domestic violence: The case for a problem solving approach. *Western State University Law Review, 27,* 1–13.
King, M., Freiberg, A., Batagol, B., & Hyams, R. (2009). *Non-adversarial justice.* New South Wales: The Federated Press.
LaFond, J. Q., & Winick, B. J. (2003). Sex offender reentry courts: A cost effective proposal for managing sex offender risk in the community. *Annals of the New York Academy of Science, 989,* 300–323. doi:10.1111/j.1749-6632.2003.tb07314.x.
Lind, E. A., & Tyler, T. (1988). *The social psychology of procedural justice.* New York: Plenum.
Littel, K. (2003). Specialized courts and domestic violence. *Issues of Democracy: The Changing Face of U.S. Courts, 8,* 26–31.
Mazur, R., & Aldrich, L. (2003). What makes domestic violence court work? Lessons from New York. *The Judges' Journal, 42,* 5–11.
McKune v. Lile, 536 U.S. 24 (2002).
Meichenbaum, D., & Turk, D. C. (1987). *Facilitating treatment adherence: A practitioner's guidebook.* New York: Plenum.
Miller, W. R., & Rollnick, S. (2002). *Motivational Interviewing: preparing people for change* (2nd ed.). New York: Guilford Press.
Monahan, J., Hoge, S. K., Lidz, C., Roth, L. H., Bennett, N., Gardner, W., & Mulvey, E. (1995). Coercion and commitment: Understanding involuntary mental hospital admission. *International Journal of Law and Psychiatry, 18*(3), 249–263. doi:10.1016/0160-2527(95)00010-F.
National Drug Court Institute (2009). *Drug courts: A national phenomenon.* http://www.dci.org/research.
Petrila, J. (2007). Civil commitment: A therapeutic jurisprudence model. *Psychiatric Services, 58,* 572–573.
Petrila, J, Poythress, N. G., McGaha, A., & Boothroyd, R. (2001). Preliminary observation from an evaluation of the Broward County Mental Health Court. *Court Review, 37,* 14–22.
Petrucci, C. (2002). Respect as a component in the judge-defendant interaction in a specialized domestic violence court that utilizes therapeutic jurisprudence. *Criminal Law Bulletin, 38,* 263–295.
Quinn, M. (2009). The modern problem-solving court movement: Domination of discourse and untold stories of criminal justice reform. *Washington University Journal of Law and Policy, 31,* 57–82.
Redlich, A. (2005). Voluntary, but knowing and intelligent: Comprehension in mental health courts. *Psychology, Public Policy, and Law, 11,* 605–619. doi:10.1037/1076-8971.11.4.605.
Redlich, A., Steadman, H., Petrila, J., Monahan, J., & Griffen, P. (2005). The second generation of mental health courts. *Psychology, Public Policy and Law, 11,* 527–538. doi:10.1037/1076-8971.11.4.527.

Reisig, M. (2002). The difficult role of the defense lawyer in a post-adjudication drug treatment court: Accommodating therapeutic jurisprudence and due process. *Criminal Law Bulletin, 38,* 216, 218–219, 221–223.

Rottman, D., & Casey, P. (1999). Therapeutic jurisprudence and the emergence of problem solving courts. *National Institute of Justice Journal, 240,* 12–19.

Sack, E. (2002). *Creating a domestic violence court: Guidelines and best practices*. San Francisco: Family Violence Prevention Fund.

Schma, W. (2003). A New kind of power: Judges gain fresh perspectives on how to steer cases toward productive outcomes. *ABA Journal, 89,* 66–67.

Schopp, R. (1999). Therapeutic jurisprudence: Integrated inquiry and instrumental prescriptions. *Behavioral Sciences & the Law, 17*(5), 589–605. doi:10.1002/(SICI)1099-0798(199923)17:5<589::AID-BSL368>3.0.CO;2-3.

Shiff, A., & Wexler, D. (1996). Teen court: A therapeutic jurisprudence perspective. *Criminal Law Bulletin, 32*(4), 342–357.

Shuman, D. (1993). The use of empathy in forensic examinations. *Ethics & Behavior, 3,* 289–302. doi:10.1080/10508422.1993.9652109.

Steadman, H. J., Deane, M. W., Borum, R., & Morrissey, J. P. (2000). Comparing outcomes of major models of police responses to mental health emergencies. *Psychiatric Services, 51,* 645–649. doi:10.1176/appi.ps.51.5.645.

Steadman, H. J., Redlich, A., Callahan, L., Robbins, P. C., & Vesselinov, R. (2010). Effect of mental health courts on arrests and jail days. Archives of *General Psychiatry, 68*(2), 167–172. doi:10.1001/archgenpsychiatry.2010.134.

Stefan, S., & Winick, B. (2005). A dialogue on mental health courts. *Psychology, Public Policy and Law, 11,* 507–526. doi:10.1037/1076–8971.11.4.507.

Stolle, D. P., Wexler, D. B., & Winick, B. J. (Eds.). (2000). *Practicing therapeutic jurisprudence: Law as a helping profession*. Durham: Carolina Academic Press.

Tauber, J. (2002). Address at the eleventh annual symposium on Contemporary Urban Challenges at the Fordham University School of Law, problem solving courts: Adversarial litigation to innovative jurisprudence. *Fordham Urban Law Journal, 29,* 1755, 1901–1905.

Trupin, E., & Richards, H. (2003). Seattle's mental health courts: Early indicators of effectiveness. *International Journal of Law and Psychiatry, 26,* 33–53. doi:10.1016/S0160-2527(02)00202-9.

Tyler, T. (1990). *Why people obey the law*. Princeton: Princeton University Press.

United States Government Accountability Office (2005). Adult drug courts: Evidence indicates recidivism reductions and mixed results for other outcomes. Washington, DC. http://gao.gov/products/GAO-05-219.

Watson, A., Hanrahan, P., Luchins, D., & Lurigio, A. (2001). Mental health courts and the complex issue of mentally ill offenders. *American Psychiatric Services, 52,* 477–481. doi:10.1176/appi.ps.52.4.477.

Wertheimer, A. (1987). *Coercion*. Princeton: Princeton University Press.

Wexler, D. B., & Winick, B. J. (1991). *Essays in therapeutic jurisprudence*. Durham: Carolina Academic Press.

Wiener, R. L., Winick, B. J., Georges, L. S., & Castro, A. (2010). A testable theory of problem solving courts: Avoiding past empirical and legal failures. *International Journal of Law and Psychiatry, 33,* 417–427. doi:10.1016/j.ijlp.2010.09.012.

Winick, B. J. (1991). Harnessing the power of the bet: Wagering with the government as a mechanism for social and Individual change. *University of Miami Law Review, 45,* 737–816.

Winick, B. J. (1992). On autonomy: Legal and psychological perspectives. *Villanova Law Review, 37*(6), 1705–1777.

Winick, B. J. (1995). The side effects of incompetency labeling and the implications for mental health law. *Psychology, Public Policy & Law, 1*(1), 6–42.

Winick, B. J. (1998). Counseling about advance directive instruments: Client denial and resistance in the advance directive context: Reflections on how attorneys can identify and deal with a psycholegal soft spot. *Psychology, Public Policy & Law, 4,* 901–923. doi:10.1037/1076-8971.4.3.901.

Winick, B. J. (1999). Therapeutic jurisprudence and the civil commitment hearing. *Journal of Contemporary Legal Issues, 10,* 37–60.
Winick, B. J. (2000). Applying the law therapeutically in domestic violence cases. *University of Missouri Kansas City Law Review, 33,* 36–45.
Winick, B. J. (2003). Therapeutic jurisprudence and problem solving courts. *Fordham Urban Law Review, 30,* 1055–1090.
Winick, B. J. (2005). *Civil commitment: A therapeutic jurisprudence model.* Durham: Carolina Academic Press.
Winick, B. J., & Perez, A. M. (2010). Aging, driving, and public health: A therapeutic jurisprudence approach. *Florida Coastal Law Review, 11,* 189–236.
Winick, B. J., & Wexler, D. (2003). *Judging in a therapeutic key: Therapeutic jurisprudence and the courts.* Durham: Carolina Academic Press.
Winick, B. J., Wiener, R. L., Castro, A., Emmert, A., & Georges, L. S. (2010). Dealing with mentally ill domestic violence perpetrators: A therapeutic jurisprudence judicial model. *Journal of Law and Psychiatry, 33,* 428–439.
Wyatt, T. (2001). Threat of jail helping keep mentally ill on medication: Domestic violence court offering program monitored probation. The Dallas Morning News. http://www.dallasnews.com/metro/stories/STORY.eaaf9ac391.b0.af.0.a4.4c9c0.html

Part IV
Epilogue

Chapter 13
The Intended and Unintended Consequences of Problem-Solving Courts

Eve M. Brank and Joshua A. Haby

> If I need some insight into the future of medicine, I might head over to Stanford Medical School. If I wanted to learn about likely directions in finance and hedge funds, I might visit Penn's Wharton. If I were looking to make investments in computing, I might arrange a tour of a lab at MIT. If I decided to learn something about where legal practice, law firms, and legal departments will be in 2014, where would I go? Not to law school (Paul Lippe 2009).

The quote stated above from Paul Lippe, the well-known founder and CEO of Legal OnRamp, suggests that there is a lack of progression when it comes to overall growth and innovation within legal training. Lippe made the above statement in an article for The Am Law Daily, in order to address faltering legal training. Lippe's comparison of the innovations in the legal realm versus those in the medical field is particularly poignant given the struggles outlined in this book that problem-solving courts are experiencing. Lippe's stance on the need for reform in certain areas involves the inclusion of more empirical education for legal students, an educational structure similar to the medical model, and the use of empirically supported findings as motivation for improvement within the legal system as a whole. Lippe is not alone in this call to reform, as other authors in this book have made similar calls (Gatowski et al. in press; Lederman in press; Redlich in press; Weisz in press). As Lippe puts it, "Law schools are extremely disengaged from professional practice," when compared to other professional schools, and we are quickly reaching a period where law schools need to "catch up" (Lippe 2009).

As mentioned previously and throughout this book, Lippe is not the only advocate for reform and improved approaches for those involved in the legal system. The old way of traditional courts focusing only on the sole issue presented has transformed into the idea that courts, and those who work within them, should serve a greater purpose and be prepared to take different approaches (e.g., Babb in press). One different approach is exemplified with problem-solving courts discussed in the preceding chapters. Problem-solving courts exist to serve either a special population of offenders or a special type of offense, yet the training for those who work in and

E. M. Brank (✉) · J. A. Haby
University of Nebraska-Lincoln, Lincoln, NE, USA
e-mail: ebrank2@unl.edu

R. L. Wiener, E. M. Brank (eds.), *Problem Solving Courts*,
DOI 10.1007/978-1-4614-7403-6_13, © Springer Science+Business Media, LLC 2013

lead these courts may not be adequate to meet the needs of these new and innovative approaches.

This chapter will be divided into three sections. In the first section, we will examine the intended consequences of the problem-solving courts by highlighting data and material presented in the preceding chapters. The second section will be devoted to the possible unintended consequences of these special courts and why those unintended consequences are virtually assured. In the third section, we offer two polemic solutions to address these unintended consequences: stop all the problem-solving courts or change legal education as we know it.

Intended Consequences of Problem-Solving Courts

As mentioned in previous chapters, the creation of problem-solving courts began with the formation of a juvenile court in Chicago, Illinois in 1899. Since then, problem-solving courts have grown to address numerous other issues such as drug abuse, domestic violence, and mental health issues, to name a few. The chapters within this book provided a well-rounded and well-articulated view of such courts.

Generally, these courts developed from an innovative and different approach to dealing with offenders. Specifically, these courts seek to deal with the root of the offense, in an effort to prevent recidivism, or the offender's reentry into the system due to the same offense. In order to deal with the underlying issues, some problem-solving courts use an integrated approach to deal with comorbid issues, such as mental health and addiction problems (Richardson et al. in press; Winick in press). Richardson et al. (in press) describe this integrated approach in Australia and New Zealand noting that these problem-solving courts seek to "address multiple problems in a holistic way" (Richardson et al. in press). Such a holistic approach focuses on using the same judge and court professionals to review the same case, which allows for consistency and enables the judge to develop a rapport with the defendant (Babb in press). Richardson et al. suggest that these lower level courts are able to be more adaptable to "economic, political, and social change" than traditional courts. This adaptability allows these courts to be more innovative with their approaches, such as developing versions of the court that are culturally specific and integrating therapeutic jurisprudence principles within these courts (Richardson et al. in press).

The integration of therapeutic jurisprudence plays an important role in problem-solving courts (Babb in press; Gatowski et al. in press; Lederman in press; Petrila in press; Richardson et al. in press; Schopp in press; Winick in press). In many ways, the process of problem-solving courts represents the defendant-centered principles of therapeutic jurisprudence by seeking to empower the defendant—giving the defendant a voice in the court's decision making (Petrila in press). This different approach has positive outcomes. Past participants in mental health courts report feeling less coerced than those in traditional courts (Petrila in press; Winick in press). Clearly, lower coercion means that the defendants are participating more because they want to and less because the court requires them to do so. Relatedly, this defendant-centered style of judging often attempts to maximize defendant autonomy as much as possible (Petrila in press). Autonomy is prioritized not only with the treatment choices but also with the outcomes from those treatments (Petrila in press). Promoting autonomy rather than paternalism increases the defendants' chances of success because such sense of control is essential in recovery (Petrila in press). Having a voice, increasing autonomy, and encouraging voluntary engagement in services are likely to improve participants' chances of success and recovery, as these feelings can act as intrinsic motivators and increase participant satisfaction (Winick in press).

In addition to giving defendants a voice in the process, Petrila (in press) notes that many problem-solving courts are not encumbered by the large case loads of traditional courts. In fact, many of the courts are considered a separate jurisdiction and have separate judges (Winick in press). These smaller caseloads allow the court to spend more time focusing on the defendant and pursuing a resolution of the underlying issue(s) that problem-solving courts aim to remedy. It seems this model can be successful. Limited studies (e.g., single site) suggest that these problem-solving courts provide participants with increased services (Petrila in press) and treatment access (Redlich in press), and increased service use (Gatowski et al. in press; Richardson et al. in press). In addition to increased service access and use, these courts are more cost effective than criminal court (Winick in press).

One major difference between problem-solving courts and regular courts seems to be the type and level of judicial involvement in the lives of the people who have cases heard before these courts (Wiener and Georges in press). For example, in a drug court, the judge can set provisions for participants (e.g., behavior contracts, periodic drug testing, community treatment program, etc.) and is actively involved in providing support, in the form of public praise or enforcing sanctions (Winick in press). Similarly, in a mental health court, the aim of the court is to persuade the participant to take medication and monitor their compliance with treatment using similar incentives to drug courts (e.g., dropping of charges; Winick in press). Proponents of these courts argue that the increased latitude provided to the courts is one of the features that makes these courts special and can lead to the courts' success. Importantly, we need to also consider whether there are unintended consequences of this extra-involvement that could lead to problems with the courts or lead to the courts being ineffective. Certainly, these problem-solving courts are not without criticism.

Unintended Consequences of Problem-Solving Courts

Moving away from an adversarial-based, traditional court to a problem-solving court is certain to have some complications. Consider the drug offender who is referred to a problem-solving drug court, where, in lieu of a conviction, the offender is offered the "opportunity" to participate in a rehabilitation program. Upon first hearing this offer, the offender may not understand the attraction of such a program. But, there is an incentive. Upon completion of the program, the offender's offense will be removed from his record—that is a highly convincing incentive. However, in order to participate in drug court, the offender must agree to the regulations set forth by the court. These regulations generally include a lengthy rehabilitation program, frequent drug screens, and frequent appearances before the court and judge. If the offender does not abide by the regulations, many courts require that the offender enter a guilty plea for the original charge and accept the resulting sanctions.

According to some critics, an unintended consequence of these problem-solving courts is the lack of due process and its inherent unfairness toward the offender. Some critics argue that abandonment of the traditional system ignores procedural rules and the defendants' rights of due process (Benaquisto 2003). Additionally, the attractiveness of potentially dropped charges could be argued to be unduly coercive for the defendant. Of course, it is not legally coercive, and thus, unconstitutional, but instead the argument is that it could be psychologically coercive. Specifically, the offenders are presented with a choice to make of their own volition (face the charges vs. participate in the program), but the potential incentive of having charges dropped essentially forces the offenders into a decision. Winick (in press) contends that the argument of coercion is not valid for two reasons. First, the choice is not made under the legal definition of coercion (i.e., a form of improper inducement), and second, the offender is in the difficult position due to her own choices. Nonetheless, it is certainly possible and plausible that the offender feels as though she had no choice but to submit to the drug court jurisdiction. Within the same vein, Weisz (in press) makes the argument that some courts effectively force families into services that may not be suited for that particular family, yet participating in the services have high stakes for the families. Consider dependency courts, the placement of the child can come down to the outcome of a service that a family never wanted and arguably never needed (Brank et al. 2002). The parents' successful or unsuccessful completion of the service (e.g., parenting classes) could determine the removal of the child, the separation of the child from his or her siblings, or the placement of the child in foster care. It certainly could feel like a forced choice for the parents.

Another unintended consequence of these problem-solving courts stems from the high level of variability between different courts and different jurisdictions. As there is no formal agreed upon standard operating procedure, there can be variability in the authority the courts have over state authorities, and vice versa (Weisz in press). Of more concern, the rules of evidence are relaxed for disposition and review hearings in most states (Weisz in press), which results in an informal admission policy that allows hearsay and subjective testimony (Weisz in press). These relaxed rules and the resulting allowed evidence is particularly concerning, considering the impact that such evidence could have on the outcome of a case—these are cases that generally involve the high stakes of children's lives and anything else related to the family (Babb in press).

Problem-solving courts are an attempt to move the role of the judge away from the mechanical rule arbiter and into a more compassionate helper. As Wiener and Georges (in press) note, the problem-solving courts move us away from the traditional criminal court model where the judge acted like an umpire handing down rule-based orders and into a system where judges act more as team leaders or case managers collaboratively encouraging the participants and working with them to find appropriate services (Wiener and Georges in press). Unfortunately, as judges move away from the criminal court model, they move away from what they have been taught, what they know, and arguably, what they are equipped to do. Although judges have continuing education opportunities, for many that is likely to be too little, too late.

Redlich (in press) notes that as these problem-solving courts are a departure from the norm and foreign to most involved, there is a natural regression toward a criminal court model within the problem-solving court system. In other words, the courts may start off with special goals and ideals, but as time passes they become more like a regular criminal court because a criminal court is somewhat of a status quo or the model from which all else are compared and derived. Although not always considered a problem-solving court, juvenile court jurisdiction is a perfect example of this regression toward criminal court. With the intention of being a different system—a system that healed the wayward youth and did not criminalize them—the juvenile court even developed a new language separate and distinct from the criminal system (e.g., dispositions rather than sentences). Nonetheless, the juvenile system now looks very much like the adult criminal justice system (Gardner 2009).

In sum, although the current benefits and potential benefits remain promising, the authors of this book and other scholars on the topic note a number of complications stemming from problem-solving courts. The courts come with some unintended consequences that seem to force defendants to submit to the alternative models and outcomes that can be much more intrusive than if the case had proceeded through regular court. This happens often with relaxed procedural rules and increased subjectivity. All the while, the courts and those involved seem drawn back to the traditional criminal court model. We believe there are two possible solutions to address these issues. The first solution is to stop the problem-solving court experiment. The second solution is to focus on the initial training of those involved and train them to meet the needs of the problem-solving courts. We detail both possible solutions next.

Two Possible Solutions

Solution One: Stop Problem-Solving Courts

If we return to a system where all the criminal cases are heard in regular criminal court, then we have certainly resolved any specific problems with the problem-solving courts. We could return to a system where judges emotionlessly hand down orders and apply rules; judges and lawyers would not get to know the defendants or victims. Mentally ill or drug abusing defendants could be executed or banned from living within city limits (Deutsch 1946). Families would be granted unbridled discretion in domestic relationships and permitted to decide how to interact with each other. Of course, this will lead to a gamut of other problems and we are back to the point when problem-solving courts began and the reason why they came to be. Clearly, these courts are attempting to fulfill a real need and we believe eliminating them is not a viable solution.

Solution Two: Specialize Legal Training

If we accept that stopping problem-solving courts is a bad idea, then it seems that we need some other way to make them work to their potential. There needs to be some way to ensure that they are not regressing back to their criminal court roots. We propose a change at the beginning: a new system of legal education. To support our proposal, we first briefly review the current system of legal education and compare that to medical education. We focus on medical education because, like legal education, it is considered a professional curriculum. Unlike legal education, medical education has a complex set of extensive steps and specialties to prepare physicians for their specific type of practice. Second, we propose a plan to undertake such legal specialization highlighting programmatic foreshadowing that includes an increase in specialized training while obtaining a J.D. (including a focus on empirical legal methods), additional legal training, dual-degree programs, and more extensive legal internships. Third, we describe the future court system if there was such specialized legal training—a utopian court system in which constitutional and psychological rights are upheld because those involved will be inclined toward and trained to do so.

The current system. The legal community is seeing record unemployment rates by law school graduates, with unprecedented low rates of employment in jobs that require bar passage (Weiss 2012). Nonetheless, the number of prospective law students taking the Law School Admissions Test (LSAT) has generally continued to increase, with clear peaks during difficult financial times (Robbins 2010). Many people see going to law school as an opportunity to advance their current career, whether that be within the legal field or not. For instance, almost 20 % of recent law school graduates were employed in business (Weiss 2012).

Obtaining a law degree—a J.D.—for most law students is a commitment of three academic years beyond a bachelor's degree. Generally, the first year curriculum is a predetermined set of courses usually consisting of all or most of the following courses: Contracts, Civil Procedure, Criminal Law, Property, Torts, Legal Writing/Research, and Constitutional Law (Association of American Law Schools 2006). The following 2 years provide students with the opportunity to sample other areas of law. Some law schools have subspecialties or concentrations. At the authors' institution, a law student can concentrate in a number of different predefined or individualized areas. For example, the Intellectual Property Law concentration requires students in their second and third year of law school to take courses like Copyright Law, Patent Law, and Trademark and Unfair Competition Law. Presumably, these specialties better equip students to practice law in these areas. Many law students after their first year of law school clerk for law firms or work in other legal positions. This too, helps expose the students to different areas of the law and, through somewhat of an apprenticeship system, helps prepare students for the practice of law.

With only a few rare exceptions, a law school graduate will need to take and pass a state bar in order to practice law. Although studying for a state bar is not technically part of the legal education, mass-produced bar review courses procure the loyalty of many a recent law school graduate. The courses effectively extend the law school curriculum for a few additional postgraduation months making the regular law school experience almost precisely three calendar years long. Add in a few months to wait for the bar exam results, and the whole experience from "no legal training" to "ready to practice law" is slightly over 3 years.

For comparison sake, a practicing physician with a medical degree (M.D.) will have completed 4 years of medical school and at least a 3-year residency. Specializations will require even more training beyond the residency. For instance, a 3-year residency in internal medicine (inclusive of the first year internship) will be followed by a 3-year fellowship in gastroenterology in order for a physician to be a gastroenterologist. Other specialties require even more time and training (e.g., a pediatric neurosurgeon will be in medical school, residency, and training for about 12 years beyond the bachelor's degree). Like legal training, medical training also includes comprehensive qualifying exams (i.e., boards).

Clearly, there is a stark difference in years of training between law school and medical school. It is not only the years of training, but also the level of specialization and organization of that specialization that provides a helpful model for specialized legal training. Medical students are matched in a residency program after completing their 4 years of medical school. For those who want to continue with further specialization they can complete a fellowship. Whether attributable to the system of specialization or something else, the unemployment rates for physicians are usually among the lowest of all professions and the expected job outlook is much better than average (US Bureau of Labor Statistics 2012). Can we learn from the medical community to better shape legal training? We turn next to examine some of the ripples of movement that suggest that a similar type of specialization system could be possible within legal training.

New legal education system. Suggestions for legal training to emulate medical training are not new. Lippe (2009; discussed earlier in this chapter) calls for more practice-oriented training in law schools, with successful practicing attorneys passing on their own real world experiences. Lippe argues that a practice-oriented approach such as a year of externship similar to the medical school approach, would increase the acquisition of marketable skills during law school (Segal 2011) and reduce the need for long apprenticeships for recent law graduates. Overall, Lippe calls for a reform to overcome the current stagnate condition of legal education and move toward a model that takes cues from the medical profession. Specifically, such programs would have an empirical approach to practice, a subject-area focused externship, and more practice orientation (see Lippe 2009 for full review).

Schopp (in press) highlights what we see as two needs for better training specifically with the mental health courts and generally with all problem-solving courts:

empirical methods and clinical training. Specifically, Schopp notes that in order to determine if the mental health courts are actually successful in reducing recidivism there needs to be ongoing data collection in both mental health courts and traditional criminal courts. Although social scientists could certainly be the main source of labor for data collection and analysis, anyone who has tried to work within the court systems knows that in order to get true buy-in, there is a clear need for judges and lawyers to have at least a working knowledge of empirical methods. Schopp also notes that there is an underlying communication barrier between clinicians and legal actors. Even basic vocabulary training would seem to be useful and imperative in moving these courts forward.

As Wiener and Georges (in press) note, judges in problem-solving courts are as much case managers as they are judicial officers. Authors in this book described some of the extra training that judges are already receiving (or should receive) who are involved in problem-solving courts. For example, Gatowski et al. (in press) discussed the therapeutic jurisprudence-based training dependency court judges often receive. Despite these special trainings, Judge Lederman (in press) argues that there needs to be more. She notes that judges and lawyers are trained in the law and not science, and that Lederman says this "is not enough." Lederman poignantly argues that judges need to be concerned with research and attempting to understand the research on adolescent brain development and other important issues the courts must address. She even says that a problem-solving court devoid of science can be "dangerous." Those are powerful words, but words true to the situation and Judge Lederman's own experiences.

In some ways, legal training is already changing because of the various options for focusing on new or specific topic areas, extending training beyond the core law school experience, and complementing the J.D. with other advanced degrees. One relatively new area of legal scholarship that has and continues to gain popularity involves empirical legal studies. Empirical legal studies provide attempts to incorporate empiricism into law-related areas. This movement of embracing scientific inquiry has led to the development of the Society for Empirical Legal Studies, as well as the creation of the Journal of Empirical Legal Studies (JELS), an academic peer-reviewed journal that publishes empirically oriented articles that are rooted in law and law-related fields. Lawless et al. (2009) wrote *Empirical Methods in Law*, a book that teaches law students to identify when empirical research should be applied and provides vocabulary that facilitates communication with scientific experts. The empirical legal movement is particularly important because it arguably runs contrary to the traditional legal education that allows students to eschew math and empiricism. Such a movement suggests that some students (and faculty) in law schools may be interested and willing to examine the law and their legal training from a new perspective. Importantly, this new perspective is one that values experimental examination and scientific research.

Furthermore, there is evidence that some students are willing to extend their legal training beyond the traditional J.D. The Masters of Law degree (referred to as the LL.M.) is becoming more widespread and diverse (Sloan 2010). Schools offer an LL.M. specialization in a number of areas including Space, Cyber, and

Telecommunication Law; Elder Law; Tax Law; International Human Rights; and Corporate Law. Even though the vast majority of law school graduates does not pursue an LL.M. degree and certainly do not need to have one to practice law, a person may pursue an LL.M. as a way to specialize in a specific area of practice, Tax Law in particular is a popular area of study (Jones 2010). Another reason the degree is gaining popularity is that foreign attorneys can gain US training. Commonly, however, pursuing an LL.M. is a path thought to help a person become a law professor. An LL.M. degree will traditionally take an additional full year of law school with course requirements consisting of mostly regular law school classes in a particular area (Sloan 2010). The American Bar Association does not track salary or employment data for LL.M. graduates (Sloan 2010), which leaves only anecdotal information about whether the extra letters are worth the tuition and time costs. Nonetheless, its gaining popularity bolsters our argument that students may be willing to invest additional time in order to specialize their education.

The popularity of dual degrees is further foreshadowing of potential future changes for legal training. A dual degree generally involves a law degree (J.D.) and a master's or doctorate degree in another field. In fact, a majority of law schools have approved dual-degree programs (Association of American Law Schools 2006; US News Staff 2012). The J.D./M.B.A. for business administration is a particularly popular option (Association of American Law Schools 2006; Hafemeister et al. 1990). Many of these dual-degree programs are ad hoc in nature such that the students are mostly responsible for developing their combined programs and attempting to integrate the disciplines (Hafemeister et al. 1990). Other programs are well-integrated with fairly stringent requirements and networks for the students. Again, at the authors' institution, there is the longest running law and psychology dual-degree program. This program integrates the traditional law school J.D. usually with a Ph.D. in one of the subspecialties in psychology.[1] The normal law school 3-year time commitment is extended with students generally finishing both of their degrees in six or so years.

Law-psychology programs produce graduates who are often not comfortable in either a traditional law setting or a traditional psychology setting, despite their new "trilingual" skills (Hafemeister et al. 1990, p. 271). Most graduates of these programs find themselves working in academic or public policy settings (Hafemeister et al. 1990). The acquired skill sets from these law-psychology dual degree programs, however, does seem well-suited for working within problem-solving courts because the dual-trained professionals are able to assess issues from different and unique perspectives (Hafemeister et al. 1990). Additionally, as more law schools adopt an empirical approach to the law, law-psychology students are not only well-situated to participate in these activities, but are also well-equipped to guide these efforts toward what is needed for making problem-solving courts successful. The notion of a problem-solving court is a paradigm shift away from the rational actor model and

[1] The University of Nebraska-Lincoln also has a very popular Masters of Legal Studies (M.L.S.) degree that can be taken with the Ph.D. We do not focus on that degree here because we are addressing the specific needs of the legal education system. The M.L.S. serves more as a complement to the Ph.D. and can be an important aspect of training psychology students about the law.

into the psychological model that recognizes the complexity of offenders and their situations (Babb in press; Wiener and Georges in press). Such a change deserves and needs a similar shift in the education of those working in the area.

Future legal training for a truly new court system. Imagining that this legal training and legal system overhaul could occur, what would it look like? We can envision a variety of configurations, but we describe only one for simplicity and brevity. What follows is a broad generalization of a plan in which law schools and legal training in general could shift to meet the needs of not only problem-solving courts, but also other areas by utilizing and expanding the J.D./Ph.D. or J.D./M.A. law-psychology systems that are already in place and adding key LL.M. programs geared toward the skills needed to be a judge or work in a problem-solving court.

First, it probably makes the most logical sense to keep the traditional first year of law school the same. Although this first year has been vilified by some, it does provide a relatively efficient system to present the general topics of civil procedure, contracts, criminal law, property, and torts. One simple addition would be to also include a semester of short electives that would be particularly useful for future possible specialization. The first year law student could then be introduced to topics such as clinical psychology, developmental psychology, empirical methods, among many others topics. Students would be able to get a taste of options and learn about the potential career paths. In the years of training to follow, the students would be actively involved in both law school classes and psychology graduate classes. In addition to the classwork, the students would be involved in research relevant to their desired career path. For instance, a student interested in drug courts would do externships and research at drug treatment facilities and programs. The end result of such an education would be a dual-trained individual equipped to make both legal and psychological decisions. For those attorneys who have already graduated, a Problem-Solving Courts LL.M. degree would be an appropriate way to provide in-depth and immersive education on topics important for the type of problem-solving court in which they will work.

We would be remiss not to mention some limitations to our suggestions. Anyone who has been a faculty in a graduate program is likely to wonder who will provide the supervision, and pay, for all these new graduate students. It is clear that this new system could not be sustained with the current level of resources. How will all of this be funded? Legal education costs are not inconsequential and the source of great criticism (Tamanaha 2012). One of the benefits to medical education is the source of funding for the residencies and fellowships. The residents and fellows learn their specialties in exchange for minimal wages and long hours at teaching hospitals. Is there a similar setting within the legal community?

Certainly within the J.D./Ph.D. model, the students are funded as graduate students. But, the demand for such students is limited by the number of professors who can mentor and advise the students—usually only a few at a time per professor. If the J.D./Ph.D. students were more actively involved within their area of problem-solving during their training, financial matters may be more manageable. Consider a student who is pursuing dual psychology and law degrees in order to be a judge in a mental health court. Such a student could gain invaluable experience working at a prosecutor's office, public defender's office, in-patient mental health clinic, and so on. The potential for rotations would be very similar to the medical residency rotations in which the resident spends a month working (and learning) in the intensive care unit, then the emergency room, and then an out-patient-clinic. The institutions benefit because they have extra help in the form of "residents."

Therefore, one source of income could come from the externship sites that would be receiving student-work. Another source of income could come from the law schools that are attempting to address the criticisms of over-priced irrelevancy (Tamanaha 2012). Still another source of funds could come from court innovation grants or the like. This last source would obviously require some government appreciation of the need for specially trained judicial officers and the potential for cost-saving benefits when problem-solving courts are doing what they are intended to do.

Conclusion

The term "problem-solving" court suggests that there is something different with these courts—something "special" that is not possible with our regular court system. The current system will likely do fine shuffling along with a hodgepodge of continuing legal education courses and judicial conferences because the judges involved in these courts are very committed to their success. Nonetheless, the very notion of a problem-solving court highlights the need for something different. We argue that a difference should start with a change in legal education.

We are encouraged by the attention that the subject of problem-solving courts has received in recent years. It is promising that others within the field (particularly those within this volume) agree that there is a need for reform and change. Such recognition, especially from the esteemed scholars in this book, suggests that we should be closer to finding a solution. We argue that the legal educational system is at a time when it can and should make some changes. Such changes can and should be done to improve the court systems—including (and especially) problem-solving courts. Attention to change at the law school level will result in what Paul Lippe (described earlier) seemed to think was an impossibility—law schools as places of innovation and discovery.

References

Association of American Law Schools. (2006). *Survey of innovations in law school curricula*. http://www.aals.org/documents/curriculum/Survey.pdf. Accessed June 20 2012.

Babb, B. A. (in press). Unified family courts: An interdisciplinary framework and a problem-solving approach. In R. L. Wiener & E. M. Brank (Eds.), *Problem solving courts: Social science and legal perspectives*. New York: Springer.

Benaquisto, L. (2003, March). Review of the book *Drug Courts in Theory and Practice*. Canadian Journal of Sociology. http://www.cjsonline.ca/reviews/drugcourts.html. Accessed 20 June 2012.

Brank, E. M., Williams, A. L., Ray, R. E., & Weisz, V. (2002). Parental compliance: Its role in termination of parental rights cases. *Nebraska Law Review, 80,* 335–353.

Deutsch, A. (1946). *The mentally ill in America: A history of their care and treatment from colonial times*. http://archive.org/details/mentallyillinamee029063mbp. Accessed 29 Apr 2013.

Gardner, M. R. (2009). *The understanding series: Understanding juvenile law* (3rd ed.). LexisNexis.

Gatowski, S. I., Dobbin, S. A., & Summers, A. (in press). Exploring the value-added of specialized problem-solving courts for dependency cases: Lessons learned from a study of dependency problem-solving court models. In R. L. Wiener & E. M. Brank (Eds.), *Problem solving courts: Social science and legal perspectives*. New York: Springer.

Hafemeister, T. L., Ogloff, J. R., & Small, M. A. (1990, Summer). Training and careers in law and psychology: The perspective of students and graduates of dual degree programs. *Behavioral Sciences and the Law, 8*(3), 263–283. doi:10.1002/bsl.2370080308

Jones, A. (2010, September 20). *The LL.M.: A valuable degree or a wasted (and expensive) year?* Wall Street Journal: Law Blog http://blogs.wsj.com/law/2010/09/20/the-llm-a-valuable-degree-or-a-wasted-and-expensive-year/. Accessed 20 June 2012.

Lawless, R. M., Robbennolt, J. K., & Ulen, T. S. (2009). *Empirical methods in law*. New York: Aspen.

Lederman, C. S. (in press). The marriage of science and the law in child welfare cases. In R. L. Wiener & E. M. Brank (Eds.), *Problem solving courts: Social science and legal perspectives*. New York: Springer.

Lippe, P. (2009, June 22). *Welcome to the future: Time for law school 4.0*. http://amlawdaily.typepad.com/amlawdaily/2009/06/school.html. Accessed 20 June 2012.

Petrila, J. (in press). Mental health courts may work, but does it matter if they do? In R. L. Wiener & E. M. Brank (Eds.), *Problem solving courts: Social science and legal perspectives*. New York: Springer.

Redlich, A. D. (in press). The past, present, and future of mental health courts. In R. L. Wiener & E. M. Brank (Eds.), *Problem solving courts: Social science and legal perspectives*. New York: Springer.

Richardson, E., Thom, K., & McKenna, B. (in press). The evolution of problem-solving courts in Australia and New Zealand: A trans-Tasman comparative perspective. In R. L. Wiener & E. M. Brank (Eds.), *Problem solving courts: Social science and legal perspectives*. New York: Springer.

Robbins, D. (2010, January 26). *Cornell law school applications increase by record 52 %*. http://cornellsun.com/section/news/content/2010/01/26/cornell-law-school-applications-increase-record-52-percent. Accessed 20 June 2012.

Schopp, R. F. (in press). Mental health courts: Competence, responsibility, and proportionality. In R. L. Wiener & E. M. Brank (Eds.), *Problem solving courts: Social science and legal perspectives*. New York: Springer.

Segal, D. (2011, November 19). *What they don't teach law students: Lawyering*. http://www.nytimes.com/2011/11/20/business/after-law-school-associates-learn-to-be-lawyers.html?pagewanted=all. Accessed 20 June 2012

Sloan, K. (2010, September 20). *'Cash cow' or valuable credential?* The National Law Journal http://www.law.com/jsp/nlj/PubArticleNLJ.jsp?id=1202472170557&slreturn=1. Accessed 20 June 2012.

Tamanaha, B. Z. (2012). *Chicago series in law and society: Failing law schools*. Chicago: University Of Chicago Press.

US News Staff. (2012). *Law school tips for success*. http://www.usnews.com/education/best-graduate-schools/top-law-schools/articles/2012/03/13/law-school-tips-for-success. Accessed 20 June 2012.

US Bureau of Labor Statistics. (2012). *Occupational outlook handbook*. http://www.bls.gov/ooh/healthcare/physicians-and-surgeons.htm. Accessed June 20 2012.

Wiener, R. L., & Georges, L. (in press). Social Psychology and Problem Solving Courts: Judicial Roles and Decision Making. In R. L. Wiener & E. M. Brank (Eds.), *Problem solving courts: Social science and legal perspectives*. New York: Springer.

Weiss, D. C. (2012, June 7). *Only 65 % of 2011 law grads have jobs requiring bar passage, a record low*. ABA Journal http://www.abajournal.com/news/article/only_65_percent_of_2011_law_grads_have_jobs_requiring_bar_passage_a_new_rec. Accessed June 20 2012.

Weisz, V. (in press). Dependency courts and science: A discussion of Gatowski et al. and Lederman. In R. L. Wiener & E. M. Brank (Eds.), *Problem solving courts: Social science and legal perspectives*. New York: Springer.

Winick, B. (in press). Problem solving courts: Therapeutic jurisprudence in practice. In R. L. Wiener & E. M. Brank (Eds.), *Problem solving courts: Social science and legal perspectives*. New York: Springer.

Index

DOI 10.1007/978-1-4614-7403-6, © Springer Science+Business Media, LLC 2013

CPSIA information can be obtained
at www.ICGtesting.com
Printed in the USA
LVOW03*1319050716
495156LV00008B/26/P

9 781461 474029